THE

ALBERT SCHWEITZER

JUBILEE BOOK

EDITED BY

A. A. ROBACK

Division of University Extension
Commonwealth of Massachusetts

WITH THE CO-OPERATION OF

J. S. BIXLER
President of
Colby College

GEORGE SARTON
Professor of the History of Science
Harvard University

GREENWOOD PRESS, PUBLISHERS
WESTPORT, CONNECTICUT

Orginally published in 1945
by Sci-Art Publishers, Cambridge, Massachusetts

First Greenwood Reprinting 1970

Library of Congress Catalogue Card Number 79-97392

SBN 8371-2670-3

Printed in the United States of America

TO THE FELLOWSHIP OF THOSE

WHO BEAR THE MARK OF PAIN

CONTENTS

PAGE

PREFACE 15

CHAPTER

PART I

PERSONAL INTERPRETATIONS

I ALBERT SCHWEITZER THE MAN
By A. A. ROBACK, Ph.D., *University Extension Lecturer*

Growth of an Ideal — The Secret of Schweitzer's
Prestige — A Humanitarian is Born — The Core of
His Personality — Truth and Logical Consistency —
Genuineness and Consistency in Art — Ethical Acuity
—Character and Personality — Integration — Simulta-
neity in Succession — Adequacy Valence — Puzzles and
Speculations — A Living Law 23

II PRODUCTIVE TENSIONS IN THE WORK OF
ALBERT SCHWEITZER
By J. S. BIXLER, Ph.D., *President, Colby College*

Dualism of Intellect and Emotion — Types of Solution
Offered — The Problem as Seen in His Treatment of
History — The Same Problem in Music — Schweitzer's
Personal Attitude 69

III ALBERT SCHWEITZER, HUMANITARIAN
By EVERETT SKILLINGS, *Professor-Emeritus, Middlebury
College; Chairman, Albert Schweitzer Fellowship*

I. Beginnings of a Great One-Man Institution — A
Resolution Takes Shape — A Momentous Step — Starting a Jungle Practice — Influence upon Natives — The
World War Interrupts Healing Activities — Returning
to Lambaréné.

CONTENTS

CHAPTER   PAGE

II. Weathering World War II — How the Albert
Schweitzer Fellowship Came into Being — The Nature
of Dr. Schweitzer's Work — Inspires All Sorts and
Conditions of Men — Touching Reactions — Growing
Interest in Schweitzer's Work — The Need of Expan-
sion — When Medical Supplies Arrive — A Host of
Admirers 87

IV THE BLACK MAN AND ALBERT SCHWEITZER
By W. E. B. DuBois, Ph.D., LL. D., D .Litt., L.H. D.
Prof. Emeritus of Sociology, Atlanta University

The Black Man and Albert Schweitzer — Dim Origins
— A Delicate Issue — A Dream to Some; A Night-
mare to Others 119

PART II

METHODOLOGY AND EVALUATION

V ON UNDERSTANDING
By Joachim Wach, Ph.D., Th. D., *Professor, History of
Religions, Brown University; formerly Professor, Uni-
versity of Leipzig.*

Presuppositions, Conditions, and Limitations of Understanding — The Act of Understanding — The Objectivity of Understanding — The Purpose of Understanding 131

VI VALUATIONS OF ACHIEVEMENTS, ACTS, LAWS
AND PERSONS
By Edward L. Thorndike, Ph.D., LL. D., Sc. D., (Hon.)
*Professor Emeritus, Teachers College, Columbia Uni-
versity*

I. Valuations of Twenty Achievements. II. Valuations
of Fifty Activities. III. Valuations of Laws. IV.
Valuations of a Person 147

CONTENTS

PART III

AESTHETICS

VII SCHWEITZER'S AESTHETICS: An Interpretation of Bach
By Leo Schrade, *Yale University* 173

VIII THE TRANSCENDENTALISM OF ALBERT
SCHWEITZER
By Archibald T. Davison, Ph. D., Mus. D. (*hon.*)
F. R. C. M., *Professor of Music, Harvard University* . 197

IX ALBERT SCHWEITZER'S CONTRIBUTION TO
ORGAN-BUILDING
By Carl Weinrich, *Organist and Choirmaster Princeton
University and Instructor of Organ, Columbia University and Wellesley College* 213

X MUSICAL DAYS WITH ALBERT SCHWEITZER
By Alice Ehlers, *Professor of Music, University of
Southern California* 227

PART IV

ETHICS AND CIVILIZATION

XI ALBERT SCHWEITZER AS CRITIC OF NINETEENTH-
CENTURY ETHICS
By Ernst Cassirer, Ph. D., LL. D., *Formerly Professor
of Philosophy (also Rektor), University of Hamburg,
Late Visiting Professor of Philosophy Yale University
and Columbia University* 239

XII CIVILIZATION
By Ananda K. Coomaraswamy, D. Sc., *Boston Museum
of Fine Arts* 259

[9]

CONTENTS

PART V

HUMANITIES

XIII THE UNITY OF MANKIND IN THE CLASSICAL CHRISTIAN TRADITION
By ROLAND H. BAINTON, B.D., Ph. D., *Professor of Ecclesiastical History, Yale University* 277

XIV LUTHERANISM, CATHOLICISM, AND GERMAN LITERATURE
By KARL VIËTOR, Dr. Phil., *Professor of German Art and Culture, Harvard University* 297

XV JUAN RUIZ DE ALARCON
By ALFONSO REYES, LL. D., *President, El Colegio de México, formerly Mexican Minister Plenipotentiary to France, Spain, Argentina, and at Various Times Ambassador to Argentina, Brazil etc.* 323

PART VI

MEDICINE

XVI THE TRANSMISSION AND RECOVERY OF GREEK AND ROMAN MEDICAL WRITINGS
By DALLAS B. PHEMISTER, M.D., *Professor and Chairman Department of Surgery, University of Chicago* . . . 339

XVII THE POST-GRADUATE TEACHING OF CLINICAL TROPICAL MEDICINE
By SIR PHILIP MANSON-BAHR, *Director of the Clinical Division, London School of Hygiene and Tropical Medicine* 359

XVIII THE STRANGE CASE OF DIVES AND LAZARUS
By CLEMENT C. CHESTERMAN, M.D., O.B.E., *Hon. Sec. British Advisory Board on Medical Missions* . . . 375

CONTENTS

CHAPTER

PAGE

XIX MEDICAL MISSIONS AND THE FUTURE
By ERNEST COOKE, F. R. C. S. I., L. R. C. P. I., D. P. H.,
L. M. R., *Physician in Charge Outpatient Clinic,
Hospital for Tropical Diseases, London* 385

PART VII

THEOLOGY AND RELIGION

XX XENOPHANES AND THE BEGINNINGS OF
NATURAL THEOLOGY
By WERNER JAEGER, Dr. Phil., D. Litt., Litt. D.,
*Professor of Classical Philology, Harvard University;
formerly Professor at the University of Berlin* . . . 395

XXI ALBERT SCHWEITZER'S INFLUENCE IN HOLLAND
AND ENGLAND
By KIRSOPP LAKE, D.D., D.Litt., Dr. Phil. *(hon.)*,
Professor of History, Emeritus, Harvard University . 425

XXII ALBERT SCHWEITZER'S INTERPRETATION OF
ST. PAUL'S THEOLOGY
By OLOF LINTON, Theol. D., *Assistant Professor of Exe-
getics, University of Uppsala* 441

EPILOGUE

XXIII THE SCHOLAR'S DILEMMA
By GEORGE SARTON, D.Sc., L.H.D. *(hon.)*, LL.D. *(hon.)*
Professor of the History of Science, Harvard University 459

A TENTATIVE BIBLIOGRAPHY OF ALBERT SCHWEITZER
By A. A. ROBACK, Ph.D., *Department of Education, Commonwealth of Massachusetts* 469

REGISTER OF PERSONAL NAMES 485

INDEX OF SUBJECTS 497

[11]

ILLUSTRATIONS

ALBERT SCHWEITZER . . . . *Frontispiece*
    (in his Study in Günsbach)

Facing Page

LOG ROLLING IN LAMBARENE 49

ALBERT SCHWEITZER AT HIS DESK IN LAMBARENE . . 49

ALBERT SCHWEITZER AT LAMBARENE IN 1930 . . . 49

THE ROMANTIC AND ARTISTIC ALBERT SCHWEITZER . . 65

ALBERT SCHWEITZER IN BERLIN IN 1928 65

THE HOSPITAL IN LAMBARENE 97

EMPATHIC INDUCTION 113
    (with native patient)

AT THE ORGAN IN THE GROOTE KERK IN DEVENTER,
    HOLLAND IN 1932 205

EXCERPT FROM DR. SCHWEITZER'S LETTER IN GERMAN . 477

FACSIMILE OF DR. SCHWEITZER'S HANDWRITING, IN FRENCH 477

PREFACE

That Dr. Albert Schweitzer's seventieth anniversary would not pass unobserved in the educated world might have been regarded as a foregone conclusion, yet at a time when millions upon millions were engaged in an attempt to exterminate each other and when the human race came as close as ever in its history to self-annihilation, presentation volumes were not likely to be thought of, much less produced. The book before us is one of the exceptions, and well it might be; for Dr. Schweitzer does not belong to a single group or coterie, but as one Dutch biographer has put it, he "speaks to all." He speaks through his deeds rather than through his words or music, although these in themselves call forth homage in all who have felt the initial impact of the man from whom they emanate.

The name Albert Schweitzer is as yet little known to the masses. Those who have read his books in English, French, German, Dutch, Dano-Norwegian, Swedish, Polish, Hungarian, Finnish, and Japanese would constitute an army of perhaps two million men and women, who, though unacquainted with one another, are yet imbibing at the same font and inspired by the same personality. This army, augmented by perhaps another million who have read of Dr. Schweitzer or listened to his recordings of Bach, form the élite of the world in every civilized country; for Schweitzer, living and working in the equatorial jungle, has, without any deliberate effort on his part, succeeded in drawing the attention of the tender-minded of all classes and climes, and certainly of the intellectual aristocracy, to the possibilities of the moral will.

In all these millions, if they but knew of it, the appearance of an Albert Schweitzer *Festschrift* should arouse a wave of enthusiasm in the awareness that something has been done to signalize the achievements of their ideal, even on the modest scale which it was possible to encompass under the trying circumstances of a war-torn world. Had Dr. Schweitzer received his full due in terms of a presentation, three volumes would not have sufficed to accommodate the contributions of the votaries in the fields which Dr. Schweitzer has cultivated so assiduously and effectively. Bulk or voluminousness, it is true, is no criterion of the cultural and spiritual values, yet it must be avowed that representation, in the full sense, implies scope, and scope physically requires space.

It was the wish and intention of the editors to make the present volume catholic in every way (although it so happens, through sheer circumstances, that the Catholic angle is missing, despite repeated efforts to invite a Catholic writer) but when countries seemed to have been separated not by boundaries, or even oceans, but by stellar distances, when all access to the occupied countries was cut off, seeking continental contributions was like reaching out for the moon; and even if some communication were established, it would have sounded almost callous, if not truculent, to broach a matter of this sort during such stress. The end of the diabolical War was not in sight when the material for the Schweitzer volume was being gathered; and even a letter via airmail to England, would, thanks to the censorship, take months to reach its destination.

For all that, the volume is still representative—representative, in the first place, of the spheres which appealed to Schweitzer, namely, New Testament research, ethics and philosophy, music, and medicine; secondly, of a number of European and American countries; and thirdly, of the best-known American universities. It was fortunate in a sense that some of the leading German scholars were actually teaching in American universities. Thus the University of Berlin is represented by Professor Werner Jaeger, while the University of Hamburg is reflected through its former *Rektor*, the late Professor Cassirer. The essay by Professor

Schrade is a contribution by a former instructor of the Universities of Königsberg and Bonn. Professor Wach was formerly associated with the University of Leipzig, and Professor Viëtor was of the faculty of the University at Giessen.

Thus Germany figures considerably in the Albert Schweitzer Book, and fitttingly through those none of whom was *persona grata* to the Nazi regime. It was through the kind offices of the Legation of Sweden in Washington (more especially, its Counselor, Dr. Sven Dahlman) that the Swedish Government, or rather its Ministry for Foreign Affairs, made itself responsible for a contribution from one of its highly reputed scholars — Professor Linton, of the University of Uppsala, sending the essay through special diplomatic channels. Professor Sarton may be said to speak for the French-speaking countries. England, of course, has its representatives in Sir Philip Manson-Bahr and two colleagues in medicine, and the Hindu point of view appears in the article by Dr. Coomaraswamy. Holland is adequately connected with Dr. Schweitzer by Professor Lake. Latin America participates through Dr. Reyes, who has distinguished himself in the republic of letters even more than in diplomatic circles, serving in the capacity of ambassador and plenipotentiary to the leading states in South America, as well as to France.

With the war crisis during the early part of the fall of 1943 becoming more acute, it is easy to understand why the Presidents, respectively, of Czechoslovakia and Portugal, as well as Premier Marshal Smuts of South Africa, could not see their way clear to undertaking a piece of literary work for the Schweitzer volume. General Smuts was at the time preparing to leave for a conference in England, while from the Chancellery of the Czechoslovakian Republic (at the time in London) the following letter was received:

I am writing to acknowledge the receipt of your letter of August 14th sent to Dr. Beneš.

[17]

PREFACE

With regard to your request for Dr. Beneš' contribution to the Albert Schweitzer *Festschrift*, the President
wishes me to say:
He welcomes the idea of publishing the *Festschrift*
and appreciates your thought in inviting him to contribute. Dr. Beneš, however, cannot say definitely at the
present juncture whether it will be possible for him to
contribute or not. It is difficult for him now to plan
for such a long time ahead, and he therefore suggests
that you should kindly write again later when the publication of the *Festschrift* is nearer at hand.
With the President's best wishes of success for your
undertaking.

A later letter made it clear that "although . . . . Dr. Beneš
originally hoped that he would be able to contribute to the volume, he now finds it impossible to do so. The reason, as you will
not be surprised to learn, is that he is so very busy at this critical
moment in the destinies of Europe. . . . ."
It would have been a serious omission to have no expression
from a Negro leader, since Albert Schweitzer's life has been
dedicated to the cause of the black race, in a practical capacity,
and therefore, of necessity, in a circumscribed area. Professor
DuBois surely is the man *au courant* with the situation, and his
plaintive note, even if it does not entirely harmonize with the
other strains, is a welcome complement, making the Schweitzer
symphony all the richer; for it leads to interracial reflection.
Dr. Schweitzer himself, it must be borne in mind, is a persistent
and dauntless critic.
As to universities, it is gratifying to see that the five which
are generally regarded as the greatest in America (Harvard, Yale,
Columbia, Chicago, and Princeton) join, not officially, but through
some of their leading figures, in paying tribute to Albert Schweitzer. That Harvard should have the largest delegation in this connection is not surprising.

PREFACE

It is with deep regret that allusion is made to Professor G. S. Brett of the University of Toronto, who, during his protracted and painful illness, made a valiant effort to write his paper "Schweitzer's Contribution to a Theory of Ethics," but died before he could set down his ideas. Professor Ernst Cassirer's death occurred just after making the final revision of his article, which covered the same general topic as that proposed by Professor Brett.

One of the things to be expected about a *Festschrift* is over-lapping, since the contributors usually have no access to each other's papers. All the more remarkable then that so little repetition occurs in the present volume, although some of the contributions might seem at first blush to treat of the same subject-matter, but then the versatility and calibre of the man Albert Schweitzer would naturally be matched by the pronounced individuality of his admirers and consequently the variegatedness of the collective production.

It may be observed that perhaps never has a publisher's devise on the title page expressed more aptly the essence of the subject treated in the book. The Hebrew words occupying each of the three corners of the Greek pediment in the seal stand for truth (*emet*), uprightness (*yosher*), and charity (*ts'dakah*). Who in our age exemplifies these qualities in a greater degree than Albert Schweitzer, whose very name seems to be assonant with the Hebrew words just mentioned?

A word of explanation is in order concerning the compromise in orthography made in the articles by British contributors only. The English forms *re* instead of *er*, as in *centre*, and *s* instead of *z* in such words as *civilise, organisation,* etc., have been retained, out of consideration for the thousands of British readers, as well as the contributors, especially where the British spelling in these instances is more consistent than our own, since we write *advertise, improvise,* and *little*. Besides, there are still many in the United States who adhere to the older spelling in such words.

Other British forms, however, like *colour, endeavour,* etc. have been modernized.

Acknowledgements are herewith made to Messrs. Allen & Unwin and A. & C. Black of London, and Henry Holt and the Macmillan Co. of New York for permission to quote from several of their publications. Most of the illustrations used were from originals in the possession of Professor Everett Skillings, Chairman of the Albert Schweitzer Fellowship. For the frontispiece we are indebted to Mr. Gilbert Loveland, of Henry Holt & Co.

A. A. ROBACK.

Cambridge, Mass.
October 12, 1945.

PART I
PERSONAL INTERPRETATIONS

ALBERT SCHWEITZER, THE MAN

By

A. A. Roback, Ph. D.
Department of Education, Commonwealth of Massachusetts

CHAPTER I

ALBERT SCHWEITZER, THE MAN

BY

A. A. ROBACK

Every individual who is not of the ordinary run of the mill, turned out by Nature in the millions, and partaking of the quality of a stamp, to use Schopenhauer's analogy, is a phenomenon; and thus an object of study. The outstanding person, however, is not merely a phenomenon to observe, but appears as an illumination, a guiding star, and is thus not simply an intellectual or cognitive matter, but an active carrier of a volitional nature — a vector of character — specifically, perhaps someone to emulate at least optatively.

It is for this reason that more than one celebrity commenced his actual course in life at the point he became acquainted with his ideal. Personal meeting is not necessary. Indeed, sometimes it leads to depreciation; familiarity with the exploits of the ideal is sufficient. All the greater my astonishment therefore, when to the question: Which is your ideal in history or biography? asked in one of the world's leading technological institutes, practically all in the large class replied that they had no such ideal. These students were too young to have become cynics. They were just "built that way." Either no one in history measured up to their standards, or else they believed it mawkish to avow such a dependent attitude. Perhaps the very nature of the technological temperament is to put one's faith entirely into the conquest of inanimate forces, while the cultured temperament draws its nourishment from human qualities.

GROWTH OF AN IDEAL

After all, our whole cultural personality is constituted of the achievements of pioneers, many famous, others obscure, and some

[25]

even anonymous. Of those known to us, some one figure fires our imagination, and we look up to him as a patron saint, or else we either consciously or unconsciously strive to identify ourself with him, though he belong to a different sphere of thought and action. We might well ponder what our life would have been, had we not learned of this or that great man at a certain age.

Perhaps even pure technologists have their heroes, only they don't worship them. In truth, however, hero worship as such scarcely exists even in the most blatant and blaring Nibelungen conceits. It is the virtues that the heroes and heroines embody which evoke our admiration. Accordingly to wave aside all heroes and historical ideals is tantamount to maintaining implicitly that there are no virtues worth prizing, or else that "there is so much good in the worst of us and so much bad in the best of us" that no one is to be held up as a model to the rest of us.

To the many "tell-me" maxims, we might easily add another, if that had not already been done, viz., "tell me who your ideal is, and I'll tell you who you are," but the obverse has scarcely been thought of, the obverse being that a figure can be judged by the kind of people who adore him. It would be both interesting and instructive to have a survey of what the first acquaintance with the name of Albert Schweitzer meant to the hundreds of kindred spirits who in time became "Schweitzer-conscious," and who, although ignorant of each other's presence in this world, are yet linked together by the very fact that Schweitzer means so much to every one of them. The relationship thus becomes something like a magnetic field, not bound, however, by the limitations of space or time.

Adopting this metaphor, let me recount the initial experience of one of the filings drawn to Schweitzer. It was in the late summer of 1924 that I found an article on our hero, reprinted in translation, from the *Neue Züricher Zeitung*, which began with the words "Albert Schweitzer is like the rainbow, which gleams in every color and yet maintains a magnificently complete unity.

No other man living has given significant literary expression to such a variety of talents."

It was with considerable avidity that I read the sketch, but not without a pang of self-reproach, as I came to realize that although the writer's name was known to me, because of Pfister's contributions to psychoanalysis, alas, the man who has called forth such admiration in him, a truly remarkable personality, had been until then a cipher so far as I was concerned; and yet among my academic and literary colleagues I rated as a well-informed individual.* Furthermore, theology and Biblical criticism appealed to me in my early youth; ethics and civilization, another field which Schweitzer cultivated, were among my studies, and music, from the non-technical angle, was occupying much of my time. How could I have missed coming across at least one or two references to such a cultural monument?

It was, however, probably not his mental endowment that thrilled this reader then so much as the conative, the characterial traits, in conjunction with his cognitive gifts, which appeared to be in a class by themselves, and served as a revelation. Pfister's attempt at somehow psychoanalyzing his subject did not enhance the picture of Albert Schweitzer; and the image of the man only gradually took subjective shape, until the actual visualization was made concretely possible through a portrait which appeared in the pages of a European philosophical journal. I was amazed at the discrepancy between my own representation of Schweitzer and his actual likeness; for here was a person who could be taken for anything but a theologian, philosopher, or missionary (although in Schweitzer's case the designation of missionary is a misnomer, and should scarcely be used). He might well have been, to judge by his physiognomy, at first blush, a lyric tenor, or a romantic

---

*I wonder how many, like myself, have come upon Schweitzer's name in this casual fashion. Mrs. C. E. B. Russell, a Canadian, who has assisted in the work at Lambaréné, writes in her *The Path to Reconstruction*: "I myself discovered Schweitzer and was led to his books, and from his books to helping him in Africa, by a chance reading of a short but admirable article in the *Hibbert Journal* entitled 'Schweitzer's Ethic' ".

actor, a dreamy poet, or a sentimental composer, but to associate him with the habits of a solemn scholar and a self-effacing minister to the underdog would have been almost unthinkable.

The strange fascination which this phenomenon called Albert Schweitzer exerted over me, and the fact that his very name was unknown to me long after I had been publishing, somewhat disspirited me as I kept reflecting on the widespread publicity which so many pasteboard heroes are assured of in this world, while a man of such Herculean stature and prowess remains obscure even to the enlightened. It had become long since almost a practice with me to ask friends and acquaintances what they knew about Albert Schweitzer, but invariably, in those years, I would be greeted with a bland but blank expression, or else a hazard which was wide of the mark. I would then proceed to tell them briefly, what was afterwards formulated in my *Peretz, Psychologist of Literature* (where the two thinkers and humanitarians are shown to bear a physical resemblance to one another), that "Albert Schweitzer may be considered as one of the greatest men living today. Not only is he a distinguished philosopher of religion and New Testament critic, but probably the foremost interpreter of Bach's music, and an organist of world-wide fame. In addition to these activities, he studied medicine, and in the capacity of a surgeon, he built a hospital, practically with his own hands, in the equatorial zone of Africa, so as to give medical aid to the neglected aborigines."

This description does awaken the interest of my interrogatees and interrogators, in turn, but usually it is not sustained unless it is followed up by the reading of some of Schweitzer's books. At any rate, within the last twenty years, Albert Schweitzer's following has spread not only among the pillars of present-day culture, but even among the intelligentsia in general. For many years I have been showing before my university extension classes stereopticon slides to illustrate various types. Schweitzer's picture is projected in order to bring out the cast of countenance which is associated with decision, alertness, and a superior type of extraversion. Out of the thousands of adult students, not a single one, until very recently, would have the slightest inkling of Schweitzer or his calling, although they might easily recognize his dynamic qualities. Whereas, however, the "little man" has been unduly neglectful of him, Albert Schweitzer, perhaps more than any other of his contemporaries, stands out as the cynosure of the élite, the "great man's great man." And that in itself requires an explanation.

THE SECRET OF SCHWEITZER'S PRESTIGE

Had Schweitzer been the foremost theologian, musicologist, or medical authority, we could easily understand the reverence in which he is held by distinguished men and women in every country. It is homage to the superlative which always makes itself felt among those who have themselves achieved, but in Schweitzer's instance, it is the rare combination of the scholar, artist, and, above all, the man, which attracts so irresistibly. In the course of my contacts and conversations with intellectuals, many of them outstanding in their own way, I have found a few, at least, who did not take kindly to Schweitzer. Their attitude almost shocked me as much as when I heard someone speak ill of Spinoza; and I would decide that because of this disagreement alone, there must be a barrier between our mentalities. Astonished, I always ask for the reason of this negative attitude on their part, and discover that at bottom they think Schweitzer has dissipated his energy and wasted his talent on trivial matters. Others, of course, in addition, question his distinction in any one of the fields which he has enriched. Discredits usually come in pairs, the man sharing the fate of his ability. Why this small minority of highly intelligent people should take such a stand toward Schweitzer is matter for further analysis, but our next step is to examine the life-course of Schweitzer himself. What is there about him which grips even the generally unenthusiastic? What makes Schweitzer different

from so many, nay, all of our contemporaries who have been
blessed with a mind to grasp and to create; so that he might
well be said to tower like a beacon in a dark age on a dark
continent?

The answer to this question hinges on, or is encased in, yet
another question, fervently posed by Dr. Karl Reiland, who apparently prefers not to answer it himself, but to let the reader
obtain the inspiring information from Dr. Schweitzer's autobiography. Yet the very question throws considerable light on the
reason for regarding Schweitzer as a man without parallel, in our
generation at least.

How comes it that one of the world's greatest scholars - -
doctor, scientist, philosopher, theologian, organist, lecturer,
author - - goes from Alsace to Africa, from a great European university to the Equatorial primeval forest, there to
found a hospital and devote his accomplished life as physician and surgeon among sick and suffering Negro tribes?
Who is this extraordinary, many-sided man, this humble
and heroic man who forsakes a thrilling career in Europe
to heal natives on the River Ogowe in the Trader Horn
country? Well, read his own remarkable story, *Out of My
Life and Thought*. You will not easily lay this book aside.
You cannot read it without being fascinated by the matter
and becoming an admirer of the man.

You will read of various great tasks all well done. You
will find Albert Schweitzer the university professor and
lecturer; the musician, playing organ recitals in London,
Paris and Berlin; the doctor among his patients in Strasbourg and Africa; the preacher and the pastor; the author,
writing epoch-making books on Jesus and Paul, on philosophy, on Johann Sebastian Bach and his music; the expert
on organ construction; the authority on comparative religions.

See him — at medicine and surgery — taming the jungle
—charring logs for hospital construction — prisoner of

war, with his brave wife, doctoring fellow-prisoners — receiving degrees in England and Europe — making journeys of mercy among Negro Tribes — receiving the Goethe Prize at Frankfort — practicing on his piano (equipped with organ pedals) late at night on the edge of the African forest — playing a Bach recital in Paris with his friend, Widor, or giving lectures and recitals all over Europe to raise funds for his hospital at Lambaréné. Was there ever such a capable, versatile, ubiquitous, and altogether human and companionable giant among men? Yet how humble and with what a sense of humor!

There are those who snicker at such sacrifice, deeming it trivial, if not paltry. A psychoanalyst *e. g.,* has written, although, fortunately, it has not as yet been published, an account of Schweitzer which places him in the category of the paranoid, those who suppose themselves to have been chosen for some special mission in the world, and to have gained this sudden impulse from a vision, dream, or ominous event.

Psychoanalysts would be apt, on scanning the portrait of Albert Schweitzer with his fist upon his chest, to note a *peccavi* posture, and see in it a colossal guilt complex, which he is making every effort to compensate by his arduous labors in Africa. Then, again, others will conclude that Schweitzer's *superego* development is the result of an extremely rigid upbringing and an overpowering awe with which his father inspired him. This is not even *ex post facto* reasoning; for the facts do not bear out these assumptions; and the chief defect of certain psychoanalytic divagations is the principle that the reasonable and the unreasonable are both to be explained by unconscious motives, whereas we should suppose that only the unreasonable, the reprehensible requires such accounting. The reasonable and the good are justified by grounds which are superindividual, objective, and conscious. Undoubtedly behaviorists, environmentalists, and other mechanists will seek to explain Schweitzer's career in terms of early associations, the environment, conditioned reflexes, and the rest of the stock-in-trade.

A HUMANITARIAN IS BORN

Anyone, however, who is at all acquainted with Schweitzer's life-history will recognize the shallowness of these attempts as based on sheer hypothesis and not on fact. Schweitzer, it must be borne in mind, did not make any hasty resolutions. His plan to render succor to the natives of the jungle has had a long maturation, "having been conceived so long ago as my student days. It struck me as incomprehensible that I should be allowed to lead such a happy life while I saw so many people around me wrestling with care and suffering. Even at school I had felt stirred whenever I got a glimpse of the miserable home surroundings of some of my school-fellows and compared them with the absolutely ideal conditions in which we as the children of the parsonage at Günsbach lived." (*Out of My Life and Thought*, page 102, English translation). It was in 1905, that he definitely resolved to study medicine so that he could serve as a physician in Equatorial Africa, but as early as 1896, he had already made the decision to live for science and art until he was thirty, and from then on to devote himself to humanitarian work.

Schweitzer's interest in missions dated from the time he was a young boy, when his clergyman father, at a missionary service, would tell and read about the life of missionaries in South Africa. The fate of the Negro had already occupied the juvenile thoughts of the later healer and comforter of the unfortunates in far-off Africa. The goal idea was initiated probably in childhood, even if it took shape gradually.

Through a curious coincidence, it was the sculptor who fashioned the Statue of Liberty which guards the harbor of New York that stirred the emotions of young Albert, through a stone figure which stood (perhaps is still standing) in the Champ de Mars at Colmar, a township close to Günsbach. Schweitzer thought this piece of work to be one of the most expressive which Bartholdi, the Colmar sculptor, ever produced. "It is a figure of herculean proportions, but the face wears an expression of thoughtful sadness which I could not forget, and every time we went to Colmar I tried to find time to go and look for it. The countenance spoke to me of the misery of the Dark Continent, and even today I make a pilgrimage to it when I am in Colmar" (*Memoirs of Childhood and Youth*, page 63).

Countless youngsters, no doubt, would, on viewing this statue, not give it a second thought. Others again might reflect on the condition of the Black Man for a while, but no lasting effect would follow. Schweitzer was constituted differently. Incubation of a course of action would begin with the first perception which provided an affective hold. The subsequent reflection was not merely a passing notion, but lingered to develop into a definite idea taking its place in a larger systematized world outlook (*Weltanschauung*) thence to be translated into a personal life-attitude (*Lebensanschauung*) and finally into a resolution for action.

To speak of arbitrariness, impetuosity, or even impulsiveness, in the instance of Schweitzer's spiritual adventure, is therefore to set one's face against the actualities, and to derive conclusions out of surface appearances. Not only the value and the intention of an act, but its very genesis cannot be judged except through the whole history and personality of the agent.

Schweitzer was born a humanitarian (just as others, in our own contemporary period, were born brutalitarians) but it required experience to draw his attention to the woes and miseries which cried for redress but encountered only ears that were deaf and eyes that were blind. It then became a life-duty for Albert Schweitzer to make this *vox clamantis in deserto* heard throughout the world by reason of his unparalleled example. The trait of benevolence which in so many people slumbers as a pious wish, or else expresses itself in devotion to wife and children, in him resided as a propensity which found its level in beneficence extended to all fellow-beings or even fellow-creatures, wherever they be. What to the generality of mankind terminates in sheer compassion, for Schweitzer became a passion to terminate through relief brought to the sufferers.

One may find adumbrations of this craving in his early childhood, which already is marked by great tenderness and sympathy and selflessness. Schweitzer, it would seem, was born with a dispositon that carried latently the psychophysical structure of the Golden Rule, either in its negative phase, as formulated by Hillel, Talmudic pillar, or the positive phase, as taught by the *New Testament*.

In his *Memoirs of Childhood and Youth,* we have a number of incidents which go to prove the prepotent (not reflex but) urge for consistency which, as I have set down elsewhere (*The Psychology of Character*), is the basis of character, in its higher forms—an urge which may be the resultant of more elementary tendencies, like sympathy, in a high degree, and aggressiveness, in a low degree. He was always afraid lest he have it better than his playmates or the rest of the village boys. It pained him to think that he was getting better food or that his clothes marked him out as a "sprig of the gentry." When a larger, and therefore supposedly stronger, boy whom he had downed in a friendly tussle, cried out to him from underneath "Yes, I should be as strong as you, if I had broth twice a week," the injustice of living conditions in this world came home to little Albert with such poignancy that "the broth became nauseous to me."

So much did equality mean to this youngster that he actually refused to wear an overcoat which was made for him, in spite of the punishment meted out by his father. None of the village boys wore an overcoat, and he was not to be an exception. The same problem presented itself when his mother took him to the shop in order to buy him a hat. He stubbornly refused to wear any of the becoming caps which were placed before him or on his head, and finally "a shop girl was sent out and she brought me from the unsaleable stock a brown cap one could pull down over one's ears." It was the kind that all the other boys wore. Albert's mother was embarrassed more than once because of this refusal to be superior. The story repeated itself in the case of gloves as against mittens, shoes as against wooden clogs. The humbler apparel always won out. "This stern contest lasted all the time I was at the village school, and poisoned not only my life but that of my father too. I would wear only fingerless gloves, because the village boys wore no others, and on weekdays I would go out only in wooden clogs, because the village boys wore their leather boots only on Sundays." It is evident that Albert was a socially-minded individualist even as a boy and did not derive that attitude from his somewhat bourgeois' parents, although he doubtless inherited some disposition which stimulated him in that direction, without the strong opposing inhibitions.

It scarcely needs saying that Albert was a very impressionable child, just as he afterwards became a most impressionable adult with a nervous system so sensitive that a mere shadow of an event not only registered but left an indelible impression, and served to enhance subsequent impressions. Schweitzer's first contact with racial and religious prejudice was gained in his first year at school.

A Jew from a neighboring village, Maushe by name, who dealt in land and cattle, used to come occasionally through Günsbach with his donkey-cart. As there was at that time no Jew living in the village, this was always something of an event for the boys; they used to run after him and jeer at him. One day, in order to announce to the world that I was beginning to feel myself grown up, I could not help joining them, although I did not really understand what it all meant, so I ran along with the rest behind him and his donkey-cart, shouting: 'Maushe, Maushe!' The most daring of them used to fold the corner of their shirt or jacket to look like a pig's ear, and spring with that as close to him as they could. In this way we followed him out of the village as far as the bridge, but Maushe, with his freckles and his grey beard, drove on as unperturbed as his donkey, except that he several times turned round and looked at us with an embarrassed but good-natured smile. This smile overpowered me. From Maushe it was that I first learnt what it means to keep silent under persecution, and he thus gave me a most valuable lesson. From that day forward I used to greet him politely, and later when I was in the secondary school (the Gymnasium) I made it my practice to shake hands and walk a little way along with him, though he never learnt what he really was to me. He had the reputation of being a usurer and a property-jobber, but I never tried to find out whether this was true or not. To me he has always been just 'Maushe' with the tolerant smile, the smile which even today compels me to be patient when I should like to rage and storm.*

THE CORE OF HIS PERSONALITY

Again, it illustrates the independence of thought as well as the spirit of tolerance, or perhaps better, equity, which dwelt in that young mind. It also goes to show that "being like the other children," was not, as some negating, if not cynical, psychologists and sociologists would be apt to suggest, merely a case of submissiveness or assimilation to the group. The more fundamental question of fairness was the underlying cause of Albert's conduct, and becomes the standard of action. He is with the boys if they are the underprivileged, but he is against them when they wrong someone else.

This concern and exertion on behalf of the underdog came to expression even before Albert was old enough to go to school.

*It is perhaps worth mentioning that his heroic life partner is of a Jewish family.

"As far as I can remember," he tells us in his childhood reminiscences, "I was saddened by the amount of misery I saw in the world around me. Youth's unqualified *joie de vivre* I never really knew . . . . One thing that specially saddened me was that the unfortunate animals had to suffer so much pain and misery. The sight of an old limping horse, tugged forward by one man while another kept beating it with a stick . . . haunted me for weeks."

Why he should pray for human beings alone seemed to him a rank injustice, so after his mother prayed with him and kissed him good night he used "to add silently a prayer that I had composed myself for all living creatures," which ran "O, heavenly Father, protect and bless all things that have breath; guard them from all evil, and let them sleep in peace."

It was during his seventh or eighth year that he was put to a test difficult for any child to withstand. A companion had induced him to use some toy catapults which they made to shoot at birds. Suddenly the church bells began to ring mingling with the blithe singing of the birds. That was little Albert's cue. He shooed the birds away; and deep in his heart, the commandment "Thou shalt not kill" became ingrained for life. "From that day onward," he tells us "I took courage to emancipate myself from the fear of men, and whenever my inner convictions were at stake, I let other people's opinions weigh less with me than they had done previously."

I have dwelt at some length on the early episodes and sentiments of Schweitzer only to disprove the impression harbored in some minds that this man was a faddist or eccentric who went to extreme lengths in carrying out an *idée fixe*. We might easily disabuse our minds of any suspicion that Schweitzer was moved by complexes, reaction-formations, or fixations, or that he was rationalizing, in the psychoanalytic sense, although his whole design for living was strictly rational, with a healthy tincture of mysticism added, at the conclusion of the process, for flavor.

In Schweitzer, the affective personality is dominated by the sensibilities, vibrant and quiveringly delicate so as to react to the slightest discomfort or uneasiness in others. In the first grades in school, he was dissatisfied with the one-finger playing of his teacher who knew no harmony. In his enthusiasm, he sat down and improvised with harmony in several parts. "Then it occurred to me that I could do something which she could not, and I was ashamed of having made a show of myself."

Well might he have said with the poet

> God with a feeling heart afflicted me
> That aches when life with others goes not well;
> I have a heart that writhes with stranger's pains
> A heart that burns in everybody's hell.*

Emotional states are often spent in idle words, expletives, and vehement language, where one feels wronged. In the case of indignation over someone else or compassion, the solitary individual is assisted, as a rule, but the principle under which the present instance is subsumed, is in the majority of cases lost sight of. It becomes a *personal* relationship between reliever and sufferer. Schweitzer can hardly be said to fall into this group; for his feelings were always filtered through the lens of reason and insight, and thus the second step in the evolution of his conduct is achieved. Then comes the third—the translation of his ethical insight into action. One might almost talk of this process as the syllogism of action—the consistency carrying over from logic into behavior.

Is the emotional or logical predominant in Schweitzer? As one who feels so intensely about music that as a child he "almost fainted from excess of pleasure" when he first heard duets sung in harmony, the emotional foundation could not be questioned,

*Kh. N. Bialik: *The Last Word* (translated from the Yiddish by A. A. Roback, and versified by Alice Stone Blackwell).

but the logical trend of all he writes about, the dispassionate analysis which almost compels conviction, is equally strong; and the daring which it sometimes takes to uphold heresies, not only in theology, but in music and philosophy too, is on a par with the determination shown in his more active pursuits.

TRUTH AND LOGICAL CONSISTENCY

What the discovery of the historical Jesus, waiting with the majority of his contemporary brethren for the end of the world to come, and subsequently realizing his mistake, must have meant to the universally respected theologian may be gathered from Schweitzer's own statement that the satisfaction of solving so many historical riddles about Jesus "was accompanied by the painful consciousness that this new knowledge in the realm of history would mean unrest and difficulty for Christian piety." After all, if Jesus was as fallible as any other man, then how can he be considered divine? And if the very Gospel is not regarded as authentic in its entirety, but thought to be pieced together by later hands than the names of the authors would suggest, then what value do we set upon the contents?

Schweitzer's mind, however, would brook no artifacts. His passion for truth and his ability to inject himself into a period or situation, no matter how remote, which implies also the knack of isolating himself from the present-day world, and divesting the subject at issue of all its accumulated mythical appendages through the centuries, forced him to accept the consequences of his far-reaching discovery, despite the torrent of religious indignation in orthodox quarters. It was evident that his *"Eureka"* was not devoid of its sting, because the body of evidence which he collected in *The Quest of the Historical Jesus* (in the German original, *Von Reimarus zu Wrede*) displaced not water but a body of dogma which was at the very foundation of orthodox Christianity.

Schweitzer, in his rôle of "Israel the wrestler" does not hesitate to criticize the pious frauds and mystifications committed in early Christianity in order to bolster up its cause, a cause which would have gained immeasurably if the truth were allowed to unfold historically, so that the intrinsic merit of the teachings of Jesus could take hold of the world without the spurious and artificial frills.

Truth is under all circumstances more valuable than non-truth, and this must apply to truth in the realm of history as to other kinds of truth. Even if it comes in a guise which piety finds strange and at first makes difficulties for her, the final result can never mean injury; it can only mean greater depth. Religion has, therefore, no reason for trying to avoid coming to terms with historical truth.

His attitude is reminiscent of another investigator who gave us a *Life of Jesus* and one whose versatility and adventurous spirit were like Schweitzer's—Ernest Renan. In that revealing autobiography *Souvenirs d'enfance et de jeunesse,* he tells of his struggle with himself on having discovered many discrepancies in the Bible, while he was training for the priesthood at the Seminary of St. Sulpice. How he would have liked being in Schweitzer's position—to find flaws in the Gospel and yet not lose caste among Christians. Protestantism makes allowance for such digressions, but Catholicism presents an iron barrier, and you must retreat the entire length or else r e n o u n c e its creed. *"Ah!"* cries out Renan somewhat pathetically, *"que ne puis-je comme un Herder, épouser tout cela et rester ministre, prédicateur chrétien"!**

The gulf between simple faith and formal dogma occurred to Renan exactly one hundred years ago (1845) as it did to Schweitzer later, and for a time Renan considered himself a Protestant. "The thought that in leaving the Church, I should remain true

* What would I not give to be a Herder, to hold all that, and still remain a Christian minister and preacher!"

to Jesus took hold of me, and were I capable of believing in apparitions, I most certainly should have seen Jesus telling me *"Abandonne-moi pour être mon disciple"* (Abandon me, so that you might become my disciple").

Schweitzer did not undergo such anguish in his crisis, yet his daring pronouncements were not likely to be forgotten when he was preparing to enter on his humanitarian career in Africa. In order to serve *gratis* as a physician in the territory of which the Paris Missionary Society was in charge in French Equatorial Africa, and to come out to that jungle at his own expense, he had to undertake something like a campaign so as to convince the members of the Committee individually, at their homes, that his sole interest in the natives was to treat and cure them, and not to preach to them. Received by a few members rather coldly, he was able to persuade the majority of them that he would, in all religious or spiritual matters, be as "dumb as a fish." Only then was the offer accepted, but not without the resignation of one member, who chose to remain adamant on the ineligibility of Schweitzer as a mission doctor.

GENUINENESS AND CONSISTENCY IN ART

It was not only in the sphere of religion, but in all that concerned life, in art as well as in science, that truth was for Schweitzer the *élan vital,* the driving force; and as we shall see later, his sense of justice was not only an outgrowth of sympathy but also a translation of truth in the realm of conduct. Schweitzer's mental endowment is not marked by a soaring imagination which displays flashes of inventive genius. It is rather characterized by a historical vision which sees things in their true perspective. It is common sense applied to the sublime and the lofty productions, which, because of technical progress, had become glamorized through the popular urge of gilding refined gold, in an age of "bigger and better" everything. What even the majority of our cultural leaders do not realize is that you cannot enhance intrinsic values by light or sound effects, that truth is truth even when heard through the still small voice within, and that Schweitzer's salvaging of old organs was in itself a manifestation of his burning zeal to preserve the truth—to see and hear masterpieces as they were intended by the creator and not as they were transformed through some new-fangled experiments.

Lest this interpretation of Schweitzer's preoccupation with organs and their construction seem an exaggeration, I wish to quote the following remarkable statement from Schweitzer's own pen. "The work and the worry that fell to my lot, through the practical interest I took in organ-building, made me sometimes wish that I had never troubled myself about it, but if I do not give it up, the reason is that the struggle for the good organ is to me a part of the struggle for truth." And even in that activity, harmless as it would appear, he was not only opposed by most of the guild, but actually made enemies because he was "the obstacle to their plan of replacing their old organ by a factory one, or was guiltily responsible for their having to cut out three or four of the stops they wanted, so that the rest might be of better quality!"

I should go a step further and suggest that Schweitzer's absorbing interest in Bach, and (according to a statement in her reminiscences of Albert Schweitzer by Madam Alice Ehlers)* his fondness for Mozart's music stem also from his love of truth; for I think these two composers (Mozart in his introverted moods only) on the classical side, and Georges Bizet on the romantic, represent the truth in music more than any others known to us; and *per contra*, Richard Wagner and Richard Strauss, with all their studied conformation to almost programmatic realism, with all their pomp and éclat, fanfares and pyrotechnics, as a rule, ring false. One need only compare Strauss's *Also Sprach Zarathustra* with Mozart's *pianoforte concerto in C minor, no. 24*, to

* This volume, page 234.

become aware of the philosophical phantom in Strauss's music and the exalted provocativeness of the other.

It was natural for a clergyman's son, himself theologically trained, to select Bach as his patron composer, but the same reason cannot be assigned for the Mozartian taste; and it is quite probable that Schweitzer would still have been the chief authority on Bach, even if his training had been along secular lines without the family tradition; for Bach votaries are born, not made; and interest in Bach is not necessarily a concomitant of a religious nature, as I have known agnostics and even atheists who were equally susceptible to his music. For Schweitzer, to be sure, music is an act of worship, but one may by the same token extend this view and say that religion, which, for Schweitzer, seems to be compounded of faith and love, is one phase of truth; and that devotion, which originally meant *a duty* devolving upon us, is a binding truth to be acted out.

It was because Schweitzer could sense the truth element in situations and things, that he could discern at once if anything was out of kilter; or *vice versa,* he could, from his transcendental vantage ground, see the aptness of a production or a course of action, although those better trained or skilled only observed in them the superficial flaws, which in reality, like the tempered instrument, are not flaws at all. A good illustration is cited in Widor's preface to Schweitzer's *Bach.* Widor, the famous French organist, once expressed to his young pupil—for Albert Schweitzer was then still in his twenties—his doubts about Bach's chorales, which puzzled him greatly, because of the introduction of contradictory moods. The melody as a whole and the contrapuntal motives elaborated in the fantasias seemed to him at variance with one another. Schweitzer said to him, "naturally many things in the chorales must sound obscure to you for the reason that they are explicable solely by the texts pertaining to them." The particular movements which baffled Widor were then shown to Schweitzer, who translated the verses to which they were set into French from memory; and the mysteries, so far as Widor was concerned, were dispelled.*

Now, it did not require unusual originality to find the solution in this case, but the fact is that masters like Widor had not thought of comparing the words with the music. The correspondence theory of truth, which, obviously, was a ready instrument in the hands of Schweitzer meant little to Widor. Schweitzer took into consideration not only the truth-correspondence of the chorale as a whole but the coherence of the parts among themselves.

It was the same striving after the truth, his hankering for consistency and his pursuance of common sense, (with the emphasis on soundness, factualness, original intention rather than on the commonness) which impelled Schweitzer to protest against the modernization of Bach's music by making use of the many stops, swell, pedals, etc., in the modern organ so as to keep constantly changing the volume and character of the sound, through repeated crescendos and diminuendos. Many performers argue that if Bach had lived today, he would have taken advantage of these improvements in the organ, and that he was unfortunately handicapped by living at a time when instrumental construction, particularly of the organ, was not fully developed. The question, however, is whether Bach, deeply religious as he was, himself so free from effects, would have succumbed to demands of a technical age instead of adhering to the spirit of his mystic evangelism. It, again, brings up the question, already alluded to, whether the musical values can be intensified by the size of the instrument, the number of the performers, the loudness of the playing, or the variety of effects. It would appear almost at first blush that such is not the case, and that such techniques are analogous to the exaggerated mimique and frequent changes in vocal inflection on the part of the mediocre actor.

Indeed, even some of Schweitzer's admirers wonder whether

* Albert Schweitzer: *J. S. Bach, le musicien-poète,* page vii.

he had not overstepped the mark in his principle of consistency. Thus, one of his biographers, J. D. Regester, writes "That Schweitzer is too consistent in his application of the eschatological principle is a criticism commonly made. His unvarying reference to this one principle of explanation for the life and teachings of Jesus seems to carry the theory too far."*

The same logical consistency is to be found in Schweitzer's *Philosophy of Civilization* and *Civilization and Ethics*, and although the slogan "reverence for life," to which it all adds up, is not by any means the novel discovery or panacea which the author feels it to be, the work, to be completed in four volumes, is a profound critique of modern civilization in all its aspects. It may truly be said that Schweitzer has deepened the concept of civilization by putting his finger on all the foibles, including the ivory-toweredness of philosophy.

In his inaugural dissertation, Karl Raab observes "It is remarkable what little interest Schweitzer takes in scholasticism and the whole philosophy of the Middle Ages, right up to Descartes. In his works, there are but a scant few references to it."** There is nothing remarkable about it once we are cognizant of Schweitzer's aversion to hair-splitting categories and casuistry. To him, logic should serve life, and not *vice versa*. What Schweitzer calls "elemental thought" is the warp and woof of the philosophy which counts, and not the cosmologies and metaphysics which do not improve living, although they sharpen one's wits.

Rejecting the intellectualism of Descartes's *Cogito ergo \sum,* he substitutes in its place the conative formula "I am life which wills to live in the midst of life which wills to live." At times, Schweitzer strikes the note of a Jeremiah sitting amidst the ruins of his battered city-state; and it is here that his strictly ratio-cinative powers occasionally make way for his strongly religious and mildly mystical sentiments, which will not carry the same

*J. D. Regester: *Albert Schweitzer,* page 114.
** K. Raab: *Albert Schweitzer; Persönlichkeit und Denken,* page 30, note.

weight with his unreservedly rationalistic readers and admirers. The thread of logical consistency, however, is followed to its extreme consequences in that Schweitzer bids us respect the life of the worm, not merely not to crush it under foot, but to guard it against danger, wherever possible, and even to treat plants with some consideration, and to feel contrite whenever destruction of a tree or twig proves necessary.

Who among us can follow the prophet to such heights of ethical conduct? Nevertheless in theory, there is no denying that life is life, and what is true of the one is true of the other, even if convention has adopted a graded system of values in accordance with the supposed sensitivity to pleasure and pain, so that royalty and the nobility were invested with more delicate feelings than plebeians, the white man or the Christian with greater reactivity than the Negro or the Jew; and of course, psychologists have long since come to the conclusion that the lower the species of the animal the less pain it feels, which belief was responsible for the cruel treatment of animals. In his autobiography, Salomon Maimon tells us in his whimsical way how Descartes's assigning a soul only to human beings rendered the dumb animals exposed to all kinds of blows at the hands of the enlightened; and the cries or yelps were interpreted as if they were the sounds given off by striking anything inanimate, e. g. a drum.

The "regard for life" to Schweitzer means more than not taking life wantonly. It applies to all that goes toward making life —the weal (and woe), the pleasures (and pains), the cultural fullness, in other words, all that enters to promote and preserve life. When Albert Schweitzer set about to deplore the decline of civilization, little did he anticipate what unspeakable fiendishness (the word *bestiality* would be an insult to the animals and beasts) was in store for the world—and all engineered in that very country which boasted of a civilization and culture surpassing all others.

Goethe has signalized this state of civilization in his oft-repeated couplet

ALBERT SCHWEITZER, THE MAN

Er nennt's Vernunft, und braucht's allein,
*Nur tierischer als jedes Tier zu sein.**

That Schweitzer with prophetic foreboding saw what was
coming even before the Nazi dragon had seized power is evident
from this significant passage in *Aus meinem Leben und Denken,*
which appeared in Germany in 1932.

> I am inwardly conscious that we are on a road which,
> if we continue to tread it, will bring us into 'Middle Ages'
> of a new character. The spiritual and material misery to
> which mankind of today is delivering itself through its
> renunciation of thinking and of the ideals which spring
> therefrom, I picture to myself in its utmost compass. And
> yet I remain optimistic. One belief of my childhood I have
> preserved with the certainty that I can never lose it: belief
> in truth. I am confident that the spirit generated by truth
> is stronger than the force of circumstances. In my view
> no other destiny awaits mankind than that which, through
> its mental and spiritual disposition, it prepares for itself.
> Therefore I do not believe that it will have to tread the
> road to ruin right to the end.

And yet, was it not through a fortunate accident, a fluke, that
the international thugs were kept from demolishing our whole
civilization, cities and states, along with the hundreds of millions
of their inhabitants? How close the fiendish V^2 and V^3 rockets
were from turning the world into a global cemetery, stalked by
ghouls, is only being discovered today; and one shudders to think
what would have happened to whole races and national groups,
not to speak of ideological adversaries, if the Nazis had succeeded
in contriving the atomic bomb first.

If logical consistency were all that distinguished Schweitzer

*Reason he dubs it; and its use, at least,
Is to be more beastly than any beast.

from others, he might have been worthy of honor, but he would have not been revered by almost all who are acquainted with his work. Nor is it because he has been able to accumulate doctorates in fields as far apart as music, theology, philosophy, and medicine that he stands out today as possibly the world's most venerated man. Versatility at a high level like his is rare, but his genius lies not in a single one of the fields to which he has made significant contributions, but in the sphere of conduct. In a youthful student essay long before I knew of the existence of Schweitzer, I argued that there were ethical geniuses as well as musical or literary geniuses. Certainly Schweitzer is one of the very few who belong to the former class. There are admittedly those who have become paragons of virtue in advanced years after leading a profligate life in youth; there were always to be found, in the words of Harold Begbie, "Twice-born men," but for a man to renounce the fruition of his gifts and to take the hardest road in order to perform services which no one else would render requires not cognitive but conative or volitional genius. The curious distinction between mental endowment and ethical practice is that while it is given to a blessed small minority to be creative, everyone can, if so disposed, do the right thing according to his own lights, but how often, even among the righteous, is the plaint of the poet true, when he sang

> *Meliora video proboque;*
> *Pejora sequor.*

Schweitzer has achieved the all but impossible by incorporating the syllogism into his mode of living. His major premise is the maxim or imperative; the minor, a specific instance, like the neglected Negroes, and the conclusion is acted out, as if it were a matter of paying a visit to a sick relative. As we examine all his known behavior, we note that each act falls into the category of a moral syllogism. The circumstances are not thought relevant

[48]

LOG ROLLING IN LAMBARENE.
(Dr. Schweitzer assisted more than once, in gratitude)

ALBERT SCHWEITZER AT HIS DESK
IN LAMBARENE

ALBERT SCHWEITZER IN LAMBARENE
IN 1930.

to the issue so as to relax his self-discipline or to reverse his original decision. The question before his mind always was: Should this be done? If so, there could be no hedging, no temporizing, nor half-way measures. This self-discipline is evidenced in all his studies. At 19, he was just able to pass his Hebraicum after much effort. "Later, spurred on again by the endeavor to master what did not come easily to me. I acquired a sound knowledge of that language."

ETHICAL ACUITY

Schweitzer's practice was to benefit from a single observation, and to apply the knowledge gained therefrom, regardless of how unbecoming it might seem from a conventional, or rather philistine point of view. A typical illustration of this translation of a perception into an act of high ethical consistency is furnished in an episode which happened at the time the Schweitzers were leaving Camp Garaison, where they were held as prisoners of war.

At the station at Tarascon we had to wait for the arrival of our train in a distant goods-shed. My wife and I, heavily laden with baggage, could hardly get along over the shingle between the lines. Thereupon a poor cripple whom I had treated in the camp came forward to help us. He had no baggage because he possessed nothing, and I was much moved by his offer, which I accepted. While we walked along side by side in the scorching sun, I vowed to myself that in memory of him I would in future always keep a look-out at stations for heavily laden people, and help them. And this vow I have kept. On one occasion, however, my offer made me suspected of thievish intentions.!"*

Every time he gained an insight into the mind of his fellow-man, through his own experience, he made it a point to remedy

---

*Albert Schweitzer: *Out of My Life and Thought,* pages 207-208.

the situation, so that he was not only a doctor to the African blacks, but an assuager of pain or distress to whomsoever he happened to be thrown in with. This particular knack might be called *ethical acuity*. It is not merely a sympathetic transitory feeling, which millions may experience, but a transmutation into a maxim, and thence into a beneficent deed, often of trying proportions. The opposite of ethical acuity is ethical obtuseness, which begins with a lack of sympathy, or else does not carry over the sympathy, if felt, into conduct.

The self-denial which Schweitzer accepted, or rather imposed upon himself, places him in the forefront of modern saints. Saintliness, we know, is a concept which lends itself to various interpretations. It is not, however, the renunciation *per se* that constitutes saintliness, but self-sacrifice in behalf of a w o r t h y cause; and what cause can be worthier than setting an example to the world, upon arriving at the conclusion that we can individually alleviate the misery of thousands of individuals if we are only willing to give up some of our own, in many cases, questionable comforts?

Perhaps it is not saintliness so much as heroism which characterizes Schweitzer; but heroism implies meeting a sudden situation or emergency. Schweitzer's stamina were proven by the long-range planning and courage which it required to execute his original decisions and to overcome both the situational and the man-made difficulties. How much of a temptation there would have been for the most self-reliant and determined person to turn back with the comforting thought "I've done my level best, and it is not my fault if the way is barred"! Patience of which Schweitzer is possessed almost to excess—although he tells us that in his childhood he would exhibit a short temper with those who seemed stupid, and therefore it must be inferred that he re-educated his primary tendencies—is an attribute of saintliness rather than of heroism, although both are linked with courage.

ALBERT SCHWEITZER, THE MAN

CHARACTER AND PERSONALITY

Here we come to the very crux of Schweitzer's character. If we accept the definition of Emerson that "character is centrality, the impossibility of being displaced or overset," then, surely few of his contemporaries can measure up with Albert Schweitzer in that respect. "A man should give us a sense of mass," he further specifies; and here too Schweitzer more than meets the requirements. In his account of the African comfort-bringer, W. Montgomery tells us that the first impression one receives in Schweitzer's presence is that of power, while the second is that of charm. His rugged constitution, which has withstood for many years the hardships of the African climate and its consequences, as well as the chagrin and annoyance resulting from the irresponsibility and backwardness of his charges, has become almost legendary. His graciousness, cordiality, and his charm have been attested by all who came in contact with him. Uusually these qualities are to be found in individuals of the primary-function type. Schweitzer is unmistakably of the secondary-function type,* and therefore the combination of such traits is a rare occurrence, like blue eyes with a dark skin and dark hair.

Schweitzer's felicitous blend of apparently divergent qualities is, it seems to me, not an indication of a duality, as argues Dr. Bixler, in his somewhat Hegelian interpretation of Schweitzer, which follows this rather common-sense approach, and although his solid and closely-reasoned essay offers sufficient evidence to make out a case for tension and polarity in Schweitzer, I still consider Schweitzer's writings as exemplified by a remarkable unity and his life and personality characterized by extraordinary inner adjustment—wholly predictable on the strength of general principles. Whatever antithesis looms in his system is soon reorganized into a synthesis without leaving a blemish or scar. In other words, we are dealing with a highly integrated psychophysical organism.

*The distinction is treated in my *Psychology of Character* pages 244-248.

INTEGRATION

A person in whom duality is pronounced would show alternating phases of his character. Schweitzer was not addicted to such oscillations. Humility and authority shone through like the sun from among the clouds during the same period. An idealist of the first water, he has not undertaken anything which was not feasible. What is more, he displayed the most practical sense in handling a situation, *e.g.,* in exchanging banknotes for gold, when he was travelling to Africa for the first time, or in the disposition of his manuscripts during the first World War, or in the simpler task of packing his cases.

No one could harbor the thought that Schweitzer is an opportunist, and yet he made use of every opportunity to further his rightful cause. He never wasted time bewailing his lot, or in protests, in useless struggles against the authorities, or in exposing the absurdity of conditions that were created through officials at the time of the war. He could smile with equanimity at the irony of the situations and would proceed to busy himself with some other activity and accomplish his objective in one or another of his several fields, as if that had been his original intention.

To illustrate, when Schweitzer was, as a result of his German nationality, forbidden as an "alien enemy," to minister to the natives, he continued his work on the Philosophy of Civilization, or he would practice on the "piano-organ," until the ridiculousness of the ban occurred even to the District Commandant, after "white and black alike had protested against being deprived without any perceivable reason of the services of the only doctor for hundreds of miles around." Schweitzer probably knew that it would come to that without spending his energy on vehement representations. The same comedy recurred in France whither he had been transferred as a prisoner of war. It did not take long before his worth was revealed to the Governor of the camp, who afterwards was glad to carry on a correspondence with his erstwhile prisoner. In this camp, as soon as a grateful fellow-prisoner, who was a carpenter, made a table for him, Schweitzer immediately set about shadow-playing on it, as if it were an organ. That Schweitzer was ever mindful of the *carpe diem* injunction is evident from the following episode. During 1923, while he was traversing Switzerland, he had to wait two hours in Zürich. To pass the time, he paid a visit to his friend, the pastor and psychoanalyst, Oskar Pfister, who welcomed him of course, and asked him to relate his childhood memories to be used in a juvenile magazine in which Pfister was interested. After Schweitzer saw the transcript of the shorthand notes, he begged his friend not to publish them, and one stormy afternoon, Schweitzer decided to extend these memories, and soon a little volume appeared first in German, then in English, and later in Swedish, Dutch, Danish, and French.

Here we have the secret of Schweitzer's tremendous achievement; for it must surely fill us with wonderment how a man could have accomplished in four different fields what would have been a signal achievement in any one of them and labor, besides, in a one-doctor hospital. The answer is that Schweitzer never wasted his minutes, hence the hours took care of themselves. Furthermore, his was a direct way of getting to the core of a subject. In his capacity for scuffing the technicalities away, he resembles the British rather than the Germans. Moreover, it would seem that he could engage in several different activities at once, as if, while his conscious was occupied with one train of thought, his unconscious would be elaborating or incubating something of a different order. "While I was correcting the proofs of *Civilization and Ethics*, I was already packing cases for my second voyage to Africa." That describes pithily the tempo of his work, almost of a synchronous order.

Clarendon's description of John Hampden as one "who was of an industry and vigilance not to be tired out or wearied by the most laborious, and of parts not to be imposed on by the most subtle and sharp, and of a personal courage equal to his best parts" would fit Albert Schweitzer equally well. He may not have adhered religiously to the *nulla dies sine linea* rule, but he certainly did not allow the day to pass without crowding into it a considerable amount of activity, or rather beneficence.

SIMULTANEITY IN SUCCESSION

It is generally expected of one who has changed one specialty for another to wean himself away from his first vocation, or at least to treat the earlier activity as an avocation. The wide gulf between Schweitzer's European life and the conditions under which he was living in equatorial Africa would more than warrant this supposition. Indeed Schweitzer himself, in his autobiography, tells us "When I first went to Africa, I prepared to make three sacrifices: to abandon the organ, to renounce the academic teaching activities, to which I had given my heart, and to lose my financial independence, relying for the rest of my life on the help of friends. These three sacrifices I had begun to make, and only my intimate friends knew what they cost me."

He likens, however, his case to that of Abraham who was spared the sacrifice, for the Paris Bach Society made him a gift of a piano with pedal attachments, so that he was able to develop his skill as a performer, aside from the balm which it meant for his soul during his jungle loneliness; his extensive lecture cycles in the various European universities, between his first and second African sojourn, gratified his academic aspirations, while the funds raised through his lectures, writings, and organ performances, which brought him the highest praise as an artist, assured his financial independence, at least for a considerable period.

Let us recall, also, that as a physician, he was not merely a doctor, a surgeon, but an organizer, and administrator, even a master-builder, to begin with—a foreman heading a group of recalcitrant and unintelligent "voluntary" workers.

While engaged in carrying out his exhausting tasks and chores, he still managed to concentrate on his music and philosophy, as if each one were his only concern. His amazing adaptability to new circumstances and conditions would secure for him the award of very high intelligence among American psychologists; but what seems more wonderful is the *continuity* of his interests, proving in part the unity of his life, his past entering into the present, and together going to shape the future. This may be considered somewhat analogous to a melody which has its significance for the listener in its simultaneity although it consists of a succession of tones. There was never any splitting but a splicing of interests in his make-up. This integratedness at a high peak, which starts with the powerful physique and culminates, through a compounded development, in the moral or spiritual, is the quintessence of Schweitzer's characteristics; and he sums up his personality very aptly when toward the end of his biography, he speaks of the things that he has to be thankful for: "that I enjoy a health which allows me to undertake most exhausting work; that I have a well-balanced temperament which varies little, and an energy which exerts itself with calmness and deliberation; and finally, that I can recognize as such whatever happiness falls to my lot".

The dilemmas which Schweitzer has been confronted with are not those of his making. They do not emerge from any conflicts within himself but from the conditions of existence, the need of sacrificing one life for another—and therein it is difficult to follow him, when, for example, he has to reflect on the destruction of the germs of sleeping sickness in order to save life, or when he buys a fish-eagle from the natives in order to rescue it and then must kill a number of small fishes daily in order to feed it.

This may appear as a sample of rationalism reduced to absurdity, but it is not so to Albert Schweitzer, who must have taken seriously the old sorites argument, which in the present case would in the last analysis ask: "At what point in the animal world does life cease to have value for us"? Obviously the answer to this is "When it menaces the existence of other beings." Social usefulness may also become a criterion of the value of life. Thus mosquitoes, germs, and other harmful organisms can scarcely arouse our compassion, even on rationalistic grounds.

But here we are probably approaching the mystical element in Schweitzer's ethicism, where everything is related to everything else in an inextricable manner. To the "naked eye", such a world outlook must smack of sentimentalism, which will project feelings into inanimate objects.

Chopin probably typifies that sort of excessive sympathy, if credence is given to the various ancdotes related about him, at its vulnerable, not to say ridiculous, level.

In the libretto of the opera *Chopin*, we find a passage which gives expression to this form of sentimentalism, without, however, the highly ethical or rationalistic aspect that is to be discerned in Schweitzer.

When his friend Elio invites him to go skating, Chopin, struck by the dull rumbling which comes from the lake, the surface of which is cut by the gliding skaters, indignantly replies:

> *To make gashes like glistening wounds?*
> *To make it weep so profoundly?*
> *At every glide of the skates*
> *A dull mournful sound is heard,*
> *There under the ice lamenting*
> *Moan the pent up waters.* *

Perhaps this ethical hyperaesthesia will some day be understood by a majority of the enlightened. At present it seems carrying

*A solcarlo di candide ferite?
A far che pianga
Profondamente?
Ad ogni guizzo di pattini un rombo
Sordo lugubre si sente:
Là sotto i ghiacci, lamentevolmente,
Gemon l'acque prigioniere.

the reverence-for-life principle to an impasse, but perhaps this is due to the tinge of mysticism which colors Schweitzer's rationalism. "Rational thinking, if it goes deep, ends of necessity in the non-rational of mysticism. It has, of course, to deal with life and the world, both of which are non-rational entities". Mysticism, according to Schweitzer, links men spiritually with the Infinite. Strict rationalists will not follow him through this conclusion, but the mystic has the advantage in that he is immune to examination. By way of retaliation, however, he is left severely alone; practically ignored or cavalierly treated by non-mystics.

In this respect, one is ready to grant President Bixler's finding of polarity and tension in Schweitzer's philosophy, but otherwise, the harmony in his life and work is unique for our generation. Schweitzer frequently speaks of *Entzweiung* (dissociation) in the world and its thinking, but, aside from the circumstances of nature (will-to-live and its complications) which place even him in a quandary, he would be the last person to be guilty of such splitting.

ADEQUACY VALENCE

Whatever the physiological reasons for such unity of purpose, integration, balance, and almost perfect adjustment to be found in Schweitzer, *genuineness* is the outcome. There are numerous schemas of personality, but in the last analysis, genuineness is the underlying criterion. The neurotic, the maladjusted, yes, even the muddlehead—they all lack that quality which sometimes is called "sterling". For every person who is genuine, there are 999 who are artificial, spurious in various gradations. Many artists, scholars, scientists, authors, and notables in other walks are incomplete in that they pose or are self-seeking, or calculating, pompous, or egotistical, irascible, ingratiating, etc. There is an inadequacy in their constitution, which manifests itself in their behavior, no matter how glorious they show themselves in their achievements. Need one mention such celebrities as John Ruskin, Carlyle, Rousseau, or Voltaire? On the other hand, some of the mediocre have been known for their self-reliance, independence, non-opportunism, graciousness, balance and other qualities which are constituents of what we might call *"adequacy"*. The adequacy valence might be taken to mean the opposite of "inferiority complex", as the phrase is understood among psychologists and psychiatrists, the concept of psychopathic inferiority dating back to J. L. A. Koch, and even long before him, if we discount the actual term.

The basic elements of adequacy, which give it its valence are three, each representing one of the larger departments of the mind. From the affective range, it is not the emotions or the feelings or the temperaments which count, but the *sensibilities* and *sentiments*. From the cognitive or intelligence factors, neither intelligence nor intellect is the determinant, but rather *insight*, which bears on the relation between ourselves and others, while in the volitional or characterical sphere, the trait of *independence* (courage, self-reliance) is paramount. A blend, then, of cultivated sentiments, fine insight, and a high independence coefficient will yield a desirable adequacy valence. A low index in any one of these qualities will spell inadequacy, or what Goethe called "incompleteness".

I don't know of any person who surpasses Schweitzer in the felicitous integration of these adequacy components. His sensibilities, if anything, are overdeveloped, his insight has proved itself again and again in his relations with the great as well as with his humblest native patients, while his independence has been such as to evoke the exclamation *"ne plus ultra"*. From his early childhood he dared to oppose his elders, if he thought his cause to be just. The humanizing of the apotheosized Jesus was, of a truth, a daring exploit for a theologian and preacher. Nor did he mince his words in protesting against the weakness of organized Christianity through the ages, and especially in recent years. "The situation today is that Christianity has completely withdrawn into itself, and is concerned only with the propagation of its own ideas, as such." And in the same vein, he takes Christianity to task for not opposing the police and prison tortures in order to extract confessions. "Similarly it makes hardly any effort to counter the superstitions of today". He denies that Christianity has any power over the spirit of the age, and concludes that "just in proportion as it gains in external power, it loses in spiritual". What critic of the Church has been more emphatic in his strictures than this theologian and preacher who frankly declares:

> What has been passing for Christianity during these nineteen centuries is merely a beginning, full of weaknesses and mistakes, not a full-grown Christianity springing from the spirit of Jesus. Because I am devoted to Christianity in deep affection, I am trying to serve it with loyalty and sincerity. In no wise do I undertake to enter the lists on its behalf with the crooked and fragile thinking of Christian apologetic, but I call on it to set itself right in the spirit of sincerity with its past and with thought in order that it may thereby become conscious of its true nature.

Schweitzer took his calling as doctor seriously. How he would like to have performed his operations on institutions and organizations, as he did on the jungle aborigines! Correct the hernias of civilization, cure the dysentery or sleeping sickness of Christianity, but just as Archimedes needed a fulcrum for moving the earth, so Schweitzer lacked the facilities for carrying out his collective surgery. He can only prescribe, but it is up to the patient to follow the instructions; and there are other physicians who drug the patient with all sorts of agreeable pills . . .

Independent thought and action like Schweitzer's is uncommon, but critics who dared to speak the truth in the face of authority, even to their own undoing, have been known in history. It is not, however, known that a man who was the friend of rulers (the talented Rumanian Queen, Carmen Sylva, tried to prevail upon Schweitzer to live at the palace so that she could listen to his playing every day), and one who had received honorary degrees from Oxford, Edinburgh, Prague, and would have been honored by Harvard at the Tercentenary Celebration, had he been willing to appear personally in Cambridge at the time, a man who had made his mark in several distinct departments of knowledge and art—that such a man would, first of all, abandon all the prospects of further creativeness in order to dedicate himself to the cause of the forlorn Negro in uncivilized Africa; and above all that such an outstanding luminary would, in order to repay a kindness to one of the timber merchants during the first World War, join the native laborers rolling timber. "This heavy work—we often needed hours to roll up on to the shore one of these logs weighing from two to three tons—was only possible at high tide. When the tide was out, I sat at my Philosophy of Civilization, so far as my time was not claimed by patients".

It is one of this calibre whom Wotton must have had in mind when he wrote

This man is freed from servile bonds
Of hope to rise, or fear to fall;
Lord of himself, though not of lands;
And having nothing, yet hath all.

It is the freedom which knows of no traditional cobwebs, which is shackled by no conventionality, except that of the heart (or, in the terminology of some, the spirit) a freedom which is tantamount to Kant's autonomy of the will, which, too, is the moral principle embodied in the adequacy valence.

When Kipling wrote his well-known "If" poem, he must have pondered whether such a standard as he has set could be met by more than a few in a generation; and we may wonder whether the designation "man" in the last line is not an example of British understatement.

> *If you can trust yourself when all men doubt you,*
> *But make allowance for their doubting too;*
>
> .   .   .   .
>
> *Or being hated, don't give way to hating,*
> *And yet don't look too good, nor talk too wise:*
>
> .   .   .   .
>
> *If you can talk with crowds and keep your virtue,*
> *Or walk with kings—nor lose the common touch,*
> *If neither foes nor loving friends can hurt you,*
> *If all men count with you, but none too much;*
> *If you can fill the unforgiving minute*
> *With sixty seconds' worth of distance run*
> *Yours is the earth and everything that's in it*
> *And—which is more—you'll be a man, my son!*

If his and Schweitzer's paths crossed, then he must have intuitively sensed, even if he should not have obtained the information beforehand, that the *rarissima avis* was before him.

The term *valence* has been employed here in the sense of a measure or coefficient which is bound to bring out the significance or colorfulness as attributes of adequacy, but the *Gestalt* connotation, The *Aufforderungs-Charakter,* i.e., the provocative character (attracting or repelling value) of objects or processes is applicable here too.

In this respect, as has been brought out, Schweitzer's adequacy valence has been decidedly positive. His ability to mingle with others in every station, in every clime, and at every time, in a strengthening way, needs no further corroboration. Yet critics there will ever be. Some, from the technological camp, are not in sympathy with Schweitzer's mystical, or even religious, trend, while others again, in orthodox circles, look askance at his bold-ness in questioning the authenticity of the Gospels and the om-niscience of Jesus, who is now cast into an eschatological Jewish mould. His views on organ music have earned for him a great reputation, but there are those who see in them only a limited imagination and an unprogressive tendency.

PUZZLES AND SPECULATIONS

His failure to cry out against the Nazi regime is broached by one of his most ardent admirers, in this volume. Alice Ehlers informs us that he politely declined an invitation, tendered by the city of Leipzig, to participate in the great Bach festival, in 1935; and then in reply to the query, which must have reached her ears more than once, why Schweitzer did not speak his mind on the impending cataclysm, she expresses her conviction that he is a persistent but not an aggressive fighter. It would be futile to thresh this issue out in Schweitzer's absence. His relation to Germany in general is not clear. Of all the Nordic countries, Germany accorded him the least attention, even if books and articles on his work did appear in German under the Nazi regime.*

In Sweden and Denmark, in England and Scotland, in Holland, Switzerland, and in the United States, Schweitzer has been almost canonized in humanistic circles. There is something significant even in the particular "Schweitzer constellation" which this group of liberal countries represents. Although Schweitzer labored on French territory for nearly thirty years, curiously enough, it is Schweitzer the musician that France has recognized.

It is perhaps not wholly fortuitous that his assistants and co-workers were Alsatian, Swiss, and British. I have not been able to trace a single German helper; and there was ample opportunity

* K. Raab, in his doctoral dissertation, *Albert Schweitzer; Persönlichkeit und Denken,* even sees a link between Albert Schweitzer and Alfred Rosenberg, the Nazi theoretician, in that both are preoccupied in their respective philosophies with elemental life!

for Germans to enter French colonies at the close of the War in 1918. Schweitzer of course preferred Berlin to Paris ("I was especially impressed by the simple mode of life of Berlin society, and the ease with which one got admittance to its family life"). Alsace, however, seems like a country by itself, to judge by the number of occasions he would single out Alsatians. There is a tinge of poetic justice in the footnote to an article on Albert Schweitzer in *Hebdomadaire*, a French weekly, which speaks *"d'un Français trop méconnu, aussi grand savant et grand artiste que grand philosophe"* (See Bibliography in this volume under Urmatt F., in Section IV). We must bear in mind that this "very much unknown Frenchman" had been in a French concentration camp for enemy aliens during World War I, and had not since become naturalized.

His uncharitable comparison of Clemenceau's physiognomy with that of an animal might have been unwittingly dictated by the feeling that it was that statesman who imposed the Versailles treaty on the Germans. Russia, too, fares poorly in Schweitzer's estimate ("I never shut my eyes to the fact that the fate of Europe had been placed by the development of events in the hands of the semi-Asiatics . . . ")* and he hints that France and Germany would have gotten along well but for the intrigues of Russia. On this point, Schweitzer's political insight, so clear and penetrating in general, seems to err; and it would be ironical to discover eventually that there was Slavic blood in his veins; for at least in some of his p o r t r a i t s, he might be taken for a Czech rather than a German—perhaps a distant cousin of Nietzsche. His world-outlook, too, with its rationalism turned into mysticism, savors of Russian elemental thought, with the call for self-renunciation so as to ameliorate and elevate the status of the peasantry. Whether or not he has changed his opinion about Russia in recent years is something worth inquiring about.

---

* But does this veiled slur not overlook the fact that the highest religion came from Asia, and that the Nazi coldblooded mass murders were products of twentieth-century *European* civilization?

Schweitzer's suspicion of all nationalism does not render him insensible to national differences; otherwise, he would not have taken the trouble to mention the origin of his workers, as he usually does, except in the case of the Jews, some of whom have been most ardent supporters of his cause. In his aversion to nationalism, Schweitzer thinks rather in terms of territory. Thus, the country takes the place of the nation or nationality, but in this substitution, some injustice is bound to occur, and certain cultural aspects are sometimes lost sight of. He himself must be a blend. The very name *Schweitzer* already implies Swiss as well as German antecedents, but undoubtedly there were other strains too in the genetic make-up, and a Slavic ancestor is at least a possibility.

Surely it is not without significance that Schweitzer's national physiognomy seems to change from likeness to likeness. In the one where he is seen with a tropical helmet he might be taken for an Englishman; in the photograph showing him at the organ, he calls to mind a French composer, perhaps Massenet, while in other portraits (hand against his chest), he appears Slavic. Certainly there is nothing typically German about any of them. It is as if divergent strains of his make-up were to reveal themselves under different circumstances.

These speculations, however, are merely slender clues which may aid the comprehensive biographer. Schweitzer's life and personality are transparent because of the man's rectilinear and forthright course, but occasionally a dim pinpoint will present itself, which may be due to the blind spot either of our subject or the observer.

A LIVING LAW

The chief criticism which Schweitzer has had to endure is, of course, his giving up his rich cultural pursuits and prospects in order to minister to the "dregs" of humanity. "In Europe" they jeered, "he saved old organs, and in Africa, he saves old niggers."

ALBERT SCHWEITZER IN HIS
ROMANTIC AND ARTISTIC PHASE

ALBERT SCHWEITZER
IN BERLIN, IN 1928

What these cynics do not perceive in their smug careerism is that aside from the saving of thousands of lives and the alleviation of excruciating pain and untold misery, Schweitzer has called the attention of the world to the sordid realities, hitherto ignored, and the boundless possibilities, but especially to the bounden duties, not merely of the white man to the black, but of man to man. He has taken the hardest road because it is the most effectual. When we honor the Lavoisiers and the Robert Mayers for proving the indestructibility of matter and the conservation of energy, we must not forget the Schweitzers for demonstrating, through their own conduct, the continuity of the ethical principle, thus exemplifying the force and validity of Kant's striking dictum *"Du kannst denn du sollst!"* ("You can; for you ought"). It had not been thought possible for a European to endure the equatorial climate and its consequences for more than a few years without a long vacation elsewhere, but Schweitzer has subordinated the physical to the moral and thus broke one of the empirical quasi-laws. It was assumed, on all hands, even by Schweitzer himself, that his arduous activities and responsibilities in the jungle would throttle all his other main cultural interests, yet he was able to continue his research, his writing, and his playing to the point of astonishing the *cognoscenti,* thus again throwing overboard an empirical rule.

Some day an intelligent cinema producer or his counsellor will become aware that the "great Ziegfelds" the "magnificent Lou Gehrigs," the "glorious Knute Rocknes" and "dazzling George Gershwins" do not offer nearly as much material of human interest as the life of Albert Schweitzer, first in peaceful Günsbach, then in the large European centres, and finally as a jungle doctor in Africa. What opportunities are missed by those tycoons, and what entertainment and instruction are denied to the millions who would be inspired and imbued with the spirit of service!

Yes, there is a great deal of entertainment in store for those who will see on the screen the most preposterous and laughter-provoking situations, as when Schweitzer, being asked by the members of the Synod in his district to express an opinion on a certain point, is told by one of the black preachers that "the matter was outside the Doctor's province 'because he is not a theologian as we are' ". The native preacher did not know that while still a young man, Schweitzer's name was one to conjure with in European theological circles.

At another time, Schweitzer, trying to make it easy for an old native woman in an examination prior to baptism as a Christian, asked among other simple questions, whether Jesus had been rich or poor. "What a stupid question!" the lady impatiently answered, "If God, the great Chief was his Father, he certainly can't have been poor." Another curious incident took place in 1924, when Schweitzer was embarking at Bordeaux for his second trip to Africa. He had taken with him four potato sacks full of unanswered letters, but the customs inspector supposed that this was a ruse for taking out of the country more than 5000 francs allowed by the law, so he proceeded to examine for an hour and a-half each sack, until coming to the end of the bottom sack, he gave up in disgust.

The French sergeant who was dumbfounded to think that his charge, then an interned German, was reading, in French, a book entitled *Politics,* until Schweitzer explained that the author, Aristotle, lived long before the Christian era, which seemed incredible to that "scholar," provides us with another good anecdote; and Schweitzer's offer to carry a stranger's suitcase being mistaken for attempted theft would surely "bring down the house."* It is not, however, as a movie promoter that I wish to present my case, but as a spokesman of the more cultivated, who find no satisfaction in the pusillanimous manner in which, with one or two exceptions, biography is treated in Hollywood. Without the least

* In his *From My African Notebook,* there are some hilarious stories about a young native who was brought to England, stories which, in addition, are most enlightening as illustrating primitive mentality.

desire to make comparative evaluations of the contributions of Pasteur and Schweitzer, I have no hesitation in maintaining that a Schweitzer film would be far more interesting than that of Pasteur because of the versatility of the latter and the variety of conditions presented.

Whether the benefactor of the mind or the benefactor of the heart is the greater blessing strikes one as an academic question. Often the two qualities go together, although in different proportions. Every genius is something of a hero and a martyr as well; for aside from the actual penalties often exacted of him by the State or the Church, as in the case of men like Socrates, Boethius, Dante, Giordano Bruno, Galilei, and many others, there can be no flowering of inspiration without the perspiration to constantly irrigate it, in numerous instances accelerating the expiration of the genius, who has set himself a pace which is too much for his frail constitution. Humanitarians, no less than discoverers, inventors, artists, and scientists, realize new possibilities through their very living.

We are thankful for the Pasteurs and the Kochs, the Listers, and the Edisons, but the saint no less deserves our gratefulness; since he atones for our shortcomings, not in any afterworld, but in our very midst. When we, in our self-centredness and bustle, omit the very simple courtesies and amenities of life, it is the saint who, through his kindness and gentleness, corrects the wrong. I think it is psychologically true that our heart goes out to the man or woman who has been extremely patient with some stupid, stolid, or awkward individual whom we cannot bring ourselves to treat more than civilly; and unless we are congenitally unfeeling we learn through such acts to cultivate a true humanitarian spirit.

The saint is not necessarily one who walks with God, but he who serves man and ministers to beast in distress; in other words, we may envisage him as the humanitarian *par excellence*. It is not his concern with man as someone to assist that makes the humanitarian what he is, but his living up to the dignity and destiny of manhood. The saint is thus the mediator between God and man, an angel, in the Hebrew sense of the word, *i.e.,* a messenger; and it does not matter whether one has in mind the anthropomorphic God (*prima causa*) of the theist or the theomorphic Man (ultimate ideal) of the humanist— pragmatically, it comes to the same thing. The saint, as he is conceived here, serves as the harbinger and interpreter of the humanity-to-be to mankind-as-is.

If Albert Schweitzer makes such a strong appeal to our imagination, it is because he has subordinated his many urges and gifts of the mind to the one call and blessing of the spirit. At the time of the Nazi "coördination" of university teachers, the Nobel prize laureate, Richard Willstätter, could have still retained his academic status, at least until he was eligible for retirement, but soon after the disturbances at the University of Munich, he decided to share the lot of his other non-"Aryan" colleagues. To the counsel of friends who urged him to cling to his professorship, because of his prospective contributions to science, he significantly replied: *"Genien gibt's genug; Charaktere sind selten"* (Of genius there is plenty, but men of character are rare). It was a tribute to the celebrated chemist to have recognized that timely fact which scientists, and technologists in particular, are wont to overlook. In this realm of character, Schweitzer has soared to hitherto unattained heights by operating in the very depths of Darkest Africa. He will always be remembered as the man who has dispelled a good deal of the darkness in Africa by lightening the burden of the black man, and by his indomitable will setting a precedent for creative minds with matching hearts of a veined humanity.

PRODUCTIVE TENSIONS

IN

THE WORK OF ALBERT SCHWEITZER

By

J. S. Bixler, Ph.D.
President, Colby College

CHAPTER II

PRODUCTIVE TENSIONS IN THE WORK
OF ALBERT SCHWEITZER

BY

J. S. BIXLER

Albert Schweitzer has entitled his autobiography *"Out of My Life and Thought"* as if to indicate that life and thought had each contributed in its own distinctive way to his working philosophy. The double emphasis is, I think, not merely a matter of rhetoric. In Schweitzer's various achievements life and thought complement each other in an unusual manner. We gain intellectually from his thought. We learn in a different way from his life, and because his life is what it is we approach his thought with a special type of interest. This essay will attempt to show that what confronts us here is a conflict of emotion and idea in Schweitzer which is not wholly resolved, yet which, in its lack of resolution, seems to afford us deeper insights than could otherwise be possible. Schweitzer appears to present us with a dualism where the lack of finality is itself a sign of fertility. Indeed Schweitzer himself often calls attention to a fundamental lack of compatibility in the demands of reason and feeling as a dualism with profound implications for philosophy.

Like the word "dialectic" the word "dualism" is ambiguous. In Schweitzer's usage it means simply that thought and feeling often cannot agree. Such an idea is of course not new. William James, for example, felt the difficulty keenly and expressed it in his famous formula "ever not quite," by which he meant the inadequacy of theory before the uniqueness of the color or the poignancy of the passing emotion. In a more general way Hegel has brought out unforgettably the struggle between thought and its object carried on not only in the individual human life, but in society, history, nature, and the cosmic process as a whole. Indeed one may ask whether the chief reason for the great influence of so obscure a writer as Hegel is not in the fact that his readers feel his own keen awareness of the constant tension between two opposing forces in the entire world of creation and respond to the genuineness of this insight in spite of the cumbersomeness of its expression. One reason, again for the deserved popularity of Brahms' Fourth Symphony may be its dramatic treatment of this dualistic theme. From the very first bar it presents a contrast between two opposing principles as if to represent an elemental struggle that can never be resolved. In our own day the issue is revived in the constant attack made on education for its exclusive concern with the verbal side of experience. Learning has two aspects, we are told — theoretical and active or practical. Forgetting this, our schools produce sterile formulas in the place of either living emotions or practical abilities, while our philosophies strive for intellectual consistency at the cost of neglecting important data provided by the feelings.

DUALISM OF INTELLECT AND EMOTION

In Schweitzer's case the problem is brought into sharp focus by his strenuous insistence on rigid intellectual procedure coupled with his frank admission that at crucial points the intellect simply will not respond satisfactorily to our demands. What interests us particularly is the honesty with which the lack of harmony is faced. The difficulty is not glossed over but is allowed to protrude in all its awkwardness from many of his written pages. It comes out with special prominence in his treatment of the difference between *Weltanschauung* and *Lebensanschauung* which we clumsily translate "World-view" and "Life-view." A world-view is an intellectual construction, a metaphysical statement of the nature of the universe reached through observation and critical analysis. A life-view is an emotional response to the demands the universe makes upon us. The element of reflection enters into a life-view but it is a particularly sensitive and appreciative kind of reflection. In the life-view we allow the currents of instinct and feeling to well up within us. We enter sympathetically into them and permit them to unfold their spiritual possibilities. But the intellect does not always coöperate as it might. We should think, Schweitzer says, yet we cannot think as we should. We should feel, but we cannot expect the intellect to justify some of our deepest and most imperious feelings.

Often Schweitzer attacks a problem as though he had complete confidence in the power of the intellect to solve it, only to discover that critical analysis must give way to a more intuitive approach. For example, he inveighs against our age because it has lost the power to think. We are assailed on all sides, he says, by advertising and propaganda, and since we are treated so often as merely suggestible automata we have begun to lose confidence in our ability to think for ourselves. This is very bad. Further, the massive achievements of science are so overwhelming in the special knowledge they require that we find ourselves passively accepting truth on authority and becoming skeptical of our intellectual independence of the experts.

All this must be changed. "The beginning of all spiritual life of any real value," he says, "is courageous faith in truth and open confession of the same." (*The Decay and Restoration of Civilization*, 102) Again: "Even if our will-to-action is destined to wrestle endlessly and unavailingly with an agnostic view of the universe and of life, still this painful disenchantment is better for it than persistent refusal to think out its position at all. For this disenchantment does, at any rate, mean that we are clear as to what we are doing." (*ibid* 104) "The true sense for reality," he says once more, (61) "is that insight which tells us that only through reasoned ethical ideals can we arrive at a normal relation to reality." And in the same book we find a spirited defense

of the rationalism of the eighteenth century. "All real progress
in the world is in the last analysis produced by rationalism," we
read. "It is true that the intellectual productions of the period
which we designate historically as the rationalistic are incomplete
and unsatisfactory, but the principle, which was then established,
of basing our view of the universe on thought and thought alone,
is valid for all time." (89) "I therefore stand and work in the
world," he remarks in his autobiography, *Out of My Life and
Thought,* (254) "as one who aims at making men less shallow
and morally better by making them think." And again: "Renunciation of thinking is a declaration of spiritual bankruptcy."
(*ibid* 258).

Yet listen to this from *Civilization and Ethics.* "Every world-
view which does not start from resignation in regard to knowledge is artificial and a mere fabrication . . . " (Preface, xi)
Again: "All valuable conviction is non-rational and has an
emotional character, because it cannot be derived from knowledge
of the world but arises out of the thinking experience of our
will-to-live, in which we stride out beyond all knowledge of the
world." (*ibid* xvi) Thus "the last fact which knowledge can discover is that the world is a manifestation, in every way puzzling,
of the universal will-to-live." (*ibid* x) And just as he claims
elsewhere that he stands as one who tries to make men think,
he says here: "I believe I am the first among Western thinkers
who has ventured to recognize this crushing result of knowledge,
and who is absolutely skeptical about our knowledge of the world
without at the same time renouncing with it belief in world-and
life-affirmation and ethics." (*ibid* xi)

Now of course it is not unusual to find a philosopher who says
that we must go beyond thought for the answers to our deepest
problems. What interests us in Schweitzer is this almost strident
proclamation of the contrasting virtues of thought and feeling
and the almost passionate espousal of thought even though it has
to be given up. It is interesting further to find Schweitzer's fre-

quent references to dualism as presenting an especially knotty problem suggesting that he himself felt that a wholly satisfactory solution is unattainable.

TYPES OF SOLUTION OFFERED

Schweitzer meets the issue partly by contrasting knowledge, as scientific and analytical, with philosophy or reason, which is more synthetic and creative. He remarks that in the nineteenth century philosophy took on a scientific and specialized character and in so doing lost what he calls its power of spontaneous and reasoned elemental thought, becoming a mere history of past events. For its specific concern with epistemology he has little sympathy. The problem of how knowledge is won is a technical specialized issue. The real job of philosophy is to show us the larger outlines of the world we live in and what our obligations to it are.

But he goes further. Philosophy is not only synthetic where science is analytic. Truly reasonable reflection is always carried on against a background of mystery. Otherwise it soon loses its vitality. Thought begins in wonder, as Aristotle said, and it ends, according to Schweitzer, in mysticism. Thus he asserts in his autobiography (273) "Rational thinking, if it goes deep, ends of necessity in the non-rational of mysticism. It has, of course, to deal with life and the world, both of which are non-rational entities." And in *The Decay and Restoration of Civilization* he says: "Reflection, when pursued to the end, leads somewhere and somehow to a living mysticism, which is for all men everywhere a living element of thought." (92) In other words, reason is a larger term than intellect. Reason includes the will. To quote: "It is in reason that intellect and will, which in our nature are mysteriously bound up together, seek to come to a mutual understanding. The ultimate knowledge that we strive to acquire is knowledge of life, which intellect looks at from without, will from within." (*ibid*, 91)

I think most readers will agree that this solution, which consists in assigning to reason other than strictly intellectual qualities, is more verbal than real. Schweitzer seems to feel this himself, for in other places he is more ready to affirm the presence of an unrelieved dualism. For example, in the preface to *Civilization and Ethics*, (xi) he comments on rationalism's failure to relate its knowledge of the world to our own moral impulses and to find a basis for our ethical action. The aim, he says, was unattainable. We are not meant to unite the world and ourselves in such harmony. "The result is that our thought finds itself involved in a dualism with which it can never finally settle. It is the dualism of world-view and life-view, of knowing and willing. To this dualism all the problems with which human thought has busied itself ultimately go back." The expedients used to get rid of it, he says, are innumerable but hopeless. In *Christianity and the Religions of the World* he puts the dilemma in a more sharply religious form. "All the problems of religion," he there says (83-84) "ultimately go back to this one—the experience I have of God within myself differs from the knowledge concerning Him which I derive from the world." But here there is no attempt at reconciliation. "All the mysteries of the world and of my existence in the world may ultimately be left on one side unsolved and insoluble." (*ibid*) Many similar expressions could be quoted from his books and articles. Finally, at the conclusion of his autobiography (279 *ff.*) he cries out: "My knowledge is pessimistic, but my willing and hoping are optimistic . . . Only at quite rare moments have I felt really glad to be alive . . . But however much concerned I was at the problem of misery in the world, I never let myself get lost in broodings over it; I always held firmly to the thought that each one of us can do a little to bring some portion of it to an end."

Here obviously we have not a verbal solution but one that is practical in the sense that we are set a moral rather than an intellectual task. The crux of the question is seen in the conflict set up between our own moral impulses and our inability to find their justification in our knowledge of the outer world, with the corollary that the problem of human suffering is intellectually insoluble and must simply be taken as a stimulus to constructive action.

Yet Schweitzer does not leave it without at least one more attempt to reach a reasonably satisfactory answer. In chapters XVII and XVIII of *Civilization and Ethics* he argues that if we cannot find knowledge of the outer world that satisfies both heart and head we can at least turn to the inner world and win consistency in our thought about what we find there. Our inner will to live is the elemental thing about us. We cannot deny it. Its presence makes pessimism finally impossible. Out of our reflective consideration of the will to live grows reverence for life. For the will to live is not sheer blind impulse, but the will to fullness of life. Feeling this in ourselves we can feel it in all around us. "In everything that exists there is at work an imaginative force which is determined by ideals." (pp 216-217) The will to live is more elemental, more basic, more fruitful than the will to find reasons. Descartes's initial datum "I think" was too abstract. Thought always has content. The undeniable content of my deepest introspective observation is the realization: "I am life that wills to live in the midst of life that wills to live." (*Out of My Life and Thought,* 186) Here is a basic datum tied up with my very existence and at the same time satisfying my deepest ethical impulses.

Thus the solution is not to grovel before the dualism but "to realize it as something which can no longer do us any harm." (*Civilization and Ethics,* preface xii) We should "bow to the fact that, as we cannot harmonize our life-view and our world-view, we must make up our minds to put the former above the latter . . . . What is decisive for our life-view is not our knowledge of the world but the character of the volition which is given in our will-to-live. The universal spirit meets us in nature as puzzling creative power. In our will-to-live we experience it within us as volition which is both world- and life-affirming and ethical." (*ibid*)

To summarize briefly: Thought is necessary, not merely pragmatically, or as a means of getting along successfully, but in response to a moral demand and as a necessary way of developing the spiritual life. Before the central religious problem, however, the question of an almighty God who supports our moral strivings, thought bogs down. Philosophy dodges the issue by going off into epistemology or history or by becoming scientific and specialized. The moral impulse which drove us to think does not appear to find in thought the satisfaction it expected. A certain amount of frustration, insufficiency, and therefore confusion is thus inevitable. Thought simply doesn't do for us all that it should. However, there is another need as deep as the need to think, as irresistible, as consonant with morality, and in a way more inclusive than the other. This is the will to live. It does not grow up in complete independence of thought, and thought should be centered on it to make our attitude toward it as consistent as possible. The will to live appears in us, when we approach it with understanding, not as the mere pragmatic will to survive, nor as a Nietzschean will to power, but as a will to perfection and in particular a will to love. It is true that my knowledge of this will is an inner or subjective knowledge, which must be contrasted with the outer knowledge to which I aspired. Yet it is not merely inner, for I am aware that what animates me animates all other individuals in the world of sentient beings. Thus while I lack the ability, so to say, with the prophet Amos to envisage the sweep of nature and history and to see a law of justice everywhere operative, I do have the emotional capacity, shown by Hosea, to probe deeply into my own experience as living, suffering, and loving existence and to find there the universal element shared by all alike. I must always have a sense of frustration until the head acknowledges the reasons for belief that to the heart are so clear. But, troublesome as this frustration is intellectually, morally I must not allow it to get me down. After all, I know, in the sense that I am aware of my kinship with other living beings. I realize my need of them and theirs of me, as surely as I know anything. I am aware, furthermore, of my obligation to improve myself ethically.

In all this I am certainly not blind to the obligation to be intellectually consistent. Indeed, my very recognition of the incompleteness and even the actual dualism in my philosophy is part of my response to this obligation. Therefore I should not reproach myself for this dualism. Neither morally nor intellectually has there been any compromise. It is better to acknowledge openly that the facts are not what I might wish than to claim unity where there is none. The frustration that the dualism stands for is not a moral frustration but a sign that the facts do not satisfy all the cravings of my heart. But I can take it. Indeed I can use this personal disappointment constructively by turning it into a stimulus to further self-mastery. This, I think, must be what Schweitzer means by urging us to absorb this dualism into our lives as something that no longer has any power over us.

THE PROBLEM AS SEEN IN HIS TREATMENT OF HISTORY

Let us now notice one or two illustrations of how a similar conflict between intellectual and emotional interests crops up in some of the specific problems Schweitzer attacks. As all his readers know, an essential part of Schweitzer's intellectual method is to build up a historical background in each field he treats before presenting his own views. In *Civilization and Ethics* he surveys the development of European thought before giving his own conclusions. In his studies of Jesus and Paul, likewise, he emphasizes historical fact in two ways. First he goes into an exhaustive discussion of the ideas held by earlier scholars in the field. Second, he explains in detail the historical setting in which both Jesus and Paul worked. But, in each case, before he is through his interest shifts from analysis of historical fact to an appreciative emotional awareness of certain truths that are independent of historical circumstances. It is as though Schweitzer began each task with enthusiasm for an exclusively intellectual approach and lost his initial confidence after the limitations of the intellectual method appeared.

Take, for example, his work on Jesus over which so much controversy has raged. Schweitzer's book, *The Quest of the Historical Jesus,* is important as a scholarly analysis of the work of earlier New Testament critics, especially those in Germany. It is also important for the light it throws on the historical facts of Jesus's own life and times. Throughout his analysis of the early Christian period one can feel the keen interest of the historian in knowing accurately what went on in this crucial epoch. Yet as he develops his own view of Jesus one begins to realize that it is not as an historical character that Jesus himself is significant. What we really gain from Jesus is a set of eternal truths which might have been set forth in any age. And Schweitzer goes further. Not only is Jesus significant as a figure who transcends history, but his own views of history were mistaken and irrelevant. Jesus expected the speedy end of the world. Events showed him to be wrong. Does this suggest that he was wrong in his religious insights also? Not at all, says Schweitzer. What we respond to in Jesus is his teaching about love. Jesus has religious authority for us because of this moral teaching, and his intellectual pronouncements, such as his ideas on the end of the world, do not matter. Indeed Schweitzer appears to go further and to say that Jesus's divinity is not interfered with by the fact that he was mistaken. Illusion as to what is need not affect insight into what should be.

Naturally this separation could be pressed too far. We should hesitate to listen to an obviously deluded fanatic even though his moral teachings were of the highest quality. Nor can our own moral ideas be completely separated from their factual context. Yet it appears to me that fundamentally Schweitzer is right in his approach to this whole problem and that his rightness is especially helpful today in the presence of the contemporary neo-orthodox movement which would insist on our accepting all or nothing in the Christian tradition. Today more than ever our theologies seem to search in vain for evidences of one increasing purpose by which the tragedy and waste in animal and human life can be justified. Nature and history alike are full of cross currents and we cannot by intellectual searching find the unified moral order which our hearts crave. Yet this should not make us blind to the presence amid all the confusion of a trend toward coöperation that calls us to align ourselves with it. To use Schweitzer's figure, there is a Gulf Stream flowing in the larger ocean and mysteriously keeping its own identity in the presence of forces that threaten to overwhelm it.

In the same way the fact that Jesus took over uncritically the thought forms and the intellectual framework of his age should not make us unaware of or unwilling to respond to the content he put into it. The effect of some of our Christian apologists today who would make him infallible and would try to square all he said and did with what would be expected of an omniscient Being can lead only to a more complete cleavage than Schweitzer's, viz., to an opposition between faith and knowledge where faith is called on to accept what knowledge knows to be improbable. Schweitzer's method is different and better. Although he does not put it this way one can characterize his approach as based on the difference between the relativity of knowledge and the absoluteness of moral insight. All empirical knowledge, including all knowledge of history, is at best only probable because it is based on sense observation and is subject to change by new discoveries and new experiments. We can only be sure that we cannot be sure of facts empirically known. But though we cannot be sure of particular facts we can always be certain that we should know as many facts as possible. Of some *values*, that is, we have an assurance that is absolute. That knowledge is better than ignorance, justice than injustice, and love than hate none of us will deny. It is this kind of assurance that Schweitzer sets before us and asks us to use as a basis for our religious faith. On the specific question as to the extent to which religious belief can be grounded on our shifting and relative knowledge of history Schweitzer appears to be in full accord with Fichte's dictum: *"Nur das Metaphysische aber keineswegs das Historische macht selig."* The metaphysical, used here in the sense of the total intellectual and personal outlook, is superior to the historical, where religious insight is concerned.

THE SAME PROBLEM IN MUSIC

If Schweitzer helps us to see the contrast in theology between the absoluteness of emotional response and the relativity and problematic character of historical or scientific knowledge he also helps us to see that in an art like music the roles of emotion and intellect are reversed. This is because in music the intellect acts not as a fact-gathering organ, dependent on unreliable sense experience and experiments which another day may reverse, but rather as an instrument of formal criticism appealing to abstract rules of thought. It is like the difference between mathematical and natural science. Mathematical science is absolute where the other is relative because the conclusions of mathematics follow rigidly from its premises and are true without exception in the sphere to which they apply, whereas natural science is experimental. In music the intellect grasps absolute formal relationships, while the emotional content is relative in the sense that it changes with each listener, suggesting this or that aesthetic value to each in terms of his own background and experience.

Because music is such a remarkable combination of Apollonian and Dionysian elements, presenting such a synthesis of mathematical form and dynamic living emotion, it is perhaps no accident that Schweitzer with his sensitiveness to the interplay of these two elements in experience should have been drawn to it more than to the other arts. One of the chief controversies among musicians of the nineteenth century was over the question whether music should be absolute or programmatic, appealing to abstract form or representing emotional scenes from every-day life. Those who believed in absolute music claimed that Bach's music was absolute. Schweitzer showed his originality as a music critic by pointing out that actually Bach's music is deeply expressive of emotion and peculiarly representative of familiar experiences. Of course Bach has also his formal aspect, but what Schweitzer showed was that Bach is a pictorial artist who writes music of a sort that translates itself into scenes readily visualized. Thus Bach has his own way of combining the intellect and the feelings. In contrast to Beethoven and Wagner, whom Schweitzer calls poets because they describe the unfolding of an emotional mood in what we may call the unity of its psychological development, Bach gives us a series of pictures illustrating the mood's various stages. In his own way Bach is thus dualistic, doing justice both to the free flow of Dionysian currents and the more static Apollonian quality, pausing at times to take stock of the emotional experience, to describe and evaluate it and preserve its pictorial aspects.

The interplay of these two factors is suggested again in Schweitzer's interpretation of what he calls Bach's objectivity. In his preface to Bach's organ works, Schweitzer shows that the organist must participate in Bach's objective attitude in the sense that he must subordinate his own impulses and reproduce in their absoluteness the musical figures which Bach with his own sense for abstract form heard with the inner ear and transmitted to paper. Yet in his life of Bach Schweitzer says that Bach's objectivity did not include complete detachment from the world around him. Bach's work is characterized by a merging with his own intellectual and aesthetic climate rather than an emerging from it. Bach wove together the threads of his musical environment and in synthesizing them brought to consummation the values of his own age. Objectivity need not mean complete aloofness from life but simply from the particularity and prejudiced nature of one's individual life. Form is not free from content any more than content of an aesthetic sort can be wholly unregulated by form.

SCHWEITZER'S PERSONAL ATTITUDE

The supreme example of the interplay between intellect and practical living emotion and the productive synthesis they may achieve is furnished of course in Schweitzer's own experience. He has excelled in intellectual achievement; he is also outstanding as a practical benefactor of his fellow men. Many a teacher and preacher must have responded with enthusiasm to the passage in the autobiography where Schweitzer speaks of the distaste he felt, after years of intellectual effort, for words, theories, formulas, and their inadequacy. He took up medicine and surgery, he tells us, glad that at last he would be able not merely to talk but to act, to use his hands, to manipulate materials in a practical cause. Surely nothing short of this kind of combination of theory and practice could have satisfied him. And it is worthy of note that his philosophy is itself a combination, providing a synthesis for the two influences, *Leben* and *Geist* which, except for Schweitzer's work, remain so completely at odds with each other throughout the intellectual history of the nineteenth century.

Notice, first of all, that Schweitzer constantly reaches up to *Geist* to provide standards for the demands made by *Leben*. His own living desires are brought under the sway of abstract reason. Religion is a warm, passionate emotional experience, yet Schweitzer once told a visitor at Königsfeld that the most important quality in religion was devotion to the truth with its rigorous academic standards. We should notice also that when he plays Bach, Schweitzer keeps his feelings rigidly under control, making his hearers forget their own prejudices in the presence of the eternal musical forms of which Bach was so keenly aware. As a lover of his fellow men he went to Africa in the name of justice, affirming that the least the white man could do for his exploited black brother was to share with him the benefits of the science of medicine. In his own personal life, that is to say, he has been governed by truth, beauty, and justice in all the detached quality of their formal abstractness. But as a thinker, instead of dealing merely with abstractions he has stepped down from the high a priori road to adapt his thought to the living currents of experience by making "reverence for life" his central ethical formula. In him Kantian idealism and Nietzschean *Lebensphilosophie* lie down together without fear that one will be swallowed by the other.

Thus Schweitzer is not a pragmatist, believing that thought arises only in the service of life, nor yet is he a philosophical idealist, holding that life is but an expression of thought. He does justice to both claims and the result, we feel, is not a compromise but a demonstration of the productiveness implicit in a dualistic view. The great criticism of dualism is its lack of finality. Now this, now that, it seems to say, and the result may easily be a wavering inconclusiveness. In Schweitzer's case we feel instead the strength that resides in tension and the power that may result from faithfulness to the polarity offered by experience as it is actually known. Indeed we may well ask whether the unity so often sought in both philosophy and religion is not specious. The happy ending is not found; complete justice is never done; the final inclusive formula always eludes us. The conclusion appears to be that the search and the struggle have their own worth when controlled by the moral ideal and that the ideal is not invalidated by the fact that we cannot always make it apply. Nature is often too subtle for any argument, but arguments must always continue. Life overlaps and outruns logic though logic in its own sphere is supreme. The moral rule to love our enemies is difficult if not impossible to observe amid the terrible conditions of modern war. Yet this does not excuse us from the constant effort to broaden the realm where it can be applied. Between life and thought there is a tension and at times even a conflict. But the tension may be turned to spiritual account. The eternal values are not within our reach but, in the words of Alois Riehl, they are our companions in the struggle to go forward just as the stars are our guides when we journey across the plains.

ALBERT SCHWEITZER, HUMANITARIAN

By

Everett Skillings

Professor-Emeritus, Middlebury College
Chairman, Albert Schweitzer Fellowship

CHAPTER III

ALBERT SCHWEITZER, HUMANITARIAN

BY

EVERETT SKILLINGS

I.

BEGINNINGS

Why did Albert Schweitzer go to Africa? People take up missionary work from a variety of motives. Few are led by the reason which impelled Schweitzer to give up his already brilliant career in Europe. Before he was thirty, he had already received three degrees; doctor of philosophy, doctor of theology, and doctor of music. He occupied two cathedras at the University of Strasbourg. He was preacher at one of the Strasbourg churches and Principal of the residential college for students of theology. He was welcomed at many universities as a lecturer; he it was, for instance, who delivered the funeral oration on Nietzsche before the Sorbonne in Paris. He was the author of several outstanding books on philosophy and theology. He was already considered one of the world's greatest organists, an authority on the fine art of organ building; the author of the greatest book that has ever been written on the music of Johann Sebastian Bach; and the organist of the Bach Societies of Paris, Strasbourg, and Barcelona.

Why did he give up all that? He tells us the reason in his autobiography, *Out of My Life and Thought.* Many great thinkers have believed it their part to write their thoughts, to inspire others to action. By ordinary standards, that is a great achievement. But for Albert Schweitzer that was not enough. He himself must translate his thought into action; he himself was in honor bound to pay for all that was good and beautiful in his life by doing all he could to bear his share of the burden of the world's woe. And he must do this by going to where there was the most helpless of all misery, *without questioning the value of the primitive lives whose sufferings he would alleviate.* In a world where nearly all of us are trying to get and to take all we can, his constant aim has been to give, and to give where there is the greatest need. Says Dr. Oskar Kraus, of the University of Prague: "Thinkers of this kind, who translate their ethical thought into action, are the most powerful factors in history." When Schweitzer was 21, there came to him on a bright summer morning as he awoke in his home in Günsbach, Alsace, the thought that he must not accept the happiness of his boyhood as a matter of course, but must give something in return for it.

> Proceeding to think the matter out at once with calm determination, while the birds were singing outside, I settled with myself before I got up, that I would consider myself justified in living until I was thirty for science and art, in order to devote myself from that time onward to the direct service of humanity. Many a time already had I tried to settle what meaning lay hidden for me in the saying of Jesus: 'Whosoever would save his life shall lose it, and whosoever shall lose his life for my sake and the Gospel's shall save it.' Now the answer was found. In addition to the outward, I now had inward happiness.

For a time he thought his decision would mean work with abandoned or orphaned children. Then he thought it might be work with tramps and discharged prisoners. Then one evening in the autumn of 1904, he picked up a magazine of the Paris Missionary Society lying on his desk. Skimming through it, his eye caught the title of an article, "The Needs of the Congo Mission." Far in the interior of Africa, on the Ogowe river, it said, there was dire need for medical missionaries, and no one could be found who was adequately trained and willing to fill the need. The article captured his imagination. "The article finished, I quietly began my work. My search was over."

A RESOLUTION TAKES SHAPE

On Friday, October 13, 1905, young Schweitzer dropped a few letters into the letter box on Avenue de la Grande Armée, in Paris. In them he announced to his friends his intention of going to Africa as a medical missionary. Was he crazy, his friends asked. They pointed out that it would take years to qualify as a physician. They urged him to stay in Europe and turn over the proceeds from his lectures for missionary work in Africa. It made no impression on them that Schweitzer's decision was born of no sudden impulse, that it had been made nine years before and had become strengthened in the intervening years. Why he chose Africa his own words explain:

A heavy guilt rests upon our civilization. What have not the whites of all nations since the era of discovery done to the colored people! What does it signify that so many peoples where Christianity came have died out and others are vanishing, or at least disintegrating? Who can describe the injustices and atrocities committed? Who could estimate what alcohol and the awful diseases we have transmitted have done to them? If history told all that has happened between whites and blacks, many pages would be turned without being read. A heavy guilt rests upon us. We must serve them. When we do good to them it is not benevolence—it is atonement.

And so for more than seven years Schweitzer studied medicine and surgery at Strasbourg. Strenuous years they were, and had it not been for an exceptional physique and iron determination, he could never have stood the strain. "That this study would mean for me a tremendous effort, I had no manner of doubt," said he. "I did in truth look forward to the next few years with dread." He had to earn his living while studying. On Sundays he preached, and throughout the week he taught a class of theological students. Besides, there were numerous concert trips in many parts of Europe. As if this were not enough, he wrote a book of over 800 pages on the music of John Sebastian Bach, an *Essay on Organ Building,* a classic in its field, and the final chapters of his famous *Quest of the Historical Jesus.* In spite of all these varied interests, early in 1913, at the age of 38, he received his fourth degree, that of doctor of medicine.

While he was preparing to become a doctor, his devoted wife, Helene Bresslau Schweitzer, daughter of Professor Bresslau, the eminent Strasbourg historian, was in training to become a nurse. They were married on June 18, 1912. Mrs. Schweitzer is a remarkable woman of unusual gifts, who shares her husband's humanitarian impulses and passion. It is beyond words to express all that he owes to her in his healing ministry to the African blacks. She is of the same heroic mould as he. He gratefully recognized his indebtedness to her by dedicating his book *Civilization and Ethics*: "To my Wife, the Truest of Comrades."

A MOMENTOUS STEP

On Good Friday, 1913, the Schweitzers started out on their long journey to the jungles of Africa. On Easter Sunday, they passed through Paris, attending St. Sulpice Church where they heard Charles Marie Widor, the famous organist, under whom Schweitzer had studied many years before. With the Schweitzers to Africa went a zinc-lined piano, built especially for the tropics, with a pedal attachment, so that Schweitzer might keep up his organ playing. It was the gift of the Paris Bach Society. "At first," he says, "I had not the heart to practice. I had accustomed myself to think that this activity in Africa meant the end of my life as an artist. One evening, however, as I was playing one of the Bach organ fugues, the idea came suddenly upon me that I might, after all, use my free hours in Africa for the very purpose of perfecting my technique."

When the Schweitzers finally reached Lambaréné, French Equatorial Africa in the Trader Horn Country, they were in a region of the world right over the equator, utterly different from the temperate zone in which they had lived in Europe. It is interesting to learn that an American missionary and physician, Dr. Robert Hamill Nassau, established the mission at Lambaréné in 1876. The station passed into the hands of the Paris Missionary Society in 1892 after the French occupied the province of Gabon, in which Lambaréné is situated, in order that the requirement of the French government, that all instruction should be in French, might be met. Great was the joy of Dr. Nassau, the aged founder of the mission, when Dr. Schweitzer sent him in America the news that Lambaréné was once more supplied with a doctor.

Someone has called the Ogowe region "the most unhealthy spot on the face of the earth." It has a hot, humid climate with little range of temperature. During the rainy season, from October until the following May, torrid, damp heat prevails with the nights as hot as the days. There are frequent tornadoes when the air is charged with electricity. Little wonder that Europeans can endure such a climate no more than two years before fatigue and anemia compel them to return home to recuperate. In this low damp country grow the giant okoume trees which make wonderful timber when they can be got out of the marshes in which they grow.

Here live the remnants of eight once-powerful tribes, where for three centuries the slave trade, rum, and exploitation by the white man have wrought havoc. Here the natives eke out a meagre existence; and there was dire need of medical facilities when the Schweitzers arrived. One of the natives said to them, "Here among us, everybody is sick." Schweitzer had surely chosen with care the place of the greatest need.

Sleeping sickness, venereal diseases, swamp fever and a hundred tropical ailments, such as malaria, leprosy, dysentery, frambesia and gangrenous ulcers rage unchecked here. Rheumatism is much more common than in the temperate zone, and Dr. Schweitzer says he is surprised at the number of cases of pneumonia and heart disease he discovers. Surgical treatment is called for chiefly in hernia and elephantiac tumors. Hernia occurs much more frequently among the African natives than among white people. "If there is no medical man in the neighborhood, every year sees a number of unfortunate mortals doomed to die a painful death from strangulated hernia from which a timely operation might have saved them. My first surgical intervention was in a case of that kind." Many are the men who are mauled by hippopotami, as they paddle their canoes through the swamps or along the rivers. To further plague them there is the tsetse fly, compared to which the worst mosquito, according to Schweitzer, is a comparatively harmless creature. But there is some consolation in the fact that cancer and appendicitis are unknown.

STARTING A JUNGLE PRACTICE

From the very first days, before he had even found time to unpack the drugs and instruments, he was besieged by sick people. At first, for some months, he had to use an abandoned henhouse as the operating room. Valiant help was given in the hospital by Mrs. Schweitzer as nurse. She assisted at the operations, looked after the severe cases, superintended the linen and the bandages, was often busy in the dispensary, kept the instruments in proper condition, and made all the preparations for the operations, herself administering the anaesthetics. "That she managed successfully the complicated work of an African household," said Dr.

Schweitzer, "and yet could find every day some hours to spare for the hospital was really a wonderful achievement." His only other helper at first was a native named Joseph. He was a great help as an interpreter, since he knew eight local dialects, as well as French.

When patients leave the Schweitzer hospital, the Doctor requires them to give something as tangible evidence of their gratitude for the help received, except where it is absolutely impossible for the very poor and aged. Among the primitives, old age always connotes poverty. What it is, or how much, matters little. It is the principle he wishes to establish. Sometimes he receives money, but more often it is eggs, poultry, or bananas. The real savages among them have a quite different conception of a present. When on the point of leaving the hospital cured, they used to demand one from Dr. Schweitzer, because he had now become their friend!

With them, as they leave the hospital, go the recollections of the simple religious services held by Dr. Schweitzer. In view of his frank and independent views about religious problems, some of the strictly orthodox members of the Paris Missionary Society objected to accepting him, but when he gave the assurance that he intended to be nothing but a doctor, and would be "mute as a fish" on religious subjects, they relented. But most of the missionaries are more liberally minded than the officials of the Society, so later he was allowed to preach the elements of the Gospel, as given in the Sermon on the Mount. At the simple service each Sunday morning, Schweitzer does not try to make the congregation sit still. He does not even take the noise of romping monkeys and of the birds as an irritation.

INFLUENCE UPON NATIVES

Music is provided by a phonograph, and Schweitzer gives brief talks in which he confines himself to a few simple sayings, repeated over and over again, and illustrated by experience from the natives' own daily lives. He describes, for example, how he preaches about Peter's question whether it would be enough to forgive his brother seven times. The primitives would not understand the meaning of that question without very specific explanation. So the Doctor pictures the day of a native who finds that his bananas have been stolen, that somebody took his boat, his good banana knife has been exchanged for an old rusty one, the man who took fruit for him to the market cheats him with the money, etc. The poor fellow gets angry every time, and wants to fight the evildoer, or denounce him to the authorities. But every time he thinks of Jesus, and of how many times he himself has sinned and needed forgiveness. So he masters himself and always tries to forgive. When the day is over he feels happy, though he has suffered so many unkind misdeeds. His heart is at peace. As Schweitzer says, "If, after a stay at the hospital, they take away with them even but three or four such sayings that give them something to think about, it is already a great thing in their lives."

He received heartening proof that even very primitive natives can follow his thoughts. Once a white helper reported a discussion he had overheard between two workers in the brush. A very savage looking man, before planting a pole, saved a few ants from it, explaining to his fellow that you should not destroy life unnecessarily. This indicated that he understood the Doctor's preaching about "Reverence for Life." The spiritual life of the natives is darkened by superstition, yet Schweitzer says he was astonished to find their minds open to the very essential questions of life. No one must think that their thought-world consists only of superstitious ideas and the traditional legal rules of the tribe. The child of nature thinks a great deal more than is generally supposed, and has a great natural capacity for taking in the elements of religion. "The distinction between white and colored, educated and uneducated," says Dr. Schweitzer, "disappears when one gets to talking with the forest dweller about our relations

THE HOSPITAL IN LAMBARENE BUILT BY ALBERT SCHWEITZER

to each other, to mankind, in the universe, and to the infinite. Christianity is for him the light that shines amid the darkness of his fears. It assures him that he is not in the power of nature spirits, ancestral spirits, or fetishes, and that no human being has any sinister power over another, since the will of God really controls everything that goes on in the world. In proportion as he becomes familiar with the higher moral ideals of the religion of Jesus, he finds utterance for something in himself that has hitherto been dumb; and something that has been tightly bound up, finds release."

However, for the primitive man to give up the common habit of lying and the readiness to steal, and to become a more or less reliable man in our sense, is something different from practicing the religion of love. Yet little can be accomplished by condemnatory expressions. Dr. Schweitzer thinks we must see to it that we put as few temptations as possible in the way of the primitive colored man. Still there are Christian natives who are in every respect thoroughly moral persons. Dr. Schweitzer tells of one such, named Ojembo. "I look upon him as one of the finest men that I know anywhere." In his fascinating volume entitled *"African Stories,"* one should read the story "Ojembo."

THE WORLD WAR INTERRUPTS HEALING ACTIVITIES

The Schweitzers were getting nicely settled, after working scarcely a year, when World War I broke out. Alsace was then part of Germany, and being Alsatians, they were informed on August 5, 1914 by the French colonial officials that they were prisoners of war. For a few months they were interned in their bungalow, under Negro guards, and informed that they must stop all intercourse with whites or blacks. But it soon became apparent how foolish such a procedure was; and the Doctor was allowed to go on with his healing work. In 1917, however, they were taken to France, and lived for ten months in prisoner-of-war camps in the Pyrenees and in Provence. As they were leaving

[97]

Lambaréné, the Father Superior of the Catholic Mission came on board, waved aside the native soldiers who tried to prevent his approach and shook hands with the Schweitzers. "You shall not leave this country," he said, "without my thanking you both for all the good that you have done it." Soon after arriving in the prison camp, it occurred to the ingenious Doctor, that if he only had a table, he could while away the long hours by practicing the organ, using the table for his manuals and the floor for his pedals. He was delighted when he found a fellow-prisoner, a carpenter, to make him a table.

Life in an internment camp has never been conducive to good health. Both Schweitzer and his wife suffered severely from ill health, and it took some years after their release in July 1918, before Schweitzer felt strong enough to undertake the task of starting all over again in Africa. In 1921 he set out giving organ recitals and lecturing on the philosophy of civilization all over Europe. Of the next three years he writes: "How wonderful were the experiences vouchsafed me! When I went to Africa, I prepared to make three sacrifices, and only my intimate friends knew what they cost me: to abandon the organ, to renounce the academic teaching activities, and to lose my financial independence, relying for the rest of my life on the help of my friends. But I was spared the sacrifice. The piano with pedal attachment had allowed me to keep up my skill on the organ, so that I returned to Europe in full possesion of my technique, and privileged to find that, as an artist, I was more esteemed than before. For the renunciation of my teaching activities in Strasbourg University, I found compensation in opportunities of lecturing in very many others. And if I did for a time lose my financial independence, I was able now to win it again by means of organ and pen . . . "

Early in 1924, Schweitzer was again ready to depart for Africa —this second time alone. His wife's health had broken down by reason of the devastating effects of the tropical climate, and the hardships of the prison camps. "For the fact that she so far sacrificed herself as to acquiesce under these circumstances in my resumption of work at Lambaréné, I have never ceased to be grateful to her." But there were with him on this sojourn in Africa two young Swiss doctors, and several nurses.

RETURNING TO AFRICA

At Lambaréné, the hospital was a mass of ruins. The tropical forest had conquered the clearing; the white ants had destroyed the buildings. After he had finished rebuilding the hospital in the autumn of 1925, a severe famine occurred and at the same time a terrible epidemic of dysentery set in. For many months these two misfortunes occupied the Doctor and his staff. This dysentery epidemic made clear the necessity of removing the hospital to a larger site. The old buildings sufficed for the fifty patients and their attendants of the earlier period. Now with 150 patients, it was impossible to keep the dysentery patients separate from the rest, and the whole hospital was getting infected. "It was a dreadful time," wrote the Doctor. With heavy heart he forced himself to the decision to build a new hospital on higher ground two miles up the river. So he rolled up his sleeves and went to work. On account of the lack of labor, it took a year and a-half before the new hospital, far more adequate than the last, was finished.

One of the most thrilling examples of faith being rewarded was this post-war experience of Schweitzer's. In the closing chapter of his book, *On the Edge of the Primeval Forest*, he tells of returning to Africa after seven years away. He faces ruins and disease. "Nevertheless I have not lost courage. This misery I have seen gives me strength, and faith in my fellow men supports my confidence in the future. I do hope that I shall find a sufficient number of people who, because they themselves have been saved from physical suffering, will respond to requests on behalf of those who are in similar need."

Three long trying years of toil are needed before the second hospital is finally established. Then he returns to Europe for a furlough, and in his next book, *The Forest Hospital at Lambaréné*, tells about the rebuilding. Compare the closing chapter of the preceding book with the closing chapter of this one. What a contrast! There a ruined hospital and a man's marvelous faith and courage; here a new and better hospital—faith become a reality!

II

Weathering World War II

Again a world war confronts Lambaréné and the Schweitzers. Already in 1937, and even earlier, it was clear to them that war was inevitable and might break out at any time, cutting off all the former sources of European support to their African work. So in 1937, Mrs. Schweitzer, "his truest of comrades," came to the United States on a lecture tour and again in 1938, raising considerable funds and contacting old friends, and making new ones.

In the spring of 1939, Dr. and Mrs. Schweitzer arrived in Bordeaux, France, for one of their periodic breaks in routine. They both needed rest and went straight to their home in the village of Günsbach near Colmar, in the upper Alsace valley, in the Vosges Mountains. But the dread of war hung heavy over Europe, and Dr. Schweitzer did not even unpack his baggage.

Desiring to shelter the people to whom he had given more than thirty years of his life, he returned to Bordeaux within a week and sailed back to Africa on the same ship which had brought him to Europe. Mrs. Schweitzer remained in Europe. The war which he foresaw with such clarity did not break out for six months, and he has been at Lambaréné ever since. What six years of toil in an exhausting climate have done to his physique is terrific, and is giving his friends great anxiety. Soon after the outbreak of the war, he wrote to American friends that he did not know whether he should stay at Lambaréné with his co-workers to continue their humanitarian work, or whether they should close the hospital and return to Europe, when that could be done. But they have remained and the hospital continues to carry on, since conscience would not permit them to leave the poor blacks who had just come to be treated by them.

Mrs. Schweitzer in the meantime, after the marriage of their daughter Rhena to an Alsatian, A. J. Eckert, lived with them in Paris until the fall of France in 1940. Then they started on a tragic flight through France for over a month, living on the roads, sleeping in their little car, and eating when and wherever they found something to eat. Finally they settled in Lyons in unoccupied France. In August 1941 the Eckerts got to Switzerland where M. Eckert found employment, and they are now living near Zürich. At the same time, Mrs. Schweitzer set out for Lambaréné and after a long, tedious, roundabout journey, rejoined her husband in October 1941, and is still there with him.

On learning of the decision to keep the hospital open, friends in America got together and formulated plans with a view to enlisting American support for the work, since most of the friends in Britain and the continent could no longer give aid.

HOW THE ALBERT SCHWEITZER FELLOWSHIP CAME INTO BEING

Thus it came about that The Albert Schweitzer Fellowship was organized late in 1939 with Dr. Karl Reiland as honorary chairman, Professor Julius Seelye Bixler, then at Harvard University, as Executive Chairman, and the present writer, Secretary and Treasurer. Why the title "Fellowship?" It was suggested by Schweitzer's use of the word in the last chapter of *On The Edge of the Primeval Forest*—one of the most eloquent and appealing pieces of writing he has ever penned. He writes about *The Fellowship of Those Who Bear the Mark of Pain.* He asks: "Who are the members of this Fellowship?" and he answers:

Those who have learnt by experience what physical pain and bodily anguish mean, belong together the world over; they are united by a secret bond. One and all, they know the horrors of suffering to which man can be exposed: one and all, they know the longing to be free from pain.

So those who have been delivered from pain and anguish are under obligation not to think that they are now free again and at liberty to take life up just as it was before, entirely forgetful of the past. "They must feel in duty bound to help overcome those two enemies of mankind and to bring to others the deliverance that they have enjoyed."

Albert Schweitzer wrote these words out of his own deep experience; for he came out of the prisoner-of-war camps a very sick man. Through five long years he knew the horrors of the suffering about which he writes, and the joy of deliverance by two major operations. His heroic wife also, by her gruelling sufferings which have made her a semi-invalid for the rest of her life, belongs in her own right in the Fellowship of Those Who Bear the Mark of Pain.

And again today after a too-long continuous sojourn in the malignant climate of the tropics—he for over six years and she for four years—they are suffering distressing fatigue and pain and anguish, from which not a single day of their life is free.

Hence the title *The Albert Schweitzer Fellowship* has deep meaning. So that even those who have not experienced the extremes of pain and anguish are coming in increasing numbers to feel the obligation of joining in the deliverance of such victims.

When the present writer told Dr. Schweitzer that his friends in the United States wished to continue the sort of thing his European friends had been doing, he wrote back: "Let me thank all my friends from the bottom of my heart for the immense service they are planning to render me. My mind is greatly relieved that I can now receive help from America. It seems to me in the nature of a miracle. I shall never be able to thank you all sufficiently."

THE NATURE OF DR. SCHWEITZER'S WORK

He went on in this letter to explain the nature of his work as he conceives it. It is not connected with any church or missionary society or other organization. Dr. Schweitzer has a deep conviction that there is nowadays an over-organization of public and social life. Personalities and ideas are subordinated to institutions, whereas it should be the other way round. Our spiritual and mental life now runs its course within organizations. In the eighteenth century, ideas had to be justified by the individual reason, but now consideration is given for the most part, only to the views which prevail in organized social groups.

The individual thus tends to take it for granted that the outlook of his nation, his creed, his political party, his group is beyond criticism. He becomes so lost in the mentality of the mass that he almost ceases to think for himself. But most people are quite unconscious that this abnormal susceptibility to group influence is a weakness. It is largely because the majority have in this way renounced the right of thinking for themselves and are guided only by the opinion of their group, that freedom of thought has to so great an extent gone out of use. Too much organization militates against spiritual life. Hence it is that Schweitzer insists on working as a free individual; and yet he is no champion of "rugged individualism." Dr. Schweitzer would dread our American high-powered publicity. So his one request was that our organization should be as simple as possible. He desires no rigid, impersonal organization, but rather direct personal touch from one individual to another, creating complete spontaneity of interest and spiritual concern for his undertaking. For this reason he sends a word of personal greeting and thanks to all contributors.

The life of Albert and Helene Schweitzer is the living symbol of what Christian brotherhood means, and is capturing the imagination of men and women from one end of America to the other. The annual appeal of the Fellowship for funds brings a constantly increasing response. The fact that most of the contributors accompany their gifts with interesting letters is testimony to the personal touch which they feel with Dr. Schweitzer's work. We send on to Dr. Schweitzer many extracts from such, and sometimes entire letters. His appreciation is shown from what he wrote in one of his most recent letters: "I always draw new energy from the evidence that comes to me of the great sympathy for my work." It is indeed a heart-warming experience to read these letters.

Here, for instance, writes a former professor of sociology in the University of Prague and at present on the faculty of Oberlin College: "I was much pleased to get a line from Dr. Schweitzer whom I love and admire . . . The enclosed check is for a token contribution—we are trying to save up something for our poor children and other relatives in the Protectorate (of Bohemia), who will be starving, if they survive this apocalyptic time at all." This from Mississippi: "The primary class are so anxious for their self-denial pennies to go to Dr. Schweitzer. We keep a picture of him on our walls. We love and pray for him." From the editor of a youth magazine: "I do not think any series of articles on modern saints would be complete without one on Dr. Schweitzer." From a Hawaiian-Japanese: "Allow me to say that it is a rare privilege for our children to have a little part in helping such a wonderful personality as Dr. Schweitzer, who transcends racial and all other barriers and shines in the glory of Christian love and brotherhood."

Last year Dr. Schweitzer wrote: "I am deeply moved by the interest of the organists of the United States in my work and in me. I still remember the day when Widor asked me to collaborate with him on the edition of Bach's organ works which Schirmer proposed to him. We both retired to my village of Günsbach, in

Alsace, and there we discussed together the authentic way of executing each prelude and each fugue. These are unforgettable weeks for me." The Warden of the American Guild of Organists wrote last April: "Our interest in anything pertaining to Dr. Schweitzer is great. It is very gratifying to me that so many organists are giving recitals and contributing the proceeds to the Dr. Schweitzer fund."

A young lady musician, a regular contributor, recently raised an interesting question in her latest letter. "My soul rebels," she writes, "at the routine work Schweitzer is doing which it seems to me natives could be trained to do. I wonder if he is a good administrator. It seems a waste of precious human capacity, for Dr. Schweitzer is a genius and saint." Probably the best answer to why he does it is because he is, as she says, a saint. Did it perchance occur to this saint that his Master set him an example of this very sort for him? Peter may have been indignant when his Master would wash his feet, because it seemed to him such a waste of precious human capacity. "I have set you an example," might be the words ringing in Dr. Schweitzer's ears. Indeed, this thought may have occurred to the young lady in question; for she closes her letter with this sentence: "I'm hardly reconciled to having the arts deprived, but I guess we need his faithful message for his Master." Then too we must bear in mind the critical situation at the hospital: the hospital more crowded than ever, and a shortage of helpers. Where was the time to be found to train these natives, whose chief fault is their unreliability? Surely the last man to load these details onto an already overburdened staff was Dr. Schweitzer. As a matter of fact, he is said to be an admirable administrator.

A young people's society bears the name, Albert Schweitzer Chapter of the Comrades of the Way. In sending a contribution it was explained that the Comrades of the Way is an organization of high school students in various churches, each chapter choosing as a distinctive name that of some one who to them represents the highest ideals of Christian character. The minister of the church writes that the spirit that led Schweitzer to become a medical missionary is to him the most magnificent witness to the essential spirit of Jesus in modern times; that Schweitzer's revelatory experience into "Reverence for Life" is the most profound expression of the spirit of Jesus, that his call to free the spirit of Jesus from dogmatic and institutional chains and reinterpret the Messianic work of Jesus is the only cure for a sick world. "I will be forever indebted to Albert Schweitzer for the contribution he has made to my mind, to my heart, and to my will."

A fellow-Alsatian, who roamed the Günsbach countryside as a boy, and is now a physician in this country, writes: "It is with Albert Schweitzer just as with Goethe, Shakespeare, and the Bible. The more you study his life, the more viewpoints you get. He is the most remarkable personality of the first half of this terrible century."

Individuals, high and low, and all sorts of groups, clubs, and organizations, send in contributions: churches, Sunday schools, missionary societies, chapters of the American Guild of Organists, college organ clubs, student bodies, and student Christian associations, C.P.S. camps, student volunteers, YMCA's and YWCA's, church and college choirs, etc.

The Manoa Mission of Honolulu (Rev. Ernest Fujinaga, Director) whose members are largely poor Japanese gardeners and their children, have been sending larger and larger gifts annually for the past five years. A fellow Alsatian, Mr. Edouard Nies-Berger, organist of one of the Brooklyn churches, who is the son of one of Schweitzer's former musical friends at the University of Strasbourg, has given numerous organ concerts for the benefit of the Schweitzer African work. A lady in the Hawaiian Islands had a serious operation and sent a contribution equal in amount to what her operation had cost her. Ever so many church school classes of small children send their gifts of pennies saved, because they have learned in this man's life a lesson of brotherly love which they will never forget. The sixth grade of the Riverside Church, N. Y. Sunday School dramatized a sketch of Dr. Schweitzer's life and African activity entitled *They Thought He Was Mad* and acted out the parts.

From far-off Australia and New Zealand come inquiries about the work of the Fellowship, expressing their great interest in Dr. Schweitzer and their eagerness to help. They sense the international importance of the Schweitzers in their work of racial reconciliation. The Director of the Presbyterian Church of Australia wrote in a letter: "It seems an amazing piece of internationalism that your acquaintance with a New Zealand chaplain, now in Italy, led you to write to me in Melbourne from Vermont about affairs in Africa!" From North Carolina comes a letter from a church school teacher with a contribution from the children in her intermediate class. She writes that, when she was preparing an article on great Christians of other races and nations, these children did all the research work on Schweitzer for her.

During the past year the youth publications, *Motive* of the Methodist youth movement and *Forward* of that of the Presbyterians have contained articles with illustrations of the Schweitzer work. The youth department of the Evangelical and Reformed Church puts on an essay contest each year on some outstanding Christian, choosing Schweitzer for this year's subject. And so who can measure the influence of the Schweitzers on the coming generation!

The activity of the Unitarian Service Committee in arousing interest and financial support in that denomination is quite outstanding.

It is interesting to know that the Fellowship has received two letters, one from a young man and the other from a young woman, expressing their intentions of going out as missionaries to Africa and inquiring about the Lambaréné hospital.

The interest in the Schweitzers has increased to such an extent in the five years of the activities of the Fellowship that friends in California formed a Pacific Coast Branch about two years ago. Dr. Walter Muelder, of the University of Southern California, has been the Chairman of this group. (He has just been called to Boston University). Among its sponsors are Thomas Mann, the novelist; Igor Stravinsky, the composer, and Dr. Alice Ehlers of the School of Music of the University of Southern California, who accompanied Dr. Schweitzer on the harpsichord in his organ recitals in Europe. The Pacific Branch has raised thousands of dollars for the African work and is stimulating ever-widening interest in the Pacific region. In this connection, we owe a debt of gratitude to Dr. Kurt Bergel of Deep Springs College, California, (whose acquaintance with Dr. Schweitzer began while living in Europe), for his tireless and fruitful activity in lecturing before student groups and churches. Dr. Bergel is also working on an edition of selections from Dr. Schweitzer's *Out of My Life and Thought* for the use of college students. He writes that he is convinced that it would be extremely valuable for American students to learn about a man whose philosophy expresses the very spirit with which we should reconstruct our world after the war.

In the East, the fine services rendered by three men should be mentioned: President Julius Seelye Bixler, of Colby College, who has done much to interpret the significance of Dr. Schweitzer for our day; Dr. Edward H. Hume, Director of the Christian Medical Council for Overseas Work, who has been in charge of the shipments of medical supplies to Lambaréné—not a single cargo has been lost because of enemy submarines—and Dr. Emery Ross, General Secretary of the Foreign Missions Conference, who has attended to the formalities of getting funds cabled to Dr. Schweitzer's account in the Bank of French West Africa.

Dr. Schweitzer, in his letters, mentions two things repeatedly: the hospital is more crowded than ever, and how great is the gratitude he feels to his American friends for their steadfast interest and contributions, without which he would be obliged to close the hospital. "I think of it every day with gratitude." His co-workers at present consist of his wife, three doctors, six European nurses, mostly from Switzerland, and ten black assistants. Of the latter, he says that he cannot pay them enough to live on comfortably, but they stay by him because of their feeling of attachment. Such a reduced staff is distressingly inadequate for the more than three hundred native patients. Besides, there is a lying-in hospital for native women who go to Lambaréné to be confined. There are also lodgings for the insane—an act of mercy; for when the insane were kept in the villages, the people were so afraid of them that they drowned them in the river.

There is, of course, great anxiety about having always on hand enough medicines and materials for operations. A large part of the patients come for operations, especially for hernia and tumors. Many have large tropical ulcers on their feet. To cure these ulcers takes weeks and months. And during the entire period the patients have to be fed. The world-wide wartime price rise has affected French Equatorial Africa too, and Schweitzer speaks in one of his most recent letters of the rise "not only for imported goods, but also for commodities that the native plantations produce. Rice is also becoming more expensive. This rise in prices bothers me a great deal."

Thus the feeding of the sick is one of the greatest problems. The hospital has a plantation and garden, so that they have enough to eat, but many things which could be easily imported before the war, they must now go without; potatoes, for example, because they do not grow in the tropics due to the heat and dampness. Likewise, in normal times milk and butter have to be imported, as they cannot raise cows in the virgin forest. Now, of course, for years they have had no milk, butter, bacon or pork on their table; and owing to this lack of fats, the staff have lost their appetites and suffer increasing fatigue.

The cost of living is so high that they can no longer feed meat to the sick. Almost all the patients are so poor that they can give

nothing for food, medicines, or operations. It happens sometimes that a patient brings with him very proudly a fowl, thinking that that is surely enough to pay for the operation. Some of
the patients come more than 300 miles on the paths of the forest,
or by river.

Owing to the shortage of help, Dr. Schweitzer feels it impossible to take a furlough until some weeks after the war has ended.
In the spring of 1945 he wrote:

You want me to take a vacation. For many reasons
that is impossible. When I returned from the holiday,
so many things would not have been done. I would
find on my desk a mountain of correspondence; building
repairs and many other things waiting to be attended to.

If the hospital is to function normally, I must be in
my place every day, for there are too few of us. I have
to do other jobs besides those of a doctor. I'm the one
who has to start the motors in the morning. It is I who
go to the plantation every day to look over what the
workers have done—or what they have not done. I'm
the one who sees that the fruits are gathered and put on
straw to keep them from rotting. Who would look after
the pharmacy, if I were away? It means a great deal of
work to see that the medicines do not spoil, that the
catgut for operations is well cared for in disinfectant
solutions, that rubber things are continually watched, for
we cannot replace what spoils.

I am unfolding for you some of the prosaic tasks of
the life I lead. But when I am a doctor, or when I study
the organ, or when I work at philosophy during the
night, I forget all these humdrum tasks.

WHEN MEDICAL SUPPLIES ARRIVE

A letter received soon after the preceding gives a typical description of the arrival of a shipment of medicines. This told

what took place when the second shipment of medicines, in 1945, reached Lambaréné on last Easter Tuesday, April 3rd. It came just as the Doctor and his assistants were operating. So one of the nurses superintended the unloading of the boxes. Everything arrived in good condition, since the packing was very well done.

Dr. Schweitzer mentions that since the arrival of the medicine, he has been busy every afternoon unpacking the boxes. He mentions that they were particularly glad to get the replacements for the little motor of the electric lighting for the operating room. Very often they have to perform urgent operations at night. It requires extreme care to have the contents put in glass bottles or tin boxes and the unpacking must be done with all possible dispatch, else the termites will get into the cartons within a few days and destroy everything.

I cannot describe to you the jubilation of all of us, doctors and nurses, at the unpacking of each box! I myself was particularly happy to possess again probes suitable for urology, Dr. Goldschmid to have sulfanilamide in compressed form, and the lady doctor sulfanilamide in injectable solution. And finally we have vaseline again! And how the rubber gloves came at the right time! The last pair for my large hands had just disintegrated! There were also three cases of shoes. We were awaiting them anxiously, for we had nothing left to wear on our feet. The news has been spread through the country that we again have reading glasses. Whites and blacks are beginning to stream in to get some. How many people for long months could no longer read nor write because they could not find glasses—how can I tell you the profound gratitude that we all have for those whose gifts have made possible the shipments of these boxes with their precious contents.

The weather at Lambaréné during the past year has been particularly bad, and has affected the health of both Dr. and Mrs.
Schweitzer. On October 28, 1944 Mrs. Schweitzer wrote:

Dear Friends:

I have not been able to write recently; and it is not
without effort that I do so now. We have had refresh-
ing weather barely one week during the dry season just
ending, where in normal times we have several months.
Now the rainy season is just beginning, and the rains
and the heat have returned. The temperature has been
rising rapidly, and already we have torrid heat such as
is normal from March to May.

At the end of last August the nurse of the pharmacy
had to go for rest in the Cameroons. The house nurse
is replacing her, and I have returned to the kitchen. But
I had to stop two weeks ago and limit myself to my
regular work and help out with the extras here and
there. Fortunately the woman doctor will come back
to us shortly after an absence of almost a year. I hope
that will be a relief for the Doctor.

At the height of this same rainy season, when the torrid heat
was intense, Dr. Schweitzer wrote:

While I am writing, it is so hot that it requires an
effort to do so. I am bathed in perspiration without even
stirring. The climate this year (1945) is particularly
bad. I have never seen such humid heat in all the long
years I have been in this country. Right now there are
only two of us doctors at the hospital. We are still
pretty well. Naturally we are increasingly tired. Sometimes our feet drag as if they were made of lead, but we
keep going just the same. Dr. Goldschmid is on vacation
for several weeks. He is spending part of it at Amer-

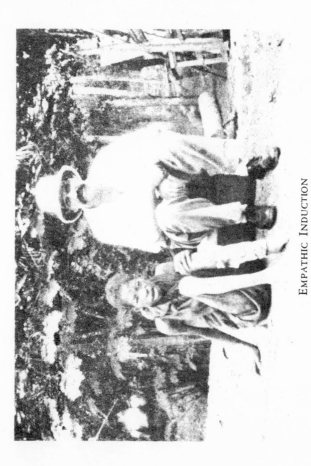

EMPATHIC INDUCTION

Dr. Schweitzer's expression assumes the suffering cast of his young patient.

ican and Swedish mission stations which one can get to more easily now, thanks to the automobile roads constructed during the last few years.

Just before the Nazi collapse he wrote:

> I received a cablegram from Alsace that my house at Günsbach has not suffered from the bombing that much of the valley of Münster has had. All the village of Günsbach is in good condition. Münster (2½ kilometers from Günsbach) is in part destroyed . . .
>
> We are all of us conscious that many of the natives are puzzling over the questions raised by the war; how it can be possible that the whites, who brought them the Gospel of love, are now murdering each other, and throwing to the winds the commands of the Lord Jesus. When they put the question to us, we are helpless. If I am questioned on the subject by those who think, I make no attempt to explain or to extenuate, but say that we are in 'front' of something terrible and incomprehensible. How far the ethical and religious authority of the white man among these children of nature is impaired by this war, we shall only be able to measure later on. I fear that the damage done will be very considerable.

HOW THE SEVENTIETH BIRTHDAY WAS SPENT

On January 14, 1945, Dr. Schweitzer was seventy years old. The date fell on a Sunday, and throughout the country many musical circles, weekly journals, churches, etc., took note of the event and many clergymen made Dr. Schweitzer the subject of their sermons. Dr. Schweitzer wrote to the Fellowship:

> Your cablegram of January 14, informing me that you are sending me funds has made me very happy. Thank you from my heart!! And how grateful I am to the donors who make this remittance possible! It was

good news for my seventieth birthday. Alas, for the work that I have to do and the years in which the hospital will still have need of me, I ought to be thirty years old instead of seventy! But I must consider myself greatly privileged to be still passably robust at seventy, and to be able to do what is most necessary . . .

For my seventieth birthday, I received a cablegram from Dr. Charles Joy of the Unitarian Service Committee, bringing me the best wishes of his Committee and also those of the General Council of Congregational Churches and of friends in the Episcopal Church; and informing me that these three groups were cabling $700.00 in gifts for the hospital. I was deeply touched and wrote them immediately . . .

In spite of the fatigue and worries, I am still in condition to work on my volume of philosophy, but only after nine o'clock in the evening until late at night; unfortunately not every day, often only two or three evenings a week. But that permits me to dwell on the subject and to advance slowly. How happy I will be when peace comes and I can free myself a little from other work and devote myself more or less continuously to this work which I would still like to finish.

. . . Sometimes I ask myself how I have ever had the strength to perform all this work during my lifetime. And these last years have forced upon me the greatest exertions. I had imagined that at the age of 65 and onward, I could entrust most of the work at the hospital to the physicians who would come to Lambaréné to help me, so that I should be able to spend a number of months from time to time in Europe, occupied with completing some books and giving concerts for the hospital. I even dreamed of once taking several weeks for a vacation.

And here comes the war to supervene and change everything. It obliges me to stay in Africa a series of years and to assume work which is beyond that I could perform normally at my age. I have known great crises of fatigue during these years, but I have kept going and able to perform my work all day long, and resist the debilitating climate. I have been able, after the day's work at the hospital, to exert myself and work on my manuscript during the evening and to practice organ pieces on my pedal piano.

I am filled with gratitude to God who has given me this health, and what benefits I have received from people, from these unknown friends, who by their gifts have made it possible that my hospital can be maintained during this war! This gives me renewed strength every day. And what a privilege to be able to help those who suffer. Thus sustained, I cherish the hope to keep going here as long as it will be necessary.

Not alone in America, but also in England, according to Rev. Edward Shillito, in his regular letter in the *Christian Century,* (under date of February 21, 1945) the people were reminded on the British Broadcasting Corporation, and in the press, that Schweitzer was seventy years old on January 14th. It was recalled that when he first played the organ in Westminster Abbey, a long queue of Londoners awaited patiently the hour when the doors were opened.

It was pleasantly remembered how Schweitzer, when the chairman at one of his lectures asked him how he should be introduced, replied: "This fellow who looks like a Scottish collie is Albert Schweitzer." "No friendlier or more unaffected visitor has ever come to this country," wrote Mr. Shillito, "everywhere he is reverenced." Dr. Micklem, of Oxford, dwelt in a radio talk on Schweitzer's eschatological interpretation of Jesus in terms of his own age, and not as if he were a child of our age, as the previous interpreters of Jesus had done. Although Schweitzer's view of Jesus has not, in Dr. Micklem's opinion, gained wide acceptance, nevertheless, said Dr. Micklem, it is a striking fact that Schweitzer is accepted as a real follower of Jesus. "This is his one purpose throughout his life: to offer his music and his medicine, no less than his theological studies, to this Divine Stranger whom he has come to know through obedience as an ineffable mystery."

The *Christian Century* of Feb. 14, 1945, wrote:

> We hope he is given strength to complete the book on which he is working—a volume of philosophy. What man is in better position than he to appraise our fratricidal civilization and to urge it to return to that "reverence for life" which has been his own guiding principle ... We have no way of knowing what he did that day, (Jan. 14) but probably it was nothing markedly different from what he did on the eleven thousand other days which have passed since he built his hospital there thirty years ago."

Dr. Schweitzer answered the surmise as to what he did on his seventieth birthday in a letter to the editors, which appeared in the *Christian Century* of May 30, 1945:

> Sir: I have just read the lines which you devoted to me on the occasion of my seventieth birthday. It was most kind of you to evince your sympathy. Alas, for the work I have to do I ought to be thirty years old, not seventy! Nevertheless I thank God that my health is still good enough to allow me to fill my post at my hospital. Naturally I have been put to something of a strain by the considerable effort I have had to make day by day for many years. I have not left the hospital even for a day over a very long time. But I am still on my feet.
>
> You wonder how I spent my seventieth birthday. That day—a Sunday—I had even more to do than ordinarily. In the afternoon, my colleague and I operated a case of strangulated hernia which had arrived that morn-

ing. And I had several heart cases which worried me greatly. Moreover, the heat was excessive, even for people accustomed to the torridity of equatorial regions.

The hospital is full of patients, white and black. With our staff reduced as it is, we are barely able to keep our regular work. But fortunately the end of the war is near, and then I shall be able to get fresh help from Europe. I myself shall be obliged to stay on here for several months after peace comes, until the hospital is restaffed and the new personnel is familiarized with the work.

I am deeply grateful for the aid its friends in U.S.A. are sending my hospital. I do not know how to express my thanks and the thanks of my fellow-workers.

ALBERT SCHWEITZER.

Lambaréné
French Equatorial Africa.

It is easy to see why Albert Schweitzer holds, and will hold such a supreme place of respect, and indeed reverence, in the hearts of so many people. "One would have to go far," writes Dr. Julius Seelye Bixler, "to find a writer whose deeds so eloquently supplement his words. We have only to turn to his life and find revealed the meaning of his deepest insights. What distinguishes him as a thinker is devotion to truth; as a doer, the practice of self-sacrifice."

Why has Schweitzer captured the imagination of Christians today? Because, as Magnus C. Ratter, in his Schweitzer biography, writes: "He is the realization of all that they would like to be; the high that proved too high for them is made visible in him. The passion to live the Christlike life that lost itself in middle age is perpetuated in him. The fatal 'then' lengthened, and in their old age they knew that they had lived good, honorable, even noble lives, but they had shirked their Calvary."

THE BLACK MAN AND ALBERT SCHWEITZER

By

W. E. DuBois, Ph. D., LL. D., D. Litt., L. H. D.

Prof. Emeritus of Sociology, Atlanta University

CHAPTER IV

THE BLACK MAN AND ALBERT SCHWEITZER

BY

W. E. DuBOIS

The attitude of Negroes toward missionaries today is tinged with bitterness. They know well that back of the aggression which we call the African slave trade and colonial imperialism with its results in ignorance, degradation, and disease, all too often lay missionary enterprise which paved the way for the merchant, the corporation, and armed Europe. With a religion that preached love and sacrifice, came a missionary who advocated work and loyalty with the one hand, and with the other hand opened the door to compulsory labor, over-taxation, the disruption of the family and the tribe, and the rape of the land and its people.

On the other hand, there are the men whom all black Africans revere like Mungo Park, David Livingstone, and Albert Schweitzer. Whatever the result of European invasion of Africa was, there can be no doubt of the personal sincerity of certain missionaries and of their utter sacrifice to great ideals. Here we have the contradiction which is the history of modern Africa, and which must be explained in order to interpret the past and condition the future.

Albert Schweitzer is a missionary and a scientist, as well as an artist. He believed in the Christian Church but not blindly in the Christian dogma. But more than that, he was acquainted with the human body. He knew how to heal disease and he was a member of the "Fellowship of Pain." As with all true missionaries, there was in him a certain naïve simplicity which saw in his pilgrimage an opportunity for him and his wife to journey to the heart of the dark continent in order to heal the victims of sleeping sickness and malaria, of leprosy and heart disease—a firm and forward step toward the millenium.

Schweitzer was trained in that contradictory nineteenth century. As student and professional man he knew little about industry and politics. He was largely, although not entirely, an economic tyro. He studied music at home and in Paris, and Theology and Philosophy in Strassburg University. During a year in the Army he read the Greek Testament. Intellectually he was interested in the historical Jesus and his dissertation for the doctorate was on the religious philosophy of Kant. He studied medicine in order to become a medical missionary. This plan, as he writes "had been in my mind for a long time having been conceived in my student days. It struck me as incomprehensible that I should be allowed to lead such a happy life while I saw so many people around me wrestling with care and suffering. I worked among destitute children, tramps, discharged prisoners, poor families. This work made it clear to me those groups of people could only be effectively helped by a number of individuals who would devote themselves to them, such as organizations. I wanted an absolutely personal and independent activity. In 1904, I became interested in the Paris Missionary Society through an article in their publication on 'The Needs of the Congo Mission'. The article hoped that readers might know workers who would help carry on the work at Gaboon."

Schweitzer spent eight years in Africa before and after the first World War. What he did not see or fully realize was the vast inhuman drama of blood and tears that had been played on the continent where he founded the Lambaréné Mission. It lay in the French Congo, North of the mighty Congo, on the Ogowe. Here in the Great Bend of the Gulf of Guinea, in the hot and humid bulge of Central Africa, this man comes, with his little band, to establish, with mites of money raised by "passing the hat," a little hospital which in time would cure the diseases of Africa and fight the mosquito and tsetse fly.

DIM ORIGINS

But what Albert Schweitzer did not know and could not easily conceive was the vast drama that had been played back of this community for many thousand years, and of which he and the natives were heirs. He met the mere remains of eight once powerful tribes, now thinned by 300 years of alcohol and the slave trade. He saw the remains of the swarms of cannibal bands who like locusts fell upon these tribes, reaching out of the black interior. He knew something of Gaboon since its discovery by the Portuguese at the end of the fifteenth century; and since that time the French had their missions there. But this was only part of the story.

Here in the bend of the Gulf of Guinea had been played a tragedy reaching down from the Egyptian Mediterranean and Red Sea, ending with the Cape of anything but Good Hope, and centering in a sense here in the Gulf of Guinea. All that happened we do not know and may never fully comprehend, but we knew of those beginnings of black men about the Great Lakes, of the way in which their civilization flourished in the eastern Sudan and beat upon the gates of Egypt until 700 years before Christ, they were rulers of the Nile Valley and among the greatest nations of the world. We know how further west, in the great bulge of the African continent, far separated from Egypt and the East, there arose an extraordinary civilization on the Atlantic Coast which was felt in Europe and influenced Asia.

Out of Asia came the Mohammedan religion in the hands of moving armies, rushing into Europe on the one hand; into black Africa on the other. In the whirling of men and ideas there arose in the Sudan a black imperialism which drove tribes south to the Gulf of Guinea and southeast to the Valley of the Congo. Here their culture flowered again until a new force appeared in the world; and that was Europe seeking the riches of India.

Out of that quest arose a slave trade, new crops from America
which reinforced that trade and made it mother of modern cap-
italism and developed an organized traffic in the bodies of men
unequalled before or since in the history of the world. For 400
years, from the middle of the fifteenth century down until the
last half of the nineteenth, the wealth of the world was based
on the stealing of black men and their driven labor. It was for
this that Europe invaded Africa and with the remains of this
invasion the slender hands of Albert Schewitzer tried to cope.

Small wonder that after years of work he saw frustration:
people reduced to poverty and ravished by disease; with a tradition of homeless wandering, which made the development of
settled culture well-nigh impossible. But Schweitzer did not despair. "I have not lost courage. The misery I have seen gives
me strength, and faith, in my fellowmen, supports my confidence
in the future. I do hope that I shall find a sufficient number of
people who, because they themselves have been saved from physical suffering, will respond to requests on behalf of those who are
in similar need . . . I do hope that among the doctors of the
world there will soon be several besides myself who will be sent
out here or there in the world by the 'Fellowship of those who
bear the Mark of Pain' ".

<h2 style="text-align:center">A DELICATE ISSUE</h2>

The little handful of people whom he helped saw in him a
vision and a promise; a white man who was interested in them
as human beings; who assuaged their bitter pain, who healed
their wounds. The thing which they did not understand was the
relation of this man to other white men. Apparently they were
brothers and acquaintances—they worked together. The merchants contributed to the little hospital. The corporations and
the government, the absent far-away colonial government, helped
to some extent this work of healing and rescue; and yet at bottom
the pattern was crazy and wrong. The European investors were

interested in the healing of disease only so far as that increased
their income. The corporations had but one object and that was
profit. The colonial governments looked upon these people as
methods by which their home cities could become more wealthy
and spectacular and their nations more powerful; and in the long
run this program was carried out, no matter how much the colonies were ravaged by disease, poverty, and drunkenness, as long
as they remained tools for the splendor of the white civilization.

But how out of this program, clear and unswerving as it was,
should come an Albert Schweitzer, standing for a religion of
healing, was more than the natives could understand. They simply
accepted it as a fact. They faced the contradiction and let it go
at that. That this man was their friend and benefactor there was
no question. If more of his people were like him, not only Africa
but Asia; not only far-off lands but near-by slums, might be raised
to decency, efficiency, and real civilization.

Why then was not missionary effort made effective, continuous,
and growing, instead of being the chance offshoot of desultory
charity? Why was it that the real thing that represented Europe
in Africa was not philanthropy, but investment? This the natives
did not understand. They do not understand it today. But the
most pitiful part of the paradox was that Albert Schweitzer did
not wholly understand it himself. His clear mind faced such of
the paradox which he saw: "Have we white people the right to
impose our rule on primitive and semi-primitive peoples—my
experience has been gathered among such only? No, if we only
want to rule over them and draw material advantage from their
country. Yes, if we seriously desire to educate them and help
them to attain to a condition of well-being. If there were any
sort of possibility that these peoples could live really by and for
themselves, we could leave them to themselves. But as things are,
the world trade which has reached them is a fact against which
both we and they are powerless. They have already through it
lost their freedom. Their economic and social relations are shaken

by it . . . In view of the state of things produced by world trade there can be no question with these peoples of real independence; but only whether it is better for them to be delivered over to the mercies, tender or otherwise, of rapacious native tyrants, or to be governed by officials of European states. Out of those who were commissioned to carry out in our name the seizure of our colonial territories many were guilty of injustice, violence, and cruelty as bad as those of the native chiefs, and so brought on our heads a load of guilt, is only too true. Nor of the sins committed against the natives today must anything be suppressed or whitewashed . . . The tragic fact is that the interests of colonies and those of civilization do not always run parallel but are often in direct opposition to each other."

He had with all this no broad grasp of what modern exploitation means, of what imperial colonialism has done to the world. If he had, he probably would have tried to heal the souls of white Europe rather than the bodies of black Africa.

A DREAM TO SOME; A NIGHTMARE TO OTHERS

Since, however, he did not comprehend this, and since nothing in his surroundings brought him any such clear apprehension, he deserves every tribute that we can give him for trying to do his mite, his little pitiful mite, which in a sense was but a passing gesture, but perhaps in the long run will light that fire in Africa which will cleanse that continent and the world.

Perhaps Albert Schweitzer heard that magnificent proclamation by Henry L. Stanley when he founded the Congo Free State for Leopold of Belgium: "On the fourteenth of August, 1879, I arrived before the mouth of this river to ascend it, with the novel mission of sowing along its banks civilized settlements, to peacefully conquer and subdue it, to remould it in harmony with modern ideas into National States, within whose limits the European merchant shall go hand in hand with the dark African trader, and justice and law and order shall prevail, and murder and lawlessness and the cruel barter of slaves shall be over-come." . . . "I am charged," he said, "to open and keep open, if possible, all such districts and countries as I may explore for the benefit of the commercial world. The mission is supported by a philanthropic society, which numbers noble-minded men of several nations. It is not a religious society, but my instructions are entirely of that spirit. No violence must be used, and wherever rejected, the mission must withdraw to seek another field."

The dream never became a reality; possibly that rapacious monarch, Leopold II, revelling in Brussels, never thought of the vision becoming real. Perhaps other nations were in part deceived like the United States; but there were countries like England and Germany who were not deceived. They knew that this rich domain in Africa, the possession of Belgium and the colonies of France, were being organized so as to keep the natives in chains, steal their land, get their ivory and rubber, and make untold millions of wealth by this method. Albert Schweitzer was neither deceived nor enlightened. He saw the pain and degradation of this bit of God's earth as something he could alleviate; for many years he gave his life to it.

PART II

METHODOLOGY AND EVALUATION

ON UNDERSTANDING

By

Joachim Wach, Ph. D., Th. D.

Professor History of Religions, Brown University
Formerly Professor, University of Leipzig

CHAPTER V

ON UNDERSTANDING

BY

JOACHIM WACH

Albert Schweitzer is a master of understanding. Without a great natural talent—or shall we say genius—no amount of acquired skill and knowledge would have enabled him to interpret so profoundly and comprehensively as he has done personalities of the past, distant periods and peoples, great religious documents and works of art, the thoughts, feelings, and emotions of human beings from the standpoint of a theologian, an artist and a physician. *Interpres non fit sed nascitur.* Yet, like all masters of a craft, he never relied on the inspiration of his genius but perfected his talents consistently and methodically by experience and study over a long period of years. His understanding, moreover, has proved to be deep and fruitful, because it is the result not only of a great and inclusive mind, but of an equally great and cultivated heart. A brief analysis of the nature of understanding, which he possesses to such an eminent degree, shall be our contribution in his honor.

All theories of understanding which try to analyze its nature and the stages of its development will have to begin with a concept of existence, and this means, implicitly if not explicitly, with a metaphysical decision. As I see it, there exist three possibilities which I should like to call the materialistic, the psychophysical and the spiritual interpretations of existence.

The materialistic conception explains the development and differentiation of the spiritual and psychic processes by evolution of matter. Its specific crucial problem is the immediate understanding of the minds of others.

The psychophysical conception admits that there is a mental existence apart from matter, so that it is possible for a man to share in the mental life of his fellows. The spiritual interpretation, like the materialistic, assumes the unity of all existence, but in a different sense. Here the basis of understanding lies in the continuity of mental life. Three theories of understanding are based on this idea:

1) The religious concept of spiritual communion, that is, communion in the Holy Spirit;

2) Hegel's secularized theory of the unity of spirit; and

3) Nietzsche's modern biologistic philosophy of life, with its idea of the unity of all life. Because we share the same spirit, mind or life, we may be able to understand what is related to us in substance *"Wie kann ein Mensch Sinn für etwas haben, wenn er nicht den Keim davon in sich trägt?"* (Novalis) ("How can a man understand anything, if he does not carry the germ of it within himself?")

I think there must be some truth in the idea expressed by Plato and accepted by Goethe in its Neo-Platonic form: *"Wär' nicht das Auge sonnenhaft, die Sonne könnt es nie erblicken."* (Were not the eye akin to the sun, it could never perceive the sun.") The religious flavor of this philosophy may be recognized in Malebranche's version: *"Nous voyons toutes choses en Dieu,"* which Ernst Troeltsch has recently taken over into his epistemology. To the extent that we are part of the divine creation do we see it in its true nature. Thus we obtain the hermeneutic principle that we cannot understand what is wholly different from ourselves. If we were also to say that we cannot understand what is wholly *like* ourselves, we would have to assume that understanding can apply only to an intermediate field, lying between what is wholly similar and what is wholly dissimilar to our nature. The wholly similar cannot be understood, because all understanding requires a certain *detachment* of the subject from the object.

We must now discuss whether we can understand equally well

everything in which we participate. It is obviously impossible to understand life as a whole, either in its infinitely varied productivity, or in its totality, which makes it more than the sum of all individuals, their experience and their creations.

The same is the case with history in its most general aspect. We may attribute meaning to history, but such an interpretation can be nothing but a subjective evaluation, an *eisegesis*, not an *exegesis*.

It is quite a different matter when we turn to particular phases of life, to specific experiences, to individual emotions and thoughts, to the history of particular cultures, periods, events and phenomena. They have a definite meaning, which we can understand and interpret objectively, provided the necessary subjective presuppositions are fulfilled.

Facts, and groups of facts, may be of two kinds: they may either arise in subjective experience only or manifest themselves objectively in expressions of that experience. There are many different stages and types of expression; beginning with the transitory expression of psychic life in facial expression, they lead up to gestures and eventually to signs. In the third stage we find a certain independence of expression from the subjective psychic experience. A signal has a special meaning, which can be understood, but which can also be misinterpreted, because it is relatively independent of the intention of the person who makes it. If someone is waving to me with his hand, I—and perhaps other persons—may interpret that sign to mean that I should go away, whereas he might want me to come toward him. His expression, the signal, is ambiguous. We see that a signal may have a meaning which may be interpreted indepenent of or even contrary to the subjective intention; therefore, we have to reckon with two possibilities: a subjective and an objective interpretation of expression.

The next stage of objectification is realized when the meaning is inherent in an expression, communicated to us through a medium: sounds, words, and phrases, for instance, may be understood in a subjective and in an objective sense; each might have a distinct meaning. The analysis of the understanding of the composition of words and phrases, which had been first outlined most brilliantly by Wilhelm von Humboldt, is the task of philology, one of the fields in which a theory of interpretation has developed. The others are theology, with its theory of the interpretation of sacred writings, and jurisprudence with its theory of the interpretation of laws.

The third stage of objectification is represented by personal *documents,* which might be of monumental or literary character. Letters are an interesting example; they contain subjective expression with an objective meaning. Now I can interpret the meaning of a letter without regard to the subjective life of the writer. I may do it rightly or wrongly. To be sure that I have the right interpretation of it, that I have really understood it as it wanted to be understood, I must see it in its subjective context. In this respect, Feuerbach once said that letters are aphorisms cut from their context in life. So we see that we are led from the interpretation of a special configuration to more and more extended subjective and objective contexts from which the original object takes its color: the whole correspondence, the character and life of its author.

So far we have dealt with types of expression of psychic experience which are rather closely related to the subjective experience from which they originate. The maximum of objectification, independent of subjective life, is reached in works to which we can do justice without reference to their originator, such as historical documents, normative (legal or religious) writings, and works of art.

Within the realm of artistic creation we see differences of degree in this respect. The development from spontaneous gestures to the artistic dance and to the drama shows that expression is more or less bound to the personality of the actor or actress, while painting and architecture represent expression of a less personal character, their mediums being tangible and material. Music again is peculiar in this respect: the meaning of a musical composition is conveyed through sound, the subtlest vibrations of matter, and is relatively independent of the personality of its author. How complicated the problems of musical hermeneutics are, we may see from the following example, taken from my book, *Das Verstehen*. In the opera *Orpheus and Euridice* Gluck composed a special melodic line for the words: "Oh, I have lost her, and it is my greatest sorrow," and afterwards replaced these words with: "Oh, I have gained her, and it is my greatest joy," without changing the music. This illustrates the flexibility of music as a medium of conveying meaning.

So, in all understanding of more or less objectified expression which is to succeed in its intention, two factors combine: the subjective interpretation, which intends to make sure the psychological meaning of an expression by relating it to its author, and the objective interpretation, which takes it as an entity in itself and tries to unfold its meaning. The objective exegesis consists of three different procedures: the technical interpretation, analysis of the material or elements of expression (sounds, letters, colors); the generic interpretation, asking for the genre or *genos*, type or form of work; the historical and sociological interpretation, which attempts to elucidate the socio-historical background and the development of the phenomenon. None of these viewpoints should be unduly stressed at the expense of others if the aim is an integral understanding.

Michelangelo's famous paintings, "The Creation of Man," may serve as an example of highly objectified artistic expression. Understanding means, in this case, to be able to answer the questions: 1) What is to be seen? The answer is: a young man, lying on the ground, and an old man, gliding, as it were, from the air toward him; and 2) What does it signify? This question is not identical with the psychological inquiry, "What did the artist intend to express?" Rather, it refers to the objective meaning of this painting, which we may identify as the same or another than the artist intended to express. The answer is: the Lord, creating Adam, the first man.

In trying to illuminate the background, we must relate the painting to three different contexts. The first, the historical and sociological, interpretation, gives it a place in the history of art, of artists, of culture and of society. The second, or generic interpretation, analyses it according to its species and its technical character. The third, the documentary interpretation, places the work in a larger context of meaning, which might possibly be beyond the horizon of its creator; it illustrates the philosopher's shrewd remark, "The artist is ever wiser than he is." Here the success of hermeneutics lies in understanding the work of the author better than he himself did.

With this last type of interpretation we have already passed not only to inference, but also to *appreciation* and *application* of the meaning of the objectification of experience, and it is a problem whether this appreciation or application is a part of the process of understanding proper.

For instance, in the interpretation of art, interpretation, and appreciation or evaluation are closely connected, more so than in the interpretation of laws. And in the interpretation of religion, it is doubtful whether the meaning of a religious message can be understood without any reference to its hortatory character. That is how the early Protestant theologians conceive of understanding: *Primum perceptio, deinde cogitatio de illa percepta notitia in praxim, tertio velle, quarto perficere.*

PRESUPPOSITIONS, CONDITIONS, AND LIMITATIONS OF UNDERSTANDING

We have now to consider which subjective and objective presuppositions are necessary for adequate understanding and what the limitations of understanding itself are. We have already

found that understanding aims at bringing into focus the unknown as an intermediate field between the entirely foreign and
the perfectly familiar. Though we cannot say we understand
the lower organisms, we succeed in interpreting the meaning of
the gestures and sounds made by animals. Scheler has defined
the dividing line between man and animals by attributing to
man *Geist,* the ability to reflect on his own nature and to become
a moral being, capable of renunciation and self-sacrifice. I would
prefer to draw the line between those beings which are and
those which are not able to create permanent expressions for
their internal experience, which may be understood independently
of subjective life. Therefore, we may say that understanding
in a technical sense is limited to the realm of human life and
human creations.

Why is it difficult for us at times to understand our fellow
men and the expression of their experience? First, because we
are—each of us—the complicated and highly individual result
of slow development from an original germ. The second thing
to remember is that the understanding subject does not live in
a vacuum; he is conditioned in many ways by his environment.
Our understanding, therefore, is necessarily limited, first, by what
we are personally, and secondly, by the conditions under which
we exist. Thus we can say that the chances for understanding
persons and things are in some respects worse and in others
better than some epistomologists think.

Two extreme attitudes, however, must be avoided: a naive
realism, which hopes to grasp the object "as it is," and a sub-
jectivistic skepticism, which dissolves the object into relations.
Not relativism, but relationism, should be the motto of all sound
hermeneutics.

The understanding of individuality is the basic problem of
hermeneutics. *"In der Individualität liegt das Geheimnis alles
Daseins,"* said Humboldt, and Dilthey agrees with him: *"Indivi-
duum est ineffabile."* That means that individuality is not only

[139]

inexpressible but also incomprehensible. In the different methods of investigation of personality, however, some methods have been developed to solve this mystery. Without doubt the theory of types is suitable in serving the understanding of personality, although exaggeration may be dangerous and lead to fantastic conclusions. If we want to understand the actions and reactions of a person, we use categories like "the hero," "the coward," "the miser," "the lover," to make his motivation and scale of values plausible to us. Dilthey has demonstrated the importance of types of human character for the understanding of personalities in literature in his thesis on Shakespeare. History and poetry present additional difficulties for an understanding. The personalities in dramatic poetry, for instance, are seen through the medium of the poet. Thus we must differentiate between the "objective" meaning and the highly personalized interpretation which the actor may give to a particular role and to individual lines in attempting to convey the specific intentions of the dramatist.

What we do in daily life, the historian practices in his study in viewing historic personalities in the light of characterological types. Furthermore, history is always related through some sources. Sometimes an actual witness describes the events and the personalities figuring in them; sometimes again we have more than one source through which we must understand historical events and personalities. Sometimes the understanding of a character presents special difficulties, particularly if we have very few objective expressions as material. If we face a person, we may interpret his speech by examining the caliber of his voice, the expression of his eyes, and his gestures, so that we are able to discern clearly whether his words are straightforward, or ironical, or ambiguous. Since all literal and historical analysis misses this advantage, the student must combine very carefully as much material as he can collect on his subject.

After these remarks on the objective difficulties of understand-

ON UNDERSTANDING

ing, we may consider briefly its subjective conditions, which are
the presuppositions for the understanding of the not entirely
foreign and the not perfectly familiar. He who wants to understand appears to be confined within the magic circle of his personality, yet is is not entirely so. I would like again to quote an
example from the history of religion. The historian of religion
deals with exotic, ecstatic and primitive cults, all of them more
or less foreign to his mind and his soul, still more to his personal
experience. He has never participated in complicated rites; he
has never taken part in ecstatic sessions or performances. He
knows animals—totems in the primitive language—only as they
occur around the house or at the zoo. Nevertheless, there exists
some means of breaking the magic circle of these limitations.
All of us are able to enlarge the limits of our empiric personality:
the first means is by availing ourselves of the immeasurable
treasure of research and the arts, which enables us, through
knowledge and comparison, to gain analogies for the phenomena
which we wish to understand. A great modern philosopher de-
fines art as an organ for the understanding of life. All natural
sciences and the humanities make their contributions to the en-
largement of the empiric self.

The second way is indicated by the words of Goethe: *"In
jedem Menschen liegen alle Formen des Menschlichen."* ("In
every man all forms of human character are potentially present.")
Goethe felt, when told about a crime, that he would have been
capable of committing it himself. Modern students have emphasized the fact that our conscious life does not complete the entire
circle of our personality. I refer to a very interesting report of
Eduard Spranger in the transactions of the "Berliner Akademie
der Wissenschaften" (1930): "Ueber die Schichten des Wirk-
lichkeitsbewusstseins," and to Jung's investigations inspired by
Freud on the atavistic structure of the mind, as it appears in the
analysis of the archaic patterns in schizophrenia. In this way the
student of primitive religion will remember the experiences of

[141]

his youth—the well-known Indian games of American boys and girls—and thus expand his understanding of the primitive mind.

The person who understands is distinguished by the ability to renew and revivify continuously his own experience as well as that of the race. The great psychologists and philosophers of the seventeenth and eighteenth centuries in France and England combined the interpretation of historical events with participation in the political, military, cultural and social life of their times. We see the result in the testimonies of the understanding of the human soul given by such French and English moralists as Montaigne, LaRochefoucauld, Chesterfield, Chamfort, Hume and Vauvenargues.

All great scientists and artists need this capacity for transcending the limits of their personal experience. The great instrument for doing this is the imagination. In his book *Königliche Hoheit*, Thomas Mann has a prince ask a poet if, in order to be able to write his novel, he had had to travel around the world. The poet immediately replies, "Quite the contrary, Your Highness!" Marcel Proust calls the artist the man of Noah's Ark, who sees and understands the world from inside his ark.

THE ACT OF UNDERSTANDING

There has been much discussion in hermeneutics on the relation of the synthetic and the intuitive methods. The first operates by combining several small details to a composite picture, and the second by the immediate act of comprehension. Some have thought that the intuitive method is arbitrary, and others that without it synthetic methods can gain only partial results. We do not arrive at a complete understanding by induction, and by combination of its results, unless this procedure is accompanied by a specific act which can better be delimited than defined. We may illustrate it by comparing this specific act with the jumping of a spark between two electric poles, or with the sudden closing of a door, or with the psychological experience behind the phrase "I get it!"

Psychologists and sociologists have discussed the possibility of the direct and immediate grasp of the personality of another. Max Scheler, for one, denied all empathy and possibility of transposition. The experience of another personality is not gained by the transposition of one's own personality, for then the other personality would be obscured. Yet we anticipate and understand by wholes. That does not mean that by an act of divination we can understand another personality completely and correctly; the important thing is to seize the dominant traits of its nature. That is done by an act of comprehension in which both methods of procedure are combined. I should like to illustrate this with another phrase of Goethe's, who said that he could successfully imitate a man for an hour whom he had heard speak for fifteen minutes. The same sentiment is expressed in the sentence: *"Ex ungue leonem,"* ("By the paw we know the lion.")

Once we have acquired the idea of the dominant characteristics, we may be able to understand and fit into the main context the secondary characteristics of a personality and its means of expression. Since we cannot build up the whole structure of a personality simply by understanding, we have to pick out representative features. Thus we see that to "understand" a person and his expression, means to grasp intuitively as well as to piece together many isolated observations, the salient characteristics affording clues to his personality.

We have already seen that understanding is not photographic. There is a subjective factor in it, which neither can nor should be removed. It could be asked whether a feeling of accord with a person or a phenomenon is a requisite of its understanding. Medieval thinkers dealt much with the relation between emotion and knowledge. Some of them maintained that emotion (love) is the basis of knowledge. Even such recent writers as Pascal and Scheler postulated an *"ordre du coeur"* to supplement the order of thought. Those opposed to this theory will quote the proverb which says that love is blind, a contention which is only correct if it is true that hatred sees clearly. Whole biographies have been written, prompted by the author's hatred of his subject. However, they are as unsatisfactory as those dictated by an uncritical admiration for the hero.

All this tends to prove that certain emotional factors are inclined to influence the understanding, Nevertheless, it is not so much the coloring as the presence of emotion which established the contact necessary for an understanding and for the mood in which it can be developed. There is a type of indifference which makes understanding difficult if not impossible. *"Graue, kalte Augen wissen nicht was die Dinge wert sind,"* said Nietzsche. ("Gray, cold eyes do not know what things are worth.") Yet the existence and the nature of the "affectus" have to be realized and, what is even more important, to be controlled if genuine and true understanding is aspired.

We must therefore now turn to the problem of the possibility of limiting and controlling the subjective factor which we have found to be unavoidable. As a final motto for this section we may quote a word of Jean Paul—that there are three difficult things: to possess character, to draw character, and to recognize character.

THE OBJECTIVITY OF UNDERSTANDING

The two extremes we have found to be erroneous are the notion of photographic reproduction and a radically skeptical attitude. History is not only a "fable convenue," as the skeptic would say, although occasionally we find in the historiography of our days a tendency to turn history into myth.

We can understand historical events and personalities and can check our results.

Some theories, for instance the radical theories of race, will not admit that there can be any objectivity in the understanding of another person, or of history, and if there were, it would not be desirable. It is true that not everyone can understand everything, but as we have already seen, there is the possibility of verification and control of the presuppositions on which understanding can be based. Students of hermeneutics have been much concerned with establishing objective criteria and thus defending the evidence of understanding. This procedure includes two factors, first an internal consistency in the process of understanding facts, and secondly the check which is exerted by weighing individual facts and instances against each other. Philosophical and psychological, historical and philological research and methodology have developed a great critical apparatus in order to guarantee the certainty of the evidence of the results of their interpretation. The aim of understanding must be defined as integral comprehension, even if only an approximation to an absolutely objective understanding is attainable.

I wish to repeat that such comprehension cannot be a simple copy of its object in the mind, but that it is rather a reproduction in perspective and an all-inclusive interpretation of its significance.

THE PURPOSE OF UNDERSTANDING

The question of why understanding is essential has been frequently answered from a purely pragmatic point of view. I wish to call attention to another aspect of the aim of understanding, advanced by the hermeneutics of the *historische Schule*. We seem to feel within ourselves an overwhelming impulse to understand, even when no "practical" issue is involved.

"Alles Gewesene ist wissenswürdig." (All that ever existed is worth knowing"). We may add: Everything that does exist is worth knowing, though to a different degree. There are priorities in this respect which vary with the understanding individual, the period and the context in which he lives.

I cannot discuss here the interesting problem of the limits of understanding which is indicated by Nietzsche's conception of creative ability, *"plastische Kraft."* He himself was of the opinion that nobody should be allowed to learn and understand more than he can well absorb into his personality without weakening his creative impulses. If I am right, that is the problem of our civilization and age. Should there not be a way between an indiscriminate incorporation of all and everything that our understanding can reach, and the dangerous simplification extolled by some false prophets as a return to the status "before the fall?"

Should we not try to be broad—by wide and sympathetic understanding—broad, but not shallow? We, as individuals, and as collective entities, can afford to be so, provided we have principles to guide us, when we choose and assimilate, strong but not narrow principles that will be strengthened rather than weakened by practicing understanding.

In summary we may say that the function of understanding is threefold. The first is preservation. He who understands what is and what has been, revives and preserves in the memory of men the sum of their experience. The second function is the guidance and direction of our thoughts and actions, education of ourselves and others according to the formula, *"So sollst Du sein, denn so verstehe ich Dich."* (Droysen) ("Thus shalt thou be, for thus do I know thee or thy true nature.") The third aim is to realize the scope and variety of human nature and personality, as well as its expression in all fields of cultural activity.

VALUATIONS OF ACHIEVEMENTS, ACTS, LAWS, AND PERSONS

By

E. L. Thorndike, Ph. D., LL. D., Sc. D.
Professor Emeritus, Teachers College, Columbia University

CHAPTER VI

VALUATIONS OF ACHIEVEMENTS, ACTS, LAWS, AND PERSONS

BY

E. L. THORNDIKE

VALUATIONS OF TWENTY ACHIEVEMENTS, a to t.*

The ranking of the achievements a to t listed below was done by a group of 22 persons of superior intelligence, nine of whom were psychologists, and six of whom were advanced students of psychology, and by a group of 44 unemployed of the white-collar and professional classes.

The first number after each achievement is the median rank for the group of 22, and the next two numbers joined by a dash show the range of ranks required to include 20 of the 22. The next number is the median rank for the group of 44 unemployed, and the two following numbers joined by a dash show the range of ranks required to include 40 of the 44. The variation is very great in both groups for all the items except curing cancer and converting Roman Catholics to Presbyterianism. The unemployed agree in many respects with the superior and psychological group, the correlation between the two rank orders being .82. If items n and o are omitted, the correlation is .94.

* Certain peculiarities in the selection of achievements a to t and of the acts, laws, and persons described later in this report are due first to the fact that they are only a fraction of the valuations that I planned to get, and, secondly, to the fact that the general plan included a study of attitudes toward certain sorts of persons and customs, together with experiments in modifying these attitudes. The general plan was not carried to completion. The reports from the unemployed groups and from some of the superior groups were received in 1934 and 1935. The majority of the reports from the persons of high intelligenece were received in 1942 and 1943.

[149]

Write 1, 2, 3, 4, etc., before each of the achievements listed below according to the value you set upon them. Write 1 before the one you would like best to achieve, 2 before the one you think next most valuable, and so on to 20 for the least valuable. If two or more of the achievements seem equally valuable, write the two or more appropriate numbers before each

a. Convert a hundred Roman Catholics to Presbyterianism	19	15—20	19	16—20
b. Convert a hundred Jews to Presbyterianism	19	13—20	19	15—20
c. Convert a hundred Buddhists to Presbyterianism	18	11—20	18	14—20
d. Convert ten millionaires to giving up all their property to the poor and spending their lives in literal obedience to the teachings of Jesus	9½	1—17	12	1—17
e. Convert ten political bosses to using all their skill and wealth and influence to do what the clergymen of their cities want done	9	3—16	11	3—18
f. Cure ten children of habitual thieving	9	5—14	7½	3—14
g. Cure ten children of habitual lying	10	7—15	8½	4—13
h. Cure ten children of occasional auto-erotic indulgences	12½	5—17	10	5—16
i. Discover a means of preventing cancer	1	1—4	1	1—7
j. Discover a means of preventing influenza	2	1—7	2½	1½—9
k. Induce a hundred women to use the time and money they now spend in beauty shops in the serious study of social and political problems	9½	5—16	12½	4—19
l. Induce a hundred women to use the time and money they now spend in playing cards in telling poor people in the slums how they should bring up their children	16	7—19	12½	5—18
m. Induce a hundred men to use the time and money they now spend in playing golf, fishing, or hunting in attending public forums and group discussions on "How a Christian should run his business"	13	9—17	13½	6—17
n. Induce a hundred students in a teachers college to be as impartial in thinking about the merits of social and political questions as they are in thinking about physical or chemical problems	4	3—12	10	3—16
o. Induce any hundred of the wives of the thousand most promising young men in the U. S. to have four children instead of two or less	6½	2—15	13	2—18
p. Make a sick child happy instead of miserable for an hour	11½	6—19	9½	3—16
q. Make a sick dog happy instead of miserable for an hour	16½	11—20	14	4—20
r. Make a hundred sick children happy instead of miserable for an hour	9	5—16	7	3—12
s. Make a thousand sick children happy instead of miserable for an hour	7½	4—15	6	2—14
t. Make a million sick children happy instead of miserable for an hour	5½	2—14	4	1—14

A remarkable fact in these rankings of achievements is the large majority assigning less value to the conversion of a hundred Roman Catholics, Jews, or Buddhists to a highly respected Protestant faith than to making a sick dog happy for an hour. q is ranked higher than a by 16 of the 22 psychologists and other superior intellects, higher than b by 16 of them, and higher than c by 15 of them. q is ranked higher than a by 38 of the 44 unemployed, higher than b by 38 of them, and higher than c by 37 of them.

The values set upon making children happy in comparison with making them good are also noteworthy. Ten hours of happiness is set above being cured of habitual thieving or lying. In the group of 22, r is rated as more valuable than f by 12, and as more valuable than g by 14. In the group of 44 unemployed r is rated as more valuable than f by 29 and as of equal worth by 1. It is rated as more valuable than g by 31, and as of equal worth by 1. The cure of occasional erotic indulgences is set clearly below the cure of habitual thieving or lying, such cure of one child being set as less valuable than making a sick child happy instead of miserable for six minutes!

Among the reformations d, e, k, l, m, n, and o, that in the direction of more scientific and impartial thinking (n) leads by a clear margin. The others are of nearly equal merit in the opinion of the 44 unemployed, and rank clearly below giving a sick child an hour's happiness and not far above doing the same for a sick dog. The psychologists and others in the group of 22 rate o (production of offspring by superior families) much higher than d, e, k, l, and m. They value the addition of one such child somewhere between five hours and five thousand hours of happiness. They rate m and l, especially l, much lower than d, e, and k. They rank the conversion of one woman from playing cards to giving advice to parents in the slums as about equal to making one sick dog happy for one minute.

Using well-known formulae and certain assumptions, it is possible to compute the amount of value attached to any of these achievements as a plus over the value of one hour's happiness for a sick dog in terms of the variability (I shall use the standard deviation) of the group in valuation, and also approximately as a fraction of the difference in value between one hour's happiness for a sick dog and one hour's happiness for a million children.

For example, h has more value than q by a vote of 15 to 7, which corresponds to 47½ hundredths of the variability of opinion (standard deviation) of the 22; g has more value than h by a vote of 16 to 6, which corresponds to 60½ hundredths of the standard deviation of opinion of the 22; t has more value than g by a vote of 18 to 4, or 91 hundredths of the standard deviation of opinion of the 22. Letting x equal the value of q, we have as the values of h, g, and t, x+.47½, x+1.08, and x+1.99. Since the value of x is less than a millionth of the value of t, we may disregard it and use .47½, 1.08, and 1.99 as the relative values of h, g, and t.*

Taking h as .24 t and g as .54 t, we may equate h to 240,000 happiness hours and g to 540,000 happiness hours. The values of any other item (except i,) can be determined in a similar manner by using the votes about it in comparison with q, h, g, or t. Using the opinions of the 44 and the variability of opinion of the 44 in a similar manner, we find h valued at 385,000 happiness hours, and g at 670,000.

If the 22 judges were replaced by 100 or more representing a high quality of knowledge and impartiality and all important points of view, and if the 20 achievements were increased by 20 or 30 wisely chosen achievements, such measurements as those given above would be not only a convenient expression of valuations in terms of happiness units, but an excellent feature of a textbook on morals or guide for human activities. They would, of course, be subject to amendment by the advancement of knowledge about the consequences of, say, d, or i. Perhaps it would be

* Using m instead of h in the compuatations, we find g=1.10 and t=2.01.

discovered that the common good was benefited more if the millionaires kept their property and used it to make more than if the poor received it while the millionaires tried to do the Lord's will empty-handed. Perhaps the discoverer of a cure for cancer would only hasten by a few years what the course of events would surely produce sooner or later if he spent his life growing potatoes or playing pinochle. Certain sociologists suggest this in their criticisms of the "great-man" theory. Until so amended, however, they would be enormously superior to the adulteration of common sense by ignorance, superstitions, prejudices, and wishful thinking that now characterizes human valuations.

II

VALUATIONS OF FIFTY ACTIVITIES

Twenty-two persons of superior intelligence, 14 of whom were psychologists, and 42 unemployed persons of the white-collar and professional classes, assigned values to each of the 50 activities listed below. The number preceding each activity identifies it and gives its position in the list given to each of the 64 subjects of the experiment. The first number following the description of the activity is the median value assigned by the group of 22. The second number is the range required to include 20 of the 22. The third number is the median value assigned by the group of 42. The range required to include 38 of the 42 is not reported, but would equal or exceed the range for the 22.

John Smith, college graduate, a chemist aged 40, married to a woman of average health, beauty, intellect, morals and temperament, with three children, aged 12, 10 and 4, worth $40,000 and earning $3600 per year, is let off from work for Thursday afternoon so that he has three hours at his disposal. This being all you know about him, consider the following ways of spending the time by him, rating each for its probable value, or merit, or goodness. Use 0 if the activity would do as much harm as good. Use 10 for the best of the first page of the list. Use −10 for the worst of the first page of the list. If you later find something better than what you called +10, or worse than what you called −10, you may use 11, 12, 13, etc. and −11, −12, _13, etc., as seems necessary.

1.	Studying chemistry.	5.5	14	5
7.	Reading a standard work on history.	2	7	5
48.	Reading *Harpers Magazine*.	3	8	5
49.	Reading the *Literary Digest*.	2.5	6	3
50.	Reading the newspaper.	2	9	5
5.	Taking his wife for a walk, a thing of which she is very fond. He cares very little about walking.	5.5	10	5
15.	Relieving his wife of care of the four-year-old by taking it to play in the park.	5	10	3
47.	Telling his wife to choose what she would most like to have him do and doing it cheerfully.	3.5	12	4.5
17.	Taking a young woman who works in his office to the movies.	—2	9	0.5
2.	Going to a prostitute.	—10	15	—10
34.	Getting the two older children excused from school and taking them to the Natural History Museum.	3	10	5.5
3.	Making out his income-tax report.	3	7	1
19.	Working in his garden.	5.5	9	5
28.	Making repairs and improvements in his home.	5	10	5
46.	Cleaning out the cellar of his home.	2.5	6	3
4.	Visiting his aged mother.	6	10	6
40.	Going with his wife to call on two poor maiden aunts.	2	9	1.5
6.	Taking a nap.	2	8	2.5
14.	Playing solitaire.	0	8	0
20.	Playing golf with his brother.	5	10	5
24.	Going to a baseball game.	3.5	10	5
27.	Listening to the radio at home.	2	9	4.5
44.	Playing the piano.	3.5	7	5.5
29.	Getting a hair-cut, shampoo, and manicure and shopping for clothes.	3	6	3.5
9.	Gambling (roulette, with small stakes, losing $4.00 in all).	—2	11	—1
13.	Taking a quart of whiskey home to his room and getting thoroughly drunk there.	—8.5	11	—8
8.	Doing extra work for $25 which he donates to the local hospital.	5	11	5

31.	Helping a neighbor who has asked advice about some chemical problems.	6	8	5
41.	Going to the office of a friend who has been ill and helping him to catch up with his work.	6	11	5
43.	Analyzing the water from the well of a farm which a friend is thinking of buying.	5	8	5
10.	Loafing with men friends.	1	9	1
12.	Reading a detective story.	1.5	4	2
11.	Praying and reading the Bible.	1	16	0
16.	Going to the park alone and talking encouragingly to unemployed men found there.	2	11	3
18.	Writing letters to the newspapers complaining about the noisiness of the streets.	—0.5	12	0
42.	Making calls to solicit subscriptions for the city's Community Chest.	2.5	12	0.5
45.	Writing a set of good resolutions for the New Year.	0	9	0.5
32.	Shooting squirrels in the woods.	1	11	0
35.	Reading literature issued by the Communist Party.	2	11	3
36.	Reading literature issued by the Socialist Party.	2	15	2
37.	Reading literature issued by the Republican Party.	0	15	0
38.	Reading literature issued by the Mormon church.	1	14	0
21.	Writing and sending anonymous defamatory letters to several men about their wives.	—10	8	—10
33.	Sitting in the park, trying to frighten any children who came near by making horrible faces at them.	—6.5	11	—9.5
39.	Teasing the monkeys in the zoo by holding out food and pulling it back when they reach for it.	—4	11	—8
22.	Writing and sending anonymous insulting letters to prominent clergymen.	—8	9	—10
23.	Writing and sending anonymous insulting letters to prominent politicians.	—5	10	—9.5
26.	Going to stores and stealing small articles.	—8	7	—10
25.	Going to a symphony concert.	5	9	8
30.	Writing poetry.	2	7	3

The variation even among the 22 individuals is very great—
14 or more for six of the activities, from 8 to 12 for thirty-five of
them, 6 or 7 for eight of them. Getting drunk is rated as an
innocent indulgence (o) by two, shooting squirrels as worse than
frightening children by two, and reading literature issued by the
Republican party as worse than writing and sending defamatory
letters to prominent politicians by three! Gambling is put above
giving the man's wife her chosen pleasure by two. Our chemist
could find among the 22 one or more defenders of any of the 50
activities except writing and sending defamatory letters to men
about their wives.

The great variation among individuals is, however, consistent
with a consensus of the 22 which probably approximates closely
to a consensus of the opinions of, say, all American college gradu-
ates, or all American doctors, lawyers, teachers, engineers, and
labor leaders.

The medians present this consensus of the 22. The medians
for the 42 are in general similar, the correlation between the two
being over .90.

This consensus lacks such surprises as characterized the consensus valuations of the achievements a to t, but the low valuations of praying and reading the Bible (1 for the 22 and 0 for the
42) and the opprobrium cast on the Republican party (0 and 0
as compared with +2 and +2 for the literature of the Socialist
party) may seem remarkable to some, and almost surely would
not have been the consensus of the intelligentsia of two generations ago. The valuations are, I think, the resultants of both
impersonal considerations of the consequences of the activities,
and more personal judgments of what one would do or ought
to do in the chemist's place. There is also some acceptance of
conventional opinion about whether the activity is praiseworthy.

The individual opinions reveal many prejudices or doctrinaire
notions such as that one should use leisure to get far away from
one's specialty (as in a rating of —10 for studying chemistry,

—5 for doing extra work for $25 and giving that to the local hospital, and —5 for helping a neighbor with chemical problems). Taking a nap is put as —10; talking encouragingly to the unemployed as —9; listening to the radio as —6; writing poetry as —8. These doctrinaire notions and individual prejudices are in part counterbalanced by opposite ones, and exert an appreciable influence on the medians only when several of them act alike upon the rating of an activity.

The general assignment of value in accord with consequences is adequate to account for a large fraction of most of the median valuations. The consequences primarily of benefit to the chemist himself are given weight, the self-improvement of activities 7, 48, and 49 being valued at 2, 3, and 2.5, the innocent indulgences of 6, 14, 20, 24, 27, and 44 averaging 2 2/3, and those of 10, 12, 32, and 50 averaging 1.4. Consequences benefiting others at some sacrifice to the chemist are set much higher; the activities in behalf of his wife, mother, aunts, neighbor, friends, and the hospital have medians from 3½ to 6, and average almost exactly 5.

The influence of more personal judgments about what is fit and proper for a man to do with an unexpected half-holiday appears in the ratings of 5.5 and 5 for "working in his garden" and "making repairs and improvements in his home," as compared with 3 and 2.5 for making out his "income-tax return" and "cleaning out the cellar of his home." "Playing golf with one's brother" (5) also seems much better than "playing solitaire" (0), over and above its greater value for health. "Telling his wife to choose what she would most like to have him do and doing it cheerfully" seems somewhat unreal and silly, and perhaps as setting a bad precedent, and so is ranked low in spite of its superior consequences.* The degradation of oneself by anony-

* The average for the three activities in favor of the wife (5, 15, and 47) are in order 5.2, 5.2, and 2.9 for the group of 22, and 3.9, 3.3, and 3.0 for the group of 42.

mous insults to clergymen seems greater than that by similar insults to politicians.

How far the low ratings for acts of religious devotion and for informing oneself about the programs and arguments of political parties are caused by low estimates of the value of the consequences of so doing, and how far by the absence of personal impulses in their favor as proper uses of a holiday, I do not know.

The influence of conventional opinion may be seen in the rating of 6 for the visit to an aged mother but only 2 for the visit to two poor maiden aunts, and in the high rating for going to a symphony concert. On the whole, the median ratings fit rather closely a happiness-welfare calculus in which the happiness or welfare of another is credited at about two and a half times the happiness or welfare of oneself.

It is of some interest to put the median valuations from 0 to 5 or 6 in terms of the variability of the opinions of the 22. The 0 to 5 difference corresponds to 1.58 times the standard deviation of opinion, and the 0 to 6 difference to 1.83 times it. For the negative valuations or penalties we have 0 to −2 equaling .37 times the standard deviation, 0 to —8 equaling approximately 1.50 times it, and 0 to −10 equaling 1.97 times it.

Seventeen persons of high intelligence and 40 unemployed of the white-collar and professional classes performed the queer task of ranking acts A to L shown below. The first number following each item is the average rank assigned to it by the 17. The second number is the average rank assigned to it by the 40. The two pairs of numbers give the range of ranks required to include 15 of the 17, and 36 of the 40, in that order.

VALUATIONS OF TWELVE ACTS

Write 1, 2, 3, 4, etc., before each of the acts described below to show your order of preference if you were compelled to do one of them. Assume that in all cases your act is known to no person save yourself, so that the only blame or punishment you can possibly receive will be from your own conscience or from supernatural sources. Assume, that is, that the interested parties in E to G and the pupils concerned in H to L are by a miracle deprived of all memories that you were the person who assisted in the work or did the teaching.

Write 1 before the act you would prefer, 2 before your second choice, and so on to 12 for the act you would do the most to avoid. If two or more seem equally objectionable, write the two or more appropriate numbers before each. Read all before you write any numbers.

A. Eat 4 ounces of cooked human flesh, knowing it to be such	8.1	8.9	4-12	4-12
B. Marry a Hottentot and live with him or her for a year	7.4	6.4	4-12	2½-12
C. Steal $500 from a rich miser who got it by deceiving the public	4.8	3.6	1-7	1-7
D. Spit on a crucifix	5.9	7.1	3-8	3-12
Spend 100 hours of your leisure time in ways described below. In each case you are paid $500 by some interested party for doing so.				
E. Assisting a campaign to increase the sales of a tooth-paste which does more harm than good	7.3	7.1	4-9	2-10½
F. Assisting a campaign to increase the sales of a patent medicine valueless except for the alcohol it contains	6.4	5.6	3-9	2-9
G. Assisting a campaign to stir up hatred of the Jews	10.8	9.1	10-12	5-11
H. Teaching high-school pupils to use cocaine....	11.0	10.3	10-12	8-12
I. Teaching high-school pupils to regard the old testament as a collection of myths	3.7	5.1	1-7	1-9
J. Teaching high-school pupils to regard the burial of the dead as silly and a foolish, wasteful custom	3.3	5.4	2-7	1-9
K. Teaching high-school pupils that marriage is a silly custom	6.6	6.0	2-10	2-10½
L. Teaching high-school pupils that wearing hats is a silly custom	3.3	3.5	1-5	1-7

The 40 appear more conventional and more self-indulgent than the 17; and there is no reason to attribute these differences to greater frankness on the part of the 40. The percentages of the 40 unemployed ranking one act above another are worth attention in the case of certain pairs. According to the reports:

Thirty per cent prefer H (teach young people to use cocaine) to A (eat 4 ounces cooked human flesh), and 7½% would as soon do one as the other. The corresponding percentages for the 17 of high intelligence are 24 and 6.

Exactly 37½% prefer G (stir up hatred of the Jews) to A, and 7½% would as soon do one as the other. The corresponding percentages for the 17 of high intelligence are 18 to 6.

62½% would rather steal $500 from the miser specified than get it as pay for teaching against the burial of the dead. Only 92½% of the 17 of high intelligence state such preference.

95% would rather steal $500 than eat 4 ounces of cooked human flesh; 76% of the 17 of high intelligence would.

50% would rather get the $500 for selling the patent medicine than for teaching against the burial of the dead; 12% of the 17 would.

The harmless or nearly harmless, and conceivably in some ways beneficial, J and L may be taken as near a moral zero, and so as comparable to the chemist's use of his time for playing solitaire (14), writing resolutions for New Year's (45), and other activities rated as doing as much harm as good. Using J and L and 14, 37, and 45 as zero points, we find that teaching high-school pupils to use cocaine is regarded as somewhat worse than writing defamatory letters to men about their wives by the more intelligent group (2.4 and 1.9 standard deviations worse than 0), and as equally bad by the unemployed (1.5 standard deviations worse than 0 for both).

III

VALUATIONS OF LAWS

Twenty-five adults of high intelligence, two thirds of whom were psychologists or advanced students of psychology, and 40 unemployed men and women of the white-collar and professional classes ranked the 20 laws described below. The first number following each law is the median rank for the group of 25; the second is the range required to include 23 of the 25; the third is the median rank for the group of 40. The two groups' rankings do not differ greatly except for *s*. Including *s*, the correlation is .85; excluding *s*, it is .93.

Write 1, 2, 3, 4, etc., before the following proposed laws to show which you would favor most, etc. Use 1 for best choice, 2 for next best, 3 for next best, and so on to 19 for next to worst and 20 for worst. You are to assume that means will be provided to enforce each law fully. All the laws are to cover the entire United States. Read all before you write numbers for any. If two or more seem equal in merit, write the two or more appropriate number before each of them.

..........*a*.	Changing divorce laws so as to make them uniform through the U. S. and allowing divorce for adultery, cruelty, non-support (in the case of the male), insanity, and comparable causes	3	8	5
..........*b*.	Forbidding the erection of any private dwelling costing more than $100,000	11	10½	8
..........*c*.	Forbidding the growth or importation or sale of tobacco in any form	17½	9	17½
..........*d*.	Forbidding any individual to retain property beyond a value of ten million dollars	9	12	5½
..........*e*.	Forbidding any individual to retain property beyond a value of one million dollars	9	17	7
..........*f*.	Forbidding any individual to retain property beyond a value of one hundred thousand dollars	14	15	10½
..........*g*.	Forbidding any individual to give or bequeath to any individual more than $25,000	14	15	11
..........*h*.	Increase the salaries of senators to $50,000 a year	16	15	17
..........*i*.	Increase the salaries of congressmen to $30,000 a year	16	14	16½
..........*j*.	Making attendance in school compulsory to age 16 in the U. S.	4	12	4
..........*k*.	Making attendance in school compulsory to age 18 in the U. S.	8	15	6½
..........*l*.	Making attendance in school compulsory to age 20 in the U. S.	13	13	11
..........*m*.	Providing free tuition and $300 a year for all children in the U. S. with IQ's above 150 until age 25	3½	8	6
..........*n*.	Providing a subsidy to private and parochial schools for each pupil educated by them equal to one half the cost per pupil in public schools in the same community	12	14	13
..........*o*.	Putting a tax of $1 per sq. ft. per year on all signboards used for advertising	7	11	9
..........*p*.	Requiring that the bodies of all dead persons be used in scientific research or be made into fertilizer	15	15	15½
..........*q*.	Requiring that every person work one year before the age of 25 as a farm-hand or domestic servant	14	16	14
..........*r*.	Requiring every person 21 or over to vote, the penalty being 1 week in jail	13	15½	9
..........*s*.	Requiring the sterilization of all individuals with IQ's under 60	7	15	14

........*t.* Transferring the ownership of all railroads to the nation, paying the owners of the stocks their present market value and making the bonds of all railroads null and void 9   15   10½

The happiness calculus that is potent in the ratings of achievements and acts of public and private nature appears here in the ranking of the law depriving people of tobacco below the odious payments of large sums to senators and congressmen (*h* and *i*), and the shocking proposal concerning the bodies of the dead (*p*).* Positive egalitarianism by requiring a year's humble manual labor of all (*q*) is put below the restriction of wealth and income by the 25, and farther below by the 40. The attempt at positive democratization of government by requiring everybody to vote (*r*) and disgracing those who do not is put somewhat higher. Ignorance or carelessness about economics is shown by both groups in the high ratings of *t*, a law which would go far toward ruining those who have invested their savings in life insurance. Both groups imply that it is worse for persons to have much wealth than to spend much selfishly (*e* and *b*).

Measured by the variability of the opinion of the 25, the difference between the average of the two best laws, *a* and *j* (which are regarded as almost equal in merit), and *n* (which is near the zero line between laws that would do more harm than good and laws that would do more good than harm) is about 1.25 standard deviations; the difference between this approximate zero and the law about tobacco is about .90.

IV

VALUATIONS OF A PERSON

A person may be valued on hundreds of scales—qua producer, consumer, citizen, neighbor, friend, husband, immortal soul, carrier of genes, bundle of habits, source of infection, and so on.

* *h* and *i* are not necessarily odious, and *p* is not necessarily shocking; nor were they to all of the 25. But they probably were to the great majority.

[162]

Twenty-five men and women of high intelligence, 17 of whom were psychologists or advanced students of psychology, and 42 unemployed men and women of the white-collar and professional classes assigned ranks to the 25 persons, *a* to *y*, described below, as husbands. The letter preceding each description is unimportant. It merely shows the order in which the candidates were listed on the sheets given to the 67 persons who made the ratings. The first number following the description is the median of the ranks assigned by the 25; the next two numbers joined by a dash show the range required to include 23 of the 25 ratings; the next number is the median of the ranks assigned by the 42 unemployed; the next two numbers joined by a dash show the range required to include 38 of their 42 ratings. The meaning of the last two numbers will be explained presently.

The rankings by the two groups are much alike, the correlation between them being .96. The 25 in the more intelligent group value the Chinese, the headwaiter, the undertaker, and the Methodist clergyman higher than the 42 do; and value the Christian Science healer, the working man, and the two men with Catholic affiliations lower than the 42 do. But even these differences are not large or very reliable.

In the seventh and eighth numbers the valuations of the two groups are combined, equal weight being given to the more intelligent 25 and the less intelligent 42. The seventh number is the valuation in units of the variability of opinion expressed as a deviation from the valuation of the architect *a* and high-school teacher (*v*). The eighth number is the same quantity expressed as a deviation from the valuation (3 standard deviations below *a*, *v*) which the great majority of the 67 persons would probably regard as no better for their daughter or sister than going without a husband. I will describe the procedures by which these last two numbers are computed for each husband and add a few comments on the rankings. In general, however, these may be left to speak for themselves.

Write 1, 2, 3, 4, etc., before the following to show which you would choose for your sister or daughter to marry. Use 1 for first choice, 2 for next, 3 for next, and so on to 24 for next and 25 for worst. If two or more seem equal in merit write the two or more appropriate numbers before each of them. The age of all is supposed to be 30 years. The amount of money in parentheses is the person's annual earnings.

f.	A factory owner, a college graduate ($7000)	2.5	1–9	2	1–13	+.21	3.2
a.	An architect ($2500)	3.5	1–8	3	1–8	0	3.0
v.	A teacher in public high school ($2500)	3	1–6	4	1–7½	0	3.0
j.	A librarian ($2500)	5.5	1–8	6.75	2–12	–.73	2.3
m.	A musician ($2500)	6	2–12	7.5	1–14	–.73	2.3
i.	A Jewish lawyer ($3000)	8	1–20	8.5	1–20	–1.06	1.9
y.	A writer of advertisements ($2500)	7.5	4–14	7.25	2–17	–1.06	1.9
k.	A life-insurance agent ($2500)	9	4½–15	9.25	5–16	–1.43	1.6
l.	A Methodist clergyman of liberal views who earns $2000 as a pastor and $500 by writing	10	4–22	14	2–19½	–1.47	1.5
p.	A poet of undoubted genius, but who earns only $1400	11	1–20	11	1–20	–1.47	1.5–
t.	A secretary of the Non-Partisan Voters' League ($2500)	10	5–14	11	5–16½	–1.54	1.5+
q.	A policeman ($2800)	13.5	9½–18	13	5½–21	–1.86	1.1
b.	A head-waiter in a hotel earning (with tips) $6000	13.5	7½–21	16	5–22	–1.88	1.1
o.	An officer in the Eastern Catholic Publishing Company ($2500)	14	7–22	14	6–23	–1.88	1.1
w.	An undertaker earning $3000	12	9–20	15	5–21	–1.88	1.1
r.	A professional stage dancer ($2500)	15	7–21	15	6½–20½	–2.02	1.0
s.	A secretary of the Knights of Columbus ($2500)	15	10–24	12.5	6–23	–2.02	1.0
x.	A working-man ($1800)	15	10–22	14.5	3½–22½	–2.02	1.0
e.	A Chinese mandarin's son aged 25 (Christian convert) with an income equivalent to $10,000	17.5	4–24	21.5	12½–25	–2.50	.5
c.	A Baptist clergyman believing literally in the Bible ($2000)	20	14–24	18.5	9–24	–2.60	.4
d.	A Christian Science healer ($4000)	20.5	14–24	18	12–24	–2.70	.3
b.	An agitator employed by the Soviet Republics to encourage dissatisfaction among American workers ($2500)	20.5	16–25	21	13–25	–2.90	.1
n.	A Negro physician, a college graduate ($3000)	21	16–25	23	13–25	–3.20	–.2
u.	A son of an old American family who is a lawyer and also an illicit seller of drugs. He makes $600 a year from the law and $1900 from the traffic in morphine, etc.	23	17–25	23	17–25	–3.50	–.5
g.	A feebleminded man (IQ70) with an income of $12,000 from trust funds	25	23–25	23.75	20½–25	–4.13	–1.1

a and *v* (the architect and teacher earning $2500) are of approximately equal merit. The factory owner receiving $7000 is rated higher than the average of *a* and *v* by 59 per cent of the 25 and by 56 per cent of the 42. $4500 more per year (or 2.8 times as much per year) does little more than counterbalance the disfavor attached to the conditions under which the $7000 is received. In terms of the standard deviation of opinion of the group in question *f* is .23 or .15 above *a* and *v*.

a and *v* are rated higher than *j* and *m* (librarian and musician each receiving $2500) by 74 per cent of the votes of the 25 and by 74.7 per cent of the votes of the 42, or, in terms of the standard deviations of opinion, by .65 and .67. *k* and *l*, the life insurance agent and Methodist clergyman ($2500 each) average .69 standard deviations below the librarian and musician and so 1.34 deviations below the architect and teacher, by the votes of the 25. By the votes of the 42, the corresponding figures are .69 and 1.36.

r, *s*, and *x*, the stage dancer ($2500), secretary of the Knights of Columbus ($2500), and workingman ($1800) are approximately equally esteemed and are .74 standard deviations below *k* and *l*, and so 2.08 standard deviations below the architect and teacher, by the votes of the 25. By the votes of the 42 they are not so far below *k* (only .50 standard deviations) and are about equal to *l;* they average .20 standard deviations below *k* and *l*, and so 1.56 below the architect and teacher.

The stage dancer, secretary of the Knights of Columbus, and working man are rated about half way between the architect-teacher pair and the lowest pair of the list, the man with IQ of 70 and the illicit peddler of drugs! But in Russia, the first would doubtless rank very high; in the votes of four Roman Catholics among our unemployed 42, the second is close to the teacher and architect.

b, *c*, and *d*—the agitator ($2500), fundamentalist ($2000), and Christian Scientist ($4000) are equally disesteemed by the

25, and average .69 standard deviations below r, s, and x, and so 2.77 below the architect and teacher by the votes of the 25. In the case of the 42, I report the facts for b separately from those for c and d. b is .95 below the r, s, x trio and so 2.51 below the architect and teacher. c and d average .42 below the r, s, x trio and so 1.98 below the architect and teacher.*

The illicit dealer in opium, etc. (u, with $2500 income), is .67 below the b, c, d trio, by the votes of the 25, and is .25 below b and .90 below c and d by the votes of the .42. u is thus 3.44, 2.76, or 2.88 below the architect-teacher pair according to the method of comparison.

g, described as feeble-minded with an IQ of 70 and an income of $12000, is .84 below u, or 4.28 below the architect and teacher, by the votes of the 25. He is .37 below u, or 3.19 below the architect and teacher, by the votes of the 42. A secured income of nearly five times that of the drug-peddler, whose superiority in intelligence is evidenced only by his having been admitted to the bar and being able to earn $600 a year as a lawyer, does not counterbalance the greater disesteem of a fool for a husband than a cheap criminal.**

Let us now place the others of the list—e, h, i, n, o, p, q, t, w, and y. That can be done roughly from the medians of the ranks, and more accurately from the votes on pairs. In the case of the votes, we have two sets of measures, in terms of the standard deviation of opinion of the 25 and of the 42, respectively. So we must either report two placements for each or combine them somehow. The latter will make the facts clearer and easier to get in mind, and there will be little loss in precision if we leave the standard-deviation measures for the 25 as they are, but

---

* It should be kept in mind that the 2.51 and 1.98 are in units of the variability of opinion of the 42 and that this may not be equal to the variability of opinion of the 25.

** This relative disesteem of the fool is not caused by a prejudice of the psychologists. The nonpsychologists among the 25 set g farther below u than the psychologists do.

multiply the standard-deviation measures for the 42 by 1.22 so
that the total difference in standard-deviation units from $a+v$
to u will be 3.44 for the 42 as it is for the 25. I combine the
determinations from the 25 and the 42 giving them equal weight.

Besides placing e, h, i, n, o, p, q, t, u, and y, I also check or
amend the valuations of a, b, c, d, etc., by fuller use of the com-
parisons by pairs. The results appear in the last two numbers
following each description. The reader may consider it highly
probable that if rankings were given by persons of superior intelligence in general, and by clerical workers and teachers in
general, neither ranking would differ greatly from the ranking
reported here.

This ranking will be used by some as a terrible example of
the prejudices of the "intelligentsia" and "middle class" of the
northeastern United States. Parts of it certainly will seem prejudiced to Russians, fundamentalists, Christian Scientists, and
Roman Catholics.

But it is better to try to understand the causes of the prejudices
that move the most intelligent twentieth of the nation or of any
large section of it, than to deride them. Let us therefore grant
that if a miracle made twenty-five hundred daughters or sisters
of the persons of whom our 25 are a random sample fall in love,
one hundred with a hundred a's, another hundred with a hundred
b's, and so on, and get married to them, the actual consequences
to them and to the world at large would show many and large
divergences from the rankings given by the 25. The consensus
of the 25 would in so far forth be wrong. Why?

One's valuations of a person as a husband are especially sensitive to the customs and prejudices of one's self, family, and
friends. It is hard to use impartial reasoning concerning the
probable consequences of the marriage of one's daughter or sister
to any given sort of person, and easy to vent one's low or high
opinion of that sort of person in one's rating. Also one knows
very little about the probable consequences in many of the 25

cases listed. For example, probably few of the 25 psychologists and other intellectuals know how much, if any, better architects receiving $2500 are mentally and morally than undertakers receiving $3000 or head-waiters receiving $6000. One does, however, have rather definite and potent expectations of how comfortable or uncomfortable one would feel in each case. The consequences that one does know about and that do figure in one's reasoning include predominantly what one's family and friends would think and feel and do about the husband.

In default of knowledge of consequences, it is reasonable to use knowledge of affiliations. Here the 25 rankers are somewhat better informed. For example, the 25 probably knew nothing about the intrinsic success of gifted poets as husbands, save perhaps that Browning was a good one and Byron a very bad one. But they knew that being a poet of undoubted genius is affiliated with intelligence, originality, sensitiveness, and artistry. The head-waiter's work is affiliated with eating and drinking, while the librarian's is affiliated with books and reading. The head-waiter's tips are affiliated with servility. The knowledge of affiliations is, however, far from complete or accurate, and does not do much to prevent unreasonable attitudes toward certain sorts of husbands in an individual or a class.

All these reported valuations of achievements, acts, laws, and persons may differ considerably from the preferences shown by the actual behavior of the reporting groups in doing or avoiding, stimulating or repressing, rewarding or punishing, and other concrete treatment of concrete cases. The observations and experiments that would tell how great such differences would be are lacking. I conjecture that there would be a close parallelism (say a correlation of .90 or more) between the valuations reported by either group and the valuations shown by the actual behavior of that group. For an individual the correlation would, of course, be less. The group of unemployed were accustomed to experiments, tests, and questionnaires of all sorts and descriptions, were very cooperative, and give internal evidence in their replies of great frankness. There was probably relatively little harm done by deliberate efforts to show oneself in a favorable light.

PART III

AESTHETICS

SCHWEITZER'S AESTHETICS:
AN INTERPRETATION OF BACH

By

Leo Schrade
Yale University

CHAPTER VII

SCHWEITZER'S AESTHETICS

AN INTERPRETATION OF BACH

BY

LEO SCHRADE

When the famous book on Bach was published by Albert Schweitzer at the beginning of our century, it aroused a vigorous discussion among historians of music, artists, and scholars of many a province of learning. Students of the history of music who, at that time, made their acquaintance with the book, still remember the excitement, quite unusual in the scholarly world. There was the comprehensive work of Philipp Spitta which, for more than a quarter of a century, every serious student had taken to be the last word on the subject of Bach. Spitta seemed to have been unsurpassable both in the nature and in the scope of his research; in fact, after his exhaustive studies, it appeared as though nothing more could possibly be added. Spitta had explored the field with such completeness and accuracy that, for some time, the effect of his work was to discourage any fresh investigation of Bach. Spitta, moreover, had established a procedure for the finding and interpretation of musical material on the basis of documentary evidence. He brought to his task the training afforded by the tradition of classical philology; he adopted methods tried out in the old discipline for many a decade; thus he, as others before him, made the history of music heir to scholarly accomplishments of long standing. Scholars have, therefore, accepted Spitta's Bach as a standard work scarcely to be excelled.

Nevertheless, in 1905 Albert Schweitzer came out with his

Jean Sébastien Bach, le musicien-poète.* In this book there was
no specially important addition to biographical data, or to the
masterly description Spitta had given of the surroundings and
conditions under which Bach's work came into being; there was
perhaps not a single "fact" newly discovered. And yet, the book
caused a stir among the historians. It was in his interpretation
of Bach's music that Schweitzer succeeded in giving his book the
aspect of a new revelation to be placed beside, if not over against,
that of Spitta. The truly vast amount of biographical, even more
of circumstancial, material which Spitta had presented for the
first time was cut down to a relatively brief biography. Far more
important than the biographical portion is the interpretation of
the music. Not that Spitta had neglected Bach's work; in this
respect, he is even broader than Schweitzer, broader, not more
profound.

Schweitzer took the work of Bach purely as a phenomenon of
art. He expanded his interpretation as it related to what he
himself called the aesthetical part of the musical composition.
Schweitzer—or rather Charles Marie Widor for him—raised a
question that made it necessary to place Bach's music in a new
light. This question appeared to be exceedingly simple: Do we
understand his music fully and on the proper basis? The answer
was negative, one that, in fact, resulted from an opposition to
Spitta. This opposition did not grow out of scholarly grounds.
Schweitzer never contested the authoritative method of historical
research which Spitta had applied; nor did he ever oppose the
unfailing historiographical procedure of his predecessor. It was
a difference in principle, one concerned with views upon music
as an art, that parted him from Spitta. The essential question
upon which the ideas of the two authors fell apart centered

* Schweitzer's *Bach* was soon translated into German and English. Schweitzer
enlarged the German version considerably. The English translation has been made
from the German. The English translation, by Ernest Newman, has here been
used for quotation.

around the problem of "symbolism" in Bach's music. In this lies
the novelty of Schweitzer's interpretation. The nature of symbolism was, however, to him essentially aesthetical; that is to say,
the understanding it granted had its origin in terms of art and,
therefore, came within the field of aesthetics.

Schweitzer truly made Bach a new theme of aesthetical thought.
When he discussed the importance of the work for the musical
life of his own day, he recognized that during the whole nineteenth century the instrumental compositions and the Passions
were kept alive, while the cantatas were forgotten. It is the cantatas, however, that offer the key to the understanding of Bach.
Consequently, they should be brought to a resurrection. Schweitzer pleaded for this in the strongest terms; he would turn away
from history toward aesthetics, where lay the core of the matter.
He took up the dispute that in his day had begun to play an
important part in so far as the revival of Bach's cantatas was
concerned. On account of the intensely religious, that is, liturgical, character of the cantata, there were those who favoured its
revival together with the liturgy out of which it had grown.
This Schweitzer rejected. We might not have expected such a
disapproval to come from him. But he held the view that religious service and art were separated from each other as a consequence of modern developments. The revival of Bach was
subject to such a divorce. Hence the liturgical performance of
the cantata had now to be replaced by some sort of sacred concert whose exclusive aim should be the aesthetical interpretation
of the work. Like all truly sublime expressions of religion, Bach's
music, according to Schweitzer, does not belong to any particular
church, but to the religious spirit of mankind. And since a
church is no more than a sacred building, the cantata will turn
any place in which it is performed into a house of worship.
Contemplation and devotion should result from the performance;
for the latent religious character of the cantatas would call them
forth regardless of any liturgical or ecclesiastical connections.

It is, then, an idea grounded in pure aestheticism that Schweitzer took as his starting point. Indeed, before setting out to interpret the individual compositions, he gave the principles which were to guide him in his interpretation. These principles comprise a body of aesthetical tenets, and on these he based his understanding of Bach.

Schweitzer wrote at a time when musical artists were still divided, some being adherents of absolute music and others, advocates of descriptive composition, that is, of the view that there should be a poetical idea, programme, or picture underlying every work. The controversy had come, of course, to its climax when Wagner and Brahms were posed against each other. Those who, along with Brahms put their faith in what was called pure or absolute music needed no particular support in holding to this tradition since the classic past exerted all its influence on the side of this conviction. The other school, however, that which took the musical composition to serve a poetical end, found itself obliged to search out works of the past that showed evidence of a descriptive purpose. And, since they found the music of the seventeenth and eighteenth centuries, properly speaking that of the baroque age, to be full of realisms through which the composers had attempted to translate any word suggestive of a picture directly into music, they looked upon Bach's music also as a direct predecessor to the most modern programmatic music—such as that of Liszt or Strauss—in so far it included descriptive, realistic, features. Spitta belonged to the other school of thought, and this Schweitzer took into full account. For Spitta, averse to the Wagnerian cult and to the ideal of musical art maintained therein; in other words, Spitta, an ardent believer in absolute, non-descriptive music, feared that Bach would become involved in the opinions held upon the music of Wagner. As a historian he knew how great a distortion such a comparison would produce. And as aesthetician he resisted even the thought that the art of sound should serve pictorial purposes.

This attitude, of course, led to his embarrassment whenever he met with descriptive elements in Bach's cantatas where they are by no means rare. He made some attempt to treat them as of slight significance, or to explain them as indicative of sheer musical wit. He evaded the issue by denying the existence of any close relationship between word and tone. He "took care that no one should be misled by this or that piece of characterization into doubting for a moment that Bach was a priest of absolute music." It was at this point, that Schweitzer turned definitely against him.

When Schweitzer sketched the history of Bach and his interpretations he came to the most influential figure of the nineteenth century: Wagner. It is characteristic of Schweitzer that he assumed it to be Wagner's musical work rather than his few remarks about Bach that had opened the way for a fuller understanding. Wagner had taught the musical world, on the ground of synaesthetical views, that composition should be poetical in establishing a profound relationship between word and tone. The novelty of the aspect under which poetry, inherent in music, would transform the composition altogether, should have had an immense influence on the understanding of Bach for whom Wagner, "though unconsciously," was fighting. That it did not, is simply incomprehensible.

And here, finally, the aesthetical doctrine that underlies Schweitzer's interpretation manifests itself. These aesthetics are to be explained.

Schweitzer was predominantly concerned with the understanding of musical sound in its artistic forms. He regarded the aesthetics of music as pitifully neglected. If they were treated, they had been made part of philosophy, and aestheticians whose interest pertained to musical art turned to Schopenhauer, or Lotze, or Helmholtz, rather than to their proper object, to the composition itself. While in the other arts the doctrine of aesthetics took the work to be the starting point for all critical observation and interpretation, in the aesthetics of music this essential point had been overlooked. And so Schweitzer begins to fill the gap by making his aesthetics center around the work of Bach. Schweitzer openly admits that his interpretation is opposed to the purely historical method of research which, as applied to Bach, has come to an end; it should now be succeeded by aesthetics. History had been taken into full account; it failed to give the answer. History had explained all that surrounds the work; but it did not uncover what is in the composition itself. Schweitzer is not hostile to historical interpretation as such; but he shows himself to be impatient with the discipline of history if and when it evades an interpretation that alone keeps Bach's work as a living force. With this he is concerned; with nothing else and nothing less. Historical interpretation has failed because—to his way of thinking—it does not lead into the inner structure and content of the composition. Aesthetical interpretation has failed because it has been limited to philosophical aspects and has been carried on in complete remoteness from the composition. Significantly, Schweitzer chooses of the two the aesthetical approach as the one that will hold the promise of success if put on a new basis. Although he does not assume aesthetics as applied to music to be derived from the philosophy of the nineteenth century, the sum and substance of his aesthetical views spring from romanticism and the afterlife it had during that century. It is through them that the work of Bach becomes to him a comprehensible phenomenon.

Schweitzer adheres to the tenets of romanticism in so far as he unifies the understanding of any one art under synaesthetic aspects. Poetry, music, painting, each originates with having a mutual share in the characteristics of the others; without coöperation of all, art will not be true to its essence. The imagination of the artist works with effects of sound, pictorial associations, and poetical images at one and the same time. Art is seen to be something of superior nature, but also of somewhat abstract character. "Art in itself is neither painting nor poetry nor music, but an act of creation in which all three coöperate." For it embodies itself in such a way as to force the power of images, the structural discipline of tones, the rhythm of language into any one medium. It is this unity of all the arts that matters, while the medium itself has only secondary significance. Thus the individual work of art becomes representative of the unity which exists before the creative act produces any concrete expression and which is, also, ever-active in the imagination of the artist. Each individual work realizes the totality of the arts.

Schweitzer finds this to be true of Goethe. He reveals the musical nature in Schiller. He expresses a deep appreciation of Boecklin's poetical painting. He interprets, most ingeniously, the sweeping prose of Nietzsche as an outgrowth of a structure characteristic of musical composition. The romantics, also, have struggled with this very possibility of unifying the arts into one. They prepared the theoretical ground for the idea that by the artistic act a new totality of artistic qualities and elements arises that turns music to poetry, or painting to music. The romantic theory of a total work of art differs in some aspects from that of Schweitzer, if we think of the ideas that Novalis, Wackenroder, Schelling, E.T.A. Hoffmann, Lamartine held on the subject. But inasmuch as their visions were directly taken up by Richard Wagner to contribute to the theoretical foundation of his total work of art, there is a complete set of synaesthetical ideas, built up by the romantics and kept alive throughout the nineteenth century, upon which Schweitzer could draw. For it is chiefly through Richard Wagner that Schweitzer experiences the understanding of art. He does not take an active share in the controversy on the principles of musical art that heated the minds of the musicians in the camp of the absolute, independent, self-sufficient music, and of those who held to the "total" work of music. Moreover, the controversy had somewhat subsided by the time Schweitzer wrote his work on Bach. Yet, he has formed his aesthetics through Wagner; he, thus, gave new expression to the enormous influence Bayreuth exercised on the French theories of art.

As a consequence of the idea that there exists as a higher quantity the abstract art which contains the unbroken unity of man's mind, as it were, the individual arts incorporate in themselves the tendency to reach out beyond their own limits and faculties. They have, furthermore, the propensity to return to their origin, that is: to the primal unity. These inherent faculties make clear that there is no such thing as an "absolute" art, in the sense Anti-Wagnerian composers, historians of music, or aestheticians have taken for granted. The advocates of absolute music do not recognize the nature of music. They may "hoist the banner of pure art over the works of Bach and Beethoven," but they will not make their works any more absolute or purer than truly artistic music can ever be. It is in the nature of music to be both poetical and pictorial, and any great composer cannot but bring out this nature. If there are musicians who, by a misconception of this essence, have tried and still try to treat music as if it were the same as painting or poetry, as if, in other words, music could give the very same image as that the canvas shows, or the concrete idea that language conveys, this merely reveals those musicians to be at fault; it does not affect the character of music. The relationship between music on the one side, and both poetry and painting on the other, is ever close. It is not so much a product of history as it is a fulfilment of the nature of music. To be sure, there was a period when composers for the first time began to speak poetically and to think pictorially when they spoke musically. This beginning means, however, that the musicians became aware of the nature of music by discovering its true essence. Hence, the discovery is bound to the music itself, and is not due to history.

The recognition of an abstract, philosophical essence of music which the composer must by necessity seek to materialize; furthermore, the notion that the compositions of any period differ from one another by the degree according to which they have fulfilled the nature of music: these are essentially romantic views. No matter which period a composer belongs to, he will be judged by the distance that lies between his work and the nature of music. He may be far from or close to it: he may have travelled along an entirely wrong path; but he cannot be placed in a category of "absolute" music or in one of "relative," that is: pictorial, representative, composition. There is only one nature of music which establishes the aesthetic value.

Any distinctive understanding of musical composition will strive to penetrate to the original totality of the arts even if the approach of one individual work only is involved. The process by which we think musically when appreciating poetry, when looking upon a canvas with a landscape as its subject, or by which we imagine a picture when listening to music, is quite common; it is even natural to anyone who perceives artistically. Whoever sees a painting with a "pine wood" and does not hear "the infinite distant symphonies of the wind sweeping over the tree-tops, sees only as half a man, not as an artist." As the totality of the arts lies in the nature of the art, so the multiplicity of impressions, pictorial, poetical, musical, lies in the nature of all artistic perception. The act of receiving the work is one of reconstructing the totality and thus seizing upon its "meaning." Any work stands for certain "aesthetic associations of ideas" which the artist conveys to us through his medium. The artistic form is merely the vehicle for such aesthetic associations. Not the ideas themselves are to be expressed; but the associations that arise in the artist together with them.*

In Schweitzer's aesthetics, this is a decisive point. For he does not expect from any art the explicit translation of concrete ideas. Were an artist to do this, he would injure the inner capacity of art. Along this line of argument, Schweitzer, also, avoids taking the expression of ideas through music into account at all. Although definite ideas can never play any part in composition, all that

* In the differentiation between ideas and associations of ideas Schweitzer is, however, not consistent.

[183]

sounds or is to be seen holds something behind or beyond the visible or audible sign. All external signs in art, be they lines, colours, letters, or tones, are symbolic because they signify something internal. Apparently Schweitzer assumes that the farther away from the ordinary, common means of communication the symbol lies, the more suggestive it becomes; in this way, he differentiates the arts from each other by the degree of their capability of being symbolical. Hence language, common to both poetry and daily life, is perhaps least capable of symbolism which Schweitzer takes to be the inner meaning that an external sign carries within itself. But as language may be least suggestive, music—on the same ground of reasoning—turns out to be exclusively symbolical. "In music the expression is wholly symbolical." Feelings, general or specific, and associations of ideas, both subject to expression in music, do not yield to indisputable definiteness if they appear in the medium of tones. The tones, therefore, as symbols abound in meaning. All is significance,—all is symbol. If the musician ambitiously endeavors to hold fast the meaning as concretely (or, realistically) as possible, the symbolism of his language becomes obvious, even obtrusive. This is, however, only a special case of a procedure that takes always place in composition. For every sound, tone, melody, harmony, carries a particular meaning, or else, we have not a phenomenon of art. Hence, also, absolute music must be symbolical, the difference being that absolute music comprises abstract feelings, while pictorial music concerns itself with more concrete associations. "It is wrong to imagine that so-called pure music speaks a language that is not symbolical, and that it expresses something of which the meaning is unequivocal."

Schweitzer shows himself in this to be a romantic of the purest kind. The work of musical art appears to be split into form and content; it must have this content, because it is its very essence. It is characteristically ambiguous. Surely, so it must be, if the visible form embraces an invisible meaning. If artistic form is thus symbolical, all the arts manifest symbolism, with differences in degree, not in kind. Herein Schweitzer follows Wagner closely. Wagner may have taken for granted that the exclusive subject to be presented in music, the only content of the musical form, consists of feelings, emotions. Schweitzer may have widened the scope of expressiveness in that he, also, admits certain aesthetical associations. In principle, the two men have the same idea of symbolism in music. The symbol is identical with the form that signifies the content. The more suggestive of meaning the tone is as a symbol, the higher stands the symbolism in the musical composition as a whole. Of course, suggestiveness acts as a continual appeal to man's powers of imagination. What is left to imagination, what remains unspoken, this in particular establishes the value of the work. "In truth, the greatness of the poet can be best measured by what he refrains from saying, in order to let the inexpressible itself speak to us in secrecy," so Wagner once declared. It lies in the logical development of his aesthetic thought that Schweitzer would accept this thesis of Wagner. In the search for the content whose character may merely be hinted at, we take the form as an element that sets the imagination free for the vision with which to grasp the inexpressible. It would seem that this visionary understanding of musical ideas or feelings is a direct offshoot of romanticism.

But the theory of music Wagner has found in the aesthetical sense by deriving its principles from romanticism, especially in *Zukunftsmusik* and *Oper und Drama*, enabled Schweitzer to look upon musical compositions under unifying aspects regardless of the historical period within which they originated. It also eliminated, to him, the fruitless disputes concerning absolute music and the descriptive, poetical composition. Symbolism comprises all music. Associations and feelings are carried by all and every composition. Only in the artistic form are there differences; they can be essential; even so, they serve one and the same end. "There are poets and painters among the musicians." This accounts for the "two main currents in music"; one does not exclude the other. The poetic music avails itself of ideas, the pictorial music of pictures; "the one appeals more to the feeling, the other to our faculty of representation." Beethoven and Wagner are seen on the side of the poets; Bach, Schubert, Berlioz on the side of the painters. We may be astonished to find Berlioz in another camp than that of Wagner; or to find Schubert at the side of Bach. The aesthetical system, indeed, pulls down all the fences set up by the delimitation of historical periods as well as by historical thought; and Schweitzer merely draws the logical conclusions from his own preliminaries. According to the natural disposition of the artist the music sets forth the emphasis on pictures or on ideas, on pictorial or poetical form. There is the parting-line; not in the historical epoch in which it was produced. And since the pictorial form springs from a stronger visual power, there are here possible, allowable, and comprehensible as well, all such expressions as tone-painting, picturesque descriptions, in brief, a realistic presentation of the subject. Schweitzer discovers in Schubert more realistic features, descriptive and painting, than in Wagner, whose hostility to realisms Schweitzer apparently accepted in so far as such features may produce a double impression, bound to the material event and to the feeling that the event contains. At the extreme end of all poetical music, there is Wagner. At the extreme of all pictorial music, there is—Bach. These are the two ends of symbolical, or "characteristic," music, limits that allow an enormous variety to be embraced within them. Bach does not act as a poetical musician. "He is the most representative of pictorial music — the direct antipodes of Wagner."*

Without this doctrine, the interpretation Schweitzer imparted to the work of Bach cannot be understood. Through it, we al-

* We may observe a certain contradiction. Schweitzer calls his work "Bach, the poet-musician." But in the original French version the chapter Le symbolisme de Bach, which Schweitzer—because of its importance for the whole interpretation —published also separately in Revue Germanique, vol. 1, 1905, pp. 69-81, begins: "Bach était un poète et ce poète était en même temps un peintre.

ways meet romanticism as well as Wagner, its offspring. Whoever traces Schweitzer's theory back to its sources, will unavoid-
ably arrive at such roots. He has, moreover, given a full account
of the source upon which he has drawn. He has made the most
serious effort to establish his aesthetics as a doctrine, free from
theoretical prejudices and systems. He may have in mind the work
of Wagner more than his theory; though it is perhaps impossible
to keep the two apart. Yet Schweitzer has succeeded in presenting his views as musical aesthetics, thus escaping the temptation
to treat the work of musical art as an issue of philosophy; for a
man who is philosopher in thought, training and profession truly
a success. His aesthetics, though expressed as a doctrine, have,
however, no end unless they are related to Bach. Rarely, if ever,
did an aesthetician limit his own doctrine so severely and so consciously as did Schweitzer. It would seem that his aesthetics of
music have no real place in his total system of philosophy. At
first sight, we are embarrassed when attempting to link the
aesthetical to higher purposes which establish its cause of necessity. Bach holds both the meaning of the aesthetics and their
superior end.

The interpretation of Bach is based on the relationship between word and tone. The form in which it is said to manifest
itself concerns, in the first place, the translation of the text into
the melody. There, Bach idealized the verse or sentence to which
he set his music, by adjusting his melody to the inner meaning
of the text rather than to its actual verbal qualities. The phrasing
Bach has achieved puts the composition, therefore, into a higher
region, regardless of the value of the poem. Bach penetrated into
the text, lifted, as it were, its true idea and expression, from
which he then derived the structure of the melody; he did not
derive it from the material arrangement of the poem. Hence,
it mattered little if Bach composed mediocre texts, since every
poem, good or bad, would go through the same process of being
transmitted into a sphere idealized according to the inner sense.

[187]

In this respect, Schweitzer arrives at his findings concerning Bach's declamation and phrases by a purely aesthetical observation. He takes no account of the historical implications in that Bach's form of melodical phraseology may be related to the vast theories with which his predecessors and contemporaries treated the structural phenomenon of melody as a subject of rhetoric whose terminology they fully applied to music.* The results of the aesthetical method and those of the historical investigation do not always coincide.

In this, then, Schweitzer discovers a first manifestation of the poetical nature in Bach who gave to the verse of the poem or to any sentence the quality of final truth according to an idealistic conception. A second manifestation becomes apparent in Bach's treatment of the chorale-melody. Schweitzer again shows an attitude that has exclusively aesthetical implications. This is all the more surprising since the deep religious associations the chorale-melody had for Bach apparently did not play any part whatever in Schweitzer's evaluation of the intensity with which Bach avails himself of the chorale for his composition. For this intensity is not supposed to spring from a religious source but from one that aesthetically involves artistic invention and imagination only. It is for the qualities of poetical imagination with which the composer seems to abound that Schweitzer takes Bach's melody as a scion of the "soul," not of the "body of the word." Evidence for this lies open to view in the way in which Bach interprets the given chorale-melody by harmonies. In true consequence of the aesthetical tenets from which he proceeds Schweitzer assumes that these harmonies do not follow abstract rules of everlasting or even ever-applicable validity under musical or tonal aspects; they follow the words. It is logical for Schweitzer, according to his theory, to say that Bach set his harmonies to the words of the chorale-melody, not to the tune as such, a

* A first attempt of an instructive interpretation according to the poetical and rhetorical treatises in music has been made by Arnold Schering who also gives a list of the treatises in question; see especially: *Bach und das Symbol*. 2. *Studie. Das "Figürliche" und "Metaphorische," Bach-Jahrbuch*, 1928, 119 ff.

statement that must have called forth much disapproval when it was made. Only the definiteness of the text deprived—for Bach —the melody of its indefiniteness; were it not for the text, Bach would have been indifferent toward the melody. Bach seized upon whatever of content the words might yield, and especially upon that part of the content that by the nature of the word must remain the inexpressible in every term of language. Bach would delve into it to bring to light the mystery to which the concrete word would not give any expression. That which the words of the chorale failed to express, that quality which transcended the capacities of language, would now be clothed in its one and only artistic form—in music. Bach chose harmony as the element through which to reveal the secret of the word. This discovery would allow him to break with the ordinary laws of harmonical progression, even with some well established rules. Schweitzer goes so far as to maintain that in the course of this process Bach did not hesitate to set to the given chorale-melodies harmonies which under purely musical aspects would make no sense. It is, therefore, a "poetic harmonisation" that he discovers in Bach, an idea which becomes particularly illuminating if we compare the different harmonical versions of one and the same chorale-melody.

Wagner has obviously guided Schweitzer's thought. For Wagner held the belief, and based his work upon it, at least theoretically, that music, in yielding to poetical tendencies must give form to the inexpressible. Although Schweitzer experienced the nature of Bach's chorale aesthetically, he characterized an attitude of Bach toward the word that we still find to be valid. We may refute the aesthetical approach, we may deny the theory, we may abandon the whole Wagnerian element, there still remains something that does not admit dispute. It is the intense devotion to the meaning and implications of the text that Bach made the tenor of his composition, especially when he constructed his work around the chorale-melody. Schweitzer, in bringing into the light this devotion, has shown it to be one of the most essential qualities of Bach's work. Instead of the poetical mystery, instead of the inexpressible which Bach is said to have searched after in the text, we may find that it is rather the religious values as established in the text that account for Bach's apprehension and intense devotion. Schweitzer has observed that there is something in Bach's relationship to the texts he set to music that has no parallel in the epoch and must have a meaning of its own. That this meaning takes on a Wagnerian colour, is significant for Schweitzer's aesthetics, though secondary for the interpretation of Bach. Moreover, when Schweitzer characterizes one or another individual feature of a composition, he comes close to its significance despite the Wagnerian doctrine which he always is frank enough to admit as his general guide.

This becomes even more obvious when he discusses the element of emotion in Bach's music. Here, too, the ground on which the interpretation is carried out appears as aesthetical, not as historical. For Schweitzer does not derive the emotional qualities he seeks in Bach from the elaborate system of "affections" which Bach followed as a man of the baroque age. Surely, Schweitzer knows the system; he knows of its historical implications, knows that Bach understood his music to be *affektvoll*. But regardless of the knowledge Schweitzer turns away from the exclusively historical connotation of this unique phenomenon. In its place he sets the aesthetical evaluation that disposes of the historical limits to be seen in "affection" and, in its stead, allows emotion to be taken as an element common to the whole of musical art. Thus the emotion acquires all the marks of Wagnerian ideas. Emotion is revealed in the text. Hence, the character of Bach's emotion must be measured, first of all, in his vocal music. The process of artistic creation presents Bach as being in search of the inner "mood" contained in the text. The text must have an emotion suitable for musical expression; otherwise Bach would not have composed it. What Schweitzer describes as the emotional content of the text is nearly identical with the poetical content he sees Bach to have expressed in his chorales. With respect to the emotion indicated in the text, it is again, according to Schweitzer, a process of intensification. Here, also, Bach would purify the emotion to its true substance, constantly transforming or freeing the text from the slag that holds the emotion down to the word. The final result of this effort is the complete aptitude of the emotion to enter into the musical form. As is the case with the poetical idea which Bach puts into a higher sphere, so the emotion appears to be lifted "to a higher power" through the music. And an emotion, reduced to its essentials, is then shown in all its various possibilities. If—with Wagner—feeling is the very subject of musical expression, Bach is one of the truest musicians since he brought out emotion in its purity. It is always something of an *Urbild* that gains artistic form through Bach, so that the manifoldness of the material world seems to be reduced to the true types. This, according to Schweitzer, holds true also for the stylistic forms Bach has taken over from established traditions. Whatever he draws from the past or from his own time into the orbit of his composition, he transforms so completely as to give his artistic accomplishment the character of an *Urbild*, of the very original type, of the Platonic idea.

However close the relationship between Bach and Wagner may be, characteristic differences are also noticed. Wagner's artistic experiences originate altogether in emotion. Whether he takes up an idea, or an impression of nature, the conception that demands the musical form will have had at the source the emotional quality, not the intellectual or rational, and not the pictorial. In this Wagner and Bach part with one another. Bach's experience of the subject to be expressed musically passes through plastic imagination; hence it calls for an image. Bach will approach a text with the images that it contains in view; Wagner with the emotion that it arouses. In consequence of this pictorial reaction to the text on the part of Bach, the descriptive nature of Bach's music is the result. Here, then, the "tone-painting" that has always been taken as the most significant feature in Schweitzer's aesthetical interpretation, has its proper place. This is too well known to be pointed out in all its details. Schweitzer has, for the first time, systematically investigated the work of Bach in search after the musical presentation of images. He has categorized them by motives: as "step" motives, as motives of beatific peace, of grief, of joy, as speaking motives, and so forth.*

But what is the aesthetical basis upon which Schweitzer has explained the tone-painting? Is this not irreconcilable with the principal ideas of his musical aesthetics if Wagner—hostile to painting in music—is ancestor to the theory? Indeed, Schweitzer escapes contradictions at this point only with a great many difficulties. Yet his aesthetical thoughts are carried to their logical end.

The texts Bach has set to music should be valued according to the multitude of images they show through their words. The more images a text might have, the more it would appeal to Bach. The quality of poetry seems to him to depend upon the abundance of images the poet admits. There are other texts, less picturesque in that the images occur merely sporadically. But in any case, Bach would seize upon the image to form it realistically by means of music. He paints in tones. The theme that he shapes becomes descriptive of the image. The poetic idea or image is carried by the theme which at the same time is said to unify the structure of composition. Bach would not, therefore, pass from

---

* Concerning the symbolism in Bach's work see: André Pirro, L'esthétique de Jean-Sébastien Bach, Paris, 1907, a work that Schweitzer took to be a support to his own interpretation. Indeed, Pirro has also based the principle of tone-painting on Wagnerian theories. Among the essays of A. Schering see in particular: Bach und das Symbol. Insbesondere die Symbolik seines Kanons, in Bach-Jahrbuch 1925, p. 40-63. See also the "Bericht über den Kongress für Aesthetik und allgemeine Kunstwissenschaft von 1927 in Halle," in Zeitschrift für Aesthetik und allgemeine Kunstwissenschaft, vol. 21.—The best and most elaborate investigation of the symbolical material is by Karl Ziebler, Das Symbol in der Kirchenmusik Johann Sebastian Bachs, Kassel 1930. (Ziebler works along the line of A. Schering.)

one word to another, from one image to the next—the result of such a procedure could not but be the most confusing piece-work; he would condense the images of a poem into the essential thematic material, as he did with poetical ideas or emotions. Such a concentration should grant unity of form, but it should also have the same effect that is to be felt in his treatment of associations and emotions. Individual images produce the "germ-idea" of the theme; in other words: something again of an original, idealistic type that is shifted into a higher sphere. "The tone-painting merely heightens the plastic impressions of the words." It is, then, nothing but the method of composition in which Schweitzer discovers the idealizing concentration that made up the aesthetical character of all the other features in Bach's work. Bach would address himself to the "conceptual imagination" with the descriptive theme that carries the image aroused by the word. It would appear that the theme and the words in the original language form an inseparable unit. Schweitzer, however, who takes for granted that ideas, associations, emotions, even images have been reduced to their ideal norms, can, by extreme logic, draw the conclusion that all translations of Bach's texts into foreign languages should be as free as possible, expressing, as it were, the very essentials of the "moods" in keeping with the *Urbilder* of the music as Schweitzer takes them to be.*

Schweitzer has finally included the actual symbolism within the forms of tone-painting. For characterization he cites, among other compositions, the famous example of the cantata "Du sollst deinen Herren lieben," in which Bach has used the chorale-melody "Dies sind die heil'gen zehn Gebot" as an instrumental *cantus firmus* with the application of contrapuntal devices and numerical symbolism.** It is especially this symbolism through which Bach succeeded in establishing religious intensities as concrete values

---

* He mentions the translations of the chorale-texts by Albert Mahaut into French as praiseworthy because of their "poetical" understanding.
** This example has continually been quoted, and all authors who have done so, accepted also the description of Schweitzer almost literally.

[193]

of the Protestant church. But Schweitzer, in full conformity with his principles, sees even this symbolism to be "fundamentally musical," that is to say: aesthetical in its nature and in its effect as well.

The interpretation of Bach is the medium through which Schweitzer has communicated his own aesthetics, his belief in the position that the work of musical art must take in the world of spirit, his confidence in the message that music can bring to man. But these aesthetics have also to be understood as a violent reaction to the predominance or even exclusiveness of history, significant of the nineteenth century which had found salutary wisdom in history. In so far as Wagner has held the work of art to be an integral part of the intellectual and moral world as a whole, in so far as he has tried to prevent the art either from being an isolated phenomenon or from becoming merely a subject of historical interests, Schweitzer is to follow him. Thus he has prolonged the life of Wagner's theories through his aesthetics as he has examplified them in Bach. He sets forth the aesthetics at all cost. Although devoted to history as a scholar, Schweitzer even speaks against it whenever history seems to put its rights above the work of art. This is perhaps the most courageous manifestation of pure aesthetics through a historical subject to be found in any work of musical criticism. For, at the time when Schweitzer brought out his Bach, the turn he made in the manner of interpretation was a venture, liable to stir up once again the antagonism between friends and foes of Wagner. The frankness with which he called upon the friends of music to move toward aesthetics and away from history is an act of courage that finds scarcely any equal in the musical literature of our day. It may be that this frankness accounts in part for the effect the book produced. Through the emphasis on aesthetics and the artistic quality Schweitzer's interpretation has become a literary achievement. To be historically right or wrong, must at times be irrelevant. It was so to Schweitzer. Therefore, he will always challenge the historian. Historical criticism, however, cannot be the only legitimate measure here.

Schweitzer set out to bring the work of Bach to his time as a living force. If men will not accept it as an active power, there will be no meaning to any interpretation. The work of musical art must stand in life, and not in history. Schweitzer brought in the promise of Wagner that the future of man's culture, of morals and ideals, will belong to music and to what we do with music. This enormous trust in the power of music marks Schweitzer's aesthetics. And here lies the issue. His aesthetics, as presented through Bach, are fundamentally ethical. They do not exist as an independent discipline for their own sake. They carry an ethical message for mankind. For the sake of the message it could be no other than Bach who must proclaim it. When Schweitzer describes Bach's attitude toward the religious texts whose servant the composer is in that he submerges himself into their depths to fathom their ideal meanings, it is the necessity of man's devotion and subordination to an ideal that alone would bring forth the message of truth understandable to all. If Bach found the message by devotion, the work of musical art is the ethical messenger of truth.

THE TRANSCENDENTALISM

OF

ALBERT SCHWEITZER

By

Archibald T. Davison, Ph.D., Mus. D., (hon.), F. R. C. M.
Professor of Music, Harvard University

CHAPTER VIII

THE TRANSCENDENTALISM OF ALBERT SCHWEITZER

BY

ARCHIBALD T. DAVISON

Among the many technical articles bearing on the career of Albert Schweitzer which will doubtless appear in this volume, I hope there may be room for one which pretends to no scholarship, but which records high admiration for a characteristic which has grown in impressiveness during an acquaintance of over thirty years with the man and his work. I have selected this single attribute, not because it is more worthy of mention than others, but because it seems to me to have ministered in unique fashion to the success of his labors, and because I am not aware that it has been dwelt upon in proportion to its merit. While my preoccupation has been mainly with Schweitzer's musical activities, such an intense interest as I have felt could not fail to lead me into those other fields of thought which have been tilled by that penetrating mind. Indeed, had I not, as a layman, extended my acquaintance with his work beyond the borders of music, I would scarcely have been able to establish that quality in him which I have later set forth.

It was during the winter of 1908-09 that I first saw Albert Schweitzer. At that time I was studying organ and composition with Widor; and anyone who at any time has had the good fortune to profit by that master's instruction, and who is reading these words, will realize at once that my studies were devoted in large measure to the works of J. S. Bach.

The Bach Society was an important factor in the musical life of Paris; and it was with the idea of further extending a first-hand knowledge of Bach's music that I joined the Society's chorus. As I look back upon it, the value of that experience lay not in the beauty of the performances, for the conductor was to my mind, even then, more competent than inspired, and the membership, at least as far as the men singers were concerned, being to a considerable extent professional, was able to dispense with a goodly number of rehearsals which would have been welcome to those of us who desired primarily a thoroughgoing knowledge of the music rather than a merely correct rendition of it. If the resulting performances lacked the fire which amateur enthusiasm would have imparted to them, that was not all loss, for the skill of the singers made it possible to bring to a hearing, within a single season, a surprisingly large number of Bach's choral works.

At the concerts, Schweitzer played the organ, and as a student of that instrument I naturally paid close attention to his share in the proceedings. We know, of course, how strongly in agreement were Widor and Schweitzer regarding the basic questions of style in the performance of Bach's works, and it may be that as I was conscious of the often mechanical and heartless perfection of the chorus and orchestra at the public concerts, my impression that Schweitzer's contribution was easily the most distinguished of all, may have arisen in part from the influence upon me of Widor's teaching.

I was struck, first of all, by Schweitzer's indifference to any "effectiveness" in registration or manner of playing, the entire process being concentrated in the presentation of the music in its proper setting without the slightest effort to make it "telling" of itself. And it must be remembered that the question was not of the great organ compositions; it was solely of the organ background to, let us say, one of the cantatas. My early studies had centered about the instrument as a vehicle of display, and from Widor I was discovering that the organ and the organist were the servants; the music, especially that of Bach—the master. The unpretentious accompanimental parts must always be a pretty routine affair to the organist who loves his playing better than the music he plays. Schweitzer, however, never once obtruding himself, lavished upon them all the scrupulous attention they deserve but all too seldom receive. I realize now that my feeling about his skillful and appropriate support was primarily a technical one, albeit an as yet undiscovered clue to the impulse that converted these stylistic marvels into an almost biographical record of Bach himself.

As far as I can remember, Schweitzer, in spite of his authoritative knowledge, was never consulted—publicly, at least, — regarding any of the questions involved in the performance of Bach's music. In fact, the only occasion upon which I remember his forsaking the near-anonymity of the organ bench was at a rehearsal when the conductor, wishing to judge an effect from the rear of the hall, put his baton in Schweitzer's hand, and asked him to direct the chorus and orchestra. At that time, at least, Albert Schweitzer was in no sense a conductor, and it is significant for the purposes of this article that he made no pretense of being one. Turning his back squarely upon both orchestra and chorus, one hand thrust in his trousers pocket, his head back, staring up into the dark of the Salle Gaveau, his arm moving in awkward sweeps and unorthodox directions, it was quite obvious that if he gave himself a thought—which I doubt —it was only to consider himself the agent who should bring the music to life. Beyond that he had no responsibility. It was for the conductor to judge whether the balance of tone or the seating of the participants was satisfactory. Above all, there was complete detachment; entire absorption in the sound of the music. To this day I can remember the intense admiration I felt for Schweitzer's indifference to externals. How I swelled with indignation at the pitying smirks of the orchestral players as they condescendingly shrugged their shoulders and ostentatiously disregarded the vague gestures of the conductor *pro tem*. It was then, I feel sure, that I first sensed the stature of the man.

A good many years passed before I saw Albert Schweitzer again. I had eagerly followed each new publication of his, and had read biographies and critical commentaries with a deep personal interest. During the summer of 1921 I was in Europe with the Harvard Glee Club, and for some days we were quartered in Strasbourg. Fortunately for me, Schweitzer was there, and in the periods between concerts and celebrations, I had several opportunities of talking with him. The most memorable of these hours fell on July fifteenth, when Schweitzer took us to St. Thomas's Church for organ music and singing. The church was dark except for the necessary lights around the organ, and a single candle in the church itself, so placed as to make my motions visible to the Glee Club which sang unaccompanied church pieces in the intervals between the organ numbers. Finally Schweitzer invited me to the organ loft to inspect and to try the organ.

There it was, very much as it was in Bach's day, devoid of all the labor-saving devices of the modern instrument, cumbersome, and, from the point of view of one who had been used to the mechanically effortless instruments of America, calculated to set up for the player almost every conceivable impediment to easy and comfortable manipulation. That was my first experience with the type of organ which had served Bach; and like many another, I found myself soberly pondering the manner in which the average "concert" organist deals with Bach's music. When Schweitzer sat down to play the G minor Fantasia and Fugue as a crown to a memorable evening, one was literally transported back into another St. Thomas's, and there came vividly to mind all of Widor's admonitions concerning speed, clarity, legato, rhythm, and dissonance in the performance of eighteenth century organ music; admonitions born not of what one might think Bach would have liked had he had at his disposal the instrument of to-day, but born, rather, of a knowledge of the organ for which Bach actually composed, and, of equal importance, the organ on which he played.

A long and practical acquaintance with Bach's music denies the possibility of separating these two elements in any consideration of how that music shall be made most life-like in performance. To any student of the Bach literature it becomes increasingly evident that Bach's musical thinking was, in the main, just abstract musical thinking, or else instrumental thinking; and though the vocal music needs no apology, it nonetheless persistently suggests another medium. The Glory to God in the Christmas Oratorio is a luminous example among many others of the purely abstract contrapuntal weaving in which the player, rather than the singer, is at his best.

I remember some years ago the late Sir Donald Tovey showing me some concerted instrumental pieces of Bach which the former had rescored. This he was led to do by considerations both of the range and the technique of the instruments involved. Tovey's impression was, as a I remember it, that Bach, consumed with the musical idea of the moment, had cast his music for one set of instruments while thinking in terms of another. Regardless of the degree of truth which may reside in that particular theory, I think that the general thesis that Bach's approach to composition was fundamentally by way of instruments, is not likely to be widely refuted; and I would qualify it further by asserting that in great measure that approach was conceived in terms of the organ. Beyond the fact that it was with that instrument that Bach was mainly associated, the truth is that a surprisingly small amount of his music fails to "arrange" itself with comparative convenience for the organ. The same may, of course, be said for Handel's music, and not a little of this may be charged off in the case of both composers, to a common denominator of eighteenth century musical language which, in its solidity and grandeur, lends itself admirably to organ style. But the two cases are not identical. Bach was a contrapuntist of a stripe different from Handel. The complexity and the texture of Bach's music are virtually a part of the organ itself.

Before Schweitzer began to play, he made sure that all was in readiness for the performance. Two assistants were to draw the stops; one at his right hand, the other directly behind him, posted at that section of the organ located in the rear. Even such stops as Schweitzer could himself reach, were in the care of a helper, as, with proper and characteristic conscientiousness, he would not allow himself for any reason to interrupt the contrapuntal lines. The omission of a brief phrase, even of a single note, was unthinkable. The music began. The "machinery" of the old organ was plainly audible, but it was clear that Schweitzer was not aware of it. Lost in the music, only the eloquence of Bach concerned him; and soon, for his hearers standing about the organ, all the mechanical intrusions disappeared in the superb playing of transcendent music. Only once, indeed, after the beginning, did any physical element make itself felt. That was at a climactic point when a considerable dynamic addition became necessary. As the music swelled up towards its peak, the assistants looked hurriedly at the music and placed their hands near the group of stops to be drawn. Suddenly the player threw back his head and shouted "jetzt!" whereupon, with a sudden and well synchronized stroke, the assistants pulled forth the required handfuls of stops with a terrific clatter. Amazingly, these diversions, not to be imagined in the "organ recital," were but dimly realized by the listener; so overpowering was the effect of the music and its registration. That was the miracle. One forgot everything for the moment, the awkward manipulation of the stops, the noise of shrunken mechanism, even the player himself. Only Bach was there. It was the complete relegation of all agencies of performance to a position of total unimportance, with a corresponding glorification of the music itself. Modern virtuosity of every type has too often created a barrier between the composer and the listener. Too often, indeed, is the music no more

ALBERT SCHWEITZER AT THE ORGAN
In the Groote Kerk at Deventer (Holland) in 1932.

than a vehicle for the self-expression of the interpreter. Of all that there was nothing on that evening in Strasbourg. For once there was the realization of that so-oft dreamed ideal, the artist at one with the composer.

Now I have made much of the matter of the organ accompaniment for the Bach Society, of a brief appearance as conductor at a rehearsal of that organization, and of the Strasbourg performance of the great G minor, not because they have anecdotal interest, but because they are conspicuous examples of what I feel to be a fundamental reason for Schweitzer's perception of all that we mean by the name *Bach*. Before I come finally to that, however, which is the real objective of this writing, I would like to point out one or two other conclusions which seem to me to be self-evident. There is, for example, the witness of a consistently selfless attitude toward the music and what it expresses; and that steady, truth-seeking approach is symbolic of a profound and persistent philosophy which has underlain every project to which Schweitzer has devoted himself. No life could have been more controlled by plan, more completely integrated than his. This fact was pointed out by A. G. Hogg, in 1925, when he wrote, "In a very outstanding degree this man's thought and life are one; . . . and no discerning reader of his recent books can fail to perceive that his self-dedication to medical work among the neglected is the morally fitting expression of his whole outlook on life and God and duty."*

In this, as in so many other details, one is reminded of Bach himself; of the fundamentally unchanged nature of his style, of the singleness of purpose which runs like a thread throughout his life. "I worked hard," said Bach**, and reading Schweitzer's account of his carefully thought out and relentlessly pursued

* A. G. Hogg, *International Review of Missions* 14 (1925), p. 47, quoted in J. D. Regester, *Albert Schweitzer, the Man and His Work*, New York: The Abingdon Press, 1931.
** C. S. Terry, *Bach, The Historical Approach*, p. 14. London: The Oxford University Press, 1930.

ideals of scholarship and service, one cannot fail, here again, to discern a significant similarity between the two men. I cannot believe that it was wholly on aesthetic grounds that Schweitzer was first drawn to Bach. Schweitzer is above all the philosopher; not, however, the philosopher who concerns himself primarily with interpretation, but rather with realization; with an application to his own life and thought of those principles which are, to him, abiding and spiritually productive. Here it is easy to substitute "religion" for "philosophy," because the animating purpose of Schweitzer's life, whether in scholarship or in humanitarianism, has been the will to serve. The healing of the body has been for him a road to the healing of the spirit. His study of Bach and his performances of Bach's works were not designed, I venture to believe, to encourage an interest in Bach's music, but rather to promote an understanding of artistic truth as Bach expressed it. The profundity of Bach's musical language, the close association of the music with religious exercise, and above all, its power to serve the spirit, all these would inevitably attract the philosopher, the theologian, the musician, and the lover of humanity, like a magnet. It is significant that as a performer, Schweitzer's preoccupation with Bach has extended itself mainly to include the work of that other great mystic of the organ world, César Franck. We cannot imagine the worldly Handel or any of the nineteenth century "virtuoso" organ composers commanding Schweitzer's unremitting allegiance.

Consistency of purpose and devotion to the truth should be the characteristics of all scholars and musicians. But beyond that there is, it seems to me, a quality in Albert Schweitzer which unites and vivifies all the rest; a quality lacking in much scholarship that is otherwise praiseworthy; too often absent from what is, in other particulars, competent musical performance. I even dare to think that to its ignoring may be charged, in large measure, this present sorry state of things in our world. I refer to what we call *imagination,* which, in this case, I take to be a kind of second sight, accepting the externals at their face value, and perceiving the real truth that lies hidden beneath what appears as truth to the unimaginative man. No modern figure has possessed imaginative power in greater degree than Albert Schweitzer; and one of the surest proofs of this is to be found in the fact that the world has sometimes accused him either of having it not at all or of exercising it to fantastic lengths.

Perhaps nowhere is a lack of imagination so apparent as in our misunderstanding of the importance for later life of the vague impressions of childhood. We insist that education is not education unless it is accompanied by understanding; forgetting that in our own experience it was the incomprehensible passage of Scripture, or of music, full of mystery, which first stimulated us effectively, which introduced us to beauty—which really is mystery—and which sowed in us the seeds of an imaginative power of our own. Characteristic is Schweitzer's belief that children should attend adult services of worship;* while an even more dramatic demonstration of the scope and force of his imagination appears in his sensitiveness to natural beauty, especially when it manifests itself as an incidental facet to an experience so crucial that for most men any peripheral impressions would be impossible.**

Most significant for our purposes, however, is Schweitzer's elucidation of the music of the chorale preludes. Bach had for many years been considered to be the final figure of an epoch which, to a great extent, viewed music objectively. He was held to be the outstanding genius of that epoch, but he was, nonetheless, framed within the aesthetic concepts of the 18th century. His chorale preludes, elaborations of the melodies of the German hymnal were the inspired commentaries of a devout Protestant and a genius among composers. It is easy now to ask why some

* See Regester: *op. cit.,* p. 33.
** See Schweitzer: *On the Edge of the Primeval Forest,* p. 93 and pp. 168-169.

earnest student should not have found a clue to the whole truth in such romantic lyricism as is displayed, for example, in the aria *Am Abend* in the Passion according to St. Matthew or in parts of the concerto for two violins. It remained for Schweitzer, however, to perceive the full import of the chorale preludes, to establish the close connection existing between the music and the text of the hymn upon which that music was based, and to reveal Bach as a prophet at least one hundred years in advance of his time.

I cannot be greatly concerned over the protest of some musicologists that Schweitzer is reading into Bach something that is not there, nor does it disturb me that certain theologians insist that Schweitzer's interpretations are often wilfull and perverse. In a world which is daily becoming more factual, prosaic, and statistical, I rejoice that someone dares, rightly or wrongly, to look imaginatively behind the exteriors.

I have given as a definition of imagination "a kind of second sight, accepting the externals at their face value, and perceiving the real truth that lies hidden beneath what appears as truth to the unimaginative man." To be keenly imaginative, to be able to penetrate beyond exteriors to the heart that lies within the seemingly true—these are, indeed, attributes which relatively few of us are fortunate enough to possess; and had Schweitzer never proceeded beyond the exercise of that endowment as it is displayed in his illumination of the chorale preludes he would have made an incalculable contribution to our understanding of Bach.

But there is a sphere beyond imagination, and I have mentioned it by implication more than once in the course of this essay. It is the sphere which lies above the mere perception of truth, and becomes the literal embodiment of truth. Where Bach is concerned, Albert Schweitzer is, as far as I know, its sole tenant. It is this that I have ventured to call his transcendentalism; the re-creation in him of the musical personality of Bach; and it reveals itself most impressively in the performance of the preludes and fugues. It makes no difference whether or not we believe that Bach was a better organist than Schweitzer. The fact remains that when I now hear a recording of Schweitzer's performance of Bach's organ music, I feel—and I cannot believe that I am alone in this—that I am listening in every important detail to Bach himself. I am sure that I may assume that no one will take this statement as suggesting that Schweitzer is Bach reincarnate; that the soul of Bach now inhabits the body of Schweitzer. Knowing what I do of both, I am certain that there is a wide dissimilarity between their characters. My conviction regarding Schweitzer's transcendentalism is based on two factors: the persistent logic of Schweitzer's approach to every problem connected with Bach's music, and the traditions of 18th century organ playing. In dealing with the first, let me refer back for a moment to the chorale preludes and to Schweitzer's commentary on them. Here is music which, according to Schweitzer, is dependent for its understanding on ideas expressed in language. It is possible that in Bach's own time, for a congregation hearing and perhaps singing the texts of its chorales Sunday after Sunday, and listening to the Cantor's elaborations of the ideas contained in those texts, no word of Bach's was necessary to establish the connection between the two. But in our time Schweitzer perceived that connection and forthwith supplied what Bach had left unsaid. This I would call a superlative stroke of imagination. In the preludes and fugues, on the other hand, where the substance, being abstract music, is prompted by no ideas expressible in words, (Bach's ideas being musical ideas and nothing else), the composer's own eloquence is all-sufficient; and Schweitzer refrains from superimposing anything of himself upon the original statement. His purpose is to present the music as it stands without benefit of interpretational niceties designed to show what Schweitzer thought Bach felt when he set the music to paper. This is consummately logical and entirely characteristic of Schweitzer.

Regarding the connection between the traditions of 18th century playing and Schweitzer's performance I may say that only those who were subjected to Widor's rigorous and conscientious training in the music of Bach can understand how important a part this element plays in Schweitzer's style as an organist. It is not that Widor had individual preconceptions, however artistically praiseworthy, as to how Bach should be played. He had, as he often told us, the Bach tradition of organ playing by apostolic succession direct from Bach through unbroken generations of teachers down to his own. That tradition was the gospel and we were meticulously indoctrinated in it. But who among us, save Schweitzer, ever succeeded in even approaching the ideal? We could not rise above our own musical personalities, our favored readings, our will to make the music evocative. We were not the voice of Bach; we were its interpreters. If one protests that Schweitzer's playing of Bach is unemotional, devoid of interest, impersonal and unimaginative, I reply if the fault lies not with the listener, then it is Bach and not Schweitzer who is to be rebuked. For a man who, more than any other, knows the methods of organ playing in Bach's own time, who is familiar with the limitations of the instrument of that day, who possesses a scholar's knowledge of 18th century style, and who can convert all this into a completely objective presentation of the music is not far from the source of truth; in this case, the composer himself.

One of the most profound musical scholars of our age, one whose independent and provocative opinion followed no traditional paths, has written, "To disagree with Schweitzer is dangerously like disagreeing with Bach."* Regardless of the extent to which one may subscribe to this statement, the possessions of mind and heart which we associate with Schweitzer are those

* D. F. Tovey: *Essays in Musical Analysis,* vol. V, p. 34. London: Oxford University Press, 1937.

which spring to our thought at the very mention of Bach. And of these, not the least, surely, is a pervasive and dynamic imagination which, projecting knowledge and consistently exercised, has risen even above itself to give us not an *interpretation*, but more than this, a powerful *revelation* of Bach himself.

ALBERT SCHWEITZER'S CONTRIBUTION
TO
ORGAN-BUILDING

By

Carl Weinrich

Organist and Choirmaster at Princeton University and Instructor of Organ, Columbia University and Wellesley College

CHAPTER IX

ALBERT SCHWEITZER'S CONTRIBUTION
TO ORGAN BUILDING

BY

CARL WEINRICH

Before proceeding to a discussion of Albert Schweitzer's contribution to organ building, it might be well to explain some of the organ terminology.

The pipes of the organ are played from a console having from one to four keyboards, or manuals, for the hands, and a pedal manual for the feet. These manuals are usually called Great, Swell, Choir, and Solo. Organs with more than four manuals have been built, but need not enter into the present discussion. The pipes are grouped into sections, each section mounted on a windchest, and each section connected with a certain keyboard. The pipes are arranged in rows, each row representing a different tone quality.

From the earliest days of the organ, the keys were connected with valves under the pipes by long strips of wood called trackers. When middle C, for example, was played, the tracker pulled open the valve under all the middle C pipes, admitting air from the windchest into the valve. Were it not for one further piece of mechanism, all the middle C pipes, one from every row on the chest, would sound at once. This mechanism consisted of a movable strip of wood running along under each row of pipes, above the valves. The strip had holes which exactly corresponded to the pipe holes. When the holes in the strip were exactly beneath those of the pipes, any air entering the valve escaped up through the pipe, causing it to squeak. When the strip was moved slightly to one side, the holes no longer corresponded, and the pipe above remained silent. With this mechanism, called a stop mechanism, any or all of the rows of pipes could be made to speak or be silent. The mechanism was controlled by the knobs or tablets, called "stops," found on every console.

During the latter part of the nineteenth century, a new type of key and stop action, called the tubular-pneumatic, was developed. In place of the trackers, the keys were connected with the valve pallets of the windchest by lead tubes. When the key was depressed, a small pallet valve at the end was opened, allowing atmospheric pressure into the inside of the tube, causing the pallets of the winchest to collapse and allowing the pipe to speak. With the advent of electricity the electro-pneumatic action was developed—the trackers and lead tubes of the other actions were supplanted by electric wiring. A new type of windchest came into use, in which the wind was admitted to each separate row of pipes. This type of chest, the usual one in use today, is still in some dispute. The advocates of the older type of chest, called the slider-chest, maintain that it is better acoustically because, as explained above, all the pipes controlled by each key on the console are fed from the same valve.

As to tone quality, the pipes may be roughly divided into four groups—diapasons, usually regarded as the basic and characteristic organ color, flutes, strings, and reeds. Diapasons, flutes, and strings are sometimes called flue stops—the dividing line between them is somewhat elastic, and varies from period to period, and from builder to builder. Reed pipes are of various kinds—some, like trumpets, are chorus reeds, used mainly as final additions to the full organ; others, like the oboe and clarinet, are solo stops.

Pipes differ not only in quality, but in pitch. If a stop marked 8' is drawn, the pitch of middle C will correspond to that of the piano. If one marked 16' is drawn, the note will sound an octave lower. One marked 4' will sound an octave higher, and one marked 2' two octaves higher. If the 8', 4', and 2' are drawn together, three different octaves can be discerned. In actual practice however, this effect is not analogous to playing three octaves on the piano. If the pipes are properly voiced, the effect will be rather that of a brightening of the fundamental tone. The diapasons, flutes, and strings of unison pitches of 16', 8', 4' and 2' are called foundation stops.

Some stops control pipes which speak off-unison pitches, fifths and thirds. Here again, the effect is not that of playing a chord on a single note. When properly used, such pipes, called mutations, form an important part of the color palette of the organ. Sometimes several pipes sounding octaves, fifths, and occasionally thirds, are mounted to speak on one note, and drawn by one stopknob. Such stops are called mixtures. They contain pipes of high pitch, which serve to give the organ brightness and clearness.

The stops on the console can be operated singly, by hand, or they can be moved in groups, by means of mechanical devices. Before electricity, these devices usually were levers placed above the pedalboard, which when pushed by the feet, caused certain stops to move. Sometimes the levers shut off the wind from a section of the chest, silencing the pipes for the time being. With the advent of electricity, these levers were often superseded by push buttons under the manuals.

While each manual has a group of stops which belong to it, the stops of one manual can be made to play on another manual by means of "couplers." Also, the stops of the various manuals can be coupled to the pedal keyboard.

In 1906, when Albert Schweitzer wrote his "German and French Organ-Building and Organ-Playing," German and French organ-building had taken widely divergent lines, though both countries had had fine organ traditions. As a boy, Schweitzer had come to love the tone of the fine old Silbermann organs in Alsace, built in the early eighteenth century. There had been considerable reciprocity between the Silbermanns and the French organ-builders; moreover, Germany and France had followed a somewhat similar development well into the nineteenth century. When the German organist, Hesse, opened the new organ built by Cavaillé-Coll at the Church of Sainte-Clothilde in Paris, in 1844, he found it very much to his liking, in fact considered it an ideal organ. Since that time French organ-building had undergone no changes.

The Germans, on the other hand, were using new possibilities offered by electricity to alter the character of the organ. They were discarding the old foot-levers in favor of the newer manual push-buttons, or pistons, and were raising the wind-pressures. Guilmant, the great French organist, could not understand these German innovations. As he put it to Schweitzer, "And in Germany do they still use push-buttons? I cannot understand it. Observe how simple it is, when one has everything under control of the feet." And, to quote his contemporary Widor, "Where in the music of Bach does one have a finger free at the right time to push a button? If one had to choose, Schweitzer preferred the French method, since one had a foot free more often than a hand, and since the piston system often led to rhythmic unsteadiness in playing. He suggested that organ consoles should combine both features—the foot levers of the French and the manual pistons of the German organs.

Schweitzer devoted much attention to this matter of console control because he realized that the method of making a crescendo and diminuendo had to do with the very essence of the organ. The Germans had developed the so-called crescendo-pedal or roller, by which the stops could be brought on or off by a foot pedal, in an order prearranged by the builder. By playing on the Great manual, and operating this pedal, one could arrive quickly to any desired dynamic level. Schweitzer admitted the convenience of the crescendo pedal in accompanying choruses, where dynamic considerations might be paramount. However, he feared that its use would have a bad effect on the artistic standards of young organists and composers, who would come to look on the organ simply as a "loud-soft" instrument, and fail to search out its varied tonal possibilities. Many discerning organists among the Germans avoided its use. Schweitzer's observations on the use of the crescendo-pedal are fully valid today, and are concurred in by many organists.

The French organist, without a crescendo-pedal, was not able to arrive at full organ in one movement, but he could vary the means of getting there. First, he could vary the order in which he coupled the manuals to the Great. Second, the mixtures and reeds on each manual could be added or taken off by individual levers. Third, the pipes of one of the manuals, the Swell, were enclosed in a box with shutters, which could be opened or closed by a foot pedal. Unlike the German Swell division, which had come to consist of just a few soft stops, the French Swell division contained stops of all pitches, colors, and dynamics, so that its opening and closing could materially affect the quality of the whole organ.

For example, in building up to full organ, the French organist could start with the foundation stops of 16', 8', 4' and 2' pitches, with all manuals coupled to the Great, and the Swellbox closed. With the box closed, the mixtures and reeds of the Swell could be added imperceptibly. Opening the box would bring out this tone-color gradually, after which the mixtures and reeds of the Choir and Great could be added, making a smooth and gradual crescendo. For a diminuendo, the process would be reversed. In playing French organ music, the signs $<$ $>$ always signified the use of the swellbox, never the addition or subtracton of stops. In general, the French used the swellbox in an architectural rather than an emotional manner. While the latter use was found in the works of Franck and his school, the mature works of Guilmant and Widor arrived at the more architectural conception.

The Germans, with their inadequate Swell divisions, mistakenly interpreted the signs <   > to mean the addition or subtraction of stops by means of the crescendo-pedal. This meant that, as the various stops came on, every crescendo and diminuendo resulted in a change of tone-color. While the organs of Bach's day did not have swellboxes, Schweitzer held that Cavaillé-Coll's incorporation of the swellbox in French organs of the nineteenth century was one of the important contributions of the century. He did not agree with those who regarded a swellbox as unnecessary on a small organ. As he put it, "Swellbox and complete pedal division (32 notes) belong to the essence of the organ, like four feet to a horse. Rather two or three stops less, since with a real swellbox, one can make two stops out of one."

Relying upon the crescendo-pedal had another unfortunate result, in that the whole organ responded as one unit. All the stops of the organ, regardless of manual affiliation, came on one by one, thus destroying the individuality of the different manuals.

In one form or another, this differentiation between the manuals has been one of the important principles of organ-building. The 17th century builders secured strong contrast as to color, pitch, and even location. One manual, called the Rückpositiv, was placed on the front of the gallery wall between the organist and the congregation. Silbermann, though he no longer built his organs with a *Rückpositiv,* did make the Great division weighty, the *Oberwerk* (Swell) penetrating, and the *Brustwerk* (Choir) delicate. The word "delicate" is not to be interpreted too literally! The Silbermann *Brustwerk* had nothing in common with the meager and ineffective Choir manual of the average American organ of the last few years. Following the lines of Silbermann, Cavaillé-Coll voiced the Great division with full and broad tone, the Choir (*Positif*) with a bright and breezy quality, and the Swell (*Récit*) with greater intensity.

The use of electricity enabled the German builders to add all kinds of contrivances to their consoles, which supposedly facilitated playing. Most of them were of the "free-combination" type, by which a piston would put into effect a certain previously prepared combination. However, since this silenced any combination drawn by hand, and since no stops drawn by hand would sound with the "free-combination," a stereotyped way of playing the organ with only a few combinations could easily result. Furthermore, since these combinations affected the whole organ, they tended to destroy the individuality of the manuals, after the manner of the crescendo-pedal. The pedal division also, which in the best organ music should be independent of the manuals, became tied up with the manual controls. Schweitzer admitted some shortcoming in the French system of lever controls, in that they brought on only the mixtures and reeds. He suggested that the Germans should develop their combination-pistons in such a way that the player could always choose whether or not he wanted the hand-drawn registration to affect the "free-combination." Beyond the speaking stops, the resources of a moderate-sized organ should include manual-to-pedal couplers, manual couplers, both super and sub, free-combinations (both to affect and not to affect drawn stops), crescendo-pedal, Great ventil (to shut wind from chest).

Schweitzer had much to say on the relative merits of the old tracker slider-chest, versus the various modern developments. He granted that the tubular-pneumatic and electro-pneumatic actions had certain advantages: ease and rapidity of touch, simplification of the mechanism, and a ready use of all the resources. But these were not aesthetic advantages.

The tubular action, he said, had a dead precision. The wind-pressure (and in the case of the electro-pneumatic action, electric energy), rather than the finger touch, did the work. It was not elastic and alive like the tracker action. The keys got into bad regulation, the drop was not deep enough, there was no contact point, and there was always danger of touching and sounding adjacent keys, making clean playing difficult. With the tracker action, the finger felt a resistance which indicated the contact point, and the key tended to press against the finger on the release. With the new actions, the keys did not coöperate with the fingers. As Schweitzer phrased it, "With the pneumatic action one communicates with his instrument by telegraph." The electric action gave pipes a very rapid speech, but this again was not a virtue. Rather than speaking out, the tone seemed to blurt out. True legato was not possible—the tones rolled out one after another like balls. In the addenda to his work which Schweitzer wrote in 1927, he still held the old slider-chest to be the best. For small and medium sized organs he would continue building the tracker action. Possibly, he said, modern builders would be able to invent a modern chest with the acoustical advantages of the slider-chest. The slider-chest and the tracker action still have advocates today, though the mechanical imperfections of the early electric action have been eradicated. Schweitzer approved of the so-called Barker lever used by Cavaillé-Coll, which consisted of a small pallet beneath the key-action, and which considerably reduced the finger-pressure required in playing the tracker action.

In the final analysis, the great question was whether the modern organ sounded better than the old organ. By "old" organ Schweitzer meant all organs built before the era of the "factory" organ, that is from the seventeenth century down to about 1870. He felt that the old organs of the seventeenth and eighteenth centuries should be carefully preserved and restored, and that many of their tone-colors should be revived. However, he believed that the improvements of the first seven decades of the nineteenth century, such as the swellbox, should become a permanent part of the organ, and were indispensable for the playing of music of Franck, Widor, Reger, and others.

And had the German organ of the early twentieth century improved tonally over the old organs? Schweitzer doubted it, and maintained that the organ music of Bach sounded better on the French organs of Cavaillé-Coll. The new organs were louder, but not as refined and beautifully voiced. The use of higher pressures, made possible by electric blowers, had not had a good effect on tone. An organ of 15 stops, on high pressures, might sound as loud as an organ of 30 stops on low, but it would not sound as well.

The combination of all the foundation stops of 16', 8', 4' and 2, pitches should sound beautiful and harmonious. With Cavaillé-Coll, this was the case. On the German organs, the foundation stops were not voiced as an ensemble. Used together, they often sounded thick and heavy, and even the combined 8' stops were often unendurable. Hence the mixtures did not blend with the foundation stops. They merely added power, instead of lightness and clarity. As a result, the Germans could not play the Preludes and Fugues of Bach with foundation stops and mixtures, which was entirely possible on the French organs. The Germans had to "interpret" these works, that is, fit them to the shortcomings of their instruments. Ironically, most organists considered these liberties, and these orchestral crescendi and diminuendi as an improvement!

"Back to the polyphonic organ of Bach, not the orchestral organ! Finer foundation stops! Harmony and unity of the foundation stops! Away with our few screaming mixtures! Many and mild mixtures!" Schweitzer's plea for a richer and more complex tone-structure has borne fruit both in Europe and America, as the increasing number of magnificent instruments built along these lines testify. All manuals, including the pedal, should have a rich ensemble with mixtures. The inadequate pedal division, with just a few low bass pipes, is unsatisfactory for any kind of music. Schweitzer believed that the day of the "powerful" organ was past, and that the day of the "tonally-rich" organ was at hand.

Schweitzer was of the opinion that the chorus reeds on both

German and French organs were too loud. Even Cavaillé-Coll succumbed to the temptation to use higher pressures for his Swell trumpets. The reeds should not overpower the foundations and mixtures, they should merely add a touch of golden sheen. Schweitzer favored the milder reeds of the German and English builders of the 1860-1870 period. They went out of fashion because they were not quite as prompt in speech as the higher-pressure reeds. The latter did not blend with the flue-work. They destroyed the clarity of the lines in polyphonic music, and for this reason the French did not use them in playing the music of Bach. The older and milder reeds could be used in playing Bach.

Much of the trouble, Schweitzer believed, lay in the commercialization of the organ industry. He characterized the last forty years of the nineteenth century as the "strife between the mercantile and artistic spirit, and the triumph of the mercantile over the artistic spirit." He pointed out that Cavaillé-Coll, working in the years of the monarchy, when money was available to the Church, had been able to build his fine organs, and later, he was fortunate in that the recommendation of organists like Guilmant and Widor made it unnecessary for him to compete. Many of the German builders lamented the new condition of things, but pointed out that in order to remain in business they had to build what Schweitzer called "factory-organs."

In the second part of his book, written in 1927, Schweitzer found that, in the main, the principles which he had advocated in his earlier work were still valid. He had become strongly convinced of the necessity for a real *Rückpositiv*. Only when this division was built out into the church, instead of up with the rest of the organ, would it have the character of a separate division. Without a *Rückpositiv*, the largest organ would lack one of its three necessary personalities, and Schweitzer regarded this absence of a *Rückpositiv* as a major shortcoming in the organs of Cavaillé-Coll. If at all possible the organ should be placed up in the west gallery, where it would have greatest freedom to sound. He emphasized again that the Swell manual must remain the most complete, and that if there was just one reed and one mixture, these must be in the Swell. The specification should be drawn with regard to the performance of music of outstanding composers. The works of Franck, Widor, and other romantic masters assume a gamba and a celeste. To accompany recitatives in Bach Cantatas, there should be an 8′ open flute, salicional, and mild diapason, on the Swell. The *Rückpositiv* should have a *"Musiziergedackt"* (a bright *lieblich-gedackt* verging on the Quintadena) for accompaniments, also a gemshorn, and possibly a 16′ bourdon. The Great should have a bourdon and flauto major 8′, and a wide-scaled salicional. Schweitzer saw no point in leaving out this stop, and favored a gamba as well, both on Great and Swell. On the Great of a larger organ, he approved of the English custom of having two or three principals. Flutes, rather than strings, should form the foundation of the organ.

While Schweitzer saw no need for a fourth manual in an organ up to eighty stops, he favored three manuals for one as small as thirty, in order to get the advantage of a *Rückpositiv*. In a very small church, a two-manual was sufficient. Nor did he favor two enclosed sections—the large amount of woodwork tending to spoil the tone.

The twenty years separating the two parts of Schweitzer's work witnessed great changes in the organ world. He tells of the countless letters written, trips made, and friends lost, in the effort to persuade organists, builders, and churches of the value of the fine old organs which many of them wanted to destroy in favor of some factory-made organ whose only qualification was newness. The appearance of his book in 1906, and the recommendations of the "International Regulations for Organ-building" in 1909, which embodied many of his ideas, helped to interest many and to clarify the issues.

By 1927, the pendulum had swung to the opposite extreme.

The German organists, builders and musicologists had made the study of the older builders of the seventeenth century an important part of their activities. To Schweitzer, who regarded as ideal the great organs of the eighteenth century as they were perfected by nineteenth century builders like Cavaillé-Coll, this new tendency to elevate the seventeenth century organ was not entirely desirable. He considered the organ on which Bach had been brought up, that of the seventeenth century, as the forerunner only of the ideal organ. He regarded the organ at St. Sulpice in Paris as the finest he had ever heard.

In the many-sided and immensely active life of Albert Schweitzer, his interest in the organ forms a fascinating chapter. The amount of time, work, and worry which his interest cost him made him wish sometimes that he had never undertaken it, but the thought of some fine old organ, saved through his efforts, and filling some church with glorious sound, made him feel richly rewarded. For him the search for the good organ was a part of the search for truth.

MUSICAL DAYS

WITH

ALBERT SCHWEITZER

By

Alice Ehlers
Professor of Music, University of Southern California

CHAPTER X

MUSICAL DAYS WITH ALBERT SCHWEITZER

BY

ALICE EHLERS

On being asked to contribute an article to the "Schweitzer Volume," I felt honored, but also worried; not that I have forgotten, after all these years, the smallest detail of my meeting this great man, for the very first time, and the many times after, but because writing is not my forte. I am afraid of being unable to relate truly the great influence and help Dr. Schweitzer—the musical scientist—and later Dr. Schweitzer, the friend, has been to me.

It was in 1928 that I met Dr. Schweitzer personally for the first time. He had just received the *Goethe-Preis,* and was on a lecture tour through Europe. I knew his book on J. S. Bach well, for it had already become my guide and musical Bible for interpretation of Bach's music. I was then at the beginning of my career as a harpsichordist, and my greatest aim was a clean break with the traditional Bach interpretation of all the piano virtuosos. His book on Bach helped me greatly in my difficult task. Dr. Schweitzer's ideas, based on thorough knowledge, were expressed clearly and with authority. Of course, I also had heard about Dr. Schweitzer the medical man, who, in the deadly climate of French Equatorial Africa, carried on the work of brotherly love. Yet for me, it was the Bach Schweitzer alone who seems to have counted.

If I am honest, I must admit that I did not attend Dr. Schweitzer's lectures because I was so much interested in Lambaréné, but mainly because I wanted to see and hear him. Everyone who has met the Doctor was most impressed by the utter simplicity of this truly great man. In 1928, my place in the world of great conductors and virtuosos was still behind the door, and I had not yet met a great man, who was so great that he could afford to remain simple, modest, and natural.

A TRANSPORTING EXPERIENCE

After the first five minutes of his lecture, I found myself listening to a man who made me forget Bach, harpsichord, and organ. I was in Lambaréné. I was assisting in surgical operations with Dr. Schweitzer, giving out food to the natives, and attending Sunday service. My face must have expressed a bit of my feelings, because a friend of mine, looking at me, said: "Please don't tell me you are giving up music and are going to Lambaréné as Dr. Schweitzer's helper." Frankly, that was exactly how I felt. With the greatest simplicity, he spoke about his work and many of his problems. The constant fight against the disease-carrying insects coming from the steaming jungles, the great difficulties in getting the needed medicine, the physical hardships they all had to endure, and the greatest problem of all—to gain the trust of the natives. It will take much patience and success to overcome their superstitions and to make them believe in him, the doctor, the white man. Yet he was confident; for he believed and knew he would succeed in his work. The little humorous details which helped to ease their daily struggle made one forget a bit the earnestness of the lecture.

Afterwards the doctor invited those who wished to join him to a nearby restaurant. I went along with the crowd and was sitting with some friends at a table from where I could see him well. Suddenly one of Dr. Schweitzer's helpers came to our table and asked me: "Are you Alice Ehlers?" Too surprised to answer, I only nodded. The assistant then said: "The Doctor would like to meet you." It is hard to describe my feelings as I approached Dr. Schweitzer. I remember that I felt like a little school girl, and I am afraid I behaved like one. Dr. Schweitzer must have understood my puzzled expression and took out his African diary, a most interesting book he always carries with him. It contains hundreds of pages of very thin paper, unbound, but held together in such a manner that new pages may be added at any time. In this diary he showed me a remark he had written while in Africa. "When in Europe, I want to meet Alice Ehlers; interesting programmes; unusual."

Then he explained that his friends kept him informed of what was going on in Europe by sending him magazines and programmes. In this way he had followed my concerts, and, as he expressed it, the quality and the outspoken tendency of my programmes had awakened his interest. No great applause or enthusiastic critic could have given me such happiness as did these words coming from Dr. Schweitzer. I told him that it was his book on Bach which had been my main guide. Amidst all his many friends and admirers, we were able to exchange a few thoughts on Bach, and when the Doctor expressed that he would very much like to hear me play, I enthusiastically thanked him. The very next day one of my harpsichords was sent to his residence, where I played for him and Mrs. Schweitzer for a full hour. I started with the *C Minor Fantaisie* by Bach, one of the Doctor's favorite pieces, and also one of mine. His encouraging remarks helped me to overcome my first shyness, and I played on and on.

When I left the Schweitzers, he thanked me and said: "Go on the way you started out and never allow virtuosity to guide you. Always listen to the inner voices in Bach's music; each voice lives its own life, dependently and independently at the same time. If you will look at Bach's music that way; if each voice will be allowed to sing out its own beauty — I am sure you cannot fail." Those words I have remembered all my life.

After touring all of Europe, Dr. Schweitzer returned to Africa, and I did not see him until 1932. He was invited to Frankfurt-am-Main to deliver an address on Goethe, who was born in that city. It was a hundred years after Goethe's death. The opera house where Dr. Schweitzer was going to speak was filled to the last seat. All of Frankfurt's society was present, and also many representatives of the arts, as well as scientists from all over Europe and America. Two days after this event, I gave a joint recital with the Budapest String-Quartet; it was one of the concerts in the series of the famous "Frankfurter Museums-Gesellschaft." These concerts were always sold out at the beginning of every season, but when Dr. Schweitzer expressed his wish to attend our concert with some of his friends, the necessary arrangements were made and chairs were put into the hall for them.

I shall never forget how the audience rose as one man the moment Dr. Schweitzer entered the hall. With him was Dr. Alice Masaryk, the daughter of the former President of Czechoslovakia, one of Dr. Schweitzer's closest friends. After the concert, Dr. Schweitzer invited me to visit him during the summer in Günsbach. To be allowed to spend a few days near this great man made me deeply happy. I was asked to stay a week, and as always many guests were expected, a date was immediately fixed. Since people came and left, the few guest rooms were in constant use, and everything had to be planned carefully in advance.

Günsbach is a little village in the Münster Valley. It is bedded between vineyards which are gently terraced along the rolling hillsides. The village roads are bordered with cherry trees; and plum trees are scattered over fields and slopes. With sadness and nostalgia, I remember the peace of the little village in Alsace which made everyone feel in harmony. Today the little village of Günsbach has again been disturbed, as often before, for whenever Alsace would change its master, either Germany or France, life in Günsbach would change too. But in 1932, Günsbach was the charming little village which the Doctor loved so dearly. He had built his house as a recreation center for himself and for his helpers when they were in Europe on their vacation from Africa.

For the last years, Dr. Schweitzer has denied himself the rest and needed change from his hard work and the strenuous tropical climate; for again, as in the first World War, Günsbach has been robbed of its freedom, being situated in a strategic military sphere. But back in 1932, life in Günsbach was quiet and simple for Dr. Schweitzer, when no visitors appeared, although they often did. During the most peaceful hours, they would drop in, often without warning. They came singly, or in groups, wishing to see the Doctor. They felt the need to talk to him, asking him questions, starting with Bach and ending perhaps in politics or religion. I pitied him because of the demands his guests would put upon his time, yet I admired him even more. Never would he allow anyone to excuse himself, but would interrupt his work and spend his time with his visitors. His calm never reflected the strain these many interruptions must have been on him, for to make up the loss of time, he often worked late at night. He used his vacation time, not so much for rest, but to work on his books which he had partly sketched out in Africa. It seemed to me as if the Doctor needed the peaceful air of Günsbach in order to bring his books into definite shape.

In spite of the many people who interrupted the Doctor's day, Günsbach still was restful to him, and perhaps I am unjust in thinking that the frequent guests were too many; for the days were all greatly enjoyed. I vividly remember the visit of the late Stefan Zweig, who was an ardent admirer of Dr. Schweitzer. He stayed only a day. When he left, he said to me: "What I am going to tell you may seem strange. This morning, when I came out on this lovely, slow, old-fashioned train, which stops and whistles more than it moves, I had in my mind, almost completed, the book on Dr. Schweitzer which I intended to write. But now, after I have spent this one day with him, I realize that I would have to be many more days close to this great man before I would dare to write a book about him; his simplicity, his modesty, the way he never does or says anything to make an impression only; —yes, his authority and modesty taught me a great lesson. No, I will have to wait with this book."

When there were no visitors, Dr. Schweitzer would very seldom come out of his study — usually only for meals. After meals he loved to sit with us for a while. He did not speak much, yet we went on talking without making conversation with him; we all knew that these were his hours of relaxation. Dr. Schweitzer is not a voluble talker; he is a great thinker, possessing the magnificent gift of complete concentration. Though the room in which I used to practice was next to his study, it never disturbed the Doctor to hear me practice; he admitted he missed it when I stopped. Often he would come in, sit down, listen to my playing, make his remarks about the music, and sometimes ask for one of his favorite pieces. When I played the piano, he almost always asked for Mozart; he loves Mozart.

After dinner, when his day's work was done, Dr. Schweitzer would go to the church to practice on the organ. This organ was built after his own design and wishes, resembling the old organs as much as possible. Those hours with him at the organ are unforgettable. I would sit with him on the organ bench listening, and he would ask my opinion, and we would discuss phrasing, tempo, dynamics. It was in those hours that I received my best musical education. The Doctor also loved these evenings; for he was always in his happiest mood when playing the organ. All responsibilities, the whole world, disappeared for him; there was only music—the organ, nothing else. He loves music and he needs it. Even in Africa, when working very hard, the day is not ended before he has his one hour of practice on his piano with organ pedals.

This first visit to Günsbach was not my only one—I spent about a week or so nearly every summer from then on. Since 1933, when Hitler came to power, Dr. Schweitzer has not set foot into Germany. When in 1935 he was invited by the city of Leipzig to speak at the great Bach Festival, he refused politely. Many people and some of his friends expected Dr. Schweitzer to make an open declaration as to his thoughts on "the new order," but I believe that the Doctor knew that no declaration of any man, no matter how great and respected, could change the course Germany had taken. Dr. Schweitzer is a fighter (he has proven it all his life) but I believe he is not an aggressive one, but rather a persistent one.

In 1936, Dr. Schweitzer lectured in England, giving the famous Dale and Gifford lectures in London, Oxford and Edinburgh. Between lectures, he gave many organ recitals. It was in this year that Sir Arthur Wauchope, the High Commissioner of Palestine, asked me to introduce him to Dr. Schweitzer. I asked Dr. Schweitzer if he could spare an hour, and his reply was, "With pleasure. I would like to meet Sir Arthur; for years I have been following his work in Palestine with great interest."

Sir Arthur and I drove to one of London's suburbs where Dr. Schweitzer was staying with some friends. He had his Scottish secretary with him as an interpreter; he understands English perfectly and reads it like French or German; but in conversation the language is not at his command so easily, and as he explained: "If two men meet because they want to know each other, and if they have only a very limited time, it would be a waste of energy and time to grope for the right expression, apologizing all the time for not being able to express oneself the way one wanted to." Not for a second was there the danger of the conversation drifting away into mere pleasantries; Sir Arthur, from the first moment, asked questions of Dr. Schweitzer, who, with the greatest concentration, tried to find answers for them. Many subjects were touched in this one hour. I recall one answer distinctly. Dr. Schweitzer said, "You asked me if I think humanity has improved? I would say, 'Yes,' the idea of Christianity, of brotherly love, seems to increasingly apply to our daily routine of life, instead of being an abstract idea.

"But what I cannot understand, and what disturbs me greatly, is that during the last sixty to eighty years there has been a drifting away, a backsliding. I ask myself: How is this possible? How can mankind give up something that it has achieved in a dark and hard struggle? How can it give up the principle of love for the principle of hate? Never can anything develop from hate; it may seem to be successful for a time, but in the end it is love, and always will be love which will win."

Such a man is Dr. Schweitzer, and thus shall I always remember him—a great musician, a great man, and a great friend.

PART IV

ETHICS AND CIVILIZATION

ALBERT SCHWEITZER AS CRITIC

OF

NINETEENTH-CENTURY ETHICS

By

Ernst Cassirer, Ph.D., LL. D.

Formerly Professor of Philosophy, University of Hamburg
of which he was also for a time Rektor;
later Visiting Professor of Philosophy, Yale University
and prior to his death, Columbia University

ERNST CASSIRER
1874 — 1945

"To state Cassirer's philosophical position is not my intent. A bald label such as *idealistic criticism* would be nondescript. Nor could I in the brief compass enumerate his works, some of which like his *Das Erkenntnisproblem in der Philosophie*, etc., and his *Philosophie der symbolischen Formen* take three ponderous volumes each. Cassirer has extended our knowledge on numerous subjects and men (Plato, Descartes, Kepler, Leibniz, Spinoza, Lessing, Mendelssohn, Shaftesbury, Rousseau, Humboldt, Goethe, Schiller, Kleist, Hölderlin) and edited the works of Leibniz, Kant, and of his own teacher, Hermann Cohen. A prodigious worker, an erudite scholar, and a profound thinker, he has practically no peer at the present time as a universal philosopher, so that when the magazine *Fortune,* publishing in its latest issue one of Cassirer's articles, represented him as "not only one of the greatest living philosophers but one of the great historians of philosophy," it was hardly overstating Cassirer's position.

"There are a few equally creative minds today, but I know of no one who is possessed of both breadth and depth to the same extent, whose scope and sweep stretch far beyond the Middle Ages and roll back into our modernistic period."

—Extract from "Ernst Cassirer at Seventy,"
by A. A. Roback, *Aufbau,* July 28, 1944.

CHAPTER XI

ALBERT SCHWEITZER AS CRITIC OF

NINETEENTH-CENTURY ETHICS

By

ERNST CASSIRER †

Albert Schweitzer's work covers a vast field. It extends over the whole range of human culture. Schweitzer began as a theologian and as a historian of religion. His early books are concerned with the quest of the historical Jesus, with the mysticism of Paul the Apostle, with a critical history of the interpretation of the Pauline epistles. At the same time, Schweitzer began to publish his works on the history of music. He wrote his book about Johann Sebastian Bach and gave his interpretation of Bach's preludes and fugues. Subsequently, all this was in a sense superseded and eclipsed by a new practical interest. Schweitzer became a missionary and a physician. He built a hospital in Lambaréné for the natives of French Africa! and he devoted his whole life to the administration, extension, and final development of this hospital. But Schweitzer's philosophical work never was impeded by these practical activities. On the contrary, it was enlarged and deepened. In an introductory note to his book *The Decay and the Restoration of Civilization*, Schweitzer tells us that the ideas developed in his book have been finally ripened in the stillness of the primeval forest of equatorial Africa.

Nevertheless mere many-sidedness is not the true character of Schweitzer's personality and of his work. All who met him or read his books must have obtained quite a different impression. What strikes us most is not the multifariousness, the mobility,

and versatility of his thought, but its simplicity. When dealing
with the most variegated and widely divergent subjects, Schweitzer
the man and thinker, always remains the same. His whole intellectual and moral energy is directed toward, and concentrated
upon, *one* point. His various activities are never dispersed; they
do not only complement each other, they are actually interwoven.

This applies especially to Schweitzer's theory of civilization.
What we find here is not what we usually call a "philosophy."
Schweitzer never speaks in a technical philosophical language.
His work is not encumbered with a complicated and obscure
terminology, and it does not contain any subtle and sophisti-
cated modes of reasoning. Schweitzer's thought is a straightforward and ingenious thought. He avoids all scholasticism.

To put it paradoxically, we would say that the man who speaks
here is rather a physician than a philosopher. That is no mere
logical analysis but a medical analysis of our cultural life.
Schweitzer sees all the inherent evils and the impending danger
of modern culture. His book was written more than twenty-five
years ago, during the first World War. But in no other book of
this period do we find such a strong presentiment of the crisis
to come and such a clear insight into the character of this crisis.
"We are living today," he says, "under the sign of the collapse
of civilization. Just below a mighty cataract we are driving
along in a current full of formidable eddies, and it will need
the most gigantic efforts to rescue the vessel of our fate from
the dangerous side-channel into which we have allowed it to
drift, and bring it back into the main stream, if, indeed we can
hope to do so at all."*

Schweitzer's *Olaus-Petri Lectures,* given in 1922 at the University of Uppsala, contain a diagnosis, a symptomatology and an
aetiology of this illness of modern culture. According to Schweitzer, the first and most alarming symptom was the ascendancy of

* In the following, I am quoting from the English translation of Schweitzer's
Lectures on the Decay and Restoration of Civilization by E. T. Compton, London
1923.

that new form of thought that is described by him as "collective thought."

Today it is the rule—and no one questions it—always to take into account the views which prevail in organized society. The individual starts by taking it for granted that both for himself and his neighbors there are certain views which are determined by nationality, creed, political party, social position, and other elements in one's surroundings. These views are protected, and are not only kept sacred from criticism, but are not a legitimate subject of conversation. This kind of intercourse, in which we mutually abjure our natural quality as thinking beings, is euphemistically described as respect for other people's convictions, as if there would be any convictions at all where there is no thought. Where the collective body works more strongly in the individual than the latter does upon it, the result is deterioration, because the noble element on which everything depends, viz., the spiritual and moral worthiness of the individual, is thereby necessarily constricted and hampered. Decay of the spiritual and moral life then sets in, which renders society incapable of understanding and solving the problems which it has to face. Thereupon sooner of later, it is involved in catastrophe (pp. 29, 74).

Another symptom of the same disease is the ever-increasing spirit of *nationalism*. Even in this respect the picture drawn by Schweitzer, more than twenty-five years ago, gives us the most telling description of all those things that we nowadays see before our very eyes. "What is Nationalism?" asks Schweitzer.

It is an ignoble patriotism exaggerated till it has lost all its meaning, which bears the same relation to the noble and healthy kind as the fixed idea of an imbecile does to normal conviction . . . When civilization began to decline, its other ideals all fell also, but the idea of nationality maintained

itself because it had transferred itself to the sphere of
reality. It incorporated henceforward all that remained of
civilization and became the ideal which summed up all
others . . . But with the decay of civilization the character
of the idea of nationality had changed. The guardianship
exercised over it by the other moral ideals to which it had
hitherto been subordinate now ceased, since these were
themselves on trial, and the nationalist idea began a career
of independence . . . That reason and morality shall not be
allowed to contribute a word to the formation of nationalist
ideas and aspirations is demanded by the mass of men today
as a sparing of their holiest feelings. If in earlier times
the decay of civilization did not produce any such confusion
in the sentiments of the various nations, this was because
the idea of nationality had not then been raised in the same
way to the ideal of civilization. It was therefore impossible
that it should insinuate itself into the place of the true ideals
of civilization, and through abnormal nationalist conceptions
and dispositions bring into active existence an elaborate
system of uncivilization (p. 49, f.)

It was, however, not enough to study the symptoms of the illness of modern culture. The symptomatology was to be followed
by aetiology. Which are the reasons for the present crisis?
Schweitzer refuses to accept those reasons which are commonly
alleged for the explanation of the phenomenon. He rejects the
historical and economic materialism of the nineteenth century;
and he does not expect the real help from an improvement of
the social and economic conditions. Of course he does not underrate the importance of these factors. But according to him they
are rather necessary than sufficient conditions.

The best planned improvements in the organization of our
society, he declares, (though we are quite right in trying to
secure them) cannot help us at all until we become at the

same time capable of imparting a new spirit of our age. The difficult problems with which we have to deal, even those which lie entirely in the material and economic sphere are in the last resort only to be solved by an inner change of character. The wisest reforms in organization can only carry them a little nearer solution, never to the goal. The only conceivable way of bringing about a reconstruction of our world on new lines is first of all to become new men ourselves under the old circumstances and then as a society in a new frame of mind so to smooth out the opposition between nations that a condition of true civilization may again become possible. In the sphere of human events which decide the future of mankind reality consists in an inner conviction, not in given outward facts. Firm ground for our feet we find in reasoned ethical ideals . . . The true sense for reality is that insight which tells us that only through ethical ideas about things we arrive at a normal relation to reality. Only so can man and society win all the power over events that they are able to use. Without that power we are, whatever we may choose to do, delivered over into bondage of them (p. 60, f).

Which was the principal ground of this loss of "the true sense of reality" that, according to Schweitzer, is a characteristic of our modern cultural life? His answer to this question is clear and uncompromising. It is the *philosophy* of the nineteenth century that is responsible for this loss. We must annul the whole work of this philosophy in order to find the way back: the way to those ethical standards that in former times governed and determined the life of men. Schweitzer's philosophy is consciously and deliberately "out of date." He speaks as a thinker of the eighteenth century, of the period of Enlightenment. "It is with complete confidence," he says in the Preface to his book *Civilization and Ethics,** that I step forward to press the claims

* *Philosophy of Civilization.* Part II; English translation by John Naish, London 1923.

of unprejudiced rational thought. I know well that our times have no affinity whatever for anything that is branded as rationalistic, and would like to dismiss everything of the sort as an eighteenth century aberration. But it will soon become evident that we shall be obliged to take up the same position which the eighteenth century defended so stoutly. The period which lies between those times and the present is an intermezzo of thought, an intermezzo which had extraordinarily rich and interesting motifs, but yet was all the same a fatal intermezzo. Its inevitable end was that we should founder absolutely in a total lack of any world-view of civilization at all, and it is the latter state which is responsible for all the spiritual and material misery amid which we languish at present."

Schweitzer does not underrate the great achievements of the philosophy of the nineteenth and twentieth centuries. New problems have come to the fore; new solutions were attempted, new methods were developed. But all this is no compensation for what was pushed away and was finally lost. Now we have a generation which is squandering the precious heritage it has received from the past, and is living in a world of ruins, because it cannot complete the building which that past began. With the disappearance of the influence exerted by the *Aufklaerung,* rationalism, and the serious philosophy of the early nineteenth century, the seeds were sown to the World War to come.

In a great deal of the opposition which is offered to rationalism the reaction of the early nineteenth century was right. Nevertheless, it remains true that it despised and distorted what was, in spite of all its imperfections, the greatest and most valuable manifestation of the spiritual life of man that the world has yet seen. Down through all circles of cultured and uncultured alike there prevailed at that time a belief in thought and a reverence for truth. For that reason alone that age stands higher than any which preceded it, and much higher than our own. (p. 87).

Theological and ethical thinkers have often charged the nineteenth century with a lack of religious and moral sense. The various schools of materialism, the "egoism" of Stirner, the "immoralism" of Nietzsche were alleged as reasons for this charge. But that is not the point of Schweitzer. He does not think of these systems; he does not even mention them. His accusation has a much more general and, therefore, a much graver and more serious import. He does not criticize or attack particular philosophic schools. His attack is directed against the very *character* of philosophic thought during the nineteenth century. What matters in philosophy is not so much the answers to certain questions as the questions themselves. And it is here that, according to Schweitzer, the philosophy of the nineteenth century has missed the point. This philosophy could no longer live up to its principal task; it had almost forgotten that universal *function* that philosophy has to fulfill is man's social, political, and cultural life.

Can we accept this radical solution, this hard and rigorous verdict? Can we forget and obliterate all the great achievements of the philosophy of the nineteenth century? Is it fair to condemn all the great thinkers of this period in a body indiscriminately? Is there no point of contact between Schweitzer's ethical thought and the systems of these thinkers? According to Schweitzer, the strongest, nay the only, influences in man's cultural life are *rationalism* and *optimism*. Without these influences all hope for a restoration of civilization is lost. "Rationalism" is much more than a movement of thought which realized itself at the end of the eighteenth and the beginning of the nineteenth centuries. It is the everlasting and inexhaustible source of all true cultural life. All real progress in the world is in the last analysis produced by rationalism. "It is true that the intellectual productions of the period which we designate historically as the rationalistic are incomplete and unsatisfactory, but the principle, which was then established, of basing our views of the universe on thought and thought alone, is valid for all time. Even if the tree's earliest fruits did not fully ripen, the tree itself remains, the tree of life for the life of our spirit." But rationalism does not mean a merely theoretical ideal. It is no mere intellectualism; it must be complemented and perfected by another impulse by the force of optimism. Of what character must the theory be if ideas and convictions are to be based on it? It must be optimistic and ethical. That theory of the universe is optimistic which gives existence the preference as against non-existence and thus affirms life as something possessing value in itself. From this attitude to the universe and to life results the impulse to raise existence, insofar as our influence can affect it, to its highest level of value. Hence originates activity directed to the improvement of the living conditions of individuals, of society, of nations, and of humanity, from which spring the external achievements of civilization, the lordship of spirit over the powers of nature, and the higher social organization." (p 93, ff.)

All this is clear and convincing—but can we really say that this judgment does justice to the fundamental tendencies of the philosophy of the nineteenth century? The objections to this view seem to be obvious. One of the predominant metaphysical systems of the nineteenth century was the system of Hegel. No other thinker has exerted such a deep influence upon our modern moral, political, and social ideas. This influence was not confined within the limit of a special field or a special school. It extended over the whole sphere of modern cultural life. By its adversaries, Hegelianism was often said to be definitely dead. But this sentence was always belied by its further development. The Hegelian system proved to be a phoenix which, after being consumed by the flames, arose from the ashes in a rejuvenated state. All the great currents of philosophic thought in the nineteenth century attest to this unbroken and enduring power of Hegel's system.

There were Hegelian "materialists" as well as Hegelian "spiritualists"; there were Hegelian theists, pantheists, and even atheists. Nor was Hegel's influence felt only in German thought. It extended over all nations. There was a "Hegel-Renaissance" in the Netherlands, in Italy, in England, in America. It is enough to mention the names of Bowne, Howland, of Benedetto Croce, of Bradley, and Bosanquet, of Emerson, of Josiah Royce, and W. E. Hocking to measure the extent and the depth of this Renaissance. But if this is true how can we charge the philosophy of the nineteenth century and our own contemporary philosophy with a lack of "rationalism" and "optimism"? Were not rationalism and optimism the strongest and predominant powers in Hegel's thought? His optimism was almost unbounded. Schopenhauer spoke of the Hegelian optimism as being not only absurd but even nefarious. It was the principal aim of Hegel's philosophy of history "to justify the despised reality," to give a "theodicy" widely superior to that of Leibniz. "Our intellectual striving", he said in the introduction to his *Lectures on the Philosophy of History,* "aims at realizing the conviction that what was *intended* by eternal wisdom is actually accomplished in the domain of existent, active Spirit, as well in that of mere Nature. Our mode of treating the subject is, in this aspect, a Theodicæa— a justification of the ways of God—so that the ill that is found in the world may be comprehended, and the thinking Spirit reconciled with the fact of the existence of evil."*

On the other hand, the Hegelian system proved to be the firmest stronghold of rationalism. What Hegel tried to prove was not only the *harmony,* but the *identity* of reason and reality. The Rational *is* the Real, the Real *is* the Rational. The Real is not and never has been so feeble as merely to have a right or an *ought* to exist without actually existing.**

The only thought which philosophy brings with it to the contemplation of history is the simple conception of *reason;*

* Hegel: *Lectures on the Philosophy of History* (English translation by J. Sibree) London 1857, p. 16.
** Hegel's *Encyclopaedia of the Philosophical Sciences (Werke)* ed Marheinecke, vol. VI, p. 10.

[249]

that Reason is the sovereign of the world; that the history of
the world, therefore, presents us with a rational process.
This conviction and intuition is a hypothesis in the domain
of history as such. In that of philosophy it is no hypothesis.
It is there proved by speculative cognition that Reason is
substance as well as infinite power; its own infinite material
underlying all the natural and spiritual life which it originates, as also the infinite form—that which sets this material
in motion.*

Schweitzer's judgment about the general character of the philosophy of the nineteenth century is, therefore, a great paradox.
Here we are caught on the horns of a real dilemma. Even if we
subscribe to the judgment itself, we cannot accept its historical
premises. On this point the analysis of Schweitzer seems to break
down. Schweitzer's accusation and condemnation is absolute and
uncompromising. It does not admit of any exception. As regards
the principal and fundamental question all the various schools
and systems are in the same predicament. None of them lived up
to its essential task; none of them had a true conception of what
philosophy is and ought to be. "The decisive element", says
Schweitzer, "was philosophy's renunciation of her duty. In the
eighteenth century, and the early part of the nineteenth it was
philosophy which led and guided thought in general. She had
busied herself with the questions which presented themselves to
mankind at each successive period, and had kept the thought of
civilized man actively reflecting upon them. But since that time
the ethical ideals on which civilization rests have been wandering about the world, poverty-stricken and homeless. No theory
of the universe has been advanced which can give them a solid
foundation; in fact, not one has made its appearance which can
claim for itself solidity and inner consistency. In spite of all her
learning philosophy had become a stranger to the world, and the

* Hegel's *Lectures on the Philosophy of History* (English translation, p. 9.).

problems of life which occupied men and the whole thought of
the age had no part in her activities. Her way lay apart from
the general spiritual life, and just as she derived no stimulus
from the latter, so she gave none back. Philosophy philosophized
about everything except civilization. She went on working un-
deviatingly at the establishment of a theoretical view of the
universe, as though by means of it everything could be restored,
and did not reflect that this theory, even if it were completed,
would be constructed only out of history and science, and would
accordingly be unoptimistic and unethical, and would remain for
ever an "impotent theory of the universe," which could never
call forth the energies needed for the establishment and mainte-
nance of the ideals of civilization. So little did philosophy philo-
sophize about civilization that she did not even notice ,that she
herself, and the age along with her, were losing more and more
of it. In the hour of peril, the watchman who ought to have
kept us awake was himself asleep, and the result was that we
put up no fiight at all on behalf of our civilization." (p. 8, *ff.*)

In order to understand this judgment, we must bear in mind
the *specific* character of Schweitzer's "rationalism" and "optimism." Hegel's rationalism was an *historical* rationalism, his is
an *ethical* rationalism. Hegel identified rationality with *reality;*
Schweitzer thinks of reason, first and foremost, as a practical
power to organize the human world. Following the way of Kant
he accepts the principle of the "primacy of practical reason."
It follows from this conception that Schweitzer, in spite of his
rationalism and optimism, emphasizes much more the *tension*
between "reason" and "reality" than their harmony or "identity."
By virtue of this alleged identity, Hegel had been led to his
theory of the historical world. "That this 'Idea' or 'Reason' is
the true, the eternal, the absolutely powerful essence"—says
Hegel in the Introduction to his *Lectures on the Philosophy of
History*—"that it reveals itself in the world and that in that
world nothing else is revealed but this and its honor and glory—

is the thesis which has been proved in philosophy, and is here regarded as demonstrated."*

Here we grasp the fundamental difference between Hegel's and Schweitzer's conception of man's ethical life. Their "rationalism" is not on the same level. We must not allow ourselves to be deceived by the use of the term: "Reason." In Hegel's system "reason" means a metaphysical, not an ethical principle. It is a substantial power which does its work and performs its task regardless of the thought, the wishes, the demands, or actions of the individual men. The individuals are not the real actors. They suppose themselves to be the propellers; but they are themselves pushed forward by another and more powerful force. Individual desires and passions, individual merits and failures, noble deeds and crimes are nothing but the means of which the World-Spirit avails itself in order to execute its design. "Against the doctrine that the idea is a mere idea," says Hegel in the preface to his *Philosophy of Right,* "philosophy preserves the more profound view that nothing is real except the idea. Hence arises the effort to recognize in the temporal and transient the substance which is immanent and the eternal, which is present. The rational is synonymous with the idea, because in realizing itself it passes into external existence. It thus appears in an endless wealth of forms, figures, and phenomena. It wraps its kernel round with a robe of many colours in which consciousness finds itself at home. Through this varied husk the conception first of all penetrates in order to touch the pulse and then feel it throbbing in its external manifestations."**

In Hegel's philosophy, "reason" is far above the sphere of the mere human world. Its true manifestations are not to be found in the sphere of the "subjective" but in the sphere of the "objective mind" and of the "absolute mind." This "more profound view" is entirely rejected by Schweitzer. According to him, the

---

* Hegel, *op. cit.,* English translation, p. 10.
** Hegel: *Philosophy of Right* (English translation by Dyde) p. XXVII.

metaphysical, the Hegelian, depth is only an apparent depth. To him there is no greater depth than the depth of individual life and individual consciousness. It is here that we have to seek the very centre of our cultural life. If we give up this centre we have not only lost ourselves, we have also lost our hold of reality.

The most striking expression of this fundamental difference is to be found in a terminological distinction that first was introduced by Hegel. Hegel makes a sharp and clear-cut distinction between what he calls "*Moralität*" and what he calls "*Sittlichkeit*." Up to his time, the two terms had been used as synonyms: there was no difference between the "moral" and the "ethical" order. But according to Hegel that was a grave mistake. "Morality" (*Moralität*) belongs to the sphere of the individual will and the individual consciousness, whereas *Sittlichkeit* (ethicalness) belongs to the sphere of the objective mind, that objective mind which is represented by and embodied in the life of the state. Both spheres cannot be judged and measured by the same standards. They are incommensurate with one another. As to the rank and dignity of the two spheres, there can be no doubt in the Hegelian system. Morality has no right of its own; it is inferior and subordinate to the only universal will, the will of the state. Hegel emphatically denies that there are such things as the so-called inviolable and inalienable rights of the individuals. As against the state, individuals have no rights and no claims whatever. "All right," says Hegel in his treatise on the German constitution, "originates from the state. It is the state that has to decide, not chance, not documents nor other legal titles. Since the rules of morality apply only to private life and private conduct, they are not applicable to political life, to the conduct of states."

By this conception, "custom" ("*Sitte*") becomes a necessary and predominant element in man's ethical life. Hegel has maintained this view consistently from the initial stages of his philosophy up to its finale. It is clearly and unmistakably expressed in one of his earliest works, in the treatise concerning the scientific modes of treating "natural right," written in 1802. "The striving for a morality of one's own," declares Hegel, "is futile, and by its very nature impossible of attainment; in regard to morality, the saying of the wisest man of antiquity is the only true one—to be moral is to live in accordance with the moral traditions of one's country."*

According to Schweitzer, such a traditionalism is the very death-blow of ethics. And it becomes so much the more dangerous if we bear in mind the special conditions of our modern social life. One of the most serious symptoms of modern civilization is the predominance of the collective spirit. Our feelings and opinions are under a constant pressure. We no longer think our own thoughts; we think the thoughts of others. Not only our life but even our judgments are regulated and canalized.

Our whole spiritual life nowadays has its course within organizations. From childhood up, the man of today has his mind so full of the thought of discipline that he loses the sense of his own individuality and can only see himself as thinking in the spirit of some group or other of his fellows. The modern man is lost in the mass in a way which is without precedent in history, and this is perhaps the most characteristic trait in him. He is like a rubber ball which has lost its elasticity, and preserves indefinitely every impression that is made upon it. Yet this abnormal subjection to external influences does not strike him as a weakness. He looks upon it as an achievement; and in his unlimited spiritual devotion to the interests of the community he thinks he is preserving the greatness of the modern man . . . During the war the control of thought was made complete. Propaganda definitely too takes the place of truth . . . If we find among men of today only too few whose human and moral sensibility is still undamaged, the chief reason is that the

* Hegel: *Sämtl. Werke,* ed. Manheinecke, 2nd ed., vol. I, p. 389.

majority have offered up their personal morality on the altar of their country, instead of remaining at variance with the mass and acting as a force which impels the latter along the road to perfection . . . And so we wander hither and thither in the gathering dusk formed by lack of any definite theory of the universe, like homeless drunken mercenaries, and enlist indifferently in the service of the common and the great without distinguishing between them. And the more hopeless the condition of the world becomes in which this adventurous impulse to action and progress ranges to and fro, the more bewildered becomes our whole conception of things, and the more purposeless and irrational the doings of those who have enlisted under the banner of such an impulse. (p. 29 *ff*, p. 97 *f*).

What has the philosophy of the nineteenth century done to avoid this danger and to struggle against it? As Schweitzer points out, it marks the greatness of the eighteenth century that fear of public opinion was then unknown. All ideas had then to justify themselves to individual reason. This great heritage was lost during the nineteenth century; and, curiously and paradoxically enough, it was not the materialism of the nineteenth century but rather the very *idealistic* systems that were responsible for this loss. For in these systems the centre of gravity was shifted. *Historical* thought definitely took precedence over ethical thought. Ethics itself abdicated its inherent rights; it submitted to the verdict of historical reality.

To say that Hegel was simply the "philosopher of the Prussian State" would not do full justice to his political and philosophical system. He did not mean to stabilize or perpetuate any *particular* stage of history. But his system became an apotheosis of the historical process taken as a whole. To him the history of the world was the judgment of the world. To contest this judgment is vain and futile; for there is no higher Court of Appeal than the Reason of history. Even for philosophy the decision of this court is indisputable and irrevocable. That follows from the very definition of philosophy given in Hegel's system. Philosophy is nothing but "its time apprehended in thoughts." It is foolish to think that any philosophy can transcend its present world. The clearest and most striking expression of this view is given in Hegel's famous words in the introduction to his *Philosophy of Law.* "To understand *what is,* is the task of philosophy; for what *is,* that is Reason. One word more concerning the information what the word ought to be; *for that end philosophy always comes too late.* Philosophy, as the thought of the world, does not appear until reality has completed its formative process and made itself ready. What is thus thought by the nation, history also shows to be necessary; only in the ripeness of reality does the ideal appear over against the actual, and builds up for itself that same world, apprehended in its substance into an intellectual kingdom. When philosophy paints its grey in grey, one form of life has become old, and by means of grey in grey, it cannot be rejuvenated but only known. The veil of Minerva takes its flight only when the shades of night are gathering."

This conception of philosophy is in flagrant contradiction with Schweitzer's "ethical optimism." He assigns to philosophic thought the very opposite rôle. He does not admit that, for the reconstruction of our social, our ethical, and cultural life, philosophy "always comes too late." It only comes too late when it begins to forget its mission and its principal duty, when it yields to the pressure of external forces instead of using its own powers and confiding in these powers. "The beginning of all spiritual life of any real value," says Schweitzer, "is courageous faith in truth and open confession of the same." (p. 102). To be sure, it would be absurd to charge the Hegelian system with a lack of this "courageous faith in truth." No thinker before Hegel had ever put philosophy on such a high pedestal as he did. It is described by him as a culmination, the very zenith of man's cultural life. It is all-comprehensive; it embraces and preserves all the former steps of the dialectic process, it is higher than art and religion. When Hegel, after a long interruption of his academic work, resumed his philosophical lectures in Heidelberg, he expressed this conviction in the most impressive manner. "The courage of truth," he said, "the belief in the power of spirit is the first condition of philosophy. Man, being spirit, must esteem himself and ought to deem himself worthy of the highest rank; he cannot esteem too highly the greatness and power of his spirit, and in this belief, nothing will be so hard and unyielding as not to be open to him. The essence of the universe at first hidden and closed, has no power by which it would be able to withstand the courage of knowledge: it must become manifest; it must show its wealth and its depth and surrender them to the enjoyment of knowledge." But the "courage of truth" and the "enjoyment of knowledge" are not the same in Hegel and in Schweitzer. Hegel purported to understand, to interpret, and justify his "present world." But he never meant to turn the tide of history. To swim against the tide was to him an impossible thought. If a theory transgresses its time, he declared, and builds up a world as it ought to be, it has an existence merely in the unstable element of opinion, which gives room to every wandering fancy. It needed a great intellectual and moral courage to attack this philosophical quietism. What Schweitzer demands of philosophy is much more. He assigns to it the leading rôle in the great process of the reconstruction of modern civilization. But to this end, it must first reconstruct and regenerate itself. It must recognize its fundamental duties before it can regain its place in modern cultural life.

WHAT IS CIVILIZATION?

By

Ananda K. Coomaraswamy, D. Sc.
Museum of Fine Arts in Boston

CHAPTER XII

WHAT IS CIVILIZATION?

BY

ANANDA K. COOMARASWAMY

From Albert Schweitzer's own writings it is clear that, aside from his more active life of good works, his theoretical interest centres in the questions: What is civilization? and, How can it be restored? For, of course, he sees very clearly that the modern "civilised" world, so self-styled, is not really a civilized world at all, but as he calls it, a world of "Epigoni," inheritors, rather than creators of any positive goods.

To the question: What is civilization? I propose to contribute a consideration of the intrinsic meanings of the words "civilisation," "politics,"—and "Puruṣa." The root in "*civ*ilisation" is KEI, as in κεῖσθαι, Skr. *śī*, to "lie," "lie outstretched," "be located in." A city is thus a "lair," in which the *cit*izen "makes his bed" on which he must lie. We shall presently ask "Who?" thus inhabits and "economizes." The root in "*pol*itics" is PLA as in πίμπλημι, Skr. *pṛ* (*piparmi*) to "fill," πόλις, Skr. *pur*, "city," "citadel," "fortress," Lat. *plenum*, Skr. *pūrṇam*, and E. "fill." The roots in *puruṣa* are these two and the intrinsic meaning therefore that of "citizen," either as "man" (this man, So-and-so) or as the Man (in this man, and absolutely); in either way, the *puruṣa* is the "person" to be distinguished by his powers of foresight and understanding from the animal man (*paśu*) governed by his "hunger and thirst."*

In Plato's thought there is a cosmic city of the world, the city state, and an individual body politic, all of which are communities (κοινωνία, *gaṇa*). "the same castes (γένος, Skr. *jāti*), equal

---

* As in *Aitareya Āraṇyaka* II.3.2 and Boethius, *Contra Evtychen.*

in number are* to be found in the city and in the soul (or self) of each of us"; the principle of justice is the same throughout, viz. that each member of the community should perform the tasks for which he is fitted by nature; and the establishment of justice and well-being of the whole in each case depends upon the answer to the question, Which shall rule, the better or the worse, a single Reason and Common Law or the multitude of moneyed men in the outer city and of desires in the individual (*Republic* 441, etc.)

Who fills, or populates, these cities? Whose are these cities, "ours" or God's? What is the meaning of "self-government? (a question that, as Plato shows, *Republic* 436 B, implies a distinction of governor from governed). Philo says that "As for lordship (κυρίως), G o d is the only c i t i z e n" (μόνος πολίτης, *Cher.* 121), and this is almost identical with the words of the Upaniṣad, "This Man (*puruṣa*) is the citizen (*puruṣaya*) in every city, (sarvāsu pūrṣu, Bṛhadāraṇyaka Upaniṣad II.5.18), and must not be thought of as in any way contradicted by Philo's other statement, that "Adam" (not "this man," but the true Man) is the "only citizen of the world" (μόνος κοσμοπολίτης, *Opif.* 142). Again, "This city (*pur*) is these worlds, the Person (*puruṣa*) is the Spirit (*yo'yam pavate*=Vāyu), who because he inhabits (*śete*) this city is called the 'Citizen' (*puru-ṣa*)", *Śatapatha Brāhmaṇa* XIII.6.2.1,—as in *Atharva Veda* X.2.30, where "He who knoweth Brahma's city, whence the Person (*puru-ṣa*) is so-called, him neither sight nor the breath of life desert ere old age," but now the "city" is that of this body, and the "citizens" its God-given powers.

These macrocosmic and microcosmic points of view are interdependent; for the "acropolis", as Plato calls it, of the city is within you, and literally at the "heart" of the city. "What is

---

* Plato's Immortal Soul (Self), and two parts of the mortal soul (self), together with the body itself, make up the normal number of "four castes" that must cooperate for the benefit of the whole community.

within this City of God (*brahma-pura*, this man) is a shrine,* and what therein is Sky and Earth, Fire and the Gale, Sun and Moon, whatever is possest or unpossest; everything here is within it." The question arises, What then is left over (survives) when this 'city' dies of old age or is destroyed? and the answer is that what survives is That which ages not with our inveteration, and is not slain when 'we' are killed; *That* is the '*true* City of God';** *That* (and by no means this perishable city that we think of as 'our' self) is our Self, unaging and immortal,*** unaffected by 'hunger and thirst," (*Chāndogya Upaniṣad* VIII.1.1-5, slightly abbreviated), "That art thou" (*ib.* VI.8.7); and "Verily, he who sees That, contemplates That, discriminates That, he whose game and sport, dalliance and beatitude are in and with that Self (*ātman*), he is autonomous (*sva-rāj*, κρείττων ἑαυτοῦ, self-governing), he moveth at will in every world;**** but those whose knowing is of what is other-than-That are heteronomous (*anya-rāj*, ἥττων ἑαυτοῦ, subject), they move not at will in any world" (*ib.* VII.25.2).

Thus at the heart of this City of God inhabits (*śete*) the omniscient, immortal Self, "this self's immortal Self and Duke," as the Lord of all, the Protector of all, the Ruler of all beings and the Inward-Controller of all the powers of the soul by which he is surrounded, as by subjects*****; and "to Him (*Brahma*), thus proceeding in Person (*puruṣa*), as he lies there extended (*uttā-nāya śayānāye*), and enthroned (*brahmāsandhīm ārūḍhā, atra-*

* The kingdom of God is within you" (Luke XVII. 21); ἐν αὐτῷ πολιτεία (*Republic* 591 E). The King survives his kingdoms and "lives forever." Just as, in the traditional theory of government, the Kingship immanent in kings antecedes them and survives them, "le roi est mort, vive le roi."

** Plato's πόλις ἐν λόγοις (Skr. *śrute*), κειμένη, ἐπεὶ γῆς γε οὐδαμοῦ (*Republic* 592 A.)

*** That eternally youthful Spiritual-Self of which whoever is a Comprehensor has no fear of death (*Atharva Veda* X.8.44).

**** This liberty, so often spoken of in the Vedic tradition from *Ṛgveda* IX.113.9 onwards, corresponds to the Platonic term αὐτοκίνησις (*Phaedrus* 245D, *Laws* 895B, C) and to John X.9 "shall go in and out, and find pasture."

***** *Bṛhadāraṇyaka Upaniṣad* III. 8.23, IV.4.22, *Kaṭha Upaniṣad* II.18, *Muṇḍaka Upaniṣad* II.2. 6, 7, *Maitri Upaniṣad* VI. 7 etc.

sada), the powers of the soul (devatā, prāṇā), voice, mind, sight, hearing, scent, bring tribute"***.

The word "extended" here states a meaning already implied in the etymology of the "city," KEI including the sense to lie at full length, or outstretched.**** The root in "extended" and ut-tāna is that in τείνω and Skr. tan, to extend, prolong, in τόνος, a string, and hence also, tone, and in tenuis, Skr. tanu, thin.

Not only are these worlds a city, or am "I" a city, but these are populated cities, and not waste lands, because He fills, them, being "one as he is in himself there, and many in his children here" (Śatapatha Brāhmaṇa X.5.2.16). "That dividing itself unmeasured times, fills (pūrayati)* these worlds . . . from It continually proceed all animate beings" (Maitri Upaniṣad V.26). Or with specific reference to the powers of the soul within the individual city, "He, dividing himself fivefold, is concealed in the cave (of the heart) . . . Thence, having broken forth the doors of the sensitive powers, he proceeds to the fruition of experience . . . And so this body is set up in the possession of consciousness, He is its driver" (ib. II.6.d).** This "division,"

***
*** Jaiminīya Upaniṣad Brāhmaṇa IV.23.7-23.10, somewhat condensed.

**** The divine extension in the three dimensional space of the world that is thus filled is a cosmic crucifixion to which the local crucifixion in two dimensions corresponds. To the extent that we think of Him as really divided up by this extension, i.e. to the extent that we conceive of our being as "our own," we crucify him daily.

* Causative of pṛ, the root in pur; and so "populates" or even "civilizes."

** .ψυχὴ μὲν ἐστιν ἡ περιάγουσα ἡμῶν πάντων, Laws 898 C; Questi nei cor mortali è permotore, Paradiso I.116; "the heart has pulled the reins of the five senses" (Rūmī, Mathnawi, I.3275). Throughout the Vedic tradition (most explicitly in Kaṭha Upaniṣad III.3 f. and Jātaka VI. 242) as in Plato (Phaedrus 246 f). Philo (LA.I.72, 73, III.224, Spec. IV.79, etc.) and Boethius, etc., man's constitution in which the spiritual Self-of-all-beings rides as passenger for so long as the vehicle holds together; mind (manas, νοῦς) holds the reins, but being twofold, clean or unclean, disinterested or interested, may either control or be run away with by the team of the senses. The "chariot," "city," "ship" and "puppet" symbols are equivalent, so that, for example, "when Mind as charioteer rules the whole living being, as a governor does a city, then life holds a straight course," (Philo, LA III.224, cf. Rgveda VI.75.6). The whole conception of yoga (yuj, to "yoke", "harness", "join") is connected with the symbolism of the chariot and team; we still speak of "bridling" our passions.

however, is only as it were, for the remains "undivided in divided beings" (*Bhagavad Gītā* XIII.16. XVII.20), "uninterrupted" (*anantaram*) and thus is to be understood as an undivided and total presence.

The "division," in other words, is not a segmentation, but an extension, as of radii from a centre or rays of light from a luminous s o u r c e with which they are con-tinuous.* Con-*tin*uity and in-*ten*sity (*samatati,* συντον'α) are, indeed, a necessary quality in whatever can be tensed and extended but, like the immanent Spirit, "cannot be severed" (*acchedya, Bhagavad Gītā* II.23),—"no part of that which is divine cuts itself off and becomes separated, but only extends (ἐκτείνεται=*vitanute*) itself" (Philo, *Det.* 90). It is then, the same thing to say that the Person "fills" these worlds as to say that Indra saw this Person "as the most widely extended (*tatamam*) Brahma" (*Aitareya Araṇyaka* II.4.3). In this way all the powers of the soul, projected by the mind towards their objects, are "extensions" (τεταμένα) of an invisible principle (*Republic* 462 E), and it is this "tonic power" by which it is enabled to perceive them (Philo, *LA.* I.30, 37). Our "constitution" is a habitation that the Spirit makes for itself "just as a goldsmith draws-out-for-himself (*tanute*) from the gold another shape" (*Bṛhadāraṇyaka Upaniṣad* IV.4.4).**

This is an essential aspect of the "thread-spirit" (*sūtrātman*) doctrine, and as such the intelligible basis of that of the divine omniscience and providence, to which our partial knowledge and foresight are analogous. The spiritual Sun (not that "sun whom all men see" but that "whom few know with the mind," *Atharva*

---

* Hence *vi-rāj*, literally a "distributive shining"="ruling power."

** Gold in such contexts is not a figure of speech, but of thought. Gold "is" (we should now say "means") light, life, immortality (*Śatapatha Brāhmaṇa,* passim, and traditionally); and to "refine" this "gold" is to burn away from our spiritual Self the dross of all that is not-Self. Hence it is a "golden" cord by which the human puppet is rightly guided (Plato. *Laws* 644) and Blake gives us a "golden" string that "will lead you in at heaven's gate."

Veda X.8.14)** is the Self of the whole universe (*Ṛgveda* I. 11.1) and is connected to all things in it by the "thread" of his luminous pneumatic rays, on which the "tissue" of the universe is woven,—"all this universe is strung on Me, like rows of gems on a thread" (*Bhagavad Gītā* VII.7); of which thread, running through our intellect, the ultimate strands are its sensitive powers, as we have already seen.*** So, just as the noonday sun "sees" all things under the sun at once, the "Person in the Sun", the Light of lights, from the exalted point and centre "wherein every where and every when is focussed" (*Paradiso* XXIX.23) is simultaneously present to every experience, here or there, past or future, and "not a sparrow falls to the ground" or ever has or ever will without his present knowledge. He is, in fact, the only seer, thinker etc., in us (*Bṛhadāraṇyaka Upaniṣad* III.8.23), and whoever sees or thinks, etc., it is by *His* "ray" that he does so (*Jaiminīya Upaniṣad Brāhmaṇa,* I.28, 29).

Thus in the human City of God which we are considering as a political pattern, the sensitive and discriminating powers form, so to speak, a body of guardsmen by which the Royal Reason is conducted to the perception of sense objects, and the heart is the guardroom where they take their orders (Plato, *Timaeus* 70 B, Philo *Opif.* 139, *Spec.* .IV.22, etc.). These powers—how-

** Sun of the sun," *Mahābhārata* V. 46, 3 and Philo. *Spec.* I.279; "invisible light perceptible only by mind," Philo, *Opif.* 31; "whose body the sun is, who controls the sun from within," *Bṛhadāraṇyaka Upaniṣad* III. 7. 9; "whose body is seen by all, his soul by none" Plato, *Laws* 898 D; "Light of lights," *Bhagavad Gītā* X II. 17, *Ṛgveda* I. 113.1; "that was the true Light . . . of the world," John I. 9, IX.5; "the Sun of men," *Ṛgveda* I.146,4 and "Light of men," John 1.4, "seated in every heart," *Bhagavad Gītā* XIII.17, *Maitri Upaniṣad* VI. 1.

*** We cannot expound the "thread-spirit" doctrine at length here. In the European tradition it can be traced from Homer to Blake. For some of the references see my "Primitive Mentality," *Q. J. Myth. Soc.* XXXI, 1940 and "Literary Symbolism" in the *Dictionary of World Literature,* 1943. See Philo, *Immut.* 35 and passim; also my "Spiritual Paternity, and the Puppet Complex" in *Psychiatry* VIII, 1945.

ever referred to as Gods,* Angels, Aeons, Maruts, Ṛṣis, Breaths, Daimons, etc. — are the people (viśa, yeomanry, etc.) of the heavenly kingdom, and related to their Chief (viśpati) as are thanes to an Earl or ministers to a King; they are a troop of the "King's Own" (svā), by which he is surrounded as if by a crown of glory,—"upon whose head the Aeons are a crown of glory darting forth rays" (Coptic Gnostic Treatise XI), and "by 'thy glory' I understand the powers that form thy bodyguard" (Philo, Spec. I. 45)**. The whole relationship is one of feudal loyalty, the subjects bringing tribute and receiving largesse, —"Thou art ours and we are thine" (Rgveda VIII.93.2), "Thine may we be for thee to give us treasure" (ib. V.85.8. etc.).*** What must never be forgotten is that all "our" powers are

* Or Sons of God. Cf. Behmen, Sig. Rer. XVI. 5 "Each angelical prince is a property out of the voice of God, and bears the great name of God." It is with reference to these powers that it is said that "All these Gods are in me" (Jaiminīya Upaniṣad Brāhmaṇa I.14.2), that "All things are full of Gods" (Thales, cited Plato, Laws 899 B) and that "Making the Man (puruṣa) their mortal house, the Gods indwelt him" (Atharva Veda XI.8.18); accordingly, "He is indeed initiated, whose "Gods within him" are initiated, mind by Mind, voice by Voice" etc. (Kauṣītaki Brāhmaṇa VII.4). We need hardly say that such a multiplicity of Gods—"tens and thousands"—is not a polytheism, for all are the angelic subjects of the Supreme Deity from whom they originate and in whom, as we are so often reminded, they again "become one." Their operation is an epiphany (Kauṣītaki Upaniṣad II.12, 13,—"This Brahma, verily, shines when one sees with the eye, and likewise dies when one does not see"). These "Gods" are Angels, or as Philo calls them, the Ideas,—i.e. Eternal Reasons.

** The double meaning of στέφανος must be remembered, (1) as "crown" and (2) as city "wall"; thus both a glory and a defence. "Children are a man's crown, towers of the 'city'" (Homeric Epigrams XIII). In the same way Pali cūlikā, usually "turban," is also a "city wall," as in Saṃyutta Nikāya, II.182 nagaram '. . . . cūlikā-baddham.
Philo's interpretation of the "glory" has an exact equivalent in India, where the powers of the soul are "glories" (śriyaḥ) and collectively "the kingdom, the power and the glory" (śrī) of their royal possessors; and, accordingly, the whole science of government is one of the control of these powers (Arthaśāstra I.6, see my Spiritual Authority and Temporal Power in the Indian Theory of Government, 1942, p. 86),—Non potest aliquis habere ordinatam familiam, nisi ipse sit ordinatus, St. Bonaventura, De don. S. S. IV.101, p. 475, being applicable to everyone who proposes to govern himself, a city or a kingdom.

*** On bhakti ("devotion", or perhaps better "fealty", and literally "participation) as a reciprocal relaionship see my Spiritual Authority . . . ., note 5 and Hinduism and Buddhism, 1943, p. 20.

not our "own", but *delegated* powers and ministries through the royal Power is "exercised" (another sense of τείνω); the powers of the soul "are only the names of His acts" (*Bṛhadāraṇyaka Upaniṣad* I.4.7, I.5.21, etc.).* It is not for them to serve their own or one another's self-interests—of which the only result will be the tyranny of the majority, and a city divided against itself, man against man and class against class—but to serve Him whose sole interest is that of the common body politic. Actually, in the numerous accounts we have of a contest for precedence amongst the powers of the soul, it is always found that none of the members or powers is indispensible to the life of the bodily city, except only their Head, the Breath and immanent Spirit.

The right and natural life of the powers of the soul is then, precisely, their function of bringing tribute to their fountainhead, the controlling Mind and very Self, as man brings sacrificial offerings to an altar, keeping for themselves only what remains. It is the task of each to perform the functions for which it is fitted by nature, the eye seeing, the ear hearing, all of which functions are necessary to the well-being of the community of the whole man but must be coordinated by a disinterested power that cares for all. For unless this community can act unanimously, as one man, it will be working at all sorts of cross purposes. The concept is that of a corporation in which the several members of a community work together, each in its own way; and such a vocational society is an organ-

* " 'I' do nothing, so should deem the harnessed man, the knower of Ultimate Reality" (*Bhagavad Gītā* V. 8). "I do nothing of myself" John VIII.28, cf. V.19). To think that " 'I' do" (*karto'ham iti*) or " 'I' think" is an infatuation, Philo's οἴησις (*LA* 1.47, 11.67, 111.33) and Indian *abhimāna*. The proposition, *Cogito ergo sum* is a *non sequitur* and non-sense; the true conclusion being, *Cogito ergo EST*, with reference to Him "who Is" (Damascene, *De fid. orthod.* I.; *Katha Upaniṣad* VI.12; *Milinda Pañha* p.73) and can alone say "I" (Meister Eckhart, Pfeiffer, p. 261). Cf. also the references in my "Akimcaññā; Self-naughting", *New Ind. Antiquary,* 1940.

"*Nichts anders stürzet dich in Höllenschlund hinein Als das verhasste Wort (merk's wohl!) das Mein und Dein*"
Angelus Silesius, *Cherubinische Wandersmann,* V. 238.

ism, not an aggregate of competing interests, and consequently unstable "balance of power."

Thus the human City of God contains within itself the pattern of all other societies and of a true civilization. The man will be a "just" (δίχαιος) man when each of his members performs its own appropriate task and is subject to the ruling Reason that exercises forethought on behalf of the whole man; and in the same way the public city will be just when there is agreement as to which shall rule, and there is no confusion of functions but every occupation is a vocational responsibility. Not, then, where there are no "classes" or "castes" but where everyone is a responsible agent in some special field.* A city can no more be called a "good" city if it lacks this "justice"(δικαιοσύνη) than it could be were it wanting wisdom, sobriety or courage; and these four are the great civic virtues. Where occupations are thus vocations "more will be done, and better done, and with more ease than in any other way" (Republic 370 C). But "if one who is by nature a craftsman or some sort of business man be tempted and inflated by wealth or by his command of votes or by his own might or any such thing, and tries to handle military matters, or if a soldier tries to be a counsellor or guardian, for which he is unfitted, and if these men interchange their tools and honors, or if one and the same man tries to handle all these functions at once, then, I take it, you too hold that this sort of perversion and being jack-of-all-trades will be the ruin of the city"; and this is "injustice" (Republic 434 B).

Thus the ideal society is thought of as a kind of cooperative work-shop in which production is to be for use and not for profit, and all human needs, both of the body and the soul, are to be provided for. Moreover, if the command is to be fulfilled, "Be ye perfect even as your Father in heaven is perfect"

* In which case, every occupation is a profession; not merely a way of earning one's living, but a "way of life," to abandon which is to die a death. "The man who has shifted, easily and unworried so long as the pay was good, from one job to another, has no deep respect for himself" (Margaret Mead, And Keep Your Powder Dry, p. 222).

[269]

the work must be *perfectly* done.* The arts are not directed to the advantage of anything but their object (*Republic* 432 B), and that is that the thing made should be as perfect as possible for the purpose for which it is made. This purpose is to satisfy a human need (*Republic* 369 B, C); and so the perfectionism required, although not "altruistically" motivated, actually "serves humanity" in a way that is impossible where goods are made for sale rather than for use, and in quantity rather than quality. In the light of Plato's definition of "justice" as vocational occupation we can the better understand the words, "Seek first the kingdom of God and his *justice*, and these things shall be added unto you" (*Math.* VI.33).

The Indian philosophy of work is identical. "Know that action arises from Brahma. He who on earth doth not follow in his turn the wheel thus revolving, liveth in vain; therefore, without attachment to its rewards, ever be doing what should be done, for, verily, thus man wins the Ultimate. There is nothing I needs must do, or anything attainable that is not already mine: and yet I mingle in action. Act thou, accordingly, with a view to the welfare of the world; for whatever the superior does, others will also do; the standard he sets up, the world will follow. Better is one's own norm,** however deficient, than that

---

* It is a commonplace of Mediaeval theory that the craftsman's primary concern is with the good of the work to be done, and this means that it must be at the same time *pulcher et aptus*. A Buddhist text defining the entelechies of the different vocational groups calls that of the householder whose support is an art "perfected work" (*Anguttara Nikāya* III.363).

** *Sva-dharma=sva-karma*, Plato's (τὰ ἑαυτοῦ πράττειν, κατὰ φύσιν) *Dharma* is a pregnant term, difficult to translate in the present context cf. εἶδος in *Republic* 434 A. In general, *dharma* (literally *"support,"* *dhṛ* as in *dhruva*, "fixed", "Pole Star,' and Gk. θρόνος) is synonymous with 'Truth.' Than this ruling principle there is "nothing higher" (*Bṛhadāraṇyaka Upaniṣad*, I.4.14); *dharma* is the "king's King" (*Anguttara Nikāya* I.109), i. e. "King of kings"; and there can be no higher title than that of *dharma-rāja*, "King of Justice." Hence the well known designation of the veritable Royalty as Dharmarājā, to be distinguished from the personality of the king in whom it temporarily inheres. One's "own dharma" is precisely Plato's "justice,," viz. to perform the task for which one is naturally equipped. Justice, δίκη (Skr. √ *diś*, to "in*di*cate") represents in the same way the ultimate Index and standard by which all action must be judged. Dharma is *lex aeterna;* sva-dharma, *lex naturalis*.

of another well-done; better to die at one's own post, that of another is full of fear. . . . Vocations are determined by one's own nature. Man attains perfection through devotion to his own work. How? By praising Him in his own work, from whom is the unfolding of all beings and by whom this whole universe is extended (*tatam*, ⟨ *tan*). Better is a man's own work, even with its faults, than that of another well done; he who performs the task that his own nature lays upon him incurs no sin; one should never abandon his inherited* vocation."

On the one hand the inspired tradition rejects ambition, competition and quantitive standards; on the other, our modern "civilization" is based on the notions of social advancement, free** enterprise (devil take the hindmost) and production in quantity. The one considers man's needs, which are "but little here below"; the other considers his wants, to which no limit can be set, and of which the number is artificially multiplied by advertisement. The manufacturer for profit must, indeed, create an ever-expanding world market for his surplus produced by those whom Dr. Schweitzer calls "over-occupied men." It is fundamentally, the incubus of world trade that makes of industrial "civilizations" a "curse to humanity," and from the industrial concept of progress "in line with the manufacturing enterprise of civilization" that modern wars have arisen and will arise; it is on the same impoverished soil that empires have grown, and by the same greed that innumerable civilizations have been destroyed,—by Spaniards in South America, Japanese in Korea and by "white shadows in the South Seas." ***

Dr. Schweitzer himself records that "it is very hard to carry to completion a colonisation which means at the same time a

* For our tradition, procreation is a "debt," and its purpose is to maintain the continuity of ministerial functions in a stable society (see my *Hinduism and Buddhism*, note 146). For only so can the bases of civilization be preserved.

** *Bhagavad Gītā.*
(III.15-35 and XVIII.18-48, slightly abbreviated.)

*** Cf. my "Am I my Brother's Keeper?," *Asia and the Americas'* March, 1943.

true civilization. . . . The machine age brought upon mankind conditions of existence which made the possession of civilization difficult* . . . Agriculture and handicraft are the foundation of civilization . . . Whenever the timber trade is good, permanent famine reigns in the Ogowe region** . . . They live on imported rice and imported preserved foods, which they purchase with the proceeds of their labour . . . thereby making home industry impossible . . . As things are, the world trade which has reached them is a fact against which we and they are powerless."***

I do not consent to this picture of a *deus,* or much rather *diabolus, ex machina,* coupled as it is with a confession of impotence.**** If, indeed, our industrialism and trade practice are the mark of our uncivilization, how dare we propose to help others "to attain a condition of well-being"? The "burden" is of our own making and bows our own shoulders first. Are we to say that because of "economic determination" we are "impotent" to shake it off and stand up straight? That would be to accept the status of "Epigoni" once and for all, and to admit that our influence can only lower others to our own level.*****

---

* The machine . . . is the achievement of which man is capable if he relies entirely on himself—God is no longer needed . . . Eventually . . . (it) transforms him into a machine himself" (Ernst Niekisch quoted by Erich Meissner in *Germany in Peril,* 1942).

** "When nations grow old, the arts grow old, and commerce settles on every tree" (William Blake).

*** Albert Schweitzer, *Zwischen Wasser und Urwald,* cited in *My Life and Thought.*

**** "I have more faith than a grain of mustard seed in the future history of 'civilization', which I *know* now is doomed to destruction: what a joy it is to think of!" (William Morris). "For, by civilized men we now mean industrialized men, mechanized societies . . . We call all men civilized, if they employ the same mechanical techniques to master the physical world. And we call them so because we are certain that as the physical world is the only reality and as it only yields to mechanical manipulation, that is the only way to behave. Any other conduct can only spring from illusion; it is the behaviour of an ignorant, simple savage. To have arrived at this picture of reality is to be truly advanced, progressive, civilized" (Gerald Heard, *Man the Master,* p. 25). It is also to have arrived at what has properly been called a "world of impoverish-reality" (Iredell Jenkins), and one that can only impoverish those to whom we communicate it.

***** Cf. A. J. Krzenski, *Is Modern Culture Doomed?* 1942, esp. Msgr. G. B. O'Toole's Introduction, and Znaniecki as cited on p. 54, note; and Eric Gill, *It all goes together.*

As we have seen, in a true civilization, *laborate est orare*. But industrialism—"the mammon of in-justice" (ἀδικία) —and civilization are incompatible. It has often been said that one can be a good Christian even in a factory; it is no less true that one could be an even better Christian in the arena. But neither of these facts means that either factories or arenas are Christian or desirable institutions. Whether or not a battle of religion against industrialism and world trade can ever be won is no question for us to consider; our concern is with the task and not with its reward; our business is to be sure that in any conflict we are on the side of Justice.* Even as things are, Dr. Schweitzer finds his best excuse for colonial government in the fact that to some extent (however slightly) such governments protect subject peoples "from the merchant." Why not protect ourselves (the "guinea-pigs" of a well known book) from the merchant?. Would it not be better if, instead of tinkering with the inevitable consequences of "world trade," we considered its cause, and set about to re-form (*wideraufbauen* is Schweitzer's word) our own "civilization"? Or shall the uncivilized for ever pretend to "civilizing missions"?

To reform what has been deformed means that we must take account of an original "form," and that is what we have tried to do in historical analysis of the concept of civilization, based on Eastern and Western sources. Forms are by definition invisible to sense. The form of our City of God is one "that exists only in words, and nowhere on earth, but is, it seems, laid up in heaven for whomsoever will to contemplate, and as he does so, to inhabit; it can be seen only by the true philosophers who bend their energies towards those studies that nourish rather soul than body and never allow themselves to be carried away by the congratulations of the mob or without measure to in-

---

* Whoever owns a single share in any manufacturing enterprise for profit is to that extent taking sides and to that extent responsible for world trade and all its consequences.

crease their wealth, the source of measureless evils,* but rather fix their eyes upon their own interior politics, never *aiming* to be politicians in the city of their birth" (*Republic* 591 E f).

Is not Plato altogether right when he proposes to entrust the government of cities to "the uncorrupted remnant of true philosophers who now bear the stigma of uselessness,"** or even to those who are now in power "if by some divine inspiration*** a genuine love of true philosophy should take possession of them": and altogether right when he maintains that "no city ever can be happy unless its outlines have been drawn by draughtsmen making use of the divine pattern" (*Republic* 499, 500),—that of the City of God that is in heaven and "within you"?****

---

* The body, for the sake of which we desire wealth, is the ultimate cause of all wars (*Phaedo* 66 C); and "victory breeds hatred, because the conquered are unhappy" (*Dhammapada* 201). World trade and world war are congeneric evils. Whatever we have said about the government of men and cities will apply, of course, to a government of the world by cooperative and disinterested nations. Every attempt to establish "balances of power" must end in war.

** *Noblesse oblige.* In a city that has fostered "true philosophers" the latter owe it to their fosterers to participate in civic affairs and so it is in the traditional theory of government it is incumbent upon the representatives of the spiritual authority to oversee and guide those who exercise the temporal power; to see to it, in other words, that might supports right, and does not assert itself. On the function of such philosophers in the regeneration of modern society, cf., Gerald Heard, *Man the Master*, and Aldous Huxley, *Ends and Means.*

*** I suppose that in the history of criticism nothing more inane has ever been propounded than Paul Shorey's comment, "But we must not attribute personal *superstition* to Plato" (Loeb Library ed. p.64). Solecisms such as this must be expected whenever nominalists set out to expound the doctrine of realistic philosophers; but *why* do men set out to expound philosophies in which they do not believe?

**** The work to be done is primarily one of purgation, to drive out the money changers, all who *desire* power and office, and all representatives of special interests; and secondly, when the city has been thus cleaned up," one of the considered imitation of the natural forms of justice, beauty, wisdom and other civic virtues; amongst which we have here considered justice, or as the word δικαιοσύνη is commonly translated in Christian contexts, righteousness.

It may be, as Plato says, very "difficult" to bring about such a change of mind as is required if we are to "progress" *in this way*, but as he also says, it is "not impossible"; and so we may "not cease from Mental Fight . . . till we have built Jerusalem."

PART V

HUMANITIES

THE UNITY OF MANKIND

IN

THE CLASSICAL CHRISTIAN TRADITION

By

Roland H. Bainton, B.D., Ph.D.

Professor of Ecclesiastical History, Yale University

CHAPTER XIII

THE UNITY OF MANKIND IN THE CLASSICAL-CHRISTIAN TRADITION*

BY

ROLAND H. BAINTON, B.D., PhD.

One world is the cry of our generation. By it we mean not merely to assert the fact of globalism, but to voice an aspiration for the spiritual unity of mankind. We differ as to how it is to be achieved. Some are occupied in the drafting of blue-prints for the external. Others regard all plans as fatuous apart from a change in values. Albert Schweitzer long ago told us that the disease of our time is moral and the cure lies in no new formula but in that balance of self-fulfillment and self-effacement in harmonious living which is the core of the classical-Christian tradition. To some extent this ideal has received historical embodiment, notably in the Roman Empire and in Christendom, a somewhat amorphous entity hovering between an idea and an area. Christendom meant Christianity and Europe, but not the whole of either. The Byzantines and the Russians, though Christian, were scarcely included. The Jews and the Arabs though European were left out. Christendom was Christian Europe.

This paper will seek to trace the course of Christendom with an eye to its contribution to the unity of mankind. The ingredients of Christendom are classical and Christian, and they lie in the realms alike of idea and of the concrete. The Greeks developed the concept of cosmopolitanism, the Romans established

* *Editorial Note*: It was with reluctance that the scores of footnotes to this article, most of them bibliographical references, in many languages, were omitted because of the technical difficulties involved. It was kind of Professor Bainton to permit this elimination.

the *Pax Romana,* in which were further elaborated the ideals of peace and humanity.

Cosmopolitanism was built up actually by an expansion of loyalties. First came the Greek city state. Then the association of Hellenes who, possessed already of a common culture, were first made conscious of their unity by a common foe. The Persians taught the Greeks to think of themselves as Hellenes. The concept which accompanied this stage of development was that of concord (ὁμόνοια). It meant not universal harmony but only pan-Hellenic unity. Wars between the Greeks were inappropriate. Their conflicts indeed should not be dignified by the name of war, but rather should be called "disturbances," to be conducted with a mitigation of asperities. Such were the views of Plato and Aristotle, who never divested themselves of the restrictions of provisionalism.

The one who expanded Hellenism until it became a name for culture rather than for race was Alexander the Great. By some he is credited with being the first to conceive of the unity of mankind. His actual program, however, did not exceed the attempt to form a ruling caste compounded of Macedonians and Persians, and among the populace the stimulation of commerce and the planting of cities with Greek nuclei throughout the East. Unmistakably after Alexander we meet with genuine cosmopolitanism. Earlier in Greece the term had been coined in the mint of Diogenes and the connotations were negative. To be cosmopolitan was to be deracinated. After Alexander cosmopolitanism came to be conceived in terms not of the eradication but of the expansion of loyalty in concentric rings from the family to the city-state and to the world. Another approach was made by Stoicism which conceived of unity among men not as being built up by stages from the bottom but as already existing and needing only to be recognized throughout the universe as a whole. The world is one; harmony is the law of its being. The heavens above, the earth beneath, and even the animals are integrated by an all-pervading Reason which is intelligence in man and meaningfulness in the world. Animals of the same species do not devour each other. How much less should men? They will be able to live in peace if they order their lives in accord with the law of nature, a concept vague in content but vast in import of a moral order of the universe higher than the laws of states, self-validating through the Nemesis which overtakes those who violate the structure of the cosmos. Justice and good faith are among its ingredients.

The Greeks were never able to give concrete embodiment to their ideal. The nearest approach was interstate arbitration in which they excelled all the peoples of antiquity. Such continuous peaceful settlement of disputes was, however, intermittent and impotent to save the Greeks from devouring one another. Nor did the empire of Alexander correspond to his ideals. Hellenism was disseminated but the peoples of the East were never so united as were to be those of the West.

Unification in fact was to be the work of Rome. She was able to achieve it partly because she did not intend to. Of real imperialism at Rome before Julius Caesar one cannot properly speak. The earlier expansion was gradual and grudging, motivated by a desire for security. Rome was aided by a policy epitomized in the words concord and magnanimity. The first was the Greek *homonoia,* and meant no more than unity at home, with the discouragement of all uprisings like those of the Gracchi, even though in the interests of justice. Magnanimity, however, applied to those without. The word itself exhibits an interesting development. To begin with the *magna anima,* the quality of the great soul, (μεγαλοψυχία) was the courage of the warrior. Under Stoic influence it came to be the imperturbability arising from the mastery of the passions. Cicero voiced the new meaning when he exhorted Julius Caesar to forego the revenge of a Marius or a Sulla by treating his vanquished rivals with largeness of spirit, with magnanimity. The word had thus become a synonym for clemency, to whom as a goddess the Senate under Julius Caesar erected a temple. To this divinity Rome had long paid homage and she had her reward. At the approach of Hannibal the Italians declined to throw off the yoke and by the end of the Republican period the Samnites, Bruttians, Umbrians, and the other Italians had all become neo-Romans.

There was one exception to Roman clemency, namely Carthage. Her demolition was fraught with ill alike for Italy and for Africa. Before the event, Scipio Nascica foretold that the elimination of the foe would leave Rome a prey to internal dissension. In the ensuing disorders Sallust discerned the fulfilment of his prediction and the explanation of Roman degeneracy. In Africa the reduction of the Punic population left a residue of resentment. The like was not true elsewhere. Despite the brutality of the conquests, Spain and Gaul became cordially Roman; and for that matter, in Africa, the Roman element was more Latin than Rome herself. Coincident with the western was the eastern expansion of Rome. Although her conquests engendered temporary bitterness—witness the butchery of Romans by Mithridates —yet many peoples welcomed the termination of their dissensions through the imposition of a single sway. The rule of Rome was accepted as a boon by all save the Jews, who were celebrated in antiquity not for avarice but for their turbulence. They alone were permanently unreconciled to Rome.

Two concepts received development under the *Pax Romana*. They were peace and humanity. The concept of peace among the Greeks and Romans was at first negative. For the Greeks *peace* was the absence of war; for the Romans *pax* was a pact to abstain from fighting. But peace for the Greeks soon came to be esteemed as the bestower of plenty. Prior to the fourth century, she had become a goddess, accompanied in art by a cornucopia. The poet Philemon hailed her as

> *The bestower, dearest Zeus, of every treasure,*
> *Weddings, kindred, children, friends,*
> *Wealth, health, wheat, wine, and pleasure."*

Peace as an ideal was associated with the prevalent notion of the Golden Age lost through the fall of man. Hesiod portrayed its progressive deterioration from the age of gold characterized by peace and plenty. In Roman letters the great popularizer of the theme was Ovid. This whole tradition was embodied in fact and in symbol in the *Pax Romana.* Then for the first time at Rome peace became a goddess with her altar the *Ara Pacis* adorned with a cornucopia. Virgil celebrated the age of Augustus as the restoration of the Age of Gold. Emperors as the makers of peace were styled the sons of God.

Another concept developed by imperial Rome was that of humanity. The idea was elaborated by a group of aristocrats in the circle of Scipio Africanus, the conqueror alike of Carthage and of Hellas, who became himself the captive of the Greeks and patronized distinguished fugitives. Among them the Stoic Panaitios undertook to reconstruct Stoicism as a code for conquerors. The key word was humanity, which meant not softness but civility, good breeding, the cultivated life, the epitome of the ideal of self-fulfilment. Under the *Pax Romana* humanity was further humanized. For Seneca it meant that man is sacred to man. Humanity became the sister of peace. Seneca combines the themes when he writes, "We punish murderers and what shall we say of wars and massacres which we laud because they destroy whole nations? . . . Shameful it is that men, the mildest breed, should delight in mutual bloodshed . . . whereas animals devoid of reason are at peace. Man who is sacred to man is even killed for sport."

The emperors were wise enough to realize that peace and humanity are not of themselves a sufficient basis for the unity of mankind. There must be some deeper spiritual bond and none is deeper than religion. The form adopted was the deification of the ruler for which there was both a tradition and a spontaneous demand among the peoples of the East, grateful for the Roman peace. With enthusiasm the cult adopted throughout the Roman world save by the Jews, who in time obtained exemption. Christianity arising out of Judaism continued the same intransigeance, and when denied the same privileges carried on the fight not merely until Christians were exempt but until emperors ceased to be gods. In place of the emperor cult as the cement of the empire stepped the Christian religion.

How well suited was Christianity to serve as the bond of the world? Back of Christianity lay Judaism, the most intransigeant, of religions and espoused by the most truculent people of the ancient world. The Jews and Christians had their contributions to make to the unity of mankind, but along lines different from those of the Greeks and Romans. The concrete achievement of the Jews was the demonstration that a people without political autonomy and without a fixed abode could for seven centuries preserve itself as a nation. But this could only be by resistance to assimilation. Here was ample proof that the unity of mankind must be achieved by some other method than the obliteration of diversity. Yet the very particularism of the Jews was derived from loyalty to the loftiest of all unities, the unity of God. Monotheism is the legacy of Israel. It was implicit in the religion of Moses when Israel at Sinai made a covenant with the god of the storm-cloud, bound to no locality and to no people. Unconstrained he chose Israel to be his people and might reject them if they failed to remember his precepts to do them. In defeat Israel was able, therefore, to draw not the obvious inference that her god was weak or non-existent but rather that he was a righteous god, chastening his chosen through the Assyrian, the rod of his anger. In that case he must also be the god of the Assyrian and of all the world. Such monotheism by no means carried with it the unity of mankind. All men indeed are the children and the subjects of God, but some are his chosen, however recalcitrant, and others are rejected though serviceable as instruments. Universalism on such a basis could be attained only through an extension of the covenant. Yahweh had brought the Philistines from Caphtor and the Syrians from Kir just as he had brought Israel from Egypt. "Blessed be Egypt, my people, and Assyria, the work of mine hands, and Israel mine inheritance."

Israel entertained an ideal of universal peace. As with the Greeks and Romans there were primitivist strains. The age of peace would be the restoration of that idyllic garden where prior to the fall the lion and the lamb lay down together. The initial concept of peace among the Hebrews differed, however, from that of the Greeks and Romans. The Hebrew peace, *shalom*, was always positive and material, almost a synonym for prospeperity, invariably religious, never a goddess but a gift of God, who should usher in the age when swords would be beaten into plowshares.

Universalism and particularism were constantly jostling each other in the course of Jewish history. Jeremiah could envisage a universal spiritual covenant. Ruth could exalt the Moabitess and Jonah took pity on the people of Nineveh. But Esther was vindictive and Ezra and Nehemiah endeavored to save Judaism from submersion by a program of exclusiveness in religion and in blood. The Maccabean struggle was largely over this issue. It was essentially a civil war and began when a Jewish purist slew a Jewish apostate. The apostate did not think of himself as abandoning Judaism. He adhered to Yahweh while suffering him to become a god among the gods, sending presents to Melkart of Tyre. The purist did not ban all fusion, but Yahweh must be the only god and fusion must take the form of accretion to his characteristics. Particularism triumphed.

In the meantime a dualism was projected into the heavenly places. There is indeed only one god but there are malign spiritual powers, the evil angels, the mighty Lucifer, who "exalted his throne above the stars of God." The demonic powers stir up conflict in heaven and on earth. Their overthrow is possible only through a divine cataclysm in which God will smite the ungodly and establish his kingdom. The unity of mankind requires a pre-

[285]

liminary purge and acceptance by the survivors of the rule of God. The only possible concrete embodiment of such a rule would be a theocracy on Mount Zion.

Christianity arising from Judaism in its most particularist period shattered the bonds and made of Judaism not the preservative of a remnant but a religion embracing the world. Though Jesus limited his mission to the house of Israel, yet at the judgment he would divide men, not as Jews and Gentiles on the basis of blood, but as sheep and goats according to their works. The Apostle Paul went further. No man of his generation had a larger series of concentric circles of loyalty. He was of the tribe of Benjamin, of the sect of the Pharisees, of the city of Tarsus, of the empire of Rome, and of the new Israel of God. For him there was no longer Jew or Greek.

Christianity gave a new quality to love, humanity and peace. Christian love is not the Greek *eros* whose end is self-fulfilment, but rather *agapé*, the utterly self-giving love of that God who gave his only begotten son for the redemption of the world. The concept of humanity in Christian hands is at once impoverished and enriched. It was dissociated from culture and equated with charity. *Philanthropia* became philanthropy. The reason may have been simply that in the poverty-stricken Orient almsgiving was the only appropriate expression of humanity. Certainly the dignity of man was not thereby diminished. The Christian Origen was the vindicator of the nobility of man against the aspersions of the pagan Celsus. Peace unquestionably was transformed by Christianity. The materialistic connotations of the Hebrew *shalom* were dropped while the positive and religious characteristics were retained. Peace was not simply as with the Greeks the absence of war, but the antithesis of contention. Positively peace is a reconciling and redeeming power, the companion of life and joy.

Yet Christianity like Judaism was fraught with the possibilities of division. That Paul who repudiated the separation of Jew and Gentile introduced the cleavage of elect and non-elect because of which Jacob and Esau strove while yet in the womb of Rebecca. And Paul carried over from Judaism the warfare in the heavenly places. One can understand how Christianity could become at once the most cohesive and most divisive force in history, and paradoxically often most cohesive in society when most divisive within itself.

Christianity was born in the manger of classical civilization as the heir of the cosmopolitanism of Stoicism and the outward peace of Rome. The fusion of all these was to become Christendom, but in the first three centuries Christianity was to be in overt conflict with certain aspects of the others. In the period before Constantine the two great unifiers of mankind, the Roman Empire and the Christian Church, were at odds. To the empire Christianity appeared as unassimilable as Judaism but easier to crush. Particularly in the third century the neo-barbarian emperors from the Danubian provinces regarded the new cult as enervating, as an expression of and an encouragement to the vices of peace. Christians looked with mingled feelings upon the empire. They appreciated the physical oneness of the world which facilitated the dissemination of their religion. They valued the peace and order of the *Pax Romana* and did not relish the prospect of its collapse. They were torn between prayers for the speedy coming of the Lord and for the postponement of the preliminary cataclysm. They looked upon themselves as strangers in the world, having no city of habitation but at the same time as the soul of the world, the cement of society, the power which restrains the impending chaos.

With Constantine the contest ended in an alliance The emperor ceased to be a god and became instead a lay bishop. The church passed from a position of toleration to establishment. Christian writers like Eusebius and in general the theologians of the East saw in the union of these two powers the guarantee of unity, harmony, and peace for mankind. The one empire with the one emperor properly belonged to the religion of the one God and the one Lord. Polytheism had been the natural religion for a congeries of city states inspired by demands to perpetual conflict. Monotheism is the religion conformable to a universal sway in which swords are beaten into plowshares. Constantine himself embraced Christianity in the hope that it would prove the cement of the empire, and great was his disillusionment when this new religion embroiled the empire in ecclesiastical dispute and in turn coalesced with divisions already existent in the social structure and lent to them a theological cast. In the West a quarrel over church discipline—the Donatist controversy—served to inflame the smouldering Punic resentment against a Romanized Carthage, while in the East, theological dissension in the Arian controversy threw whole populations into ferment. The emperor would have been still more deeply disheartened could he have lived to witness the contribution of Christianity to the dissolution of the East where the peoples, never really fused by Hellenism, disintegrated along ancient racial lines into Copt, Syrian, Armenian, and Greek, but under theological captions. The Christian West, however, like the classical, was to exhibit greater cohesion. The Donatist schism was the only one of importance. Arianism never obtained a genuine hold, and when the Nicene theology became dominant in the empire and Arianism was taken up by the barbarians, St. Ambrose could feel that Rome had become identified not only with Christianity but with orthodoxy.

Then came the barbarians. The West was overrun. Government broke down. In the midst of this debacle, Christianity was to exhibit its greatest power of cohesion. At the outset of the new period, St. Augustine essayed a reappraisal of the relations of Christianity to society. In so doing he drew together all the threads of the classical and Christian traditions and thereby did more than any other to forge the concept of Christendom. Naïve identification of Christianity and Rome he could by no means accept. Neither for him was the deepest cleavage that between Roman and barbarian, nor even that between Christian and pagan, orthodox and heretical. The great gulf for Augustine, as for Paul, was that which separates the elect from the non-elect. This difference runs through all history and leads to a perpetual conflict. Yet history is more than a tug of war. It is also a decline and an ascent. The fall of society began when Cain killed Abel and continued through the murder of Remus by Romulus and the demolition of Carthage by Rome—Augustine is the first to combine these themes of Roman degeneracy into a scheme of progressive decline. The upturn came not with Augustus and the founding of the empire, which was only a necessary evil due to the failure of small states to live at peace. The first improvement came with the conversion of Constantine, for great states apart from justice are but robbery on a large scale and justice is possible only in a Christian state. Peace, however, will never be completely possible on earth even in a Christian state, but only in heaven. To equate the *Pax Romana* with the beating of swords into plowshares is sheer nonsense. Yet man's lust for domination can be restrained through the coercive measures exercised by the state in accord with the principles of natural law and the Gospel. At this point all of the classical, Jewish and Christian strains are drawn together: justice, the law of nature, humanity, concord, peace in the cosmos, among the animals, and among men. Yet none of these is ever perfectly realized because of the discord between faith and unbelief, the *civitas dei* and *civitas terrena*. The approximation to a synthesis could be accomplished in practice only when the forces of disorder were restrained through a state directed by the church. In other words, the method must be the one foreshadowed in Judaism of a theocracy.

The medieval church was eventually to take that way, but centuries had first to elapse in which the church proved to be the great unifier of the West. Truly Constantine had his reward. The church performed the marriage for the northern and southern peoples and could do so more easily because each presented already a relatively unified culture. But political unity there was none. When the *Pax Romana* collapsed, the West, which from this point on will be our sole concern, presented a welter of separate principalities. The church then assumed the role of her former partner, the empire, and from the outset held together the old Roman population and gradually won the barbarians from Arianism to orthodoxy or from paganism to Christianity. Centralizing tendencies in government as represented by Pippin and Charlemagne received ecclesiastical sanction. The result even in the early Middle Ages was the achievement of something approaching a universal culture. Latin became everywhere the tongue of the learned, and among the common folk the *langue d'oil* spread until the Normans took it to England, Spain, Sicily, and the Holy Land.

But, despite the abortive empire of Charlemagne, in no sense did the West ever enjoy political unification, and the peoples were very conscious of their differences. The Celts had no dealings with the Saxons. The Norman conquest injected still further division into England. In Germany the Frisians, the Saxons and the Bavarians were separate entities. South of the Rhine the Normans and Bretons, the Aquitanians, the Provençals, the Basques and the Spaniards had diversities marked enough. Besides in Spain there were the Arabs who had in common with the rest of Europe only the classical and not the Christian tradition. Nor were these peoples at peace. Feudalism was a system devised in the interests of security, but security was never attained. Not even the faith proved a common bond, for in Spain the Christian and Moslem fought the Moslem and Christian. The church then girded her loins in a new effort at unification and peace. Two institutions in particular were fostered, the Peace of God and the Truce of God. The former increased the number of non-combatants and endeavored to insure their immunity. The second limited the time for fighting until scarcely more than one quarter of the year remained as an open season. When the rules of the

Peace and Truce of God were not observed, churchmen to enforce the peace raised armies which became themselves so unruly that the cities were constrained to raise other armies to put them down. Then the popes bethought them of that ancient device for promoting peace at home by provoking war abroad. The Crusades began with a plea for the old Greek concord applied to Europe.

No doubt the Crusades did manage to promote a sense of Christendom against the Turk. Before the movement was spent in the thirteenth century came that period of Europe's history in which the Israelitish theocratic ideal was most fully realized. The West had become more genuinely unified in thought and act than ever before since the collapse of the *Pax Romana.* The pope was the overlord, claiming jurisdiction wherever sin was involved, and where is it not? The courts of the church and the canon law provided a universal legal machinery. No secular monarch was so widely and so well obeyed as was Pope Innocent III. In the realm of thought Aquinas gathered up the strands from classical, Christian, Jewish and Arabic sources and constructed a pattern of society ruled by the pope and the emperor in accord with justice, reason, and the law of nature.

But we must not wax too lyrical over the thirteenth century and suffer ourselves to be deluded into regarding it as a golden age, by returning to which we shall achieve our felicity. It was scarcely so peaceful as the age of the Antonines. Pope Innocent III managed only to keep the lid from blowing off the cauldron of Europe, not to prevent the brew from spilling over. The fourth Crusade, instead of recovering Jerusalem, captured Constantinople and further embittered the relations of Greek and Latin Christians. The crusading ideal itself was transferred to Europe to envenom the conflicts of European states. The very age of unity witnessed the revival of a long dormant sectarianism in the Albigenes, Waldenses, Fraticelli and their ilk. The church then endeavored to enforce unity by extermination or segregation. The

Jew was sent to the Ghetto. Yet the Inquisition, devised to insure unity, became a tool of the rising national state before which at the turn of the fourteenth century the papacy itself succumbed. Dante's dream of world peace under a universal monarch was only an epitaph, and the intellectual synthesis of Aquinas disintegrated in the hands of Scotus and Occam.

The age of the Renaissance in the fourteenth and fifteenth centuries was marked by divergent tendencies. On the one hand the unity of Christendom was disrupted by the rise of a new principle of cohesion operating only within limited areas, namely nationalism. In that day it was a step toward unification. In France, for example, such peoples as the Aquitanians, Provençals, Normans, Bretons, Burgundians and the French proper were welded into a single nation. Unmolested travel favored the exchange of goods and ideas and the building up of a common vernacular. Nationalism up to a point marked a distinct advance over the particularism of feudalism. But it collided with and weakened the universalism of the empire and of the church, which itself became nationalized.

To offset the divisive tendencies of the new nationalism the humanists endeavored to revive the ancient classical picture of the unity of mankind. Petrarch resuscitated *humanitas* as an ideal of the man both cultivated and humane. Erasmus was the spokesman of the state as a moral organism within and without. The new nations should be the components of a single Christendom bound with adamantine chains in that harmony which holds not only men but also the stars and the beasts in the unity of the spirit and the bond of peace. Erasmus represented that cosmopolitan outlook which after the demise of Christendom has remained to us as "European culture." It is very largely a secular culture and for that reason is ceasing even to be culture and is powerless to unite. The process of secularism had its inception in the Renaissance when even a pope could seek an alliance with the Turk. Into the midst of such a church fell a flare from Wittenberg.

The Protestant Reformation has frequently been represented as the great disruptor and Luther as the render of the seamless robe. In a sense unquestionably he was, and here appears the paradox that Christianity is never more cohesive than when it is divisive. Christian unity is based not so much upon an expanding sense of kinship among men as upon loyalty to the single truth of God. And when differing concepts of that truth divide, still the common assumptions may unite. Protestantism arrested secularism not only in those areas which broke with the church of Rome but even within Catholicism itself. The Catholic Church is never so alive as when confronted by a vigorous competitor.

Outwardly, of course, Christendom was unintentionally partitioned. Luther meant to reform the church as a whole. Instead he provoked a proliferation of sects and a disruption of outward unity in which Protestants themselves were not to acquiesce for a century. At the same time they took to themselves the existing divisions of society and thereby intensified the strains. In Germany they buttressed themselves by an alliance with feudal particularism against the universalism of the empire, in Poland and France with the ancient nobility against the centralizing tendencies of the crown, in England the reverse, but in Hungary they welcomed the Turks against the less tolerant Hapsburgs. The seamless robe indeed was rent. At the same time Protestantism exhibited a cohesion of its own even in the political sphere. Calvinsim, for example, served as a bond between French Switzerland, France, Hungary, the Low Countries, Scotland and England, and the political unification of the two latter was made possible only by the adherence of Scotland to the reform. Yet to say all this on one side or the other is to leave unmentioned the point of greatest significance. Protestantism revived Christianity. Protestantism made religion a dominant concern of men even in politics for another century and a half. Luther stripped the peel and saved the core of Christendom.

The same thing happened twice over in the course of English

history in the seventeenth and in the eighteenth centuries through the Puritan Revolution and the Methodist revival. Puritanism saw another flowering of sects, Presbyterian, Congregational, Baptist, Quaker, Ranter, Seeker, Familist, Fifth Monarchy, etc., down even to individuals like John Smythe who believed that no one was competent to baptize him save himself. Surely here was the knell of Christendom. Nevertheless, when before had England ever been so truly and so consciously a Christian nation as during the Puritan Revolution? If today in Parliament, in labor unions, in assemblies of social scientists, an appeal to Christian norms is not irrelevant, to the Puritan Revolution goes largely the credit.

Yet not wholly. The eighteenth century saw another split in the outer structure—the emergence of another sect and at the same time another welding of the nation in the Christian mould through the Methodist revival. John Wesley kindled the total religious life of England, and above all he won the working classes for the faith. That is why the labor movement in England did not embrace dialectical materialism. The workers and the employers alike talked in the vernacular of the Gospels.

Unquestionably, however, Christian divisions after the sixteenth century did present difficulties with regard to common programs of action. As a basis for international relations not only the canon law of the Catholics but even the Bible of the Protestants appeared too controversial. For that reason an attempt was made to establish the unity of mankind upon the classical, divorced from the Christian ingredients of Christendom. Grotius formulated an international law on the basis of the natural law of Stoicism which is valid also among non-Christians, valid even if there be no God. The eighteenth century witnessed the flourishing of this tendency which cannot be called secularist in the full sense. Often the persons who espoused the divorce of certain areas of life from religion were themselves men of piety who, in the interests of unity, introduced this dichotomy. One senses that notably in the attitude of the framers of the American Constitution who excluded prayer from political deliberations. The age witnessed the achievement of some measure of European unity, especially in the cultural sense. Erasmus came into his own, religious persecution died down, science was cultivated across national boundaries, and for the first time Russia came within the orbit of European culture. The leaders of thought occupied themselves with plans for universal peace.

But the nineteenth and twentieth centuries have been marked by ever widening fissures of national jealousies, issuing in a death struggle between rival views of life. The cleavage is often described as one between Germany and the West. Differences of opinion are evident in the attempts to discover precisely wherein it consists. Some see the rift primarily as an example of the divisions of Christendom. Germany is Lutheran, marked by a supine acquiescence in political control. The West is Calvinist, intransigent and democratic. Others point to the suppression of sectarian Anabaptism in Germany in favor of a sole established church in contrast to the triumph of the sects in England and North America. Another writer points to the diverse outworkings of Methodism in England and Pietism in Germany. Methodism consolidated England, Pietism engendered in Germany a high pitch of emotional enthusiasm at the very time when "the quest for the historical Jesus" was injecting doubts as to the objects of religious veneration. The enthusiasm then shifted to the nation. Despite social equality in the Pietist cells the masses were not enlisted and drifted into anti-religious Marxist Socialism. Germany has known nothing comparable to the British labor movement manned often by Methodist lay preachers. These interpreters thus see the difference in terms of Christian divisions.

But this is not the deepest difference, affirmed Ernst Troeltsch. The great gulf between Germany and the West lies in this, that she has rejected the classical tradition of natural law as the basis for the unity of mankind. The Romantic Movement in Germany swept out the law of nature, valid for all men and accessible to all through the light of universal reason, and erected in its place an irrational dynamism welling up in peoples endowed with vital energy and empowering them to forge their own morality. This is the true secularism, the true paganism, which has demolished alike the Christian and the classical unity.

Yes, but this is not exclusively a German disease, and the gulf is not simply between Germany and the West, declares Gerhard Ritter. And the rift did not begin with the Romantic Movement but rather in the period of the Renaissance. The secularist attitude was that of Machiavelli. The Christian-classical view in the same period was espoused by Thomas More. In the course of the succeeding centuries small and isolated nations have talked in terms of political moralism and universal right, such as the Dutch and the English. By no accident was Thomas More an Englishman and Grotius a Hollander. On the other hand the great states on the Continent have been readier to trample on all scruples for the sake of security. Now one, now another, has been the exponent of Machiavellianism. Under Napoleon it was France, under Bismarck, it was Germany.

The cleavage is as old and as deep as that which Augustine discovered between the *civitas Dei* and the *civitas terrena*. It is a conflict capable of multiple manifestations, of the church against the state or the state against the church, of Germany against the West or of the West against the East. It is a conflict which lies within the breast of every man. In order to unite, Christianity must first divide. He who came to bring peace cast fire upon the earth. With the ideals of a secular paganism there can be no truce. But that power which is so divisive is of all the most cohesive. Our hope lies in the classical-Christian tradition of the unity of mankind. And no institution in these crumbling days has exhibited such constancy in resistance to tyranny, no institution has preserved its own international structure and mentality so faithfully as has the Christian church.

LUTHERANISM, CATHOLICISM, AND GERMAN LITERATURE

By

Karl Viëtor, Dr. Phil.
Professor of German Art and Culture, Harvard University

CHAPTER XIV

LUTHERANISM, CATHOLICISM, AND GERMAN LITERATURE

BY

KARL VIËTOR

One of the few classicists among the German writers of the present, Hans Carossa, relates in the story of his youth how he attended school in the Bavarian provincial city of Landshut in the nineties of the last century, and how depressing it was, when one day it dawned upon him and his fellow-Catholic schoolmates that the German Catholics had little reason to be proud of the contribution which they had made to the political and intellectual history of the nation during the nineteenth century. Among the great poets, philosophers, statesmen and soldiers there was scarcely one who was not a Protestant. It looked as if the intellectual strength of the Catholic world had spent itself. "A truly free spirit seemed incapable of breathing in it any longer, at most one could hope to become a saint in it." ("*Kein wahrhaft freier Geist vermöge mehr in ihr zu atmen, höchstens zum Heiligen könne man es allenfalls noch in ihr bringen.*")

The Austrian Catholic, Grillparzer, had already said in his *Family Strife in Hapsburg* (1872): "And let me say the ablest men, the bravest, are heretics, explain it, if you can" (Transl. by Arthur Burkhard). What had it profited that the Catholics had remained victors in the "Kulturkampf" against Bismarck's regime? At the end of the century a young Catholic, Karl Muth, posed the question: "Does the Catholic belletristic literature come up to the best standards of the period?" ("*Steht die katholische Belletristik auf der Höhe der Zeit?*") (1898). He went so far as to make the true but venturesome statement that the

[299]

very modest niveau of modern Catholic novels was characteristic of the inferiority of the whole of German-Catholic literary production. The courageous attack aroused attention; it rudely awakened the Catholic intelligentsia from its slumber and gave rise to the activity which in turn led to the founding of *Hochland* (1903), a periodical which has eminently represented down to our time those Catholic groups who ventured forth from the cultural ghetto into the arena of modern ideological struggles and in the whole domain of the cultural sought to speak for a decidedly Christian *Weltanschauung*. However, even this highly respectable renaissance movement still could not succeed in producing a great poet, who was at the same time both Catholic by birth and a representative of the church in his works.

The inferiority of German Catholicism in the field of literature and philosophy is not a recent condition. It would be false, if one were to say it is as old as the religious schism. But between 1700 and 1900, leaving out of consideration the later period of Romanticism and its after-effects, there was no first class Catholic writer in Germany. This is especially true of the eighteenth century, that time in which an original German literature of deepest significance was first created. The Catholics had no share in this achievement. Lessing, Klopstock, Wieland, Herder, Goethe, Schiller, W. von Humboldt, Jean Paul and Hölderlin, all these were Protestants. The same is true of the authors of lesser significance: Haller, Hagedorn, Gleim, Gessner, Gellert, Lenz, Klinger, Hölty, Bürger, Claudius, Voss—and it is true in the last analysis of the philosophers and aestheticians: Leibniz, Christian Wolff, Gottsched, Bodmer, Breitinger, Winckelmann, Hamann, Kant, Fichte, Schelling, Hegel. Tardily and hesitantly the Catholic districts of the West and South followed the rise of the sciences, which was led by the Protestant universities. They gradually became receptive, to be sure, to the new literature; but their own contribution was so slight, that it was incapable of influencing the course of this German Renaissance.

Vienna is a pertinent example, that city in which, if anywhere at all, an inherently Catholic literature might have developed. In 1761 Nicolai, the Berlin rationalist, wrote that Austria had still not produced a single German writer who merited the notice of the rest of Germany. Literary taste, he said, was only just then at the level which the Protestant territories had already reached thirty years before. As an answer to this challenge there was founded in Vienna in the same year a "German Society." It was supposed, like the other societies of this type, which were started on all sides after Gottsched's example, to serve the cultivation of the German language and the promotion of original German literature. The man who was responsible for its foundation was Josef von Sonnenfels, grandson of a Berlin rabbi, son of a Jewish scholar. His father had emigrated from Prussia to Austria and turned Christian. Sonnenfels was a learned cosmopolite, rationalist and reformer. His efforts to enliven literary life were so disconcerting, that he was suspected of wanting to introduce Lutheranism. For the South German Catholic, German literature was identified as a Protestant product. Sonnenfels at this time was giving voice to a point of view very much similar to that of Gottsched, who had already become a man of yesterday in North Germany. The authors, whom he named as models in the "German manner" (*"deutscher Art"*), ranged from Opitz to Klopstock. All of them were "foreigners," were Protestants. Nicolai rightly thought: "Had there been in existence one single native, indeed, had there only been a single Catholic, he would certainly not have neglected to mention him." As characteristic of the intellectual situation in Austria it may be mentioned in addition that the most important critical periodical of the German "Enlightenment," the *Allgemeine deutsche Bibliothek* was still banned in Austria in 1777; the theological section obviously appeared to the censorship to be too dangerous. Before the ban this periodical had 64 subscribers in Austria and Hungary. In Hamburg alone four times as many copies were sold. The reforms of Joseph II (who was, incidentally, no connoisseur of German literature, even if he was a champion of the German language) introduced the new development, which thirty years later led to the intellectual union of Austria with Germany. The poets of Vienna at the end of the eighteenth century were, in spite of their enthusiasm for the new literature, only modest imitators of Klopstock and Wieland or partisans of the Ossian fad and the bardic poetry, that strange vogue which had significance only as a symptom of the re-awakened interest in the Nordic, the German tradition.

Then came Romanticism, through which the intellectual unity of Germany was finally achieved. But this was also the work of Protestants. Even here, a Catholic literature was not yet created, though the return to the Middle Ages, the revival of Christianity among the intellectuals and the conversion of individual North German romanticists all once again confirmed the dignity of Catholic tradition, the significance of the old church and the intrinsic worth of Catholic piety in opposition to rationalistic skepticism. The voice of a genuine Catholic is to be heard for the first time in Clemens Brentano's poetry and in the work of the great Joseph von Eichendorff. Not until this period, when the Romantic movement was already beginning to decline, did Vienna become for a short time a literary centre. Now there appeared, too, an Austrian, who was worthy of being compared with the great poets of the Protestant North, Franz Grillparzer (his first drama appeared in 1817). But this upward surge did not hold to its course. It was swallowed up in the political and realistic temper of the new period. The nineteenth century restored the Jesuit Order, it directed the strengthened church to ever-greater political triumphs. It succeeded, too, in defending and securing the Catholic world against the rationalism of the natural sciences, against modern Bible criticism and against the materialistic atheism. But again, as in the Counter-Reformation, the victory of the Church was paid for with a loss of cultural authority. Annette von Droste-Hülshoff is certainly a sensitive poet, but one would hardly call her great. Even so, she was still the only poet of the nineteenth century who was Catholic not by baptism and descent alone. And for the others it should be remembered that a literature written by Catholics does not need on that account to be Catholic literature. The greatest Catholic author among the German narrators of the nineteenth century, Adalbert Stifter, was educated by Benedictine monks. Nevertheless, he belongs more to the classical tradition than to that of his native Catholic environment. For him Goethe, with whom he believed himself to possess an "uncommon similarity," was "one of the greatest men who ever lived." The "Catholic standpoint," so he writes, is in art only *one* among others. It was not his.

But there is, of course, another side to the matter. Both popular poetry and the folk theatre continued to flourish during the eighteenth and nineteenth centuries *only* in South Germany. It is of particular significance, moreover, that even if the Catholics were "inferior" in the field of elevated literature and philosophy during the age of bourgeois culture, they were, on the other hand, superior to the Protestants in music and sculpture. The "sensual arts" blossomed in the eighteenth century only in *Catholic* Germany. That is especially true of architecture. The inward Christianity of Protestantism did not favor a culture of the senses. Lutheranism and Calvinism did not need any ecclesiastical art. In Calvinistic Holland, to be sure, painting flourished in spite of this with unprecedented productivity. Why it degenerated precisely in Luther's Germany is a difficult problem, not to be explained in a few words. In the eighteenth century (as Goethe pertinently expresses it) the Protestant North was the "cultured but formless part of Germany" (*"der gebildete aber bildlose Teil Deutschlands"*). Georg Dehio, the historian of German art, says that Bible-reading had ruined the eyes of the Protestants. The architectural gems of the eighteenth century stand on South German soil: all the beautiful castles and churches in the style of the Baroque and Rococo.

Then as to music. At first it seemed as though music were destined to become *the* Protestant art par excellence. Schütz, Bach, Händel—German Catholicism of the same period has nothing of equal quality to rank with the work of these masters. But when the impetus to cultural activity was finally given to the Catholic regions as well, then in music they proved just as creative as did contemporary Protestant Germany in literature. Gluck, Haydn, Mozart, Beethoven, K. M. v. Weber and Schubert—what a group of masters! All are Catholics by origin, most of them Austrians. Yet the Protestants continue to be represented, and in this period, by Mendelssohn and Schumann. But here, too, we have the same picture as in literature: the Augustan age of Catholic music does not last. The two greatest German composers of the following era, Wagner and Brahms, are both Protestants. When one views the whole situation, the contribution which the Protestants have made to the incomparably rich treasure of German music is scarcely less than that of the Catholics.

In this essay, however, only some considerations concerning the problematic significance which the church schism has had for the development of *literature* in Germany, are to be presented. However familiar the fact, it will always remain one of the most astounding phenomena in European history, that, in the only land where a Catholic and a Protestant culture developed side by side, the Protestant area has shown such great superiority in the field of "belles-lettres" (as well as in philosophy and to a certain extent in the field of the sciences in general).

II

In the writings of the theologians and historians one finds, as is well known, a multitude of assertions and opinions about the *universal effect* which Protestantism has exercised upon the development of European spiritual life. It has been said, and rightly so, that a religion, founded not upon cult or deeds, but rather upon the life of faith, a religion which gave primary emphasis to the decision of the individual conscience, must lead to an individualistic ideal of personality, must advance independent thinking, and favor the unfolding of the inner life. The break with the old doctrine was a break with tradition in general as a principle of authority. The search for truth became an act of supreme significance. What had been learned from Bible interpretation, namely, the ability to find the meaning independently, without leaning on objective authorities, became gradually a general intellectual attitude and ability. Critical as well as speculative power could develop freely here, where they were no longer controlled by a rigidly organized church. There was no other authority save God and one's own conscience. "Who could possibly know what God wants to reveal to *you*" (*"Wer weiss, auch, was dir Gott wolle offenbaren"*.) (Butzer). An individualism, at first limited to the province of religion, extended in the end to a complete autonomy of the individual. Protestantism made intelligent reading, finished interpretation, its chief concern. "Without being able to read, one could no longer properly be a Christian" (Fichte).

Ascetic, world-denying tendencies also continued to exist in Protestantism. But a disparagement of the sinful world, on traditional principle, was joined here to the tolerant acceptance and unabashed enjoyment of divine creation. On the whole, the relationship with the existing order and manifestations of secular culture was more positive and more liberal. Lutheranism was unable to create a culture, organized and regimented by the Church like that of the Catholic Middle Ages. The life of the Protestant Christian in the world, his vocation was not supervised here, the field for "Adiaphora" was wide-open. Not so in the case of original Calvinism. Yet one must not make the mistake of thinking that Luther wished to promote or even to tolerate anything like free-thinking or an autonomous, secular culture. In contrast with the more liberal conditions which the Renaissance had already brought into being at that time, Luther's

thought and influence appear rather as the attempt to re-establish
the supremacy of religion over the whole of life. The Catholic
Church of the Counter-Reformation had the same aim. In Luther's
relation to Humanism, in his initial struggle against "heathen"
philosophy ("Philosophy is incompetent in divine matters"),
that is shown clearly enough. It is well-known what evil consequences the Reformation had above all for the German universities and Latin schools. It is well-known, too, that the first
Lutheran preachers had a tendency to reject all scholarly study,
because they maintained that for the proper understanding of
the Divine Word only intuition was necessary. These phenomena
of a time of crisis soon passed, the school system was zealously
promoted, new universities were founded. But even here there
was no enthusiasm for the "Arts and Sciences," no will at work
to achieve educational reform, but only theological and practical
considerations. Luther's essay "An die Ratsherren" (1524), which
contains his school programme, demands linguistic and historical
training, so that one may learn to understand God's word and
gain knowledge of the course of the world, as is necessary for
the three estates, especially for the ranks of churchmen and politicians. Where will one get trained pastors, preachers, councilors,
officials, if one does not educate children "in doctrine and Art?"
Classical languages must be learned, because they are the sheath
"in which the knife of the spirit rests" (*"darin das Messer des
Geistes steckt"*). One was to read the ancient poets in order to
learn language and eloquence from the example of their style,
and wisdom of life from the content of their writing. Virgil,
Terence, and Cicero seemed particularly suitable for this purpose.
Language instruction completely dominated the Lutheran schools.
Just as Luther's own poetic productions were intended merely to
serve the Church, so all secular literature had value for him solely
in the practical benefits to be derived from its contents: knowledge and eloquence, not culture. There was only one way to
the understanding of God and the world, that of religion.

Melanchthon thought in more humanistic terms. But his philosophical and aesthetic inclinations did not determine the further development of Protestant schools. Orthodox theology did not subjugate science and literature to the supervision of the Church; but it also showed little interest in educational problems and did not produce a single pedagogue of importance. Under its domination the Lutheran Latin schools and the universities were behind those of the Jesuits and Calvinists.

The German Reformation certainly did not usher in the development of an autonomous secular culture with design and intent. Religion and Church, piety and salvation—it was concerned with nothing else but these. For all that, however, forces were released through it and the practical possibilities created, from which secular culture (and with it literature) emerged. The Reformation unintentionally liberated these forces, so that they were now able to develop according to their *own* laws. The *How* of this long and complicated process is not at all simple to interpret and to understand. Research has until now not seriously endeavored to do this.

III

If one goes back to the starting point and investigates how a Lutheran and a Catholic ideal of culture develop through the controversy between Reformation and Counter-Reformation, one soon sees that at first the two agree in at least as many respects as they differ. The Lutheran like the Catholic school and university originates in Humanism. It was the chief aim of Humanism to renew modern culture by connecting the *'vera philosophia'* of the Ancients with the Christian doctrine. Both churches seek to break this tendency by opposing to it the claim of the Church to absolute authority. In his opposition to an autonomous humanistic education, even if it called itself *'humanitas christiana,'* Luther was no less positive than the Counter-Reformation. Autocracy of reason in opposition to faith was for Luther the work of the devil. "Pious people strangle reason . . . , this beast, which otherwise the whole world cannot strangle." Ignatius, too, excluded from the schools of his Order the Christian Humanism of Erasmus, which Luther opposed. The chief difference was that on the whole the Jesuits ventured to use the 'Litterae Humaniores' with less bias and pursued them more intensively. The alliance which came into being between Humanism and the Church of the Counter-Reformation proved more lasting than that between Humanism and the Reformation, to be sure at the price of humanistic studies remaining a mere accessory to the program of religious education up until the time of the dissolution of the Jesuit Order (1773). The Lutheran school and university did not succeed in achieving such a successful compromise. After attempts like that of Johann Sturm to gain an equally balanced synthesis of religion and Ciceronian eloquence had failed, Church and Humanism went their separate ways; the schools became technical institutions, Humanism in its later form became an affair of erudite specilization, in which the Church no longer took great interest.

Of particular importance, however, is the fact that in Lutheranism the organization of higher education was no obligation of the Church. Since here ecclesiastical and political power, the kingdom of God and the realm of the world were for all practical purposes separated (even if alike in their final goal), this organization was left to the regional princes and to city councillors. The Church defined the spirit in which instruction was imparted and it defined its purpose; it also made a feeble attempt to supervise its activity through "clerical supervision of the schools" (geistliche Schulaufsicht). But in the long run it could no more control the independent development of this cultural domain than it could that of others which it had relinquished to the protection of political authorities. It was, indeed, one of the most striking and consequential characteristics of Lutheranism that here the State was released from control by a hierarchy above it. It had to be of course a *Christian* State, which was authorized to provide for instruction, because that also belonged to its Christian duties. But the young Church was much too weak to influence the political authorities in this work. The princes had defended the Reformation against Kaiser and Pope. They became protectors, finally masters of the Church, which, as an institution, was a regional church. When the political development then led more and more towards absolutism, the Church finally lost all control over the functions of the State. It no longer depended on the Church, but on the *princes,* what paths intellectual life in Lutheran regions should set out upon and follow. The end of this development was the Protestant cultural state (*Kulturstaat*), which existed independenly *side by side with* the Church. A church like Luther's in which forms of organization had comparatively slight importance, could not develop any disciplinary institutions, which could have given solidity to a theocratic arrangement. The so-called "church discipline" (*Kirchenzucht*), which early Lutheranism still knew (even if not in the rigorous manner of Calvin) could not assert itself. As a rule only moral transgressions were punished, mostly failures to observe the sixth commandment. The Church would not have been in any position to exercise disciplinary control over intellectual life. The censorship of the theological faculties, moreover, was concerned solely with the purity of doctrine.

IV

Whatever the provinces of secular culture may have gained then and later from the complex innovations which the Reformation brought about, it all happened without intention and led to unforeseen results. The religious Renaissance was the centre from which everything took its motion; from this centre waves pushed forth into separate fields, overcame old obstacles and gave the impetus to developments which ran their course for a time in conjunction with the main stream, but then took their independent directions.

That is true, too, of the effect of the Lutheran Reformation upon that field which was necessarily more important for the future of literature than any other: the *linguistic* field. For Luther the German language, language in any and every sense, in fact the whole of language, was not a cultural property of any independent value whatsoever, but a mere vehicle and tool of '*sapientia Dei*'; a vessel which was destined to contain God's message. When Luther translated the Bible into High German, which he developed from the Saxon dialect, he had in mind no other purpose than to make the fundamental book of Christianity comprehensible to Laymen. German now joined the three older languages as a fourth "holy language." The "mother tongue" became the chief weapon of the new church through its ecclesiastical and controversial usage (in the polemics). But this expression itself, which was first used in 1522 by the Augustinian monk, C. Güthel, a friend of Luther, then later by Luther too, did not yet have the venerable sound which it received from the national enthusiasts of the seventeenth and eighteenth centuries or from the scholars of Romanticism. The German language found no place in the Protestant school system. Here, too, as in the humanistic period, Latin was completely dominant. In addition, Greek, some Hebrew as well, was taught. Only in the teaching of catechism was the use of German permitted. The scholars in the law and humanistic faculties, who developed more and more independently in the age of orthodoxy, looked down with the same contempt upon the language of the country as upon folk-literature.

Among the various means whereby this aristocracy of scholars distinguished itself as a class was the peculiar idiom, in which they alone were accustomed to express themselves in teaching and writing: Ciceronian Latin. It was not otherwise in the colleges and schools of the Jesuits. But in Lutheran districts there were other forces which were preparing the way at least for the future development of a High German: the use of Luther's Bible in private and Church life, the hymn and devotional books. The supremacy of Latin was broken; it was still, to be sure, the idiom of scholars, but no longer the language of the Church. The cultured *Catholic* knew only his regional dialect. The cultured *Protestant*, on the other hand, lived in continual contact with a common German language, standing above the dialects. As a clergyman he used it in his sermon; if he was a layman, he learned to understand it when reading. When the age of Humanism with its Latin literature came to a close and an artistic literature in German language began to take form, then this epoch-making transition could take place nowhere else but in the Protestant North and East. The innovations of a spiritual kind as the Reformation brought them about, constitute the most important general prerequisite. But it is in the very nature of literature that it depends upon the material which gives it life, upon language. Where the organic connection, the lively interchange between the living language and literature is forcibly cut off, no Art-poetry (*Kunstdichtung*) can develop.

In Germany the situation was different from that in England, France, Italy and Spain. Only here, where heresy had started, was the church of the Counter-Reformation opposed by an adversary as dangerous in cultural matters as in those of faith and ecclesiastical life. Scholarship, school, literature, poetry—all this became the zealously protected domain of militant orders. In Germany the old church thought its only means of rescue was to separate the regions which had remained loyal and had been regained with great effort from the Protestant area so completely as possible *culturally* as well as otherwise. Even in the linguistic field it ventured no concession. From now on there were not only two different Christian churches; there were from the middle of the sixteenth to the end of the eighteenth century also two

different *languages* and *literatures* in Germany (and only here):
a *Protestant* and a *Catholic*.

V

Modern German literature was not created through the Reformation and it did not originate contemporaneously with this movement. Its foundations were laid a century later by Opitz and other intellectuals of his time. But the prerequisites for this act of reform were created by the Reformation. Among these the fact must be reckoned that in the course of the sixteenth century a group of academically educated intellectuals was formed —a type of humanistic laymen along the lines of the Renaissance tradition, who were no longer limited by theological thinking. The second preparatory factor was that only in Protestantism could the values of a secular culture be nurtured without church control. The third factor was that in the Protestant regions alone the formation of a literary language was in progress. Of course it was no more than this. From the condition which the Protestant drama of the sixteenth century and the prose of Wickram and Fischart indicated, it was clear that a literary "Hochsprache" could be developed only under the impetus arising from some other level of tradition. The difficulty of writing verse in German in the style of the Romanesque and Humanistic poetry was so great that first of all one had to create a new vocabulary and a new word-technique by translating foreign literary works. These first Baroque poets speak just as frequently and emphatically about the material of the German language, about its venerable age and its adaptability to versification as about poetry itself and its problems of form. One had to be created along with the other: "Poetry in our mother-tongue" (*"Poesie in unserer Muttersprache"*). Among the laws which Opitz establishes in the code of the new movement, his *Deutsche Poeterei* (1624) is found this, too: that the poet, in order to speak "purely", should avoid the regional dialect and express himself in "High German." By this Opitz understands the language aiming at a common German, as it was used in the charters of the chanceries, especially the imperial chanceries. Further, of primary importance, the "Lutheran" form of speech: the purified Upper Saxon. Of the latter he says that it has for the Germans the same significance as a norm, as did the Attic for the Greeks (*Letter to B. Venator*, 1628). That could of course be only a preliminary stage. Neither in vocabulary nor in stylistic expression could the language of Luther's Bible and of the Protestant Church satisfy the poetic intentions of the new movement.

Along with Opitz and his friends and pupils the *language societies* worked for the great goal of a High German language and an artistic literature in this language. Among them the "Fruchtbringende Gesellschaft" played the leading role. Protestant (and among them Calvinistic) princes directed them. The members were noblemen, representatives of the middle class, and men of the world. With few and unimportant exceptions they were all Protestants. The historical significance of these associations, the inspiration for which goes back to the academy plans of the Renaissance, can be fully comprehended only if one understands that the cultivation of the language was, as it were, merely the practical basis of a much more extensive plan. (I may refer on this subject to my *Probleme der deutschen Barockliteratur*, Leipzig 1928, and also to the excellent book of Ernst Manheim: *Träger der öffentlichen Meinung*, Brünn, 1933).

In a time of fanaticism among creeds, of political struggle and cultural disruption, middle-class and titled members of the Protestant élite united here in secular gatherings, which had their own rites and symbols. To be sure, the leading members were faithful Christians, loyal to their Church. But the spirit of peaceableness and tolerance was at work. Above particular class and church there appeared here for the first time a national enthusiasm for culture which was not limited by creed. A German type of "virtue" and "wisdom" was to constitute the fundamental attitude; the cultivation of the "High German language" and of literary production in this purified idiom was the concrete task by which these first citizens of a German cultural realm gave practical proof of their convictions. The devotional books of Lutheran orthodoxy (Thomas Grossbauer and J. Lütkemann), the popular scientific writings of Leibniz, Gottsched, and Christian Wolff carried further the work commenced by the language societies. Leibniz, in his memoirs about the founding of a scholarly "Academy or Society," assigned these organizations the task of "increasing and improving the arts and sciences, encouraging the talents of the Germans . . . to improve *rem literariam"* (*"Künste und Wissenschaften zu vermehren und zu verbessern, die Ingenia der Deutschen aufzumntern* . . . Rem literariam *zu verbessern."*) That was a broader program than the language societies had been able to accomplish in practice. But it had grown out of the same way of thinking.

With sound historical justification, Jacob Grimm called New High German "the Protestant dialect." Beyond their marked achievement in the development of language these influential societies formed in the first half of the seventeenth century (the decisive period when the ground was broken) the nucleus for all literary efforts. The idea of an autonomous world culture was the driving force in this. In Germany, this could happen only within Protestantism, only here could it unfold without hindrance. The further development of German literature was determined by the fact that this beginning was made at a time when the influence of the French language and culture had not yet become too powerful.

It is significant that the Protestant churches had no practical control over the advance of Baroque literature. Here, unlike the situation in Catholic or Calvinistic regions, neither theatre nor printing-press was held in check. It was not in the eighteenth century that Protestant clergymen began to take active part in literary life. In the seventeenth century a great portion of German "belles-lettres" was already created by pastors and pastors' sons (a man like Johann Rist is the prototype of the poetic pastor). The church poetry adapted itself to the prosody and metric system of the new secular language-style (*Sprachkunst*). The reform-bent theologians of orthodoxy protested against the intrusion of an artistic worldly style into the music of the Church. But did they object to similar phenomena in the sphere of religious poetry? The boundaries were not clear-cut. Now there came into being something like a harmonious marriage between theological and humanistic culture, a far-reaching intimate union between Protestanism and secular literature in Germany. How differently did these matters develop in England! In Germany the scholars and men of the world who wrote also produced works of ecclesiastical content, the theologians in their writings also included secular works. Thus the development of a purely secular literature could proceed easily and smoothly in the Age of Enlightenment.

VI

These manifestations which show the ground being prepared for the great process of secularization in the 18th century, cannot be properly understood in their true light until one compares the literature which *Catholic Germany* produced in the same span of time. At the beginning of the seventeenth century there are two Jesuits who wrote poetry in the German language. Conrad Vetter (1613) of Regensburg, is one of the first who already has, besides the conventional didacticism, the tone of ecstatic emotional piety. His poems are in content and language forceful, with popular appeal. The other is Friederich von Spee, the Rhenish Jesuit. His Christian eclogues (written in 1629) follow the church hymns and the erotic figurative language of the Song of Songs. Like Opitz, he wants to prove that one may also speak poetically in the German tongue. Spee attempts to create a non-Lutheran literary language by adopting such words from the dialects as are "customary among good Germans." Judged by the language level of North German writers, Spee's German is backward, not fully grown out of the dialect. That is true to a greater degree of the Catholics, who during the second half of the century wrote in native idiom. They are all members of Church Orders (there are no longer any lay-poets in Catholic parts of the country): Benedictine and Capuchin monks. In language and style their verses show a combination of Baroque delight in figure and allegory with mystic fervor and unsophisticated grace. But they never overstep the level of the slightly stylized Upper German dialects. As charmingly and characteristically South German Baroque as their songs are, there was no way leading from them to an *artistic* poetry of particular Catholic type. One might consider as an example the collections of sacred songs which the Munich priest, Johann Kuen, published. Everywhere the situation is the same: a uniquely Catholic poetry in strongly dialectic language.

Nietzsche has said the Counter-Reformation was "a Christianity of self-defense with the acts of violence of a state of siege" (*"ein Christentum der Notwehr, mit den Gewaltsamkeiten eines Belagerungszustandes"*). That is certainly true of Germany, where the Catholic Church found itself in a fight for life or death against a very powerful enemy. It could less afford here than anywhere else to modify the rigid barrier in the spiritual and literary domain. A German-writing Jesuit like Spee remained a unique phenomenon. In the course of the century there is still only Jesuit poetry in Latin, for whose style classical poetry (Aristotle and Horace) and rhetoric (Aristotle, Cicero, Quintilian) remained prototypal. The representative collection, the "Parnassus Societatis Jesu" (1654) shows the worthy standard of this poetry.

Among the authors of the Society of Jesus was a poet who

surpasses the majority of Protestant poets in intellectual and artistic rank, the Bavarian Jesuit Jacob Balde (a native Alsatian). The odes of this Baroque Horace were still admired by Herder and Goethe. His poems and dramas are brilliant models of what the Humanism of the Counter-Reformation, what clerical classical poetry could achieve at that time. Balde praises the dignity of the mother-tongue (in Latin verse). He is just as good a patriot as the Protestants who write in German: proud of ancient Germania, an enemy of servility to foreign countries and to the mingling of languages in vogue. In stately "threnodies" he lamented the fate of the fatherland, laid waste by war. But, like other poets of his Order, Balde showed no sympathy for the efforts of the language societies. His models are Horace, Virgil, and the poets of silver Latinity, not Petrarch, Ronsard, DuBellay, Heinsius, or even Opitz. It seems that he did not become acquainted with the writings of the reformer of German literature until later. In an unpublished manuscript (written in 1654) he declines to accept the new school: its subjects are vulgar, the language banal. There is also a small number of poetic writings by Balde in the German language. Obviously these attempts deserve particular interest, for here must be shown what a great poet of the Catholic Baroque could accomplish in the language of his country. The historian will appreciate the peculiar qualities of a Catholic Baroque style. But if one judges these works by the artistic and linguistic standard, created by Opitz and his successors, one can term their style only backward and without promise. Balde does not seem to have a very accurate knowledge of either Luther's language or that of the new Protestant literature, but only of the German of the imperial chancery. Thus, the man so skilled in Latin verse, persists in writing predominantly Upper German dialect. Even the censor of his Order criticized: "Phrasis Germanica est dura, poesis durior." Another, somewhat better disposed: "Carpit Opitium et alios poetas Germanicos, quibus ipse non herbam porrigit."

In a condition of linguistic isolation the Catholic South remains restricted until the middle of the eighteenth century. It was thereby cut off from the development of secular literature which came to its fulfillment (without Catholic participation) in Protestant Germany. A literature, no longer of popular appeal, but one which sought to attain the character and quality of European literature, as it had developed in the nations of the West and South, could do so only by turning to the tradition of this literature which it hoped to equal. The only solution for the artistic problem was for the German authors of the Opitz generation to pattern themselves on the Romanic poets. Of course, there was a national tradition, the *"altfränkische"* tradition of the fifteenth and sixteenth centuries, which however belonged to another level: that of the popular and Meistersinger literature. In style it was, if one wishes to call it that, German late Gothic. This is the source from which the few works in German language produced by *Catholic* poets of the seventeenth century spring.

In the field watched over by the cultural dictatorship of the Counter-Reformation, the break with this popular tradition and an alliance with that other tradition of secular literature of the European Renaissance was impossible. For here there was nothing but clerical literature, which in content and form could not overstep the orbit of Humanism prevalent in the Church Orders, (so that the most flourishing new genres, the *"Gesellschaftslied,"* the sonnet and the courtly novel were entirely excluded.) For its language it might not accept the more mature, richer Lutheran German as a basis and criterion. Only in the field of drama, where native tradition was powerless in contrast to the humanistic, and where the classical models were equally binding for Protestants and Catholics alike, did the Jesuits create something which excelled the achievements of the Protestants in general. But the Jesuit drama, as significant as the works of J. Bidermann, J. Masen and N. Avancini are in themselves, was after all an offshoot, which grew up, blossomed, and passed away outside the great stream of development. For the very reason that it was written in Latin and was designed to meet the special facilities of the stage of the Jesuit Order.

There was one field of Baroque where the division caused by difference of creed was overcome by a mediating tendency: in the new *Mysticism*. This flourished equally in Catholic regions (where it commenced) and in Protestant parts of the country. Until towards the end of the seventeenth century one finds in religious songs and devotional books of *both* creeds the new expression of an ardent personal "religion of the heart." The Baroque character of this spiritualism is most clearly evident in the "Jesusminne" songs. (Marie-Luise Wolfskehl has treated this subject in a scholarly investigation). But if Catholic and Protestant poets struck up the same melody here, it was only in the Pietism of the Protestants that those effective forces which produced the first poetry of personal experience (*Erlebnis-Dichtung*) remained continually at work, finally flowing over in the eighteenth century into the poetry of secular emotion. Although the "irrational" forces continue to exist in purer form in the less intellectual culture of the Catholic South, it was nevertheless only within Protestantism, and deriving from an originally highly esoteric Baroque mysticism, that a powerful lay movement developed in Germany, just as it was also true that only in German Protestantism did there arise a rationalistic attitude of individual autonomy, and from it the "Enlightenment."

That was decisive for the destiny of Catholic literature. Whatever the great Orders, especially the Society of Jesus, had still been able to create in the seventeenth century within the walls of the cultural ghetto (and that was certainly commendable in its own way), Catholic intellectual life in the eighteenth century fell into an exhausted state of decline. It had become completely out of joint with the times. Even before the Order was dissolved (1773), its universities were hopelessly backward, its literary life long since sterile.

VII

The extraordinary fact that German literature, in its development from the seventeenth century to the end of Romanticism was created exclusively by Protestants is not the only unique feature in German history. No less striking is the other fact, namely, that simultaneously in the Catholic nations (Italy, Spain and France) a secular literature in the vernacular could arise, which was much more significant artistically and intellectually. An explanation for this cannot be undertaken here. I wish only to express the conjecture that the circumstance of a flourishing Renaissance literature already developed among the Latin races before the politics of the Counter-Reformation began to take effect, may have played a significant part. In *Germany* Humanism had developed belatedly; it was overwhelmed by the religious movement before it had blossomed. A Renaissance literature of high quality had not yet begun to develop when all spiritual forces were needed on the Protestant side for the enormous work of creating the new faith, organizing and defending the new Church, and on the Catholic side for the defense and salvation of the old Church. But still other complications were added. The territorial conditions, the lack of a central political power, proved of great consequence. These interconnections have not yet been sufficiently investigated in detail. Protestantism itself was not a unified structure in Germany. Apart from Calvinsim and the part it played in Germany (which cannot be discussed here) there was no *one* Lutheran doctrine but diverse varieties. There was no *one* Church, but many "regional churches" (Landeskirchen), whose cultural life was after all more or less influenced by the regional prince. If the history is to be written of the long and involved process, in the course of which the new German literature was produced as a work of Protestantism, then one must investigate and present the conditions in the separate territories more thoroughly than heretofore (as Herbert Schöffler recently has done it for Silesia). Only in this way can one hope to surmount the state of affairs existing up to the present time, where generalities and hypothetic explanations must serve as a temporary substitute for accurate historical insight. Obviously the conditions in Catholic domains must be simultaneously investigated. Only by comparison will it clearly emerge how different in substance and form are the literary creations here and there, which nevertheless existed at the same time in the same realm.

JUAN RUIZ de ALARCON

By

Alfonso Reyes, LL. D.

*President, El Colegio de México, formerly Mexican Minister Plenipotentiary
to France, Spain, Argentina, and at Various Times Ambassador
to Argentina, Brazil, etc.*

CHAPTER XV

JUAN RUIZ de ALARCON

BY

ALFONSO REYES

I

During the 1620's, while Philip IV, patron of the theater, sat on the throne of Spain, the public developed an exaggerated liking for comedy, which was at once its cinema and its daily newspaper, its spiritual food and its commentary on current events. To satisfy the demand, authors would improvise plays in twenty-four hours; or several of them would join together and parcel out a certain number of scenes between them. The genius of Lope de Vega enabled the theater to create for itself an economical, expressive and easy formula. Horsemen would say that the theater had "struck a steady gait." Even so, it is astonishing that, despite this haste, a high percentage of worthwhile works were produced along with those other immortal plays, which everybody knows and which, naturally, were wrought more leisurely. The public was not content with seeing the plays; it wanted to read them. This appetite produced piratical practices on the part of publishers, who employed individuals endowed with extraordinary memories. These terrible "memorizers" were capable of learning a play at a single performance. They would write it down, patching it here and there with verses of their own invention. Thus, what with corruptions, and even false assumptions of authorship, the work appeared promptly, and was included in theatrical anthologies of some sort.

The "fancy" are never content with the play itself, but focus their curiosity on the skillful fencers, on the holders of the championship. The literary warfare between the playwrights interests the public as much as the plays themselves. As in ancient Greece, the theater continues to be virtually a public contest. The prize is not, to be sure, a tripod, nor a crown. The guerdon is the ovation, the acclaim which the work receives. The streets of Madrid are filled with inscriptions in red, with panegyrics and names. These have nothing to do with candidates for public office; they concern writers of comedy. Suddenly, there appears an ironical lampoon. It ridicules two poets:

> *Long live Don Juan de Alarcón*
> *And the Mercedarian friar!*
> *(To befoul the wall,*
> *If for no other reason.)*

It is evident that the jibes come from the Lope de Vega faction and are aimed at Alarcón, whom the incorrigible Phoenix of the Geniuses has singled out for attack, and against the Mercedarian Fray Gabriel Téllez, known in the world of letters as Tirso de Molina. They form, the two of them, a band apart.

But who is this man, Alarcón, who has so greatly fluttered the noisy literary dovecot, and around whom what we would today call the "world of the footlights," stirs up such a clamor? He is a colonial from the Indies, born in Mexico. At the age of twenty he was a student at Salamanca, where he graduated as a bachelor in both branches of law. He practiced as a pettifogging lawyer at Seville, and then went back to his native land, where he graduated as a Licentiate of Law and held office as Lieutenant *Corregidor*. Later on he decided to return to Madrid as a "suitor at Court." And as the achievement of his ambition was delayed, and the scanty savings he had brought with him did not apparently go very far, he blossomed out as a dramatic author. His first attempts showed that he was clever enough to hold his own with the best of them.

However, if nature had been kind to him in the matter of brains, she had been niggardly as regards other gifts. He was undersized, a hunchback and pigeon-breasted. His hair was blond, verging on ginger, and his face was rather sallow. His appearance was far from imposing, and he utterly lacked that presence that would have helped him so greatly to obtain the longed-for posts in the Audiencias of the Americas or the Council of the Indies. The somewhat debased gentry of the pen, who, since they were able to live by their trade, thanks to the boom in the stage, were recruited from the ranks of laymen more or less well equipped, and no longer, as in the preceding century, from the world of humanists, clergymen, captains and ambassadors, scurrilously assail our colonial. They liken him to an ape; they compare him with Soplillo, his Majesty's buffoon, or with the diabolical beings depicted by the fantastic brush of the Dutchman, Jerome Bosco. They said that with a hump in front and another behind no one knew whether he was facing them or had his back turned; that his pigeon breast was like a false witness; that he was a poet sandwiched between two plates; that he was a knock-kneed bard and the satyr of the Muses; and lastly, that the "D" of the "Don" he insisted on using before his name was his own portrait cut in half.

It need hardly be said that he paid his adversaries back in kind, in the verses of his plays, and reminded them that it was only too easy to overlook one's own failings, to mock the physical deformities of one's fellow-man. He said that God "did not bestow all His gifts upon one man alone" and thus made it up to an ugly duckling by endowing him with wisdom to disdain the insults of the foolish. As regards the use of the title *Don,* he alleged rights of descent and birth, and said that if a ragamuffin with a long string of surnames was a bore, in contrast the *Don* before the name of a *hidalgo* was like the robe of a military order on the breast of a nobleman.

The scandal reached its height one night, when Alarcón's

Antichrist was being played. Someone smashed a phial of evil-smelling liquor in the middle of the theater. There was a great commotion. The performance was very nearly ruined. Vallejo, in the character of the hero, had to swing across the stage on a rope, but he lost his head and did not venture to do his act. Luisa de Robles, a comédienne, snatched his cloak and crown from him and launched herself into space. She saved the situation, and her feat was later recorded by Góngora in a sonnet. Lope de Vega and Mira de Mescue wound up in jail as the authors or instigators of the outrage.

Despite all this, it was not long before our man, after being so much in the public eye, withdrew into obscurity and forsook the petty triumphs of the moment, to aspire to something more enduring. His meteoric passage across the Spanish stage lasted but a decade. As soon as he obtained a post as reporter to the Council of the Indies he gradually dropped what he himself described as "making a virtue of necessity."

He had an assured income, something like two thousand dollars a month, and although he left an illegitimate daughter, happily married in a village of La Mancha, he led a bachelor existence in a bijou house on Calle Urosas. He kept his carriage, a retinue of servants, and an assembly of select friends. This discreet and well-regulated existence suited both his temperament and his office of minister, which he seems to have taken very seriously. About 1636, three years before he died, an Italian man of letters wandering about Madrid, one Fabio Franchi, prayed Apollo to run him to earth and exhort him to write clever comedies, as formerly, and "not to forsake Parnassus for the Americas, nor ambrosia for chocolate."

II

The fact is that Don Juan Ruiz de Alarcón y Mendoza, for that was his full name, had not been born for the daily scrimmage on the public square, but for study and serene cultivation of the Muses. Financial need, however, compelled him to earn his living by roundabout ways, until he made himself independent. The poet came from an illustrious though not wealthy family. On his father's side he was descended from a noble house of Cuenca, and on his mother's he was related to some of the most highly placed families of Spain. His maternal grandfather, one Hernando de Mendoza, had settled in New Spain, perhaps seeking the patronage of the first Viceroy, the worthy Don Antonio de Mendoza, of whom he was a relative. To their noble Spanish origin the Ruiz de Alarcóns added the further distinction of being one of the first families of the colony. Our poet's father appears as a mine operator in the Tasco camp, which had drawn the Spaniards from the very first, because of a report that Montezuma's tribute of gold bars had been won from its mines.

Alarcón, throughout his whole life, stands out as a man who was dependent on the support of powerful patrons, and who was always endeavoring to obtain this or that post or office to live upon. The bonanza at Tasco was perhaps declining when our poet was born, for his parents had already moved to the City of Mexico.

He managed to go to the University of Salamanca and to get his bachelor's degrees, thanks to the foundation instituted on his death-bed by an Alderman of Seville, Gaspar Ruiz de Montoya. This worthy had founded a scholarship for such of his relatives as were desirous of going to Salamanca but lacked the wherewithal. If Alarcón failed to get either of his degrees in law, it was perhaps due to the fact that the festivities ensuing upon graduation were far beyond his modest means.

When he decided to practice law at Seville, in the hope of better times, he may have sought the interest of his cousin, Father Diego Ruiz de Montoya, a brother of Gaspar of that ilk, and an eminent churchman who was looked upon as an oracle in that city. When he made up his mind to return to Mexico, he raised funds from open-handed friends, and obtained an appoint-

ment as servant to Fray Pedro Godinez Maldonado, Bishop of
Nueva Cáceres, in the Philippines, so as to travel gratis as a
member of the ecclesiastic's suite. But as the expedition never
set sail because the ships had to be diverted to fight the Dutch,
Alarcón went on practising law at Seville.

Finally the longed-for day arrived, and even then he applied
for permission to take three servants out with him to Mexico,
but he was finally content with one only. He doubtless wanted
the permit in order to sell the man to a fellow-traveller, thus
reducing his expense. It is assumed that this time he took the
journey as a member of the retinue of Archbishop Fray Garcia
Guerra, which likewise included Mateo Alemán. The Archbishop
was later to attend, in Mexico City, the ceremony of Alarcón's
graduation as a Licentiate of Laws. If he later succeeded in being
released from the pomp and circumstance incidental to the ceremony of the doctorate, although this degree he never did obtain,
it was because he was "so very poor, as Your Honor well knew."

Alarcón thereupon thought of going back to Spain, tempted
perhaps by the hope that the Viceroy, Don Luis de Velasco, a
friend of the family's in Mexico, who had returned to the metropolis in 1611, might extend to him his protection. But there is
nothing to show that he ever did secure that interest, nor that
of his relative, the celebrated ecclesiastic, Fray Diego Ruiz de
Montoya, nor of his college companion at Salamanca, Dr. Gutierre Marqués de Careaga, Lieutenant Corregidor of Madrid, nor
approved of of Don Diego de Agreda y Vargas, whose father
sat on the Supreme Council and was a member of the King's
Chamber.

It is known that he occupied himself with some petty family
business and in collecting or paying accounts between Spain and
Mexico. In any event, it was then that he made up his mind to
engage in play-writing. The theater attracted him in theory, as
a literary exercise. It may be that in actual practice he grew to
hate it, because of the many unpleasantnesses caused by contact

with all that gilded canaille of the world of letters. When he published his collected comedies he defied the populace in the prologue and haughtily said "To thee I speak, thou savage beast." Thanks to the interest of Don Ramiro Núñez Felipez de Guzmán, the son-in-law of Count and Duke de Olivares, (the great court favorite of the King) and Chairman of the Council of the Indies, Alarcón obtained two successive appointments to that high body, first as acting reporter and after that as the regular holder of the office.

In fine, throughout Alarcón's life one can see that his decline was governed by that of his protecting Maecenas, and that he was compelled to travel its path by resorting to the shifts forced upon him by poverty.

III

Although our poet did occasionally write fair verse, when he had to, he did not aspire to fame as a lyric poet. His work was done for the stage. Alarcón's comedies in some ways are ahead of his time. They even crossed frontiers, and influenced Corneille's dramatic work, for *La Verdad Sospechosa*—Alarcón's most popular and best liked work—was by the French dramatist paraphrased in his *Le Menteur*. Through this play of Corneille's, even Molière and French comedies of manners were influenced. In Spain itself, Alarcón, although a very celebrated and famous playwright, can hardly be said to have left any immediate tradition behind him. Still, the "reformers of taste" who marked the transition from the eighteenth to the nineteenth centuries, were destined to view him sympathetically.

The explanation is obvious. In the riotous world of Spanish comedy, Alarcón struck a muffled note, in a minor tone. Where all the others, from the mighty Lope de Vega downward, stood out because of their rich inventiveness and lyric power—even though at times they confine the psychological treatment of their characters to the elementary mechanics of personal honor—Alarcón appears more concerned with true problems of conduct; he is less inventive, and far less lyric; but he created the comedy of manners. His dialogue rises to pinnacles of unrivalled perfection; his characters do not know how to sing, they are not heroes, they never indulge in soaring flights of fancy. They do nothing but talk, they are men of this world, their feet are planted on the solid earth.

That is why it has been said that Alarcón is the most "modern" of the dramatists of the golden century. In his plays there are no deeply tragic situations, but rather peaceful discussions of ethical issues, so discreetly developed in a minor key that at times they seem to be scarcely more than problems of mere urbanity. Alarcón's cleverness as an observer, the serenity and intimacy of certain conversations, his touch, never exaggerated, in defining characters, his preaching of virtue, his faith in reason as the sole standard of life, his respect for appointed station in all orders of humanity; these are his outstanding qualities. His characters are pleasant neighbors, with whom one would be delighted to have a chat in the evening, in a cosy inner apartment, or at sunset, from a gallery overlooking the Manzanares.

All this means that Alarcón departed to a slight extent—not more than slightly, for he never overdid anything, and only went just far enough to assume an unmistakable tinge—from the standards which Lope had imposed on the stage of his day. Where all the others improvised, he was slow, patient, with a fine consciousness of artistry; where all extricated themselves from difficult situations by dint of ingenuity and even left things half done, Alarcón tried to confine himself to the inner claims of his subject, and never ceased until he obtained that wonderful smoothness which make of his verses, even though not musical nor lyric, a delight to the understanding and examples of perfection in his best comedies. Where they all of them turned out comedies in the thousands, Alarcón wrote a scant two dozen.

How complex and refined a personality! A nice feeling for

human dignity seems to underlie every other quality. As we advance from his intimate ego to the social and aesthetic aspects of his work, we find the following strata: a virile love of sincerity, which never degenerates into crudity; an enthusiastic fondness for reason, by which he wished to install on earth the reign of intelligence, as he invariably endeavors to bring home to us the confusion resulting from any conduct that departs from this higher law. He evinces a certain chivalrous pride in his name and lineage, born of fondness for greater dignity of living, an outward manifestation of an inner quality; his liking for courtesy and the cultivation of good manners, as a perpetual check on brutality, to keep men ever alert and make them strive unremittingly after perfection. He evidences his distaste for the routine and conventional expedients of his art, but without ever allowing himself a single revolutionary outburst, because of his worship of moderation. His words are clothed in epigrammatic elegance, and a discreet objectiveness is discernible in his portraits. His attitude towards life is mistrustful, due perhaps to his deformity and personal defects, and even to his colonial origin, which he was never allowed to forget. Lastly, his appeal to all the organizing forces which man has at his command, his undying faith in harmoniousness, his longing for greater human cordiality, all these stamp his life and work with the seal of ingenuousness. In the midst of the howling literary pack, that mocked and hurt him, he is not convinced that human nature is essentially bad, and seeks by every means an outward and impersonal foundation for his optimism. He was satisfied with his reputation as a poet, and demanded his share of the world's good things with decent naturalness. And then he aspired to become a good councillor. But we doubt whether he ever felt really happy.

IV

In any gallery of Mexican worthies the opening chapter must perforce deal with Alarcón. His work is the first eminent and internationally valuable manifestation of what may even then be called the Mexican spirit. This spirit antedates our political autonomy very considerably. Despite the ups and downs, and vicissitudes of history, it continues to be our standard, and our ideal, as evidenced in Alarcón.

This new mode of feeling and construing life is already evident among the sons of the conquistadors, if we are to believe the testimony of observant travellers of that day. It is also apparent from the literary satires or contests in verse between the long-settled and the recently arrived Spaniards, as preserved in ancient chronicles. Even if we confine ourselves to the Spaniards of Mexico, without considering ethnic mixtures, it is undoubted that they had undergone changes due to the altered environment, and the unwonted financial situation that turned former gold-seekers and adventurers into great lords. Another factor was contact with a solemn and ancient race, which never ceased to make them feel that they were on their guard, and served as a stimulus to reform. Lastly, we must not omit from our purview something equally potent, viz., the urge to differentiate, a consequence of that "mysticism of the first occupant" which opposed the claims of an aristocracy of conquest to those of the ancient aristocracy of noble descent, and set up the pride of eyes fixed on the future of New Spain, against the pride of eyes that looked back to the metropolis. And these new men deliberately did their best to be different from the older generation, and to stress the contrasts between them and it. While the Indies, to the man from the Peninsula, were something like a jumbled-up paradise of lucre and pleasure, the native son looked upon them as a land naturally lordly. If even today, when the world has been so shaken up together, we can distinguish perfectly between a Basque and an Andalusian, an Englishman or an Australian or a Canadian, what must it not have been in those days, when a Spaniard would transplant himself to Mexico bag and baggage, to hear no more of Spain except through the symbolical relations of political or ecclesiastical institutions? In these

[334]

early differentiations, which would ere long beget a sense of national hostility in the children of Cortés the Conqueror, the germs of future independence lay dormant.

Even from a cultural standpoint Mexico had already developed her own idosyncrasy by the year 1596, when Alarcón joined the University.

A half-century before, Francisco Cervantes de Salazar, in his *Latin Dialogues,* described for us a City of Mexico that was both monumental and imposing. Balbuena, circa 1603, visualized it through the curved lenses of a poet, as clothed with singular charm. The University, founded about the middle of the sixteenth century, had become a fair copy of its model at Salamanca. Once the greater part of the land had been conquered, letters as a career began to be more attractive than the life of a soldier, to the scions of good families who aspired to posts in the State.

From Spain, men as learned as Cervantes de Salazar himself had come to teach at the new University, the jurist Bartolome Frías de Albornoz, celebrated for his *Brocense,* and the Aristotelian philosopher Fray Alonso de la Vera Cruz, the great friend of another eminent monk, Fray Luis de León. The ample prospects of life in Mexico had enticed poets and men of letters like Gutierre de Cetina, Juan de la Cueva, and Eugenio Salazar de Alarcón, to say nothing of missionaries and churchmen who brought with them ample cultural equipment, or the many chroniclers who came to narrate what were then called the "exploits of the Church." Shortly afterwards, during the youth of Alarcón, Luis de Belmonte, Diego Mejía and Mateo Alemán alighted on Mexican shores. Poets like Francisco de Terrazas and Antonio de Saavedra Guzmán worthily testify to the advance of native culture. In the sixteenth century alone, one can count more than a hundred Mexican literary men. Early in the following century González de Eslava makes one Donna Murmuración say without embarrassment that poets were commoner than clods. Both Eslava and Balbuena owe everything to their Mexican training.

The printing press, introduced in the first half of the sixteenth century, had already turned out hundreds of books. And the stage, lastly, originally introduced by the missionaries for catechizing purposes, was already, by 1597, housed in a building of its own. Balbuena remarked that new feasts and comedies were staged every day.

When Alarcón left his native land for the celebrated University of Salamanca, he had already spent the first twenty years of his life in an environment that wore an unmistakable stamp of its own. This was more than enough time in which to build up a mental physiognomy.

In Alarcón's works we find scarcely any references to things Mexican, or suggestive of the atmosphere of the Americas generally, except his recollections of the Canal draining the Valley of Mexico, or his allusions to the vanity and ostentation of enriched colonies. But, on the other hand, the penetration of a certain moral and sentimental atmosphere can be noted throughout his work. This atmosphere is decidedly Mexican, and this can easily be verified by a certain impression of "strangeness" which the *littérateurs* of Madrid never concealed when alluding to Alarcón's plays. A contemporary critic has even gone so far as to call him an "intruder." The peninsular Spaniards disliked Alarcón's exquisite urbanity and refinement; they thought him tiresome and snobbish. They laughed to his face at his petty vanities of a provincial seigneur sunk into bohemianism.

One can only wish that the great and harassed poet had been as fortunate as the obscure writer of these lines, for when his fate cast the latter on to the shores of Spanish literature, he encountered nothing but help and understanding, and discreet commiseration for his misfortunes! Newspaper men and writers behaved like brothers, ever ready to share with him their honestly earned bread and their congenial labor!

PART VI
MEDICINE

THE TRANSMISSION AND RECOVERY

OF

GREEK AND ROMAN MEDICAL WRITINGS

By

Dallas B. Phemister, M. D.

Professor and Chairman Department of Surgery, University of Chicago

CHAPTER XVI

THE TRANSMISSION AND RECOVERY OF GREEK AND ROMAN MEDICAL WRITINGS

BY

DALLAS B. PHEMISTER

Modern medical progress has been so great and so rapid that the accomplishments in ancient times appear, by comparison, to have been trivial and sluggish and are seldom mentioned in current literature except by way of historical review. The contrast is particularly great as compared with the sustained interest in Greco-Roman accomplishments which obtains in certain fields of humanistic learning. Medical books and journals of two or three decades ago are for the most part outmoded at present, whereas medical books of antiquity often remained standard for generations and even for centuries. However, careful scrutiny reveals that the debt which we owe to the more slowly accumulated ancient contributions that have been woven into the fabric of common medical knowledge and to which specific reference is no longer made is undoubtedly great. By far the greatest obligation is to the Greeks who steadily advanced both the science and the art of medicine during the period from approximately 600 B.C. to 200 A.D. Progress ended with Galen (139 to 201 A.D.) and subsequent writings consisted mainly of rehashes of previous works. The Romans, despite their great civilizing influence, added extremely little to medical knowledge and throughout the life of the Roman Empire, the most efficient medical education and research were conducted in the Greek medical schools of the Eastern Mediterranean region.

There was a decadence of medicine with the decline and fall of the Empire and throughout the Dark Ages in western Europe, both the Greek literature and the Greek standards of practice were so reduced that they exerted very little influence. It is of more than usual interest to inquire how the legacy of Greek medicine was transmitted from the ancient to the modern world across the near-hiatus created by the Middle Ages. Where were the manuscripts stored, and how and by whom were they recovered? Who conducted the practice of medicine and how much of the old tradition was recovered? What other peoples acquired a knowledge of Greek medicine and how much of it was reclaimed from their writings? What were the effects of the recoveries from the various sources upon subsequent medical dedevelopment? Many of these questions remain unanswered and further searchings will be necessary before all of the light which is veiled in existing libraries and documents is brought to shine upon the subject.

Of Greek medical literature, it has been estimated that probably half was lost to the modern world. The most important works of the creative period are: the Hippocratic Corpus, before 300 B.C., the Alexandrian writings which are known only through citations of subsequent writers, Dioscorides, Aretaeus, Rufus, Soranus, Antyllus and Galen.

After the creative period came Oribasius (4th c.), Aeteus, Alexander of Tralles, and lastly Paul of Aegina (7th c.).

Of Roman medical literature, the only work that showed any originality was that of Celsus (first half 1st c.) known for its contributions to surgery. After the decline and fall of the Empire, most medical writings in the West consisted of breviaries, compends, or epitomes of existing works. The best known author was Caelius Aurelianus, who composed two works of his own and translated into Latin the eight books of Soranus entitled *De Morbis Acutis et Chronicis*. They filled a great popular need and in contrast with the buried Greek works remained in continuous use throughout the entire period of the Middle Ages. Vindicianus, Theorodorus Priscianus, Cassius Felix and Marcellus Empiricus are a few of the compiles of documents devoid of originality. A breviary of the practical medicine contained in the Natural History of Pliny the Younger had a great influence on lay medicine.

The Catholic Church, both Roman and Greek, was an important agency in the transmission of the legacy in which the libraries of the monasteries and cathedrals played prominent rôles. With the establishment of monasteries in the West in the sixth century, the monks became active in the practice of medicine. St. Benedict founded the first order at Monte Cassino in the year 529. He was a man of limited education but his monks were instructed in the care of the sick which became a large part of their duties. They also had to copy manuscripts, some of which were medical, "to fight against the temptations of the devil with pen and ink." As monasteries of the Benedictine and other orders sprang up over Europe, there was an expansion of practice by monks and of medical literature since the monastic libraries all acquired collections of books on medicine.

Vivarium monastery near Squillace Calabria was established between 546 and 555 by the nobleman and scholar, Cassiodorus, heir to the classical and pagan traditions which he regarded as complementary but not hostile to Christian learning. There he built up a congenial community embued with enthusiasm for classical and Christian learning and a library rich in classical and Christian literature which greatly influenced the intellectual development of Europe throughout the Middle Ages. A scriptorium was established in which both Greek and Latin works were translated, including many on medicine. This is indicated by his statement to the monks in the *Institutiones* that "If Greek literature is closed to you, then read Latin translations of Dioscorides, Hippocrates, Galen, Caelius Aurelianus and many other books

[343]

which you will find in the library." While the fate of the library of Cassiodorus is veiled in obscurity, the indications are strong that a spread of copies from here as well as the transfer of the originals and of translations played a considerable role in both the popularization of medical knowledge and the preservation of ancient traditions and documents. Thus Beer advanced evirium collection was transferred to Bobbio monastery during the seventh century. Some of the Bobbio manuscripts are in the Beneventine script employed at Vivarium and some of the palempsests were written on parchment from which works of Galen and Dioscorides had been incompletely erased.

While it has been possible to find evidence that medical books were contained in the libraries of many western monasteries and cathedrals during the Middle Ages, still knowledge as to their numbers, authors and ultimate fate is in most cases very scanty. The early cataloguers stressed the patristic and slighted the secular and as medicine usually came at the end and they were "blessedly ignorant" of it, the lists of medical books were often lamentably slashed and mutilated. J. W. Thompson's *The Mediaeval Library* and Th. Gottlieb's "Mediaeval Libraries" contain a great deal of information on the subject.

The theory that refugees to Ireland and Britain from the Continent, during the barbarian invasions, carried medical books among others with them which one or two centuries later were returned to the Continent at the time of establishment of the Irish and Anglo-Saxon monasteries, is based on conjecture rather than established fact (A. C. Clark, *Trans. Bibliographic Soc.* 1921). The evidence is that the monks took with them psalters, hymnals, etc. which were necessary for their religious mission and that the medical books which the monasteries acquired came from Continental sources. At least it is not known that the Irish monasteries, including St. Gall and Bobbio, or the Anglo-Saxon monasteries, including Fulda and Corbie, contained medical manuscripts written in the Insular script.

With the Carolingian revival of classical learning, it is logical to conclude that there must have been a growth in the medical literature of the monastery and cathedral libraries. If so, according to Thompson, it is scarcely reflected in the extant catalogues of the times. St. Requier in 831 contained *De Medicamentis* by Quintus Serenus. Reichenau in 822 had an interesting collection on medicine, including treatises by Galen, Vindicianus, Eupate, Democritus, Publius Vegetius Renatus, Rabenus Maurus, Soranus and Caelius Aurelianus. A ninth century catalogue of Lorsch contains 590 books with the authors and titles listed except the "three volumes of medical works."

Nothing is known of classical manuscripts in England before the Norman Conquest and no catalogues of libraries of that period have been preserved. In Norman and Angevin England both church and monastic libraries thrived and catalogues of most of them record medical books in variable numbers, nearly all of which are in Latin. The only record of a Greek manuscript is Galen's *Tegni* which Richard of Bury (1286-1343) obtained from the Bishop of Durham and translated into Latin at Oxford.

Beginning with the eleventh century, the cathedral libraries of the Continent came to the fore since the cathedral schools then surpassed those of the monasteries. But if the inventories of all these libraries as catalogued by Becker are examined for medicine, the rewards are very meagre indeed. At Reichenau, there were twelve medical codices, all but four identifiable. At Regensburg, there were ten unnamed books on the medical arts. Treatises of Hippocrates and Galen were in the library of St. Peter's monastery at Salzburg in the twelfth century.

The eastern Mediterranean proved to be a much more favorable and important field for the preservation of the classical medical legacy than did western Europe. There was less destruction of property and institutions and the Greek-speaking Byzantine Empire went through a period of cultural development while the West was submerged in the Dark Ages. Both state and private libraries were established in the principal cities but especially in Constantinople which were the repositories for both Greek and Latin manuscripts. The monasteries of the Eastern Church which remained free from molestation for centuries built up libraries which contained important Greek manuscripts on medicine. It is noteworthy that despite the existence of these storehouses of medical knowledge, the general cultural decline and the hostility of Christianity to the Hellenic spirit of inquiry were such that no new contributions were made to medicine by the Byzantines. Also the sack of Constantinople in 1203 by the fourth Crusaders, during which according to Villehardouin and Nicetas "splendid palaces, filled with works of ancient art and classic manuscripts, were destroyed" was, according to Montague James, far more disastrous in its obliteration of works of art and of literature than was the capture of the City by the Turks in 1453.

An early event in the East that had great bearing on the preservation of Greek medicine was the expulsion of Nestorius from Constantinople in 431 because of the variety of his Christian faith. The Nestorian Christians migrated to Edessa in Mesopotamia where they established a school and hospital and translated the chief works of Greek philosophy and science, including medicine, into Syrian. But the Byzantine government in 487 closed the school and the exiled teachers were given asylum at Nisibis, Persia. There under the tolerant Sassanidae they prospered and soon established an academy, medical school and hospital at Gondisapor which remained the most important Eastern medical center for centuries. Although the country was under the rule of Islam, the school remained in possession of the Nestorians. Translations of Greek medical works into Syrian and Persian were carried on and the rapid development of Arabic medicine owed a great deal to this particular school.

ARABIC TRANSMISSION

A good example of the conservation of energy is afforded by the fact that when medicine ceased to progress in Byzantium, the Greek torch was taken by Islam and carried to a height unsurpassed during the Middle Ages. The Abbassides caliphs in the second half of the eighth and ninth centuries brought together in Mesopotamia a large collection of manuscripts including medical, and an efficient group of translators, for the most part Syrians, Persians, Greeks and Jews, most of them practitioners of medicine, and it was this art mainly which aroused the enthusiasm for translation.

The Arabic translations were at first from the Syrian, later directly from the Greek. Among the numerous translators, the most prominent were Mesue and Johannitius. All of the important medical works were rendered into Arabic, including Hippocrates, Dioscorides, Archigenes, Rufus, Galen, Oribasius, Philagrios, Alexander of Tralles and Paul of Aegina. This led to the development of a school of Arabian medicine which expanded over the Moslem world and continued to flourish for four hundred years. Schools, libraries and hospitals were set up in Mesopotamia, North Africa, and Spain and a literature was created which was characterized more by erudite scholarship than by new discoveries. Avicenna, Rhazes, Haly Abbas, Maimonides and Albucasis are some of the outstanding men whose works display the Greek influence to a marked degree.

The revival of Greek medicine in the Western world had its beginnings during the tenth century in remote southern Italy where foreign influences from the east made themselves strongly felt. This region was the seat of lingering Greco-Roman medical traditions and of scattered units of Greek-speaking immigrants who had found refuge there from the barbarian invasions. It was a meeting point of western Europeans, Moslems, Byzantines and Jews. There was no lack of diffusion of medical knowledge outside the church and it was under these circumstances that a lay medical school came into being at Salerno in the tenth century which became a Mecca of medical practice and learning for western Europe in the eleventh to thirteenth centuries comparable with those of ancient Cos and Alexandria and the Mayo Clinic of recent years in the United States. The spirit was that of a Civitas Hippocratica in which emphasis was placed on accurate clinical observation and simple interpretation of symptoms and signs as a background for a simple, mechanical, dietetic or medicinal therapy as an ajunct to the healing power of nature. There is little known of the Greek manuscripts which may have been at hand in the earliest development of Salerno: Archbishop Alfanus of Salerno, who rendered into Latin "The Nature of Man" by Nemesios, may have been the first Salernian to translate a Greek medical work. But that Latin translations and compilations of Greek works were freely available, has been amply demonstrated. The most important ones were *Dioscuridea Langobardus, Passionarius Galeni,* attributed to "Gariopontus" and the *Practica* of Petroncellus.

In the second half of the eleventh century came the first known recovery of works of Galen and Hippocrates. Constantinus Africanus (1018-1087) was born in Carthage where he received his early education. He allegedly spent thirty years in the Moslem East and about the last fifteen years of his life at Monte Cassino Monastery where under its scholarly abbot, Desiderius, he devoted his time to translation. Constantine was possessed of a full knowledge of Latin and Arabic and a modicum of Greek. He translated from Arabic into Latin the Aphorisms of Hippocrates and the Ars Parva and the Commentaries on the writings of Hippocrates of Galen; also the works of the Arabic authors, Ali Abbas, Ibn al-Djezzar, and Isaac Judaeus. These new sources of knowledge helped to free the choked well-springs of antiquity and to hasten the advance of Occidental medicine. Salerno reached its high point of development in the twelfth century and the writings of Bartolomaeus, Copho, Johannes, Platearius, Petronius and others bear testimony to the Greek influence exercised by the translations. But the influence of Constantine was almost entirely local and it required a further development in Spain to awaken the West to the significance of Arabic writings as a source of recovery of Greek medical knowledge.

The extent of the cultural possessions of the Arabs was realized by Westerners through the Near-East contacts with them during the Crusades and on the international highway in southern Italy. Also after the Moors were driven out of Castile in 1085, the Christian population came into possession of a territory that for three centuries had been the seat of a highly developed Moorish culture. Toledo, principal seat of learning, with its fine Arabic libraries, soon became the center for study and attracted large numbers of scholars from various parts of western Europe. Mozarabs and Jews who had a knowledge of Arabic, Spanish and Latin were of great assistance and early in the twelfth century, a school of translation was established by Archbishop Raymund under the direction of Gundisalvi. Some of the workers at the school were Plato of Tivoli, Herman of Corinthia, Robert of Chester, Hugh of Santilla, Alfred the Englishman and Michael Scott. But Gerard of Cremona (1114-1187) was the real king of Arabic translators. Under the protection of Emperor Frederick Barbarossa, he went to Toledo while in search of Ptolemy's astronomical work, the Almagest. But on finding there a multitude of treasures of Arabic literature, he became rooted to the spot and spent the remaining and better part of his life at learning, teaching and translating. He acquired a knowledge of Arabic and utilized the services of a Mozarab, Galippus. His translations from Arabic into Latin, variously estimated from 70 to 90 in number, covered the different fields of learning but dealt especially with mathematics, astronomy, philosophy and medicine. The works of Hippocrates, Galen and Serapion of the Greek school, and of Avicenna, Rhazes, Isaac Judaeus, Alkmaien and Abenguefit of the Arabic school, were the most important translations. Aristotle might also be included as his scientific and philosophical writings influenced the course of medicine during the succeeding age of Scholasticism. Marcus of Toledo also translated some of the works of Galen and the Isagage of Johannitius.

The translations in Spain were finished by the year 1300, some of which contained a great many inaccuracies that were only remedied after comparison with other translations from Arabic and Greek sources. Latin renderings of Arabic works made subsequently in Sicily by Faradj provided little new knowledge of the medicine of antiquity but were somewhat more accurate than those of Gerard.

The effects of the Arabic translations upon western medicine were two-fold: many facts, principally of Greek origin, were acquired which were helpful in the recognition and treatment of medical and surgical conditions; and the medical schools of the universities made use of the works of both the Greeks and the Moslems as shown by the lists of prescribed texts in use. But the spirit of Galen rather than that of Hippocrates had permeated Arabic medicine and fostered dogmatism and submission to authority rather freedom of inquiry. The result was to smother investigation in the schools of medicine of the universities of the thirteenth century which were already steeped in scholasticism and to choke intellectual activity and independent observation with dazzling dialectics.

Fortunately for the future of medicine, a desire was kindled for an acquaintance with the Greek texts from which the Arabs had derived their scholastic lore. This eventually came about as a part of the general revival of ancient learning in the fourteenth and fifteenth centuries for which reason it is difficult to treat medicine separately. The patrons of learning and the discoverers of manuscripts were usually more interested in the humanities than in other fields and like the cataloguers of monastic libraries, often left little or no record of the medical works collected. Famous authors were frequently recorded for which reason there is much more information about the recovery of the works of Galen and Hippocrates than of the other medical writers.

The greatest interest in the revival of ancient learning arose in Italy and credit for the recovery of the Greek and Roman manuscripts and for their translation into Latin belongs principally to the Italians. Sabbadini in the Historical Library of the Renaissance (*Le Scoperti dei Codici Latini e Grece n'secoli XIV e XV*, Florence 1905 and 1914) has made the most outstanding investigation of the subject. The earliest impulse originated in Sicily and the southern end of the peninsula where translations of Greek manuscripts were made in the twelfth century. During the same period in northern Italy, Jacobus Venetiusm, Moses Bergamo and Burgundus Pisano rendered six of Galen's works into Latin. Robert, King of Sicily (1309-1342), obtained a collection of eleven manuscripts of Galen and four of Hippocrates from the Byzantine Emperor Andromicus III which the Calabrian Greek physician, Niccolo de Deoprepio, translated into Latin. Gido da Magnala, physician to the King of Cyprus, collected a Greek library which in 1362 was acquired by the University of Bologna. It contained one book each of Hippocrates and Galen. However, the effect of the translations on existing medicine was very slight.

Pertrarch (1304-1374) and Boccaccio (1313-1375), were fired with enthusiasm for the literature of ancient Rome by studies of Virgil, Cicero and Tacitus which led to searches for ancient manuscripts in the monasteries of western Europe. and in Byzantium that were destined to have far-reaching effects. In addition to valuable Latin works, Petrarch found a Plato in Greek, apparently in France, and Boccaccio a Homer and other Greek works in Italy.

An important event for the mobilization of Greek manuscripts was the slow Turkish occupation of the Byzantine Empire. Toward the end of the fourteenth century Greek manuscripts began to arrive in Italy from the East. They were brought by refugees and by Byzantine envoys sent to solicit aid for defense against the Turks. A Dominican monk, Bandino, had a collection of manuscripts in Florence at the end of the fourteenth century, including four books of Galen in Greek. Manuel Chrisoloras, a nobleman and scholar, was the first envoy to bring manuscripts. He arrived in Venice in 1394 and was established as a teacher of Greek in Florence from 1396 to 1404. One of his pupils, Angili da Scarperis, accompanied him to Constantinople in 1397 and returned with Greek manuscripts of Plato, Homer, Plutarch and others. In 1403 Guarino Veronese accompanied Chrisoloras to Constantinople and remained in Byzantium for five years collecting Greek manuscripts. After returning home, he continued to add to the collection until it eventually numbered 54 manuscripts, including works of Hippocrates.

From the general standpoint of Greek literature, by far the most important discoverer of and dealer in manuscripts was Giovanni Aurispa, a Calabrian, with a knowledge of Greek, whom Sabbadini called the greatest bibliophile of the fifteenth century. He made trips to Byzantium and the eastern Mediterranean between 1404 and 1415 and recovered some of the choicest works, including those of Euripides, Sophocles and Thucydides. In 1421 he went again and remained eighteen months, returning in the company of the Emperor John Paleologus. While there he succeeded in collecting the most precious lot of profane Greek works ever obtained on one mission. They came principally from the monasteries both of the mainland and of the islands. Some of the manuscripts were sent back to Florence and Messina while he was still at Constantinople. According to his record there were about 300 in all, 238 of which were of such importance as to constitute a well rounded library. If so, then medicine must have been represented but, alas, no medical authors appear to have been mentioned in the catalogue of the "principal works" which he recorded in three letters to Traversari. The only direct reference to medicine in connection with the acquistion is that of Paremonti Rinuccio da Castiglione who reported that while on the return voyage with Aurispa, he saw a work of Hippocrates. Also Hippocrates was represented in Aurispa's library twenty years later at the time of his death. Aurispa translated some manuscripts but he was more of a collector and dealer than a scholar and had perhaps greater interest in the commercial than in the cultural value of his collections. Hence he may have been as little inclined to mention medical works as had been the cataloguers of the monastic and cathedral libraries.

Francisco Filelfi was another of the well-known Italian collectors to explore the East (1420-1427). He is recorded as possessing 40 odd manuscripts "some of which were medical." Ciriaco saw and acquired Greek Codices both sacred and profane at Chios, Leucosia, Salonica, and most important, at the Island of Taso. Among them were works of Aristotle, Hippocrates and Galen. Benzio translated Dioscorides into Latin (De Herbarum Notione) in 1433 at Padua but the source of the manuscript was not recorded.

As the collections grew, most of them found their way into the libraries of the princely classes, the Vatican, and to a small extent, the medical schools. Few of the cathedral and monastic libraries made acquisitions. Little detailed information has been found about the medical contents of these collections aside from the library of Lorenzo de Medici. A learned Venetian physician, Pietro Tommasi, possessed a Greek library in which Traversari in 1433 found manuscripts of Paul of Aegena and Galen. Francesco Barbaro had a collection in Venice containing a Galen which later went to St. Michael's monastery in Murano. The Orsini Library in Florence acquired Hippocratic works from a monastery of St. Basil on Mount Athos in 1444. Valla, who had a large Greek library, was in 1448 in possession of the works of Hippocrates which had belonged to King Robert of Sicily and had been translated into Latin three times—by Azzolini of Rome, by Raymond of St. Germain, and by the famous Niccolo de Deoprepio.

The library of Niccolo Niccoli (1363-1437) contained about 100 volumes in Greek which after his death went to Cosimo de Medici and later to Lorenzo de Medici (1449-1492). Pope Nicholas V (1447-1455) very greatly enlarged the Greek section of the Vatican library and established a very important school of translation. Lorenzo the Magnificent brought together in the Medici library by the end of his life approximately 500 Greek manuscripts which was the largest collection of the fifteenth century. For twenty years beginning in 1472 he employed a refugee Greek, John Lascaris, whose name is intimately associated with the history of Greek manuscripts and studies. John made two trips to the East and others to various parts of Italy for the procurement of manuscripts. The autographed notebook of his second Eastern trip and perhaps other trips, uncovered in the Vatican library by Mueller (*Zentralblatt für Bibliothekswesen* I, 333, 1884) documents the largest number of Greek medical works ever recorded. There are four lists in the notebook, namely, books needed for the library, books already in the library, books gotten on the trips, and books to be found at the time of writing in the hands of Lascaris, which was before April 8, 1492 when Lorenzo died.

The list of medical books desired was as follows: Oribasius (with a note to get all that could be found) and Philothenous of Alexandria.

The list of medical works in the Medici library to begin with was as follows: Aetius, Alexander of Aphriodisias, Dionysius, Galen, Hippocrates, Metrodorus, Paul of Aegena, and Theophanes Nonnus—(On Foods).

The list of medical books procured on the trip consisted of—Aetius, Alexander of Aphriodisias, Alexander of Tralles, Actuarius, Dionysius, Galen, Herophilus, Hippocrates, Metrodorus,

Moschion, Nicander, Paul of Aegena, Rufus, Soranus, Theophilus. They were found in the various locations distributed as follows: At Corfu—Alexander of Tralles; from the library of Archiatros Andromicus, probably at Corfu—Actuarius, (Seven books on the Urine and Six books on the Epitome of Medical Art), Theophilus: (On Urines and on Excrements), Galen, five books ("There were several other things of Galen which we did not see because the padre was away.") There was also an anonymous work "The Great Therapeutics" consisting of 14 books which he stated "must be by Galen"). Also Stephanus, (Differential Diagnosis in Fevers) Alexander of Tralles, Soranus, (On Gynecology), Moschion, (On Gynecology), Aetius, (The Diagnosis and Cure of Fevers), Rufus, (On Diseases of the Bladder and Kidneys, On Plague; and On Satyriasis and Gonorrhoea). Herophilus the Sophist, (A Course on the Qualities of Food). At Mount Athos a total of 27 books of Galen were found in two monasteries. In Venice—Actuarias, (On Medical Problems), Alexander of Aphriodisias, and two books of Nicander (Alexipharmaci and Theriaca). Several other places were visited where important works were obtained in other fields but none in medicine. It is notable that none came from Constantinople which place had probably been drained of its supply of books by that time.

No account was found of the recovery of the works of some of the lesser lights in Greek medicine but it is most probable that they entered in collections from the East without being specifically recorded.

The story of the recovery of the ancient manuscripts from the libraries of Western Europe in the fourteenth and fifteenth centuries is a fascinating one in which such notable characters as Niccolo Niccoli, Poggio and Lascaris played the leading rôles. But in the case of medicine it is of little interest because of the absence of Greek manuscripts and the striking unimportance of the Latin ones. An old codex of Celsus was found in the Ambrosian library in Milan by Giovani Lamola in 1427. It was bound with the "Genicia" of Vindicianus, of which a copy was then made. A second Celsus was obtained by the Vatican library about the middle of the fourteenth century, probably from Bologna. Theodorus Priscianus was copied in the Middle Ages under the name of Octavius Oratianus and corrected anonymously in 1456. Appolonius Ratinek of Rheinberg who worked at the Universities of Cologne, Prague and Erfurt collected 636 manuscripts which he catalogued in 1412 and gave to the library at Erfurt. Of these 101 were on medicine which included the important Latin translations of the Greeks from Arabic as well as Latin literature from other sources.

Before the Renaissance, the libraries of the universities had accumulated Latin translations of most of the Greek and Arabic works. With the recovery of Greek medicine, they usually acquired Latin translations soon after they were made. Also with the recovery of the Greek manuscripts, the medical profession was confronted with the laborious task of comparing the various copies of the different works with those of the Latin translations from the Arabic in order to make sure, if possible of the original text. By this procedure, a great many errors in copying and translation were detected and corrected. Also many omissions and losses of parts or the whole of various works in the different languages were brought to light. Probably the most serious loss was that of the Alexandrian writings. Walsh ("Galen's Writings and Influences Inspiring Them," *Annals of Med. Hist.,* vol. 6, p. 1 and 143, 1934) estimated that about half of Galen's writings were lost. While Greek manuscripts were found of the great majority of the works that have been preserved, still certain portions were recovered only from the Arabic such as the ninth to the sixteenth books on Anatomy of Galen.

Latin translations were usually made from the Greek soon after the manuscripts were recovered. The end of the period of recovery closely approximated the beginning of the age of printing; consequently most of the important works were printed within the next 75 years, first in Latin, and then in some cases in Greek. The dissemination by the printed book of Hellenic medical knowledge and particularly of the Hippocratic spirit, aroused a new interest in medicine and helped to create the modern era which was inaugurated by Vesalius in 1543.

THE POST-GRADUATE TEACHING

OF

CLINICAL TROPICAL MEDICINE

By

Sir Philip Manson-Bahr

Director of the Clinical Division, London School of Hygiene and Tropical Medicine

CHAPTER XVII

THE POST-GRADUATE TEACHING OF CLINICAL TROPICAL MEDICINE

BY

SIR PHILIP MANSON-BAHR

"Whatsoever a man soweth, that shall he also reap"—Galatians VI. 7

THE SHAPE OF THINGS TO COME

The unprecedented progress in air travel which the present world-wide conflict has brought about must necessarily affect the lives and fortunes of all, and should influence the plans for post-graduate education of doctors from overseas and tropical countries. With Central and West Africa within three days flying time of England, India and the Far East on an average well within a week, the time saved on travel is reduced to a mere fraction of what it was formerly. In the New World the air lines and the approaching completion of the Pan-American highway have brought the republics of South America to the front door, so to speak, of North American science and culture. All this tends to change the face of things to come. Not only will the visits of foreign students to our universities be facilitated and simplified, but more intimate consultations and exchanges of opinion will follow, and immense opportunities for research will open up so that it will be possible to conduct field studies on a large scale and thereby obtain data of comparative value under varying conditions of country and climate.

IMPROVED COMMUNICATIONS AIDING MEDICAL STUDIES

The collection of specimens for study and for museum purposes illustrating tropical disease will also be facilitated, so filling a need, as these are notably deficient in most pathological collections, and in Great Britain, at any rate, the main exhibits have been destroyed by enemy action.

It is possible to envisage a time, not remotely distant, when it will be possible to arrange extensive tours for clinical instruction in the main tropical diseases, such as malaria, dysenteries, ancylostomiasis, kala-azar trypanosomiasis and a whole host of ancillary subjects, for specially selected advanced students, whilst research students in the pathological or biochemical fields will be enabled to work for extended periods on special problems in well-equipped laboratories now to be found in most tropical countries. This applies especially to the far-flung outposts of the British Empire. All these factors are bound to influence the attitude of general medicine to the specialised branch dealing with the diseases of the tropics, so that a wider conception of responsibilities must ensue. Many of the principles which emerge in the realm of diagnosis and treatment of tropical ailments should influence progress in more familiar general diseases, and, naturally, the converse will also take place. There will in fact be a general levelling up of knowledge and pooled experience. For instance, the science of nutrition and dietetics should find a far richer opportunity for intimate and comparative enquiry amidst the more primitive and backward peoples of the tropics than in the more intricate and well-trodden fields in the centres of civilisation. One of the probable beneficial results of the present world war will be the wider appreciation of the principles.

INFLUENCE OF THE PRESENT WAR ON MEDICAL TEACHING

There will be many thousands of the younger generation of doctors who will have found opportunities for acquiring first-hand experience of tropical diseases in their natural environment and, indeed, already the results of their observations are becoming apparent. The door for more intensive investigation by modern methods has been flung wide open. Thus we see the desire for more accurate diagnosis in blood infections by sternal puncture, the attention being paid to the character of the cerebrospinal fluid in malaria and other tropical infections, and in the immense subject of virus diseases.

Biochemists, too, have opportunities in the extraordinary metabolic changes which occur in subtertian malaria, blackwater fever and yellow fever, whilst equally dramatic changes found in most tropical diseases will afford further fields for research.

It thus becomes incumbent on us who have had to remain at home to plan out this better world for those who will soon be returning from many strange, hot, and humid lands.

These problems plead for a more sympathetic and statesman-like handling. Our system of teaching foreign students from overseas, many of them of different race and varying color surely calls for a wiser, more sympathetic and more regulated organization than heretofore. This should express itself in the relationship between teacher and student. Up to the present the colored student is apt to be thrust into an assembly of post-graduates from which he differs in upbringing, tradition and sentiment. He has many difficulties to overcome. He finds himself in a new environment with attendant perplexities of customs, climate and traditions. His teachers stand on platforms and address the assembled students *en masse* in a manner which is deemed intelligible and acceptable to all. The professors, referring to those of Tropical Medicine in particular, are busy men and have many engagements to fulfill. Their tendency is to talk down to the class for the prescribed hour or so and then dash away for some other appointment. The intimate association between the lecturer and the body of students who look to him for guidance and inspiration is apt to be glossed over. The old idea of the professor sitting in his laboratory with a happy band of students of all nationalities working in brotherhood together is usually, in the stress of modern times, unobtainable. The result is the absence of that individual attention so much cherished and appreciated by foreign peoples. It is undoubted that in points like this we fail to impress the colored races with our sincerity and leave ourselves open to that charge of hypocrisy which is indeed partly justified. It is to be hoped that in the new and better world we will be prepared to make sacrifices and be resolved to tackle this problem afresh and make a better contribution to the cause we all have at heart.

The intellectual and spiritual needs of exotic students—Indians, Africans, and others from the Far East and South America—will have to be satisfied. Immediate requirements differ in individual cases.

SPECIAL PROVISION FOR OVERSEAS STUDENTS

These must be made to feel at home; they must be brought into more intimate contact with the personalities and individualities of their teachers; they must come to regard their professors as human beings intimately concerned with their future welfare. They must be brought more into the home life of their teachers, so that, returning to their homelands with an ardent desire for progress, they will have no *unhappy memories* of their student years in foreign lands.

It is perhaps no exaggeration to state that well-meaning but ill-directed post-graduate study is worse than none at all, for it leads to a sense of frustration and dissatisfaction which reacts in less stabilized, but nevertheless intensely nationalistic, minds, and produces at times not friendship, but hostility, suppressed or overt, to our democratic regime and way of life. All this appears very idealistic, but we must provide some constructive ideas as to how improvement may be attained.

It is undoubted that the language difficulty is insufficiently realised and therefore adequate provision is not made for it. English is the *lingua franca,* but many of our students are poorly acquainted with many of its terms and idioms, so that a simplification of language (or the simplest words) should be used for them in lectures and demonstrations. The idea has occurred that it would be more advantageous to segregate those who have difficulty in this respect into a separate class for special instruction, but it is realised that this would be liable to give rise to administrative difficulties. Spanish-speaking postgraduate students should receive special attention as they are vitally interested in many of the tropical problems with which we deal. In Germany, for instance, tuition in the Spanish language was organised and conducted with success for these students, but in England this aspect of the subject does not seem to have been sufficiently considered. These several thorny questions which have been raised require for their solution adjustment in our machinery of administration. In many cases the material and spiritual needs of our overseas students are cared for by their own national associations, clubs and Young Men's Christian Associations, and, in addition the Indian and African students in England are supervised in a general way by the government departments concerned.

Under our present establishment the Dean of our tropical schools has a full-time appointment, and he is so overburdened with work that he cannot concern himself with details of study or research, and he certainly cannot concern himself with the social side of the student's life.

The first difficulty to overcome is that of housing the student. The hostel idea which was introduced by Manson in 1899 in his original conception of a tropical school appears to be ideal. Such a hostel, which would provide adequate and comfortable accommodation for 50 or more foreign students, should be situated in the vicinity of the postgraduate hospital and within easy reach of the research laboratories. There must be, of course, communal dining and common rooms. For recreation there should, if possible, be tennis and squash racquet courts attached.

ALBERT SCHWEITZER JUBILEE BOOK

DIRECTOR OF HOSTEL, DIRECTOR OF STUDIES, OR SUBDEAN

The Director of the hostel should be a medical man who has himself had considerable experience of practice in tropical lands. He should be qualified to direct studies whenever required and to guide the students into chosen paths of research. He should have a sympathetic outlook on the student mind and, in fact, should constitute himself their guide, philosopher and friend. Ideally such a director should be selected by Government, or actually chosen for his quilifications from the Government Medical Service. In this position he would be quite impartial, and he would assist the students, not only in their immediate studies for the degree in Tropical Medicine, but could also guide their steps on their way to higher qualifications. For special research work and theses, the student would be enabled to work on some particular problem in the adjoining hospital; being in a favorable position to obtain material at any time, both by day and night, he would have the facilities of the clinical laboratory in order to work out his results. This was the method Manson employed in his heyday, and it was the method by which he directed the minds of so many men into fruitful avenues of research and obtained results of immediate value to the studies which he himself had in hand. Of course there are no limits to which this directive idea may not be expanded. But the main point would be that the student would feel that, so far from being a wanderer in the wilderness, he had become an important cog in the machinery of medical science and a subject of intense and active personal interest.

Then there is the political and social side, the importance of which cannot be exaggerated. These men will be guided into high intellectual channels and will meet those with an understanding of their difficulties who will tend to uplift rather than repress them. They will be guided into the right social circles and meet people who are sympathetic instead of becoming attracted by the less social-minded and less educated as so often happens. The personal contact is so valuable that the Director of Studies should dine as often as possible with the students and therefore meet them on the same social plane, and what is equally important, the lecturers or professors should also take their meals in the hostel as often as is possible. The importance of these personal contacts cannot be overestimated.

THE TEACHING OF RESEARCH

Objections may be raised that the machinery of research has become so intricate that no line, however simple, can be attempted without long preliminary training and intricate and elaborate apparatus. This attitude, undoubtedly, is fallacious and is apt to have a stultifying effect, for in the realm of tropical medicine there are still many important problems which can be solved by means of simple microscopic investigations and the expenditure of patience on the Schaudinnian model. The exact method by which the malarial sporozoite enters the red blood corpuscles has never been really finally settled, nor have Schaudinn's original observations been confirmed. Here is a subject which should provide material for an eminently fruitful research, and there are many other problems of similar nature.

An organization which would stimulate, organize and carry out researches of this nature should be our aim. It should eventually light a beacon of knowledge whose rays, illuminating the four continents, will attract enquiries from every corner of the earth.

APPOINTMENT OF SELECTED OVERSEAS STUDENTS TO RESPONSIBLE POSITIONS

Another and equally important matter is the assumption of responsibility by foreign students in our hospitals and universities. There exists here a solid basis for complaint against our existing system. To put it plainly:— we educate these students in the methods and mysteries of modern medicine, but when they request the opportunity to assume responsibility in the actual treatment of patients, they are informed that no suitable position for them can be found. This attitude naturally gives rise to a good deal of antipathy, so that a solution of the problem must be sought. Naturally it would be totally unfair to deny students of our own race and tongue their share of junior hospital appointments, but it should be possible to appoint certain selected foreign postgraduates to act as clinical clerks to clinical teachers and thus to take an active share in the practical treatment of patients in the ward. Later special internships might be reserved for more prominent students in wards where clinical teaching and research are undertaken. In the Dock area of London where the patients are drawn from many races of colored people and where no color bar exists, a scheme of this nature could be carried into effect.

CLINICAL TROPICAL MATERIAL FOR TEACHING AND RESEARCH

It has been frequently stated that an almost insuperable hindrance to the teaching of clinical tropical medicine in temperate countries, or at least zones outside the actual tropics, is the lack of suitable clinical material, and also that with the advance of knowledge, better instruction in tropical medicine and the opening up of communications, the supply of tropical patients which has hitherto been available will dwindle away. It is most unlikely that this will happen, but rather that the number of tropical patients will be much increased and their complaints be of greater variety than formerly.

The exigencies of air travel via West and Central Africa and in many other localities in the Middle and Far East render the air passenger liable to become infected with subtertian malaria, amoebic dysentery and other diseases. Quite a proportion of these patients will not exhibit the infection until some weeks after arrival in England, or other temperate climates. This has already happened to a considerable degree. One night spent in a mosquito-ridden locality, like the Gambia or parts of South Nigeria, is quite long enough to acquire a virulent subtertian malarial infection declaring itself under so many varied disguises that it confounds those doctors who are not versed in the strange ways and habits of *Plasmodium falciparum*.

There must be a more widespread appreciation of these dangers and necessities together with the establishment of machinery for obtaining information and instruction from a tropical centre or hospital. Furthermore, with the development of air travel and the establishment of ambulance planes, it will become the custom to transport patients presenting critical or obscure symptoms to medical centres for investigation and treatment unprocurable on the spot. Although facilities in the tropics themselves may be beyond reproach, *complete* restoration to health is certainly hastened by treatment in temperate climates.

CLINICAL INSTRUCTION BY THE COMPARATIVE METHOD

It is safe to predict that with these developments material will be adequate and should supply the demand for clinical investigation and research. It must be emphasized that the best method of encouraging malaria investigation, for instance, is by a constant supply of fresh strains of malarial parasites for therapeutic inoculation and for chemotherapeutic research. It has often been asked how it is found possible for any band of teachers, however energetic and enthusiastic, to collect sufficient patients of tropical interest to provide instructive clinical demonstrations to a large class of students, some of whom, it may be, have already had a considerable experience of medicine in their native lands. The author has always held that it is much more instructive to stage a clinical demonstration on one well worked out and scientifically treated case than to expound on a larger series less completely investigated. A case of malaria, for instance, can be discussed from the clinical, pathological, parasitological, and biochemical aspects, if not comprehensively then, at any rate in part, by different members of the staff who specialise on these particular lines. Moreover, one of the greatest advantages of tropical patients is the value of teaching by the *comparative method*. One often feels that over-specialisation in tropical diseases tends to give the impression that the ordinary ills of mankind either do not exist, or are of no pressing importance in tropical lands, whereas the converse is really the case. For instance, tuberculosis is of overwhelming importance, so is diabetes, renal calculus and every other malady to which the human flesh is heir, so that to real efficiency differential diagnosis should be the key. What then could be better than lectures and demonstrations based on this theme? For this, one or more patients with tropical complaints are necessary as the text. Thus malaria with splenomegaly can be demonstrated and compared with other diseases, such as, splenic anæmia, pernicious anæmia, acholuric jaundice and other diseases in which enlargment of the spleen is associated with blood changes. Patients with kala-azar, of which one or more are usually available in the Port of London, are always most suitable for this purpose.

Dysentery is another subject in which accurate differential diagnosis is essential. Here there is a prolific field in ulcerative, mucous and other forms of colitis patients which are usually available. Then there is pyrexia, which can be best illustrated by means of temperature charts (of which a standard selection should always be kept at hand) and clinical demonstrations of tuberculosis, endocarditis, fevers of the salmonella group and their differentiation from liver abscess or chronic malaria. Skin diseases, rashes and their manifestations in their affinity to tropical dermatoses and the exanthemata of tropical fevers (trypanosomiasis, the typhus group, dengue, etc.) form excellent subjects for demonstration. The writer has always felt convinced that, in order to make teaching impressive so that finer points of differentiation should be driven home, a clinical demonstration should be accompanied with pictorial and microscopic displays of bloodfilms, faecal specimens, etc. To do this efficiently and to be able to organize adequately such teaching demonstrations three times weekly entails a considerable amount of thought and organisation, and, therefore, it is almost impossible for the head clinician or Director of the unit to encompass it all.

APPOINTMENT OF CLINICAL DEMONSTRATORS

It is important then in planning the future to envisage the appointment of a whole-time assistant whose main duties should be directed towards this organisation and who should be capable also of conducting the postgraduate students round the wards in small parties to impart bedside instructions in spare moments and whenever some long-sought for opportunity arises.

MUSEUM FACILITIES

One of the greatest assets to this form of clinical teaching is the provision of a suitable museum stocked with pathological specimens, photographs and paintings. There are, or were, very few complete museums of this kind in existence. As far as the teaching of tropical medicine in London is concerned there is the magnificent and unrivalled Wellcome Museum in the Wellcome Institution which is within a short distance of the School of Hygiene and Tropical Medicine. There all the tropical diseases are illustrated in ordered sequence and, not only this, but almost the whole of medicine is treated in the same exhilarating and exhaustive manner with a wealth of detail. The paintings of clinical conditions are all of the very best. It is hardly necessary to stress the invaluable character of a collection such as this. It is possible to conduct classes in the greatest comfort and seclusion; going from one section to another, and so to illustrate still further clinical cases which have been studied in the wards. Moreover, the material is presented in such an agreeable, succinct and palatable form that the students preparing for their final examinations find that the collection presents the best facilities for this purpose.

TEACHING OF THERAPEUTICS

Then there is the question of drugs and medicaments. This all-important question of the correct treatment of tropical diseases by *specific* drugs, which have been a stirring example of progress in this branch of medicine, is apt to be neglected. It does not suffice to name the drugs, or to roll out an impressive list of synonyms. The mere committal to memory of the complicated and varied names of these compounds is beyond the realms of human endeavor. Some international agreement on synonymy must be reached, or else confusion will be more confounded.

The scheme which most commends itself is one where the drugs themselves are demonstrated together with the source-plant, mineral, etc. from which they are derived, together with details regarding their dosage, tolerance, spacing, toxicity, etc. In such a collection as the Wellcome Museum this method has been adopted and has proved eminently popular and instructive.

THE TRAINING OF OVERSEAS NURSES

Together with the scheme outlined above there should be scope in our future planning for the training of nurses from overseas, Indian, African, Chinese, and of other nationalities, in the principles and practice of Western nursing and for them also, as well as for our own nurses, proceeding overseas to India, Africa or to the Colonial nursing service, short courses in tropical medicine should be arranged. This course of instruction should include the origin, methods of conveyance and spread of the main tropical diseases, together with the principles of clinical investigation. The underlying idea is to interest the nurses in their work and instruct them in the main methods of treatment. It has the further advantage of instructing them in methods of collecting specimens for various investigations and their conveyance to the laboratory. In order that the scheme outlined above may come to full fruition the special needs of these nurses will have to be met and they should lead to the establishment of a special institution for this purpose. This overseas nursing institution will have to be combined with the main plan for a tropical medicine centre such as has been here outlined.

CONCLUSION

Lest it should be assumed that the suggestions which have been put forward in this tentative scheme are too idealistic, it is urged that they are simply the natural evolution from what has already gone before. The main criticism which has been launched against the teaching of Tropical Medicine in England and other northern countries is that it tends to become too theoretical and the present courses too overloaded with a jargon of scientific names, imponderable details and morphological data which are almost impossible to digest and remember, unless they are combined with their practical application in the actual treatment of disease. Because of the practical difficulties which have been encountered in the past, the importance of the clinical side has tended to become neglected. If this attitude is allowed to persist it is conceivable that the whole organization will tend to wither and die. The direction of clinical Tropical Medicine can no longer be a haphazard affair; it must be organized on sound lines. This can and will be done and we must begin to do so now and without delay. The progress in the treatment of tropical diseases and the entirely original methods employed have redounded to the glory of Tropical Medicine and to the advancement of medical science as a whole.

THE STRANGE CASES

OF

DIVES AND LAZARUS

By

Clement C. Chesterman, M.D., O.B.E.
Hon. Secretary British Advisory Board on Medical Missions

CHAPTER XVIII

THE STRANGE CASES OF DIVES AND LAZARUS

BY

CLEMENT C. CHESTERMAN

CASE NOTES

NAME	DIVES	LAZARUS
Age	Good old	Early middle
Occupation	Gentleman	Beggar
Residence	Gated palace	Doorstep
Diagnosis	Plethora	Full of sores.
Diet	Sumptus (daily)	Crumbs (occasionally)
Treatment	Most modern	Dog licks
Result	Also died	Died
Disposal	Hades Crematorium	Abraham's bosom.

"There was a certain rich man, which was clothed in purple and fine linen, and fared sumptuously every day.

And there was a certain beggar named Lazarus, which was laid at his gate, full of sores,

And desiring to be fed with the crumbs which fell from the rich man's table; moreover the dogs came and licked his sores.

*And it came to pass the beggar died . . . .
The rich man also died . . . ."*

LUKE, xvi, 19-22.

These are evidently two very interesting cases, but what on earth have they to do with Dr. Albert Schweitzer? Let him answer this question himself, from the following opening sentences of his book *On the Edge of the Primeval Forest*:—

> The parable of Dives and Lazarus seemed to me to have been spoken directly to us! We are Dives, for, through the advances of medical science, we now know a great deal about disease and pain, and have innumerable means of fighting them; . . . Out there in the colonies, however, sits wretched Lazarus, the colored folk, who suffers from illness and pain just as much as we do, nay, much more, and has absolutely no means of fighting them.

That modern interpretation of an old story is no mere bit of abstract philosophy. It led Dr. Schweitzer to thirty years' devotion to a life of concrete philanthropy; it was instrumental in leading a man of forty to dedicating the rest of his life to the service of suffering Lazarus.

I first read these challenging words twenty years ago, when I had done my first tour as a medical missionary in the heart of the primeval Congo forest. I had already had first-hand experience with Lazarus, and this case had become one of absorbing interest to me. Dives meant nothing to me—the rich we have always with us. And besides, there are always crowds of physicians tumbling over themselves to treat Dives.

Two things particularly attracted my attention in the unusual case of Lazarus; first, the fact that he had been picked up on somebody's doorstep, and secondly, that though full of sores, he had such inadequate treatment.

A black man on a doorstep, full of sores—not a very pleasant picture. Of course, I remembered that the majority of Africans I had known were healthy, happy, robust specimens of humanity. But despite all that governments and missions are doing, there are far too many who fit the picture—full of sores.

It reminded me of David Livingstone's passionate cry "Let anyone, Christian, Turk, or Jew, come in and help to heal the open sore of Africa!" *He* referred to the slave trade as the open sore of Africa. But black Lazarus is still a slave. He is a prey of parasites, under the tyranny of torturing diseases, and fettered by frightful fears. Left to himself in the unequal struggle, he comes to grief. The *V* sign for him is *V* for Victim.

Let us proceed to a clinical examination of the case. He is not lying betwen clean sheets on a hospital bed in a spotlessly clean ward. He is just lying huddled up under a cheap trade blanket, with bits of him showing through the rents. His white-soled feet attract attention—for they are full of sores. He is jiggered, and that's no joke. The old slave ships which carried his ancestors to the New World had nothing to bring back to Africa except ballast. They dumped this on his shores, jiggers and all, and now these little burrowing pests play havoc with the feet of anyone who is too careless, too tired, or too sick to remove them.

But some of his toes are missing—suspicious sign that. The ends of his fingers are worn away, and the lobes of his ears are thickened. He is full of this sore, and it is leprosy. Actually he doesn't mind that much, for leprosy only kills slowly; and besides, one in twenty may be lepers in the part he comes from! He did try to cover up those brown patches on his skin with oil and charcoal, but they beat him, and now he is more brown than black. Fortunately leprosy is not such a rapidly progressive and mutilating disease in tropical Africa as it can be in other parts of the world.

Every now and then, as you watch him, his whole shrouded form heaves with what *he* would call "a devil of a cough." Surely not the white man's scourge, tuberculosis? All too probably it is, and it may indeed have been the white man's present, or at least the legacy of a new civilization which tends to drain men away from the bush population of 5 to 10 to the square mile, where germs cannot so easily find the next victim, and crowd the compounds where respiratory diseases can so easily propagate themselves. He and his race are not yet as used to the germ of tuberculosis as we are, and so have little resistance to it, and the increasing incidence of T B is an alarming fact in Africa.

Let us ask him a few questions. You'll be lucky if you can find someone who knows his language. Maybe he is one of a few thousand people who have a language all to themselves. His little tribe has been tucked away in an isolated corner of the uplands, or in the depths of the forest, for centuries; and now no one from the outside world understands them. Probably, however, he knows one of the *linguae francae*, and you try that. But he doesn't seem to hear you. Shake him up a bit and try again. You can't rouse him. With a shudder you realise that his lethargy may be a sign of African sleeping sickness. He may be just one of the 100,000 who die annually of that dread disease.

"Thank God," you say, "that's not our fault!" But wait a bit. In many parts where sleeping sickness is now epidemic, natives say that it is a new scourge. Their fathers had no name for what is now called the "killing disease." Strange black men brought it there in their blood, and the tse-tse flies picked it up, bred it, and passed it on. But the strange black men were porters or steamer crews in the service of the white man, who was opening up the country. Unfortunately he opened up graves in the process, and 300,000 died in Uganda alone in a few years. Sins of ignorance,—granted, but mortal sins nevertheless.

Already we seem to have diagnosed enough diseases to keep us busy with this case for a long time. Yet the list is far from complete. Before, however, we add to it, it is necessary to study one of the aetiological factors, viz., On whose doorstep was Lazarus to be found? If he is on a doorstep, it is certainly not his own; for his hut is level with the ground; of the earth, earthy. You have only got to look inside the ample panier he has been carrying to answer this question. Those bright red palm nuts and those brown ground nuts are for someone whose soap and margarine are rationed and who needs tons of glycerine for the manufacture of explosives. Those yellow lumps of raw rubber are only useful to him for muffling his drum sticks, but will serve a thousand purposes in modern war. Those ingots of copper and tin he could use as ornaments for his women, but others claim them as armaments for their men. Dives wants the gold he digs out of a hole in the earth in Africa, to bury it in another hole in the earth in America. And Dives' wife wants the diamonds so assiduously sifted from his soil to add lustre to her charms.

So there is no doubt about it; it's our doorstep he is on, and we have called him there. And if we have treated him at all like a human being he has generally responded willingly to our call. For his raw materials we have too often given him a raw deal, or we have paid him in gin or truck. After that we have been inclined to slam the front door (varnished with his copal) in his face, and leave him lying on the mat (his "cokernut") and let him and his sores go "to the dogs." "Let his wife come and look after him," we say. Certainly he has a wife, but she is left behind in his village, a thousand miles away and five thousand years behind the times. She is now doing a man's work as well as her own. But her hut is not so weatherproof now that he's away. There was no one to catch for her the best fish or to fetch her meat from the forest when carrying her last baby. She was not too strong when it came to birth, and labor was slow and hard. The attendant hags bullied her and accused her of having been unfaithful to her husband, but failing to get a confession they had to be content with placing salt on the ground and charging the spirits to take it and leave the woman alone, and allow her child to be born safely. At long last, the mother, completely exhausted, the frenzied midwives quite frantic, the child was born, and lay quite still on the broad banana leaf.

They blew down its nostrils, and shouted in its ears and stung its chest with nettles, but never a gasp from the babe. In desperation they bore it to the chief's big drum and laid it over its vibrant mouth, hoping that the deep notes would awaken it to life. But the labor was in vain, and she buried the still-born child, not near the hut, but just across the stream, lest its hungry spirit should return and cry for its milk and weary her.

She still had her first-born to comfort her, but what a repulsive object he was to any but his mother. His whole body was covered with yellow crusted sores, and he sat in the shade and whisked off the flies. "It's only yaws," she'd say, "every child has got to get them!"

She was more worried about her little girl. Her black skin had turned a light dirty brown, her frizzy hair was lank and reddish, her face and eyes puffy, her belly swollen, and her legs like spindles. Had she transgressed a taboo and eaten an egg, or was it the witchcraft medicine of her barren sister who was so jealous? Malaria, hookworm, and malnutrition are obviously what have bewitched her. But there is no quinine for fever for blacks in wartime, and how can a mother know anything about hookworms? They never crawl out of the nostrils like round-worms, or appear in the stools like threadworms. She'll be lucky if an attack of pneumonia or dysentery doesn't carry her off before the child is many moons older.

Yes, Lazarus and his family are full of sores. The primeval forest is a paradise for parasites, and the average native has ten to fifteen different sorts of germs and worms sharing his hospital-ity. In fact, no man liveth unto himself in tropical Africa. They all take in P.G.'s, uninvited guests, who believe in sharing, but who only pay evil for good. These pests and parasites are part of the black man's burden.

But the tragic fact is that, whereas Dives knows how to prevent himself from getting infected, and to cure himself of nearly all of them, yet the application of this knowledge lags so far behind its acquisition.

Of course it is not so simple as it sounds. The problem of freeing him from this slavery is bound up with a dozen different questions affecting his soil, his home, his work, his habits, his customs, and is often complicated by his ignorance and superstition, aye, and his vice. For though he is human he is but human, and is apt to make a mess of even his primitive life. He is a man of like passions with ourselves, only more so. Nevertheless, it just isn't fair that Dives in his lifetime should receive all the good things of medical science, and Lazarus the evil things. At least, that's how Luke, the doctor disciple, sees it. A few crumbs in the shape of a medical service or the eye-wash of dog-licks in the form of native hospitals at the large centres is not good enough.

Missions have had the honor of pioneering a rural medical service for Africa, and they can be proud of that fact. Nowadays the excellent government medical services are striving more and more efficiently to discharge their responsibility in this respect.

The survival of the voluntary principle in an increasingly socialised state is however greatly to be desired, and missions will continue to make their contribution to healing the sores of Lazarus, and saving Dives from a fate even worse.

Albert Schweitzer says "A single doctor out here with the most modest equipment means very much for the many." "Never did so many owe so much to so few" could be said of men like Albert Schweitzer also.

MEDICAL MISSIONS

AND

THE FUTURE

By

Ernest Cooke, F. R. C. S. I., L. R. C. P. I., D. P. H., L. M. R.
Physician in Charge Outpatient Clinic, Hospital for Tropical Diseases, London

CHAPTER XIX

MEDICAL MISSIONS AND THE FUTURE

W. ERNEST COOKE

"Tho' they haven't any haloes, only holes slashed through
*   the ear,*
And their faces marked with tattoos and with scratch pins
*   in their hair,*
Bringing back the badly wounded, just as steady as a hearse,
Using leaves to keep the rain off, and as gentle as a nurse,
Slow and careful in bad places on the awful mountain track,
And the look upon their faces makes us think that Christ
*   was black."*

The above lines written by an American Naval man to com-
memorate the work of the Papuan stretcher-bearers are sufficiently
arresting to cause the reader to give a few moments' thought to
missionaries and their work.

While the ordinary man may not agree that Christianity should
be the universal religion and while he may argue that the native's
own religion suits him best, he will generally admit that all men
should be able to get medical aid when needed, even the most
primitive savage.

Even in these days the missionary pioneer is not extinct. Not
many years ago three missionaries gained the martyr's crown at
the hands of Indians in Amazonia, and more recently a lady
missionary suffered death in Africa. For some time to come
pioneer missionaries will still be required to carry the Gospel
Message into the considerable areas of the world still unevangel-
ized.

The question at once arises what is the best equipment these
pioneers should be given? Should they have a medical training
or not?

Experience dictates that they all should have some knowledge of medicine. The work of such institutions as the Livingstone College and the Missionary School of Medicine in London is an acknowledgment that such education is a necessity, and the grateful tributes from former pupils of these institutions as to the usefulness of the knowledge and practical experience gained through them, provide unanswerable arguments. Not only has their training enabled them to alleviate the sufferings of the primitive peoples among whom they work, but also, they have been able to better preserve their own health and that of their families and so to work harder and for longer periods in their various fields abroad.

Few people have any conception of the menace of the insect world to health in the tropics and the value to the informed man of the knowledge of how to master and defeat the powers of the disease-carrying-and producing insects and other small creatures.

Whether the missionary goes abroad as a preacher, teacher, or technician, unless he is working in a country where the health services are accessible, or at a station well staffed with medical personnel, he will be constantly faced with the sick and the diseased. They will be brought to him as to the Great Physician in days of old, and their need will often delay him in carrying out his formal duties. He will gain immensely if previous training enables him to deal with them quickly and organize his labor to attain the best results,

All mission fields have shown the importance of medical work as a means of winning a way for Christian teaching and breaking down the antagonism of other faiths and native administrations to the missionary and his message.

This raises the important question as to whether in the future medical work should not be put in the forefront of missionary effort in all backward countries and among primitive races. Should the building of the hospital precede that of the church?

The most eloquent sermon or interesting teacher will fail to hold the attention of the man with severe toothache, and the non-Christian mind will be more ready to give attention to discussion and teaching when the bodily ills have been assuaged and cured. Countless instances are on record of the effect of medical aid on important and leading individuals, as in China today, where the friendship and personal contact with missionary doctors has exercised a powerful influence on not a few of China's present band of Christian leaders, as well as on whole communities bringing them under Christian influence. This has been particularly the case with certain nomadic peoples who formerly shunned the white man. Granted the importance of medical work in this way should the mission hospitals not be increased and used as pioneer agencies rather than waiting for the time when a certain amount of success has been gained?

Again, these hospitals should be adequately staffed. The lone doctor or nurse inevitably becomes overworked with lack of time for teaching and too often resulting illness. Adequately staffed and fitted hospitals, thus enabled to deal with large numbers of patients and to undertake full medical procedures, in the end prove their worth in attracting patients from much larger areas and in saving time and loss through illness of their medical staffs.

Full staffs for such hospitals in certain countries could be furnished by the coöperation and pooling of staffs and resources of the various missions working in such areas where conditions make such an arrangement desirable. It would also be of value where native administrations are assuming more responsibility in government, in that it would render coöperation with them more easy, the state having to deal with only one missionary organization rather than with several.

Work in all mission hospitals should be done with a single motive, that of unselfish service in aid of the patients, to the glory of the Master and without thought of fame, commercialism or propaganda. This was the ideal which inspired Dr. Schweitzer, and he stressed it by pointing out the teaching of the parable of the Good Samaritan as the standard for the missionary doctor, and which he not only emphasized by word and writing but by his life surrendered in the service of his African brothers.

An enormous extension of air travel must be expected in the future. This will affect the medical missions in many ways. Already the Australian bush doctor has demonstrated what the airplane can do in bringing medical help quickly to the acutely ill patient, and the war has shown how quickly patients needing major operations can be conveyed by air to the nearest theatre for surgical aid. The radius of the hospital's service will be greatly extended, and with the perfecting of the helicopter, patients will be brought from otherwise inaccessible regions. Doctors and nurses will be able to travel more quickly to any areas where additional aid is needed and the problem of conveying medical supplies will be largely solved.

The acceleration of travel by air and on the new roads and railways constructed during this war will lead to dissemination of diseases now localized in various countries but capable of being spread to regions hitherto protected by distance or inaccessibility. The remembrance of diseases such as leprosy and yellow fever spread by the slave trade, and in more recent times the introduction of malaria into Mauritius and Barbados, and again the transporting of disease-carrying insects, such as *Anopheles Gambiae* from West Africa to Brazil, where it has caused outbreaks of malaria, all emphasize the need that will arise for increased medical supervision and preventive measures in which medical missionaries will be called to bear a part.

As in the past so in the future the medical missionary will contribute in the fields of scientific research and applied medicine. The work of missionary doctors such as Muir, Lowe, Cochrane and others on leprosy; Gamble, Chesterman, Kellersberger, Acres and Keevill on trypanosomiasis; Chesterman and Fisher on bilharziasis, and Pugh, Somervell and Orr on duodenal ulcer; to mention only a few names, will be carried on; and many conditions remain to be investigated. Leprosy has always appealed specially to the endeavor of the missionary doctor, and it has been pointed out that better results have been attained in mission than in government hospitals. This is attributed to the effect of hope on the patient. In the atmosphere of the mission hospital the leper loses his feeling of being an outcast and of despair, and sees and realizes that the Great Physician can still cleanse the leper.

The collecting of man-power in labor camps and non-combatant units and the assembling of increasing numbers of natives in mines and factories in certain areas are causing disintegration of village life and customs particularly in Africa. In these communities, the ancient beliefs, taboos, and moral restraints of village life lose their hold and are too often replaced by the evil results of Western freedom, and the diseases accompanying large and overcrowded communities. The depleted villages also present new social problems.

It may be argued that these are matters for the Government Medical Services but the medical missionary will be inevitably involved, and with missionary nurses and social workers will have to meet the challenge, and this not only in the congested areas but also in the depleted regions. As their work will not be solely medical but will carry with it the uplift of the Savior's message, it should be of special value.

Another problem of Africa, the color bar, is not recognized by the medical missions in their work. Mission hospitals should be the training grounds of doctors, nurses, and hospital assistants in sufficient numbers, in those countries where state medical services do not exist, in the true spirit of brotherhood and service, to meet the vast needs of the native populations. This will contribute its aid to the solution of a problem that can only be solved by the adoption of the teachings of Jesus.

Recent years have been increasing government recognition and coöperation with missionary work. One remarkable instance is that the present British Government has conferred a certain status on the missionaries by giving them preference in obtaining travelling facilities when returning to their stations abroad. In countries where state medical services already exist, it would be well if the coöperation with these of the mission medical services could be effected, the knowledge and experience of consultants in both services be made interchangeable, and the native Christian personnel trained by the missions be contributed in increasing numbers to the state medical, health, and social services. Where the state or missions plan new undertakings or reorganizations, mutual consultations should be held to see how each may participate in or modify the plans of the other to the greatest ultimate benefit of all.

That the health of the people is a governmental responsibility is already recognized in civilized states, and already some governments are showing themselves ready to aid and subsidize medical missions. This is good, and will be generally welcomed as closer association between government and missions in medical and educational work is desired by many educated natives.

Planning is needed to remedy the differences in status and remuneration between government and mission workers doing similar work. But here there are perils as in so doing, the great aim of the medical mission services must not be submerged. Increased emolument and change of status may be deserved and due, but their adoption must not be allowed to destroy personal disinterestedness and attract those lacking the steadfast aim and ideal of the true missionary. The two services are not antagonistic to or inconsistent with each other, but they are not identical. Coöperation should not be shunned owing to such difficulties, but it will call for an intensified loyalty to the fundamental missionary principles until the day dawns when both can be merged in the service of the Highest, and humanity.

PART VII
THEOLOGY AND RELIGION

XENOPHANES AND THE BEGINNINGS

OF

NATURAL THEOLOGY

By

Werner Jaeger, Dr. Phil., D.Litt., Litt. D.

*Professor of Classical Philology, Harvard University;
formerly Professor at the University of Berlin*

CHAPTER XX

XENOPHANES AND THE BEGINNINGS
OF NATURAL THEOLOGY

BY

WERNER JAEGER

One of the essential contributions of the nineteenth century to the knowledge of Greek philosophy was the rediscovery of the Pre-Socratic thinkers. This achievement was due in part to the fact that the "historical century" was no longer contented with discussing only those documents of ancient thought which were preserved to us in their complete form by the school tradition, most of all the works of Plato and Aristotle. Instead, it set itself the new task of reconstructing the historical development of Greek philosophy in its entirety by collecting the scattered fragments of the authors who are lost, ranging from the earliest thinkers down to the philosophical systems of the Hellenistic age, the Stoics, Epicureans, Sceptics, etc.

Insofar as the Pre-Socratics were concerned there were other reasons also for this intense concentration on a vanished period of thought. During the first half of the nineteenth century, the time of Hegel and the flowering of speculative idealistic philosophy, there was a veritable renaissance of Heraclitus and Parmenides. When this era gave way to the age of positivism, a new generation of historians of ancient philosophy eagerly turned from Plato's ideas and Aristotle's metaphysics to the Pre-Socratic "materialists" and interpreted them—the φυσικοί in Aristotle's terminology—as the first physicists, the heroes and founders of modern natural science. Such was the picture of the earliest

Greek thinkers presented by Theodor Gomperz and John Burnet
who thus distinguished themselves from the older type of the
historian of Greek philosophy, rooted in the late Hegelian
school and represented, in its best form, by Eduard Zeller.

One need not blind himself to the comparative merits of this
realistic point of view which has added new life and variety to
our view of the intellectual history of Greece, but one cannot
help feeling today that it showed a certain trend toward a one-
sided modernization of the Pre-Socratic philosophers. In reality
they were still far from the methodical abstractness of modern
science and from its conscious empiricism, even though they were
concerned with the material world. For this it is sufficient to
quote as a witness the medical writer of the Hippocratic school
who composed the brilliant manifesto *On Ancient Medicine*. In
this work he violently opposed the progressive penetration of
his field, the medical art, by the spirit of sweeping generalization
and mere speculation on first principles which, he says, dominated
the natural philosophy of his contemporaries, Empedocles and
others like him. [1] These philosophers of nature pretended to give
a total view of the universe; they laid the emphasis on the
explanation of the whole rather than on the exploration of detail.
They competed with the traditional powers of myth and religion,
and although there existed no separate branch of their philosophy
under the name of metaphysics, their bold attempts at solving
the enigma of the world were, from our modern point of view, of
a truly metaphysical nature.

The aspect of their thought which reveals this most clearly is
what we may call by a later word their theology. The nineteenth
century which did so much to stress the scientific side of the
Pre-Socratic philosophers, was at the same time inclined to mini-
mize their theological tendencies, because they did not seem to
agree with its concept of the Pre-Socratic philosophy as the
"awakening of the scientific spirit." Scholars were at variance
with St. Augustine, who, in his *De civitate Dei*, surveyed the

development of the theological trend in Greek philosophy and started his record with Thales and the Milesian school. [2] And yet, Cicero in the first book of his *De natura deorum* held the same view, which he borrowed from the Epicureans and Stoics. As to the Stoics, they opposed the philosophical view of nature, "natural theology," to the theology of the poets and the state religion [3]; and by calling it "theology" they referred the "physics" of the earlier thinkers to the highest problem with which philosophy since its beginning had been wrestling. The term itself was coined by Plato, and the fact that it was generally accepted by all succeeding generations of Greek philosophers proves that it revealed an essential feature of all Greek thought. [4] When Aristotle in his historical survey of Pre-Socratic philosophy contrasted the "theologians" and the physicists, he had in mind the pre-philosophical speculation of Hesiod and the theogonic epic. [5] But the physicists had a theology of their own. It is true, it was based entirely on rational thought; nevertheless, their speculation on nature and cosmology had a creative theological function. A fresh approach to this side of their mind is desirable, although a full appreciation of the theological element in Pre-Socratic philosophy must be left to another occasion. [6] We intend here to single out for a treatment from this point of view Xenophanes of Colophon, who is interesting as a particularly pure representative of the theological strain of Pre-Socratic thought.

The ancients distinguished two schools of Greek philosophy, one in Ionia, the other in Italy, and thought of the Italian school as including Xenophanes, Pythagoras, and Parmenides. [7] This geographical classification is not altogether unjustified, but it is rather superficial. Of course, it is true that these men lived in southern Italy and Sicily and evidently devoted considerable energy to coming to terms socially and intellectually with their environment. But the mere fact that Italy was the region of their chief activity tells us nothing about their real intellectual antecedence, which was determined far more by their

ancestral background. Xenophanes came from Colophon on
the coast of Asia Minor, Pythagoras from Samos; both were
emigrants. The former left his native city after its conquest
by the Medes; the latter left Samos to escape the tyranny of
Polycrates. Elea, the southern Italian home of Parmenides,
was a colony newly founded by refugees from Asia Minor, who
had abandoned their homes for the same reasons as Xenophanes,
and whose exodus to Italy was made the subject of an epic by
Xenophanes himself. Whether Parmenides was one of these
emigrants or merely a son of emigrant stock, is of little importance. In any case, he is intellectually a child of Ionia like
the rest. All three men are obviously in close contact with the
Ionian philosophy of nature, and carry its ideas forward in various directions.

Xenophanes is the first Greek thinker whom we can know as
a personality. The human contours of the older natural philosophers have either vanished behind the monuments of their
intellectual achievements or survived only in anecdotes. The
comparative intimacy of our acquaintance with Xenophanes is
directly connected with the fact that he was no such original
thinker as they, even though his influence was of inestimable
value in the dispersion of their philosophy. His struggle in behalf
of philosophy brought him fame; and in those of his poems
which have come down to us, he is always an impassioned warrior in this cause. [8] By this time Greek poetry had long since
become an instrument by which the poet could publicize any of
his convictions about the common welfare, whether critical or
didactic; and it is characteristic of Xenophanes that, unlike Anaximander, he did not set forth a complete theory of the world
in the new untrammeled form of prose composition, but took
his stand on the problems of philosophy through poetry. At this
time it was customary for all poetry to be recited in public, and
tradition states explicitly that Xenophanes recited his own poems
in person. [9] What is new in this is that his verses are not con-

cerned with practical or personal matters, but with problems of *Weltanschauung*—the nature of the gods, natural phenomena, the origin of all things, truth, doubt, and false authority. In these fervid pronouncements the poet's ego emerges quite unabashed and at the slightest excuse. Thus we learn that even as an old man of ninety-two he is still wandering all through the Greek speaking lands, and has been leading this irregular life for the past sixty-seven years—presumably ever since his migration from Colophon to the Greek west, where he seems to have spent most of his time. [10] He recalls the elegance of the Ionian culture in his old home, describes the Medic invasion, and tells of sitting by the fire in wintertime, engaged in pleasant conversation, and being asked how old he was when the Medes appeared. [11]

The poems in which all these things are expressed can hardly have been devoted to presenting a philosophical system. Xenophanes was not the man to write a connected didactic poem, like Hesiod or Parmenides. In the main his works were quite unphilosophical. This is obviously true of his great historical epic on the founding of his native city Colophon, for which he may have found a stimulus in the tales of the city's history by another fellowtownsman and equally famous contemporary poet, Mimnermus. We have already noted that Xenophanes also wrote an epic on the colonization of Elea in southern Italy—an event that occurred in his own lifetime even if he did not take part in it himself. [12] Thus even these two long narrative poems were decidedly personal in their origin. But this personal character of Xenophanes' work is most clearly revealed in his invention of a new type of poetry—the *silloi*. [13] These poems were satirical in character; while they were sometimes written in distichs, hexameters mixed with iambics, they often took the form of pure hexameters such as we find in Xenophanes' later imitator Timon, author of a collection of caustic satires on all the important philosophers. To be sure, it has long been customary to assign the hexametrical fragments with philosophical content to a lost didactic work by Xenophanes *On Nature*; but it is probable to me that no such didactic poem ever existed. [14] The mere fact that two late grammarians speak of Ξενοφάνης ἐν τῇ περὶ φύσεως no more proves the e x i s t e n c e of a didactic epic of this sort than Plutarch's similar reference to Σόλων ἐν τοῖς φυσικοῖς proves that Solon had a system of physics or wrote a philosophical poem on nature. [15] Plutarch's statement means nothing more than that somewhere in his poems Solon spoke of lightning and thunder or of a storm stirring the deep sea—that is, of φυσικά. So if we find that Xenophanes is the very same satirist and critic in his purely hexametrical fragments as he is in the distichs, we can only conclude that both verse-forms were used in the satires or *silloi*, and that a philosopher Xenophanes with a system of his own never really existed. We possess no fragments by Xenophanes of purely philosophical content which compel us to assume the existence of a coherent didactic epos by him on the nature of the universe. What we do have points rather to a discussion of certain natural phenomena and problems in his *silloi* in which he criticized the views of other philosophers and poets. [16] Even Aristotle and Theophrastus did not count him as a natural philosopher; Aristotle called his thought "rather primitive," and Theophrastus excluded his views from his great historical work on the theories of the natural philosophers, because he seemed to belong to a different category of thought. [17]

But then what sort of man was he? Gomperz has called attention to a testimonium which reads: "But he also recited his own poems like a rhapsode." [18] At that time the rhapsode's profession was well esteemed. The rhapsodes gave public recitations of the Homeric epics; and as I interpret this statement about Xenophanes, it means nothing more than that he recited his own verses, just as the itinerant rhapsodes recited those of Homer. But Gomperz lays special stress on the little word "also": "he recited his own verses *also*." Gomperz concludes from this that Xenophanes was primarily a reciter of Homer, and read his own poems only as an added attraction.[19] But the *silloi* are well known to be full of mordant satire and scorn directed against Homer and Hesiod — a fact quite out of accord with the assumption that Xenophanes was a rhapsode. The easiest way out of this difficulty for Gomperz is to suggest that while the poet spent his days in the marketplace reciting Homer and eulogizing him, he spent his evenings at the banquets of the rich and mighty (of which he has given us a detailed picture [20]), where he voiced his own enlightened views, castigating the very gods to whom he was forced to render public allegiance in order to earn his daily bread.

Of course examples of such double-entry bookkeeping are by no means lacking in the history of later periods of enlightenment, but the age of Pindar and Aeschylus did not call it forth; and if there ever was a man with whose character this game of hide-and-seek was incompatible, that man was Xenophanes. We must abandon any attempt to think of him as a rhapsode. He was not at all as Gomperz depicts him [21]—a counterpart of Plato's rhapsode Ion, wandering through the cities of Greece solemnly attired in purple, with the plaudits of the crowd continually ringing in his ears; still less was he a man to sweep his listeners off their feet with counterfeit enthusiasm for Homer, only to unmask himself with cynical abandon in a small circle after his public performance. This bold champion, brusque to the point of intolerance, was himself and utterly himself. His sole enthusiasm was his championship of a truth which he saw emerging from the ruins of all previous ways of viewing the world; and this enthusiasm was genuine and natural. The only mistaken idea in our conception of him is the one which modern interpreters have erroneously read into it—the supposed rhapsode's professional relationship to Homer. For the chief business of the rhapsode was to maintain Homer's official classical prestige, and this is what Xenophanes attacks most vehemently. Only by this polemic against the *laudatores Homeri* can he really be understood.

Xenophanes was an intellectual revolutionary. The earlier philosophers had taken their stand simply and straightforwardly, presenting their new conceptions of reality to their contemporaries in a plain, well-rounded whole. [22] But Xenophanes was a man of an altogether different sort, who perceived the devastating novelty of their approach and loudly proclaimed that it was irreconcilable with the traditional views. At this time the dominant intellectual and moral tradition had no more distinguished representative than Homer, by whom, as Plato remarks, all Hellas had been educated. Xenophanes himself thought likewise: to him Homer was the man

"From whom all have been learning since the beginning." [23]

These words reveal a very clear awareness of Homer's authority throughout the realm of Greek culture. And it was precisely because of this awareness that Xenophanes felt compelled to attack Homer as the mainstay of the prevailing errors. At this historical moment the latent antagonism between the new philosophical thinking and the old world of myth, which had dominated the earlier achievements of the Greek spirit, now broke into open conflict. The clash was inevitable; and while the first great explorers of the new philosophy had not insisted on the importance of their discoveries, Xenophanes made this opposition a focal point for his thought. It was not for nothing that he, the poet, should be the one to see in this situation implications which spelled disaster to all previous poetry. He saw them because it seemed to him self-evident that the poet is the one real educator of the people, and his work the only genuinely responsible authority of *paideia*. And so it is with Xenophanes that the work of deliberately transfusing the new philosophical truths into the intellectual bloodstream of Greece begins.

It is characteristic of the effect of the Ionian philosophy upon

the most enlightened contemporary minds that the problem of
God is central for Xenophanes. This is the best evidence of the
extent to which the new doctrines of the origin of the world were
felt to encroach upon the domain of religion. Naturally Anaximander must have sensed his own opposition to the traditional
anthropomorphic deities when he boldly asserted the Boundless
to be the Divine [24], and thus refused to let divine nature take
the form of distinct individual gods; but it is Xenophanes who
first declares war on the old gods with the words:

One god is the highest among gods and men;
In neither his form nor his thought is he like unto mortals. [25]

By this negation the poet gives his new-discovered knowledge a
fixed direction and propulsive force which it has hitherto lacked.
These are words which catch men's fancy far more than those of
Anaximander, despite the genius with which he first expressed
his knowledge. For not only has Xenophanes chosen to put his
message in poetical form, but he consciously applies his philosophical insight to the whole world of the anthropomorphic gods of
Homer and Hesiod—a world which has previously counted as
plain historical fact, but which now is collapsing. In these two
lines the bearing of the new knowledge upon the old divinities is
made explicit for the first time, not only in its positive aspects,
but also negatively and critically. Of course this philosophical
intuition of a single world-ground involves new riddles more
difficult than those for which it provides an answer. Xenophanes
himself points out in another context that even when one sees
the truth, this knowledge can never give its possessor complete
assurance of its validity; about these highest questions there must
always be widespread doubt. [26] This insight, which, while
tinged with resignation, is still far removed from the thoroughgoing "scepticism" of later centuries, is one which inevitably
appears whenever man first starts to reason about these problems.
But one thing at least is certain to Xenophanes: the human mind

is an inadequate form through which to comprehend that infinite, all-governing unity which the philosophers have recognized as the principle of all things. It never occurs to Xenophanes to suggest that God may be without form altogether. It is significant that in all the time that the Greeks give their philosophical attention to these matters, the problem of the form (εἶδος) of the Divine is one that never dies down. It always remains an essential part of the problem *De natura deorum,* and in the Stoic philosophy these considerations acquire new impetus in the doctrine of God's immanence in the world, which is represented as a sphere. 27 But Xenophanes does not express his views of the divine form in positive terms. He does not say that the world is God, so that God's form is merely the world's form; for Xenophanes is not to be dismissed with the word "pantheist." He merely makes way for a philosophic conception by denying that God's form is human.

In other respects he retains the conventional Greek pluralism. For understandable reasons Christian writers have always tended to read their own monotheism into his proclamation of the one god; but while Xenophanes extols this god as more than human, he also describes him explicitly as "the greatest among gods and men." Of course this manner of speaking, with its polar juxtaposition of gods and men, follows the old epic formulas; but it is still perfectly clear that besides the one God there must be others, just as there are men. On the other hand, it would be wrong to conclude that these must be the anthropomorphic gods of the epic, which would thus rank side by side with the one highest god and would enable Xenophanes to compromise with the popular religion. It is more plausible to think of the dictum of Thales that all things are full of gods, or Anaximander's doctrine of the one divine primal ground and the innumerable gods 28 that have come into being (that is, the innumerable worlds), even if we have no right to ascribe to Xenophanes any specific dogma of this sort. In any case the one all-embracing

God is so far superior to all the other partial divine forces that he alone could really seem important to Xenophanes.

But Xenophanes goes even further in draining off the slag of anthropomorphism from his conception of the one god. He writes that God "sees as a whole, thinks as a whole, hears as a whole." [29] Thus God's consciousness is not dependent upon sense organs or anything comparable. On the other hand, Xenophanes' God is unquestionably represented as a conscious personal being, and this distinguishes him from what Anaximander calls "the Divine." The philosophical attempt to divest the gods of their forms, which Stenzel sees in Anaximander's conception, is something of which Xenophanes is quite innocent. He does speak very definitely of the one god who is more than all others, and this is hardly to be explained as a mere reversion to traditional poetic language. One would not be likely to say of Anaximander's "Boundless" that it sees as a whole, thinks as a whole, hears as a whole. Moreover, Anaximander, unlike Xenophanes, does not attack the gods in order to supplant them with his own divine Being. But no one can doubt that Xenophanes actually prays to his god; we could be sure of this even if we did not have his banquet elegy to show us how seriously and directly he puts his religious ideas into practice. [30]

As we read on, however, these ideas keep unfolding in sharp opposition to the prevailing faith, just as if they intended to become a prevailing faith themselves. God, says Xenophanes,

. . . . ever abides
In the selfsame place without moving; nor is it fitting
For him to move hither and thither, changing his place. [31]

Here Xenophanes is again criticising the Homeric representation. In Homer the gods' quickness of movement is construed as a very token of the divine power. Xenophanes, however, demands that his God shall be immobile; he sees in this a mark of the highest dignity, as is clear from the words "nor is it fitting for him to move." (We meet this same religious intuition again in the contemporary statues and paintings which represent the gods as sitting in full majesty upon thrones, though naturally this insight must here be expressed in anthropomorphic terms.) Furthermore, the idea of God's absolute calm and immobility leads inevitably to an altered conception of his manner of acting upon things:

> But effortlessly he setteth all things astir
> By the power of his mind alone. [32]

This conjunction of omnipotence and repose is of great importance in paving the way for the idea of God that we meet in later years. We think at once of the Aristotelian unmoved mover, an idea which really originates here—a brilliant attempt to give greater plausibility to this noble conception of the divine action upon the world by adopting the Platonic formula κινεῖ ὡς ἐρώμενον. But in Aeschylus we find some much earlier evidence of the power and vigor of this conception, particularly in the great prayer of Zeus in *The Suppliants*. Here the divine dominion is depicted in a way that reveals not only the critical significance of Xenophanes' pioneering for a purer conception of God, but also its positive religious significance for his own time. In Aeschylus the notion that God can sway the world merely by the power of his mind, is shifted from the cosmic sphere to the ethical. [33]

> Down from their high-towered hopes
>   He flings poor wretched mortals,
> Donning no armor of might,
>   For gods act without effort:
> High from their hallowed seats
>   They somehow make their own thinking
> Come all at once to pass.

Aeschylus' expressive but almost prosaic word "somehow" (πως) shows that he is moved by a great and difficult idea which is readily perceptible to his religious feeling, even though his reason cannot grasp the "how" of this activity. This is not the only place in which the poet reveals that he has been directly influenced by contemporary philosophical thought or scientific discoveries. When he imagines the divine powers dwelling on high, he still clings to the old conception of the gods as throned in heaven; but we must bear in mind that even Xenophanes, as Aristotle declares, conceived his idea of the one god by "looking up at the sky," thus bringing the divine unity before his very eyes. [34]

According to Auguste Comte, the metaphysical stage, which follows the mythical stage of intellectual development and is itself superseded by "positive" science, is the critical reservoir through which the mythical consciousness must pass. We need not discuss the value of Comte's construction as a contribution to intellectual history; but it does at least help us to formulate the relation between Xenophanes' metaphysical thought and the mythical religion in a manner quite consistent with his own genius. In Xenophanes the critical side of the new philosophical theology becomes fully conscious. The idea of an omnipotent being, transcending all the other powers in the world, even the gods themselves, was one which the later epic writers had already associated with their highest god. In the eighth book of the *Iliad* [35], for example, the poet makes Zeus say to the other gods:

> . . . . *And if*
> *You should try to dangle a cable of gold from the sky,*
> *And hang on it, all of you goddesses, all of you gods,*
> *You could not drag great Counsellor Zeus from his*
>   *heaven*
> *Down to the plain, no matter how mighty your strain-*
>   *ing.*

But I—were I once in the mood for some lifting, I'd pull
The whole pack of you up, with all of the land and
the ocean,
And fasten the cable to one of the peaks of Olympus,
Leaving you swinging.

Aristotle cites this passage as the first intimation of the power
of the unmoved mover in the early history of Greek thought. [36]
But the all-too-human form of this conception would have struck
Xenophanes as childish, and in his century thinking men had not
yet learned to hunt for their primitive forebears. Xenophanes' god
has no need to nod his head like the Homeric Zeus to make
Olympus quake with terror. And only the bold phrasing [37]
νόου φρενὶ πάντα κραδαίνει betrays the unconscious persistence of
the old Homeric tendency to humanize the sublime.

The fragments reveal still further evidence of Xenophanes'
critique of anthropomorphism. He finds his task easiest in the
realm of ethics, where the way has already been largely prepared
by the progressive moralization of the gods during the sixth
century.

. . . . . . *Homer and Hesiod say that the gods*
Do all manner of things which men would consider
disgraceful:
Adultery, stealing, deceiving each other . . . . . . [38]

Godhead must be free from any moral weakness which even men
consider blameworthy: this is a point on which Xenophanes and
all his more thoughtful contemporaries would agree. But his
criticism is not content with so easy a victory. He launches another attack at the conception at the very root of the epic theogonies: [39]

. . . . *But mortals suppose that the gods undergo*
generation;
They dress them with clothes like their own, as well
as with voices
And figures . . .

The idea of the unending and the un-becoming, with which Anaximander has characterized his divinity, the *apeiron*, has put an end to such notions. Xenophanes merely works out some of the consequences of this philosophy in detail. And this is what must have brought him up against the problem of the origin of anthropomorphism: 40

> . . . . . *But if cattle and horses had hands, and*
>   *were able*
> *To paint with their hands, and to fashion such pictures*
>   *as men do,*
> *Then horses would pattern the forms of the gods after*
>   *horses,*
> *And cows after cattle, giving them just such a shape*
> *As those which they find in themselves.*

Then there would be theriomorphic gods as well as anthropomorphic ones. Apparently Xenophanes was not aware that there were already just such animal-gods in Egypt, and man-made at that; but he would have found this only a little disturbing to his theory, which he proceeds to develop with further ethnological details: 41

> . . . . . *The gods of the negroes are black with*
>   *snub noses,*
> *While those of the Thracians are blond, with blue eyes*
>   *and red hair.*

Thus each race apotheosizes its own type. The gods of the Greeks, to be sure, are more beautiful; but this does not give them any better claim to be regarded as the only true gods. They too are merely copied after one particular human race, and so they confirm the words of the poet: 42

> *Dass jeglicher das Beste, was er kennt,*
> *Er Gott, ja seinen Gott benennt.*

Xenophanes was the first to formulate that religious universalism which, both in later antiquity and more especially in the Christian era, was an essential feature in the idea of God, indispensable to any true religion.

This does not mean, of course, that its opposite, religious particularism, was ever a conscious article of faith even in the earlier mythical stage of Greek religion; Homer himself thought of his Greeks and Trojans as praying to the same gods, despite the division of their sympathies between the two warring parties. Since Homer's time, however, the Greeks came to recognize how various the ideals of the gods have been with individual nations; and this realization could only lead them to deduce, from the very fact of this particularism, the vanity of all such distinctions between gods, however naturally they may have come about. In the Western world universalism began neither with the Christians nor with the prophets of Israel, but with the Greek philosophers. When Saint Augustine in his *De civitate Dei* speaks of Greek philosophy in this connection as the precursor of the Christian religion [43], he is giving a thoroughly correct account of the historical relationship here involved.

In this development Xenophanes was not an isolated phenomenon. He merely brought to the full light of consciousness the inevitable consequences of the philosophical revolution in religious faith to which the Ionian theories of nature led; from his time on, his universalism had a place in the theology of all the Greek thinkers as one of their basic assumptions, whether or not they took the trouble to express it. It is true enough that the time was not yet ripe for the new conception to play any decisive role in the history of Greece as a nation. The public status of the *polis*-gods in the Greek city-states was as yet unimpaired, although a personage like Xenophanes had already broadcast his criticism of them far and wide. And even Xenophanes still thought of his own refined conception of God in connection with the *polis* and the problem of its legal order; this is clear from an elegy that has come down to us in its entirety, where he praises the cultivation of the intellect (σοφίη). This wisdom is something which Xenophanes considered himself uniquely equipped to propagate in his new home in the west of the Greek world; and it is only because he saw in it the highest *political* virtue that he considered his own efforts justified. 44 Not until the fourth century, when the gods of the *polis* had died and the *polis* itself was losing its identity in the world-empire of Alexander, did the universalistic theology come into its own and emerge from the background of philosophy to cushion the collapse of all established authority.

While we have already pointed out that Xenophanes' utterances presuppose the new and profoundly disturbing experience of Anaximandrian cosmology, it should now be clear that they also contain something peculiarly his own. Anaximander's conception of the Divine was deduced by pure speculation from the conception of an absolute beginning, and from this it acquired its attributes—its boundlessness and its property of never having become. 45 But in Xenophanes we find a new motif, which is the actual source of his theology. This is nothing that rests on logical proof; it is really not philosophical at all, but springs from an immediate sense of awe at the sublimity of the Divine. This feeling of reverence is what leads Xenophanes to deny all the finite shortcomings and limitations laid upon the gods by the traditional religion, and what makes him an unique theological figure despite his dependence on the views of the natural philosophers. Only as a theologian, indeed, can he really be understood. This religious motif—the demand for utter sublimity in the godhead—is expressed with particular clarity in the assertion that it is *not seemly* for God to move hither and thither.46 Unrest is not appropriate to the divine majesty. The word ἐπιπρέπει, which Xenophanes uses here, is not, as a matter of fact, repeated in any of the other fragments; but it reveals the criterion on which his entire criticism of anthropomorphism is based: all these human frailties are *out of keeping* with God's essential nature. The misdeeds of the Homeric and Hesiodic gods are incompatible with the moral elevation of the Divine; nor are clothing, speech, human form, and birth any more appropriate. In the concept of the appropriate, which here appears for the first time in the Greek tradition, we strike one of the distinctive aspects of the Greek genius, whose significance for later ages is incalculable. It originates in that feeling for harmony and proportion which is peculiarly characteristic of the Greek artistic temper. [47] But it is no less important in the realm of ethics and politics and in the theoretical approach to reality. And in the history of this basic category of the Greek spirit a special chapter (and a particularly important one in the light of its enormous influence) should be devoted to its application to the problem of God [48]—the problem of what things befit the divine nature and what things do not.

Such a chapter must begin with Xenophanes. His own formulations are so striking that nothing is left for posterity but to quote his words and ring the changes upon them. We need only mention a few secular stages in the history of his influence. Euripides' treatment of the gods in his tragedies is largely determined by Xenophanes' insistence on the inappropriateness of the way in which they were represented in the traditional myths; [49] and so are Plato's recommendations for the use of myth as an educational device in *The Republic*. [50] Xenophanes' doctrine provides the basis of the discourse of the Stoic in Cicero's dialogue *De natura deorum*. [51] The Stoic distinction between mythical and philosophical theology, which has reached Augustine by way of Varro, eventually goes back to Xenophanes; and in Augustine's critique of the gods of the heathen poets (where he follows Varro rather closely)—*ut furati sint, ut adulterarint* [52] —we hear the ring of Xenophanes' words κλέπτειν μοιχεύειν τε nearly a thousand years afterwards. Late Greek even invents a special term to designate the theological category of that which befits the divine nature — the θεοπρεπές. Probably this new word was coined by the Stoics; at any rate, through them it came down to the Church Fathers, who made it one of the cornerstones of all Christian theology. The postulate of the θεο-πρεπές is fundamental to the allegorical interpretation of Homer's tales of the gods in Stoicism. In the first century of our era, when the Greeks, artists and philosophers alike, sensed a greater need for sublimity in conceiving of the divine nature, the author of the treatise *On the Sublime* (whose taste was much too refined for this allegorizing) rejected the Homeric gods as falling short of his standards of true sublimity, and pointed to the Mosaic account of Creation with its 'Let there be light' as a far more satisfactory model. [53] Of course the conception of the Creation has little to do with Xenophanes; but clearly his philosophical theology has done more than anything else to smooth the way for accepting the Judaeo-Christian monotheism.

Xenophanes' conception of the one God has always roused the interest of monistic philosophers (oἱ ἐνίζοντες) because he was the very first, as Aristotle tells us, to teach the unity of the highest principle. This has seemed to give him some close connection with Parmenides' theory of the one *Being* and thus with the philosophy of the Eleatics; and inasmuch as he wrote an epic of the founding of Elea, the ancient historians of philosophy, who were on the watch for school successions, saw in him the father of Eleaticism. [54] The *one God* of Xenophanes was thought to be an earlier version of the *one Being* of Parmenides, as if the religious intuition of the all-one had preceded the logical conception of the ὄν.

This view long dominated our own histories until it was upset by Karl Reinhardt's pioneer work on Parmenides. [55] Reinhardt triumphantly demonstrated Parmenides' complete originality, and succeeded in showing that it was he and not Xenophanes who created the Eleatic theory of unity. This broke the traditional link between Xenophanes and the Eleatics, and allowed the problem of his position in history and his chronological relations with Parmenides to come up again for discussion. But Reinhardt has also tried to give this problem a new solution by supplementing the direct fragments with the anonymous later work *On Xenophanes, Melissus, and Gorgias* as source material. [56] Modern historians of philosophy, such as Zeller, Burnet, and Diels, had questioned the authenticity of this work so far as it dealt with Xenophanes' teachings, and accordingly refused to make any use of it. The little treatise was generally regarded as a product of the school philosophy of the later ancient period, and no one was ready to believe that its material came directly from Xenophanes' poems.

It seemed much more likely that its author had taken Xenophanes' well-known assertions about the one God and his attributes, combined them with certain constituents of Parmenides' logic of being, and thus tried to bring them into a strictly systematic dialectical form. But Reinhardt saw it all quite differently. Nothing seemed to him to exclude the possibility that Xenophanes, supposedly a rhapsode and inveterate popularizer, quite devoid of philosophical originality but clever enough to learn from everybody, had also borrowed a large number of Parmenides' ideas, and that therefore the strange hodge-podge of the tract *On Xenophanes,* the derivative quality of which had been rightly recognized by the critics, actually went back to Xenophanes himself. If this view should prove correct, then we already possess not only the few fragments of Xenophanes on which we have relied heretofore, but also a whole theological system after the Eleatic pattern. In that case, Xenophanes' idea of God would be nothing but the *Being* of Parmenides in a theological mask; for the theological arguments of the tract *On Xenophanes* actually do not demonstrate the one god at all but merely the one Being. Thus, far from having been the father of Eleaticism, Xenophanes would simply have been a follower of the school, and not a particularly original one.

This view fails to explain Xenophanes' enormous influence on the later religious development. But the only ideas that have exerted such an influence are those with which the remaining fragments of his poems have given us some familiarity; this is by no means true of the elaborate theology ascribed to him by the author of the tract *On Xenophanes* with its dialectical arguments and systematic structure in such striking contrast with the more intuitive reasoning that we meet in the fragments. The only kind of work upon which this elaborate connected treatise could have been based, must have been a sizable didactic poem; but, as we have seen already, it is quite impossible to prove that such a poem ever existed. Even if Xenophanes had written a work 'On Nature', it is hard to imagine how this theological dialectic would fit into it. Certainly its logical form never gives us the impression of being immediately derived from Parmenides. From him, of course, comes the list of attributes which the alleged Xenophanes tried to deduce as the properties of his God; but the inferences we find in his arguments could hardly have been possible before the century of Plato and Aristotle. [57] We must therefore charge them to some later writer, presumably the author of the treatise himself. What is worse, we must discount this unknown writer's authority as against the plain statements of Aristotle. To be sure, while Aristotle is still our most valuable source of information about the pre-Socratics, the weight of his testimony has been decidedly impaired during the last fifty years as we have become more and more clearly aware of his inability to grasp the ideas of his predecessors except in the fixed categories of his own system. But here we are dealing with facts that are nearly unmistakable. Let us examine them briefly.

Aristotle reports [58] that Parmenides thought of the One in terms of its οὐσία or essence, while the Eleatic, Melissus, thought of it in terms of its matter, so that for Parmenides the One was limited, for Melissus unlimited. But Xenophanes, Aristotle continues, knew nothing of such a problem and did not definitely aim at either the logical or the material One, but merely looked up at the whole heaven and said that the One was God. Now if we are to believe the author of the tract *On Xenophanes,* we must regard this account as false, for he says that according to Xenophanes the world is neither limited nor unlimited. 59 If that is true, then Aristotle simply cannot have read Xenophanes; otherwise he could not have maintained that Xenophanes fails to distinguish between the logical and the material One, and *therefore* says nothing about whether it is limited or unlimited. But it is really much more probable that the author of the late tract has not read Xenophanes at all but has taken his data from Aristotle and misunderstood them. 60 After reading this good witness's statement that Xenophanes neither called the One limited nor called it unlimited, he has drawn the absurd conclusion that according to Xenophanes the One was neither limited nor unlimited. Out of Aristotle's merely negative statement he has thus fashioned an utterly preposterous positive dogma, which he now puts in Xenophanes' mouth. This is quite enough to prove the untrustworthiness of this author. It is undoubtedly true that some of the arguments for the One which he attributes to Xenophanes actually point to the Being of Parmenides and not to the one God; but this merely proves that he has interpreted Xenophanes' God as the Parmenidean Being.

On the other hand, we can well understand how the author of the tract *On Xenophanes,* writing at a later period, can have come to devise this Eleatic *rationale* for that philosopher's idea of God. Evidently he felt that Eleaticism was precisely the sort of thing that Xenophanes stood for. Like all of us, he had learned in school that Xenophanes was the father of Eleaticism, and accordingly he attempted to understand the theory of the one God in terms of the Eleatic logic of Being. He thus had some reason to suppose that the Parmenidean ontology must have been potentially present in Xenophanes' theology from the first. But as a matter of fact, the God of his Xenophanes is only the Being of Parmenides in disguise, and has nothing to do with the historical Xenophanes, just as it is by no means the germ cell of Parmenides' philosophy. This whole theological Eleatic Xenophanes is a chimæra. He is purely synthetic, the product of a doxographical attempt to build up a set of teacher-pupil relationships which, as Reinhardt himself has admirably shown, never existed in the form we have always imagined. But if Xenophanes is far from being the father of Eleatic philosophy, he is just as far from being its unoriginal devotee; we cannot even think of him as a person who has translated this philosophy into theological terms. Here Reinhardt himself has not sufficiently escaped the Eleaticizing view of Xenophanes which he has himself refuted. He has accordingly made him a popularizing eclectic—an hypothesis rendered possible only by Gomperz' view of Xenophanes as a rhapsode. Each of these theories is as impossible as the other. The fragments of Xenophanes' poems tell us something entirely different. It is these that we must follow; and the reports of the best authorities, Aristotle and Theophrastus, agree with them throughout. Xenophanes was never a philosopher of the type of Parmenides, least of all an eclectic pseudo-philosopher. He had many interests, as his poems reveal. To the extent that he participated in the philosophical thought of his time—and this did not yet include the Eleatic doctrines but merely the Ionian philosophy of nature—he was an enlightened man with an alert sense for the natural causes of all phenomena. But above all he was profoundly impressed by the way in which philosophy was disturbing the old religion, and it was this that made him insist upon a new and purer conception of the divine nature. His peculiar piety alone is enough to assure him a place in the history of ideas. Accordingly we cannot really understand him as an historical figure except by tracing the development of rational theology as it emerges from Greek philosophical thinking.

NOTES ON XENOPHANES

1. 'Hippocrates', *De vetere medicina* c.20.

2. Augustinus, *De civitate Dei* l. VIII c.2.

3. See Augustinus, *op. cit.* I. IV c.27, who takes this Stoic trichotomy from his source, M. Terentius Varro's *Libri rerum humanarum et divinarum.* Cf. Dombart's edition of the *C. D.*, Vol. I, p. 180, 6.

4. See my Aquinas Lecture for 1943 delivered at Marquette University, Milwaukee: *Humanism and Theology*, p. 46 sq., and the second volume of my *Paideia: In Search for the Divine Centre* (Oxford and New York, 1944).

5 Aristotle, *Metaphysics* A3, 983b29 and B4, 1000a9.

6. The present essay is part of the Gifford Lectures delivered by the author at the University of St. Andrews, Scotland, in 1936. The complete series will be published in book form by the Oxford University Press. In this final form the text will be based on ample footnotes which have been omitted in the present article. Only the most necessary references have been given here.

7. Diog. Laert., Prooem. 13.

8. Xenophanes discussed and criticized the views of poets and philosophers in his poems; see Proclus *ad Hesiod. opp.* 284 (A22 Diels). I shall quote the testimonia about and the fragments of Xenophanes from H. Diels, *Fragmente der Vorsokratiker*, Vol 1.

9. Diog. Laert. IX 18 (A1 Diels).

10. B8 Diels.

11. B3 and 22 Diels.

12. See Diog. Laert. IX 20 (A1) on the epic poems of Xenophanes.

13. See the testimonia on his poetic works A18-27.

14. Even H. Diels lists fragments 23-41 under the title *On Nature*, and K. Reinhardt in his book *Parmenides* (Bonn, 1916), in which he discusses Xenophanes also, has followed him in this regard. Doubts were expressed by J. Burnet, *Early Greek Philosophy* (4th ed.), p.115; with most of his arguments I agree. Recently K. Deichgraeber (*Rheinisches Museum* 87, p. 1-31) has defended the existence of the didactic epic *On Nature*. I shall give my reasons against it more completely elsewhere.

15. Plutarch, *Solon* c.3.

16. 16. See Note 8.

17. Aristotle, *Metaph.* A5, 986b18 sq. (A30, Diels), Theophrastus ap. Simplic. *Phys.* 22, 22 sq. (A31 Diels).

18. Diog. Laert. IX 18 (A1, Diels).

19. In reality the remark of Diogenes that Xenophanes 'also recited' his own verses is logically opposed to the preceding part of the sentence which says that he wrote elegies, epics, and iambics. 'He wrote poems and he even recited his own verses.' We must not press these words to make them mean that he *not only* recited *his own* poems but was primarily a reciter of Homer, as Gomperz read between the lines. That he ever was a rhapsode in the professional sense is stated nowhere in our tradition.

20. See the sympotic elegy (frg. B1), especially lines 11-12 and 21-24, which deal with the gods.

21. Th. Gomperz, *Griechische Denker*, Vol. I, at the beginning of the chapter on Xenophanes.

22. Anaximenes and Anaximander wrote books, only Thales wrote nothing.

23. B10 D.

24. Anaximander 15 D.

25. Xenoph. B23 D.

26. B34 D.

27. See Cicero, *De natura deorum* II c.1 and 17.

28. Anaximander 17 D. See Note 24.

29. Xenoph. B24 D.

30. See Note 20.

31. B26 D.

32. B25 D.

33. Aeschylus, *Suppliants* 96-103 (Murray).

34. Aristotle, *Metaph.* A5, 986b18 sq.

35. *Iliad* VIII 18-27.

36. Aristotle, *De motu anim.* 4, 700a1 sq.

37. B25 D.

38. B11-12 D.

39. B14.

40. B15.

41. B16.

42. Goethe, *Gott, Gemuet und Welt.*

43. Augustinus, *De civitate Dei* l.VIII, especially c.11. The main reason for the superiority of the philosophical theology of the Greeks over the mythical religion of the poets and the state religion of the Greeks and Romans is, according to St. Augustine, the fact of its universal validity and truth.

44. Xenoph. B2, 11-22.

45. See especially Anaxim. 15 D.

46. Xenoph. B26.

47. In the more recent literature on Greek rhetorical and poetical theory the concept of the befitting (*prepon*) has played an important part; see the special investigations by Stroux, W. Kroll, Pohlenz, and others.

48. This chapter has not yet been written.

49. See, for instance, Euripides' *Herakles* 1345, a passage obviously influenced by Xenophanes.

50. Plato, *Rep.* 378c sq.

51. The words of the Stoic Lucilius Balbus in Cicero's *De nat. deor.* II 28, 70, refer literally to the same passage of Xenophanes which Plato quotes, *op. cit.* 378c sq. See Xenoph. B1, 21 sq., B11 and 12.

52. Augustinus, *De civitate Dei* VI 5 (Vol. I 253, 1, Dombart.)

53. Anonymus, *De sublimitate* c. IX 7.

54. This opinion is to be found for the first time in Plato, *Sophist* 242cd. It is repeated by Aristotle, *Metaph.* A5, 986b18 sq. Plato gives it only as a half-ironical combination; Aristotle passes this conjecture on as the 'opinion of some'; the later doxographers take it as a dogma without questioning it.

55. See Note 14.

56. This treatise has come down to us under the name and among the works of Aristotle. It is not a genuine product of the great philosopher. The part of it which concerns Xenophanes is printed in Diels, *Vorsokratiker* Vol. I, Xenophanes A28.

57. The late origin of the contents of the treatise *De Xenophane* would be made evident by a thorough analysis of its logical and argumentative structure.

58. *Metaph.* A5, 986b18 sq. (Xenoph. A30).

59. Xenoph. A28 (7) Diels.

60. Probably he has not read Aristotle directly but has taken his information about Xenophanes from a doxographic handbook which was based, in the last analysis, on Aristotle's statements. That would explain the misunderstanding.

ALBERT SCHWEITZER'S INFLUENCE

IN

HOLLAND AND ENGLAND

By

Kirsopp Lake, D.D., D.Litt., Dr. Phil. (hon.)

Professor of History, Emeritus, Harvard University

CHAPTER XXI

ALBERT SCHWEITZER'S INFLUENCE IN HOLLAND AND ENGLAND

BY

KIRSOPP LAKE

I

What is theology as distinct from religion? By etymology, it is the doctrine of God, but it has come to mean the ideology not only of religion but also, at least to a great extent, of the current view of the universe,—the *Weltanschauung*. It should be as true as we can make it at any given time, but we must never forget that truth is a goal at which to aim,—not a final possession to which to cling. In the days of Scholasticism Thomas Aquinas formulated Christian theology in the light of the knowledge of his contemporaries. In the nineteenth and twentieth centuries it became obvious that this formulation was untrue,—but instead of revising an obsolescent theology in the light of growing knowledge, the Church has tried to fit nascent knowledge into the frame of a dying theology.

Religion, on the other hand, is a necessary element in the composition of most men, though not of all. It is a reaching out to something not ourselves, and a willingness to serve that something at whatever cost. In the light of subsequent events it may be good or it may be bad. It is not necessarily theistic,—for theism is a part of thought, not of religion; and it is not necessarily ecclesiastic,—for ecclesiasticism is a form of politics, not of religion. The fanatical devotion of the Fascists and the Nazis (as well as of their opponents) is just as much religion as was the devotion of the opposing parties in the war of 1641 in England.

This may seem a shocking statement, in view of the atrocious cruelties and persecutions of the Nazis and the Fascists, but history records that no wars and no persecutions have been so cruel as those of religion. Consider, for instance, the Albigensian Crusade in France, the Marian persecution in England, the Thirty Years War in Germany, or the suppression of the Old Believers in Russia. It is sadly true that religion has produced the greatest miseries as well as the greatest blessings of humanity. That is one reason why periods of peace and widespread content, such as existed in England in the eighteenth century or in Rome under the Flavians and the Antonines, were ages of toleration and not of active religious feeling,—for toleration is one of the least religious of virtues. Religious people often desire it for themselves, but rarely practice it toward others, unless the police compel them to do so. Bills of Right seldom are written by the clergy, but more often by a non-ecclesiastical laity.

Religion was, and, in my vocabulary, is a strenuous effort to serve some purpose higher than ourselves, which seems of paramount importance and supreme good.

In the eyes of others this purpose may be unimportant or even evil, but to the religious man it seems immensely good, and for it he will willingly surrender everything, even his life; he will die in torture, yet happily. So the early Christians refused to satisfy the law by burning a little incense to the emperor, and died happily, though in torment, rather than do so.

In Holland the first years of the twentieth century were interesting but confused. The country has always been theological, if not religious, and theology has consequently played a predominant part in the affairs of the nation. So it was at the beginning of the century.

At that time the Liberals had had a long reign in politics and the Moderns in theology. This was broken by Abraham Kuijper, an ambitious man gifted with political skill and theological acumen. He realized that only by attracting the votes of the "fundamentalists" among workmen and peasants had he any chance of an important career as a politician or cleric, since the Liberals and the Moderns controlled the pulpits in the great cities and education at the University of Leiden, the stronghold of Modernism, as well as partially at Groningen. Utrecht, the third of the national universities, was under the control of the conservative aristocrats and of the party which in politics was called the "Historical Christian," and in theological circles the "Ethical Christian."

Kuijper was disliked and vilified, especially in private, by the leaders of both the Modern and Ethical movements. He therefore founded a private university in Amsterdam which, by a stroke of political rather than actual genius, was called the Free University, being in practice limited to Calvinists.

In the election of 1902, Kuijper pulled off a coup of such magnitude that it changed the political and ecclesiastical complexion of the country. He established an "unholy alliance" between the Calvinists and the Catholics. The price was the control of education, and the immediate result was the complete and disastrous defeat of the Liberals and Moderns. This soon was clear in University circles. Kuijper became chief minister and as such had to fill vacancies in the hostile faculties of the national universities. One of the first theological vacancies was at Leiden, where the health of Prof. van Manen had collapsed. The faculty proposed Prof. W. Bousset of Göttingen to succeed him. Kuijper refused and, with the expressed desire to kill off the Modern movement, proposed to nominate his own candidate.

In the theological faculty at Leiden there were two Moderns, neither of whom had agreed with van Manen. One of these, Prof. B. D. Eerdmans, was a vigorous and keen-sighted politician; the other, Prof. F. Pijper, had an intimate knowledge of mediæval history but none of modern affairs. His great contribution

[429]

to progress was his belief in the importance of documentary evidence. The most adroit member of this faculty, however, was an importation from Utrecht, Prof. Chantepie de la Saussaye, an eloquent preacher, a gifted writer, and a great power in court circles. He was president of the Royal Dutch Academy and used his position to exclude from it those who, like Eerdmans, were known to be Modern, while co-opting those who supported his own Historical Christian principles. At this juncture he tried to obtain the nomination of a Dutchman, who was anti-Modern but also anti-Kuijper, to succeed van Manen at Leiden. The result was a compromise. Kuijper vetoed any German: the faculty vetoed any Dutchman agreeable to Kuijper. Thus an Englishman was indicated, and Kuijper agreed. As he explained, all Germans were known to be Moderns and he would be discredited among the Dutch Calvinist clergy if he accepted one, but the English were either orthodox or unknown and the nomination of an Englishman would raise no suspicion.

Rendel Harris, a Quaker, was first chosen. He accepted but almost immediately withdrew. Burkitt of Cambridge and Conybeare and Charles of Oxford were nominated, but refused. Finally I was chosen and was accepted by Kuijper. Had I been older I should doubtless have declined, but I did not foresee the dangers ahead and that I was able to surmount them was rather the result of ignorance than the reward of knowledge.

I found myself in the midst of a deadly struggle, not between Modern and Orthodox, but between two sections of Moderns. The main point of dispute was the historicity of Jesus. Van Manen, who doubted the authenticity of the Pauline Epistles and the historicity of Jesus, had been the leader of one of these which based its position on the Gospel of Matthew. It had followed Strauss, had rejected Holtzmann, and had decided that the evangelic figure of Jesus was a figment. The other section was more in agreement with the liberal school in Germany, and had therefore desired Bousset, Burkitt or Conybeare. I was a *pis aller*.

Just at that moment came Schweitzer's book, *Von Reimarus zu Wrede*, translated by Montgomery as *The Quest of the Historic Jesus*. Its influence was much greater than had been foreseen. Most of the younger Moderns, with the exception of a little group headed by van den Bergh van Eysinga, accepted the priority of Mark and the probability of its historical nature. With this recognition most of the markedly unhistorical features of Matthew dropped out of the picture. But of course the fight was not over. Mark may be the source of Matthew, but, it was said, what evidence is there that the Jesus of Mark ever existed? Mark may be an ecclesiastical fiction, just as John certainly is. Perhaps neither is based on history, but on the purely fictitious figure which the Church of the second century, which was already in most respects the Catholic Church, had created in order to satisfy its own practice.

So far as John is concerned they were doubtless right. John may contain a few remnants of true tradition, but in the main it is fiction, and the Moderns in Holland contended that the same thing is true of the Gospel of Mark. The material for confirming their view of the Johannine problem was reiterated and amplified in the eighth chapter of Schweitzer's book. It is obvious that the Johannine gospel implies the sacramental system of the Church and that the Gospel of Mark does not. The claim of van Manen and his pupils that Matthew was just as fictitious as John rested on a few passages, such as the beginning and the end of the Gospel. Directly, however, the theological public accepted the truth of Holtzmann's theory, supported and almost mathematically proved by Sir John Hawkins in his *Horae Synopticae* and popularized by Schweitzer, it was obvious that Mark was in a different category from John, and even from Matthew. Then the question arose, is not Mark nevertheless fictitious? The advocates of Mark's historicity were asked to show that Mark contained narratives which could not be fictitious.

The challenge was immediately taken up. If, it was said, Mark is fiction it is of course Christian fiction, but if it contain passages which no Christian would have invented, these cannot be fiction, but must be history. Take, for instance, the opening of Mark. It describes a crowd of Jews coming to be baptized by John the Baptist and confessing their sins. Jesus also came to be baptized. The implication is clear that Jesus was also conscious of sin, confessed it and came to John to be baptized for the remission of sins. This is quite contrary to what soon became the established Christian doctrine, that Jesus was sinless. It cannot be fiction, least of all Christian fiction. Similarly, according to Mark, the last audible words of Jesus were a cry of despair, "My God, my God, why hast thou deserted me?" That cannot be Christian fiction.

These conclusions are confirmed by a study of Matthew. To those who followed Holtzmann it was clear that Matthew is a second and enlarged edition of Mark. The editor of Matthew did not like the opening of his original. He felt that the baptism of Jesus with a baptism for the remission of sins had to be explained, not merely related. He therefore put in a story to the effect that John was reluctant to baptize Jesus, until Jesus explained that in his case he desired to be baptized not for the remission of sins, but "to fulfill all righteousness." Further evidence could hardly be required that the Gospel of Mark is not wholly a Christian fiction, or indeed a fiction at all.

It may be asked why this change in opinion should be attributed to Schweitzer's *Von Reimarus zu Wrede* rather than to Johannes Weiss's *Die Predigt Jesu vom Reiche Gottes*. The essential point in both books might seem to be that Mark portrays Jesus as an historical personage who was wrong in the main point of his message, and that therefore this picture of Jesus must be historically correct. Nevertheless there is a profound difference between the two books. The conclusion to be drawn from Weiss's book, especially the first edition, might well be "Jesus was wrong: very well then, we shall drop Jesus." But the conclusion which

Schweitzer himself drew from his own studies is given in the last paragraph of his book: "He comes to us as one unknown, without a name, as of old by the lake-side He came to those men who knew Him not. He speaks to us the same word; 'Follow thou me' and sets us to the task which He has to fulfill for our time." Schweitzer dropped the ecclesiastical doctrine about Jesus, but wished to follow the example of Jesus himself.

The process which has been described in the preceding paragraphs was, of course, extremely controversial. The orthodox said in effect, "all true religion is based on the revelation in the Bible, the Moderns reject this, and therefore they have no true religion." The Historic-orthodox in turn contended, and indeed I once heard Chantepie de la Saussaye say, "We are Christians because we regard Jesus as our Saviour, and salvation through Jesus is the historical basis of all true Christian religion. The Moderns are not Christians and have no true religion."

Of course the Historic-orthodox position was disputed not only by Moderns but also by the "fundamentalists" (the *Gereformeerde*), who insisted that Calvinism is the only sound basis of the Christian religion, but it became, numerically at least, predominant.

Finally the position of the Moderns was peculiarly similar, but with the values changed. They said "true religion must be based on truth, or as near to truth as we can reach. The Orthodox refuse to accept historical truth, and therefore their religion is based on falsehood, not on truth, and is itself false." Quite especially was it held that this was so in the case of the Historic-orthodox, who could know, and did know, but shut their eyes and closed their minds.

The Moderns held that a Church which was based on false history was not a religious but a mythological institution. There is, they maintained, no more real religion in a Church based on the infallible work of St. Peter, or on the alleged saving death of Jesus, than in one based on the cult of the Roman Emperor or on the saving death of the Bull of Mithras. Well then, it was asked, what is religion if it be not faith?

The answer was often a mere Babel, but perhaps a quotation from Galsworthy represents fairly what the Moderns were trying to say: " 'What do you mean by God? There are two irreconcilable ideas of God. There's the Unknowable Creative Principle —one believes in That. And there's the Sum of altruism in man —naturally one believes in That.' 'I see. That leaves out Christ, doesn't it?' Jolyon stated. Christ, the link between those two ideas! Out of the mouth of babes! Here was orthodoxy scientifically explained at last! The sublime poem of the Christ-life was man's attempt to join those two irreconcilable conceptions of God."

That clear statement of Galsworthy fairly states the position which the Moderns reached when they did not any longer doubt the existence of a kernel of history in the gospels, but rejected all belief in the doctrines of the Incarnation or of Salvation by the death of Christ.

In many ways these Moderns were the most truly religious party in Holland. They believed, but were unwilling or unable to define their belief, in an element of unity which brought men together, revealed to them something which not only guides individuals but also groups of men and women, breaks down the barriers which separate, and makes them conscious of a purpose which unites. It is this uniting purpose which our forefathers had called God, inheriting the phraseology from a mythological period, just as they personified as the Devil the barriers which divide them. The Moderns believed neither in God nor Devil in any sense in which their ancestors would have accepted the words, but they did decognize the 'Purpose', called it 'God', and tried to serve it. Many of them, influenced directly or indirectly by Schweitzer's work, came to the belief that Jesus, a real man who had really lived in history, had shown them a model of how to do this.

II

In England Schweitzer probably had more influence than even in Holland. In the beginning of the nineteenth century the Church of England was deeply Protestant and largely Erastian. It believed in the doctrine of the Atoning Death of Christ and it preached little else. Then came the Oxford Movement, which tried to be Catholic, refused to be Erastian, and emphasized the doctrine of the Incarnation. It still believed in the Atonement but it rarely emphasized it. One of the most significant notes of the time was that the book on the Atonement which most influenced thought, both inside and outside the Church, was written by Dale of Birmingham, a Unitarian.

The earliest form of the doctrine of the Atonement, or of Redemption, was that man by the sin of Adam was forfeit to the Devil, and God, by sending his Son to become a man, paid the Devil's price and so rescued humanity. By the eleventh century, Christian consciousness rebelled against the idea that God had trafficked with the Devil, but retained the idea of a "transaction." The transaction, however, was between God's justice and God's mercy. The classical presentation of this view, which was dominant until the nineteenth century, is Anselm's *Cur Deus Homo*. In the nineteenth century a "transaction" of any sort became repugnant and Dale's *Atonement* led to its abandonment and helped the rapid decline of the Evangelical movement.

The doctrine of the Incarnation as preached by the early leaders of the Oxford Movement was put into clear and captivating form by Canon Liddon. It was an accurate account of the doctrine formulated at the Council of Chalcedon—the last meeting of the whole undivided Catholic Church—which in 451 revised and established the creed accepted by the Councils of Nicaea, Constantinople and Ephesus. This doctrine stated that the Logos, the Mind of God, was the eternally generated son of God, who came down from heaven to save mankind, and for this purpose became man and lived and died on earth. Thus the Logos became Jesus, and his incarnation, rather than his death only, was the divinely instituted means of salvation. The Bible is the record of this plan of salvation,— the Old Testament foretelling it and the New Testament describing it.

But while Liddon was at the height of his powers, of utterance rather than of thought, a great revolution was being effected in Oxford and Cambridge. This dealt with the treatment of Biblical Literature. The revolution really started in Scotland, where Robertson Smith, who knew German and Dutch, had studied the epoch-making work of Wellhausen and Kuenen and expounded it in his lectures in Edinburgh. He was promptly arraigned for heresy and for the duration of the trial all England and Scotland listened. The court held that beyond a doubt he was a heretic, but the public felt that equally beyond doubt what he had said was true. He was expelled from his professorship, but the lay members of Cambridge University, more interested in truth than in orthodoxy, secured him a position in the University Library, and there grew up in Cambridge a generation of young men,— Wright, Kennett, Bevan, Burkitt and others,—who had been inspired by Robertson Smith. In Oxford, Cheyne, Driver and Sanday had not indeed been influenced by personal acquaintance with Robertson Smith, but perhaps had been inspired by his writings and certainly by the same German sources. The result was that by the end of the century the "critical" position with regard to the Old Testament was firmly established both in Cambridge and in Oxford.

At this point another element entered into the situation. The most influential teacher in Oxford was T. H. Green, an Hegelian philosopher, to whom flocked many of the ablest young men, including Charles Gore, a fellow of Trinity. He and his friends became Anglo-Catholic and also Greenite. They came to see the probable truth of the critical position in the Old Testament but, oddly enough, one of the least important points raised the most disturbance. It was generally conceded that very few of the Psalms were the actual work of David. But, it was said, we have the evidence of Jesus that David did write them. For in Mark xii, 35 he asked, "How say the scribes that Christ is the son of David? For David himself said by the Holy Ghost,—the Lord said unto my Lord, 'Sit thou on my right hand until I make thine enemies thy footstool,' David therefore himself calleth him Lord." This quotation Jesus specifically attributes to David. Can the omniscient son of God make a mistake?

Intellectual salvation was found in a verse in the Epistle to the Philippians. In Philippians II, 6, St. Paul wrote of Jesus "Who, being in the form of God, thought it not robbery to be equal with God, but emptied (ekenosen) himself by taking the form of a slave and became in the likeness of men." The exact meaning of Paul has always been doubtful, but Gore and his friends held that it meant that Jesus emptied himself of the superior knowledge and power of the Logos, reducing himself to the level of knowledge obtainable by men of his time, and therefore Jesus did not know who wrote Psalm CX. This came to be called the Kenotic theory; and bad exegesis proved the bridge by which the higher criticism of the Old Testament passed into the citadel of orthodoxy, much to Canon Liddon's horror and disgust.

But of course the question could not stop there. The doctrine of the limited knowledge of Jesus came to the front simultaneously with the application of the principles of source-criticism of the New Testament. Almost unconsciously, under the leadership of Dr. Sanday and the enlightened criticism of Dr. Estlin Carpenter and F. C. Conybeare, the Synoptic problem was accepted and it brought to light the eschatological question.

Is the world moving on to the Day of Judgment? Did Jesus say so? Of course the New Testament replies by a loud affirmative, and adds that both Jesus and Paul expected the great day to come within the life of that generation. Unfortunately the only serious argument against Jesus and the New Testament was the evidence of history, which generally proves superior to that of documents, however sacred. In Oxford the result was an effort to use the weapon of source-criticism to show that Jesus was not responsible for eschatological pronouncements which can be attributed to Jewish interpolators. Thus there was a tendency to regard the Sermon on the Mount as the historical utterance of Jesus and the rest, if unacceptable, as interpolation, or to be explained by Kenotic theories.

The result was a curious reversal of roles. Those who were conservative in criticism and believed that in the main the Gospel of Mark is history and that the teaching of Jesus was eschatological became radical in theology and, going beyond the Kenotic group, were branded by the orthodox as Unitarian.

On the other hand, the theologically orthodox selected those passages in the Gospels which suited their doctrines, and claimed that the rejection of the rest was justified by source-criticism, or by the Kenotic doctrine.

Thus the whole doctrine of the Divine Nature of Jesus collapsed, if the evidence for it was sought in the Gospels as studied in the light of Synoptic criticism. Of course, there were many who felt that the Church as an institution was more important than any theology, and the old game of explaining away what could not be accepted was played to perfection. Jesus was divine but his divinity was tempered by human ignorance. Naturally this deceived only those who wished to be deceived, and the whole theological structure of the Church collapsed.

This was largely, though not wholly, the result of Schweitzer. It was much what had happened in Holland. Men began to perceive that religion is not theology; that, indeed, an untrue theology is the worst enemy that religion has, except perhaps a theology which is preached but not believed. In England F. C. Burkitt saw the importance of Schweitzer's emphasis on the fact that the Marcan picture of the eschatological teaching of Jesus is historically correct.

Very few followed Burkitt, but by his example rather than his writings, Schweitzer had immense influence. He had used his wonderful powers of absorbing knowledge by completing in three years the course supposed to take seven years for the medical degree in the University of Paris. I believe that if at this time Schweitzer had been offered a chair of theology in one of the great American universities, he would have accepted it. Just after the last war there was a strong movement in Harvard to obtain him, but the French Ambassador warned the President of Harvard that to appoint a man of German origin would appear to be an unfriendly act, for Schweitzer is by birth an Alsatian and the French claimed that he was German, the Germans that he was French.

He then decided to go to central Africa as a medical missionary, and he was soon either imprisoned as a spy or so generally ostracised that he nearly starved to death. Nevertheless, poor and hungry, he did much good, and incidentally did much to change the opinion of white men held by the natives.

This was, I believe, his great constructive work. His *Von Reimarus zu Wrede* had gone far to destroy Christian mythology: his work as a medical missionary went far to show the possibility of a Christian practice. It may not be accepted by the orthodox as Christianity, but Schweitzer had seen the figure of "One unknown", saying "Follow thou me", and had obeyed.

ALBERT SCHWEITZER'S INTERPRETATION
OF
ST. PAUL'S THEOLOGY

By

Olof Linton, Theol. D.

Assistant Professor of Exegetics, University of Uppsala

CHAPTER XXII

ALBERT SCHWEITZER'S INTERPRETATION OF ST. PAUL'S THEOLOGY

By

OLOF LINTON

The interpretation of St. Paul's theology involves a multitude of problems concerning his letters, their authenticity, integrity, chronology, his language, his relations to the Apostles before him and to his communities, his Jewish antecedents and his conversion, his travels and the trial against him, his personality and the origin of his conceptions, etc. As is to be seen, problems of different kinds—literary, historical, psychological, and theological crop up. Above all, however, one can discern two dominant problems: the one dealing with the inner coherence of Pauline theology—his "system," if he has one; the other, treating of his relations to the Christian faith of his environment, his place in the history of theology. The task is to find a coherent solution of both these problems, the theological one and the historical one as well.

In the history of the investigation of St. Paul's theology, one observes how these problems influence each other. About a hundred years ago, F. Chr. Baur, one of the most prominent fathers of the modern exploration of St. Paul's theology, solved both problems in the light of Hegel's dialectical philosophy of history. First, thesis: the Jewish-Christian theology of the original community of Jerusalem with its loyalty to the Jewish Mosaic law; second, the antithesis: the theology of St. Paul with its polemic against circumcision and law-obedience and its proclaiming of the Gospel for the heathens; third, the synthesis: the theology

[443]

of the rising Church, in which the older dissonance is brought into harmony, as is to be seen already in *Acts*. This view involved a certain solution also of literary problems. The authentic polemical Pauline theology was, according to Baur, not to be found in all those letters which were ascribed to the Apostle, but only in the four principal letters: *Galatians*, *Corinthians*, I and II, and *Romans*.

This coherent solution of Baur had a great influence on subsequent investigations. But the Hegelian background began to fade. By and by there came another idea of evolution, the idea of a gradual evolution without great leaps. This can be observed also in the investigation of Paulinism. To Baur, the evolution was a dialectical one; and therefore the fact that two opposite systems were contemporary, created no problem. For the scholars, however, who came after him, with their idea of a gradual evolution, it was difficult to make place for the different New Testament theologies within one century or even less. In scholars of the nineteenth century, one can therefore observe a widespread tendency to postdate some or all New Testament writings as much as possible, in order to fit in the time for the supposed great changes.

It was another prominent tendency of these scholars to work out very sharply the differences within the New Testament, between Jesus and St. Paul, Synoptics and St. John, etc. A radical group of Dutch scholars even challenged the statement that the Pauline theology could not belong to the first century, which consequently implied that no Pauline epistles were genuine. But this statement was nothing but an exaggeration of a tendency which can be observed everywhere. The New Testament theology was broken up into several different theological views virtually becoming a history of New Testament theologies. To combine the New Testament sayings in a dogmatic way was considered an impossible task. The one thing possible was to combine them in a historical view. But even this task was difficult. The time between Jesus and St. Paul, the Synoptics and St. John, seemed too short to explain the great incoherence.

It was, however, possible to find another explanation of these differences. The New Testament world was a world of great contrasts. On the one hand, stood the Old Testament and the Jewish religion with its monotheism, its theocracy, its claim to be the one true faith; on the other, there was the confused Hellenistic world with its mixture of Greek and Oriental ideas, its polytheism, its different cults and myths. Also this manifold Greek-Oriental culture was being more and more explored, and many scholars challenged the idea that here a new and better explanation of the incoherence between the diverse New Testament writings was to be found. The differences within the New Testament were thus explained not so much by an evolution as by a transition from Jewish to Greek ground.

Here St. Paul evidently was at the crossroads. Scholars such as Reitzenstein and Bousset pointed out a great conformity between Pauline passages and documents of Hellenistic mystery cults. The term "in Christ" was considered a typical mystic term and subsequently of Hellenistic, and not of Jewish, origin. The idea of death and resurrection with Christ suggested cults of mystery-gods; the opposition of flesh and spirit seemed more Greek than Jewish, and so on. Thus the statement was put forth that St. Paul was really not a genuine but a Hellenistic Jew, who already before his conversion had been acquainted with the ideas of the Hellenistic world. And Bousset tried to show that not only St. Paul but already the community of Antioch, as well as other centres of the earliest Church, was to a great extent of Hellenistic character. Even before Paul there existed a Hellenistic cult, in which Jesus was worshipped as Kyrios.

In this conception the historical problem of St. Paul's theology had gained a sort of solution. St. Paul belongs to two worlds, his theology being a mixture of Jewish and Hellenistic elements. On the one hand, he had broken down the validity of the Mosaic law, promulgated the Gospel of the Heathens, and adopted Greek ideas; on the other hand, he preserved the Old Testament for the Church. The way to the Hellenistic world was opened, and at the same time the continuity with the Old Testament, Jewish monotheism, and Jesus himself was conserved. Thus Paul exerted his great influence and importance even as the man at the crossroads. It was even challenged that Paul himself had a deliberate missionary method of adapting his Gospel to the Greek mind, trying, as he himself says, to be a Jew to the Jews and a Greek to the Greeks. The majority, however, seemed to hold to the statement that St. Paul had not felt the discordance in his own thinking. Belonging to two worlds and being from youth bilingual, he spoke both Aramaic and Greek, and thought in both Jewish and Greek terms. But in any case, the solution of the theological problem of Paulinism was in this conception not very satisfactory. St. Paul had become a Janus.

This statement however did not trouble most scholars of the first two decades of the twentieth century. Many of them had but little sympathy for the Apostle; and the proof that Paul was a poor theologian they willingly accepted. Even his friends found the item that Paul was no theologian very convenient, for in those days, even among theologians, it was hardly *comme il faut* to be a theologian. Thus it was put forth, by Deissmann and others, that Paul was no theologian but a missionary and a religious genius. He was an intense Christian personality, not a man with a rigid system and a dead dogma. In this debate even the strange argument was brought forward that St. Paul could not be a theologian, because he surely had neither interest nor time for such a theoretical job. One might as well argue that Soederblom or Schweitzer himself surely could not have written the theological works which bear their names—for when should they have gotten the time for this task? The alleged coherence of the Pauline theology was thus said to be a dogmatic arrangement without correspondence to fact. Paul himself had no theological claims, and his real mind came to the fore rather in the *Epistle to Philemon* than in the *Epistle to the Romans*—also a very strange argument. This conception, however, did not mean that there was no consistency at all. There was a combining element. But this was not to be found in the Pauline theology but behind it, in the mind of St. Paul. Thus the theology of Paul was valued not because of the theoretical claims but in spite of them, only as mirror of the great and zealous mind of the Apostle. It was impossible to combine his sayings in a theoretical manner. The one thing possible was to combine them in a psychological way. The theological and historical approach to Paul was completed by a psychological one.

Thus it was accepted that there were great clefts in New Testament theology and also a great cleavage in St. Paul's theology. Most scholars were satisfied with such statements.

But not Schweitzer. In his interpretation we find a new effort to give both the historical and the theological problems of Paulinism a coherent solution. In three rather polemical theses his position can be summarized:

1) Schweitzer set forth, against the anti-theoretic view of Deissmann and others, that St. Paul is a theologian, a thinker of great originality, consistency, and depth, the first and greatest of all Christian theologians.

2) Against the Hellenistic theory of Reitzenstein, Bousset and others, Schweitzer argued that St. Paul as a theologian is absolutely non-Hellenistic, thoroughly dependent on Jewish, or Jewish-Christian, conceptions.

3) The conditions are those of eschatology, common to early Judaism, Jesus, the original Christian community, and St. Paul. Pauline mysticism is a realistic, eschatological mysticisim, not the symbolical, timeless kind found in India, Hellenism, and most of European mysticism.

This view of St. Paul's theology is only a part of Schweitzer's total interpretation of the foundations of Christian theology—only a fragment of a greater connection, expounded in several books. First, there appeared, in the year 1901, two studies, one about the Lord's supper and one on the Messianic claim of Jesus: *"Das Abendmahl in Zusammenhang mit dem Leben Jesu und der Geschichte des Urchristentums.* Part 1: "Das Abendmahlsproblem auf Grund der wissenschaftlichen Forschung des 19. Jahrhunderts und der historischen Berichte." Part 2: "Das Messianitäts-und Leidensgeheimnis. Eine Skizze des Lebens Jesu," reprinted 1929, (English translation 1925: "The Mystery of the Kingdom of God: The Secret of Jesus' Messiahship and Passion").

Already here you find two characteristic elements of Schweitzer's scholarship. First, the putting forth of eschatology as the starting-point of all New Testament exegesis; second, the method which was to become his habit, the expansion of his own suggestions in discussion with earlier investigations in question. He consequently tries to show that New Testament research results in forced interpretations of the texts, until it is acknowledged that Jesus and his Apostles as well as most Jews of their time shared the conviction that a thoroughly new era, the "days of the Messiah," the "Kingdom of God," or "the Age to Come" was soon to appear.

In his most famous work, *Von Reimarus zu Wrede: eine Geschichte der Leben-Jesu-Forschung,* 1906 (English translation 1910: The Quest of the Historical Jesus, 2nd-5th ed.) *Geschichte der Leben-Jesu-Forschung,* 1913, 1921, 1926, 1933 (English translation 1931), Schweitzer realizes his interpretation of the Gospel of Jesus in the light of *"konsequente Eschatologie"*: Jesus himself shared the eschatological expectations of his time. His task above all, was not, as most scholars believed, to spiritualize the crassly material and national expectations of the Jews, but to proclaim the coming of the expected Kingdom of God, which no longer was far off but drawing immediately near: "The Kingdom of God has come near." By his journey to Jerusalem and his death, Jesus wanted to force the appearance of the Kingdom. But the Kingdom did not come. How has the Christian faith overcome this disappointment? That is to Schweitzer the great problem of the oldest Christian theology. And so he is compelled to complete the interpretation of the Gospel of Jesus by an interpretation of the original Christian theology. Here however St. Paul has a key-position. Thus Schweitzer is impelled to set forth a new theory of Pauline theology.

The first result of this task had already appeared in the year 1911, as usual, in controversy with earlier interpreters; *Geschichte der paulinischen Forschung von der Reformation bis auf die Gegenwart* (English translation 1912: *Paul and his interpreters: A critical History*. Here Schweitzer criticized the whole earlier investigation as failing to lead to the goal. It is therefore necessary, he argues, to try the eschatological solution of the Pauline problem. In his first book on this subject, Schweitzer, however, is occupied more with the critical survey than with the expounding of his own interpretation, which was reserved for another volume. This however kept people waiting. His critics found a natural explanation—the program of Schweitzer had failed: it was not possible to realize the eschatological solution of St. Paul's theology, an eschatological mysticism being an absurdity. Schweitzer's competitors *viz.,* Deissman, Reitzenstein, and Bousset had more success, their proposals being accepted in wide circles not only in Germany but also in other countries. It was contended that St. Paul's theology, to a large extent, was influenced by Hellenistic conceptions, especially from the mystic cults, and that his theology was not coherent but dominated by heterogeneous ideas. It was almost taken for granted that the eschatological program of Schweitzer had failed.

Now it is certainly quite true that Schweitzer's eschatological interpretation had many difficulties to overcome. You cannot carry through a new interpretation of a great historical problem without meeting obstacles. And surely also the theory of Schweitzer has its weak points. But the delay of Schweitzer's second volume on St. Paul's theology was due to other causes.

Schweitzer was on his now famous expedition as missionary and physician in Central Africa; and, moreover, became occupied with works on ethics and civilization. Under these conditions it is really most remarkable, not that it was late but, that the book appeared at all. The antagonists were so far put to shame. But they were not convinced, finding the book virtually antiquated on its very appearance. That would have been very natural. But, in fact, if the book had appeared about the year 1915, it would have been in advance of its time; in the year 1930, it was just in time. This is to be seen in the critical reviews. The book of 1911 was seldom understood; frequently overlooked or rejected. The book of 1930, *Die Mystik des Apostels Paulus* was, in spite of much criticism in wide circles, welcomed as a very noteworthy contribution to the understanding of Paul's theology. An English translation, *The Mysticism of Paul the Apostle,* appeared in the year 1931. And, in fact, here we have a new and very important effort to find a coherent solution of both the problems mentioned at the beginning of this paper. Here the Pauline theology is seen in its connection with the development of the oldest Christian theology, and in addition, also the problem of the inner coherence of Pauline theology is attacked with great energy.

Although Schweitzer's position is very original, he is concerned with many modern scholars in taking his starting-point not from the justification by faith, but from the mysticism of Being-in-Christ (*Sein in Christo*). From here Schweitzer sets forth his interpretation: With the death and resurrection of Christ, a totally new situation in the whole existence of Man is achieved. In the death of Christ, the order of the present world has begun to dissolve, and in his resurrection the World-to-Come has begun to appear. He who through faith and baptism has entered the Christian Church already belongs to a new existence, a new order, partaking of the body of Christ, thus being "in Christ"—taken out of the present demonic world. In consequence, the Christians, though still living "in the flesh," are participants of a new existence. And this to Paul is not only a likeness but a reality. Therefore he cannot use a symbol of rebirth, which occurs in Hellenistic mystery-religion and in St. John. The faithful are dead with Christ to this world, to law and sin, and resurrected with Christ to a new life.

This mysticism is not, like other types of mysticism, possible at all times. It cannot exist before a certain moment, the resurrection of Christ. Likewise, it is without meaning after his second coming, as in the World-to-Come, the Christ-mysticism is followed by God-mysticism, when God becomes "all in all." Now only Christ-mysticism is possible. The peculiarity of this conception is that a special sort of mysticism is possible alone in a certain era, the "days of the Messiah." It is thus "eschatological mysticism." This term, being often scorned, in truth corresponds to fact. The question as to whether Paul is a mystic or not, which otherwise has little meaning, is here answered in a reasonable manner. If you say Paul is a mystic, you must attach restrictions. Otherwise you suggest that Paul is a mystic in the ordinary sense. But he is not. Nor will it help us to say that Paul is not a mystic, for you find in him the idea of a real union with Christ, not only a faith in Christ.

Therefore, according to Schweitzer, the doctrine of the Being-in-Christ is a better starting-point in comprehending Pauline theology than the justification by faith. This idea had already been regarded by Wrede as a polemical doctrine of second rank. Schweitzer is on the same road; but he does not mean that the idea of justification by faith is a quite independent doctrine. On the contrary, it is connected very closely with the main idea of Being-in-Christ. In his suggestive world-picture, Schweitzer compares the doctrine of justification by faith with a crater on the side of the volcano, the idea of Being-in-Christ with the chief-crater. Even the law of Moses belongs to the conditions of *this* world, which by Christ are abolished. That the law of God can be suspended within the historical development of this world is to Paul an impossible suggestion. Only in the eschatological region of Being-in-Christ is the law suspended. Man cannot alter the law of God. On the contrary, everyone must remain in the condition in which he has been called by Christ. Did any man called happen to be circumcised, then must he remain so; if when he was called he happened to be uncircumcised then he must remain in this state, and likewise whether he was free or a slave. This Schweitzer designated as the Pauline doctrine of "status quo."

A further argument that the Christ-mysticism and not the justification by faith is the centre of Paulinism, Schweitzer notes in the fact that the ethics of St. Paul is derived from the Being-in-Christ. He who is in Christ and partakes of the body of Christ must conduct himself in a suitable manner. Thus the coherence of the Pauline theology comprises also his ethics. Here also it is proved that Paul is an important thinker; for very few Christian theologians, Schweitzer points out, have been capable of bringing dogmatics and ethics into harmony.

Schweitzer thus discovers a great consistency in the Pauline theology. Starting from the conviction of the predominant importance of eschatology, he combines sayings, which other scholars found at variance, into a coherent system. That is a very noteworthy solution of the doctrinal problem of St. Paul's theology. And now Schweitzer from the same starting-point will find a solution also of the historical problem of St. Paul's theology.

The eschatology is Jewish; and if Paul's thinking is thoroughly dominated by eschatology, it is evident that his "system" is not of Hellenistic but of Jewish character. There is no cleft between Jesus and St. Paul. But how can it then be explained that St. Paul's theology in many respects differs from the Gospel of Jesus? The primary reason, according to Schweitzer, is that time had elapsed. After the death and resurrection of Christ, a new era had begun. Accordingly Paul tells us but little about the historical Jesus. St. Paul is sure that he is living under absolutely new conditions, and he will draw the consequences of this fact. It is thus that he is so independent of Jesus and dares to work out his thought in inherent logic. What Jesus expected Paul has experienced.

The bases of St. Paul's theology thus are: the Jewish eschatology, the conviction of having reached a new situation within this eschatology, and St. Paul's logical mind. In the Jewish eschatology there was namely a latent mystical element in so far as also the Jews longed for a time where the present distance between God and Man is abolished. To Paul, the days of Messiah are already at hand, and, in consequence, the Christ-mysticism is realized. It is then useless to set forth Hellenistic ideas to understand St. Paul On the contrary, nothing but the conditions of Jewish eschatology are necessary.

But how are we to understand the importance of the Pauline theology for the subsequent Christian theology? Was the Christian faith Hellenized independently of Paul? That is not the meaning of Schweitzer. Certainly St. Paul's system was soon forgotten. But his sayings conserved in his letters were by the subsequent thelogians understood in an Hellenic manner. Thus Paul, although he himself was absolutely non-Hellenistic, paved the way for the Hellenizing of Christian theology, as is to be seen in Ignatius, Justin, and St. John, whom Schweitzer puts very late.

These are but a few outlines of Schweitzer's suggestive interpretation of St. Paul. Much more might be added. But it is not possible within this essay. What has been mentioned must be sufficient to show the importance of the work. It is a very learned work built on an extensive knowledge of the literature on St. Paul. It is moreover a very forceful work with an intensive effort to penetrate the problems. It is finally a very original work, in which received opinions often are discarded by a few critical words.

It is, therefore, natural that the critics did not fail to appear. Above all, they have put forth the following three arguments. First: the theory of Schweitzer is a construction. The scholars, who found themselves content with an incoherent Pauline theology remained of the opinion that the thinking of Paul was twofold—or even manifold—and that the consistency found by Schweitzer was his own invention. Second, the critics say, the theory of Schweitzer involves a large number of fanciful and strange suggestions which are impossible. Third, it has been said, Schweitzer is guilty of many exaggerations. His eschatological solution is very interesting, and surely the eschatological element of the Pauline theology has been undervalued. It is to Schweitzer's credit to have drawn attention to these forgotten facts. But we must also escape the exaggerations of Schweitzer.

I cannot here discuss these questions. Many objections can be raised. But I think that a great number of objections are due to the fact that even scholars change opinions with some difficulty. Especially, however, is it necessary to draw attention to the fact that also the Paul of Schweitzer is a zealous and fervent man. The criticism of Deissmann and others against the assumption of a stiff and dead dogmatic system in Paul cannot be levelled against Schweitzer. According to the author of *The Mysticism of Paul the Apostle,* the theology of Paul is a living theology born out of the very situation of the Apostle. Therefore you can read in Schweitzer's work an exposition of Paul's mind and life as intensive as in Deissmann's presentation of the Apostle.

It is to Schweitzer's contribution that we must turn for all future research on St. Paul. In several respects, reservations and corrections might be necessary, but above all, it is necessary to complete and carry out Schweitzer's suggestions. The eschatology of St. Paul is, as Schweitzer himself sometimes intimates, a part of a consistent dramatic view of the whole history and the whole existence of Man. The eschatology is the most conspicuous part of this conception but not the whole of it. But, I think, even taking these facts in consideration, the future research of St. Paul must acknowledge the supposition of Schweitzer that there is a close connection between Paul and Judaism, and also the other supposition, *viz.*, that the consistency of Paul's theology is greater than usually assumed. And the importance of the eschatology is now evident to all.

But must not the theory of Schweitzer remove Paul from the modern mind? Of course it must, but it is a primary interest of Schweitzer to carry out the investigation absolutely historically, without concern for such things as might seem strange to the modern mind. But having completed the purely historical investigation, Schweitzer finds in Paul ideas of everlasting value. Two things, particularly, according to Schweitzer, we must learn from Paul: first, Paul is the champion of Christian thought. Paul dared, in his situation, to draw the consequences of Christian faith, and so, we in our situation have to do; secondly, in St. Paul's theology, Schweitzer finds an intrinsic coherence between two fundamental Christian settings: the faith in Christ and the doctrine of the Kingdom of God. In modern times, he contends, these two doctrines are separated. On the one hand stands orthodox conservative theology, which preserves the faith in Christ but does not know how to deal with the doctrine of the Kingdom. On the other hand stands modern theology which accentuates the teaching of the Kingdom of God but has no understanding of the doctrine of Christ. The former is too limited, too passive; the latter threatens to substitute a general idea of the Kingdom for the Christian.

Thus I hope to have shown that Schweitzer's interpretation of St. Paul is a very important contribution, not only to the investigation of the Apostle's theology, but also a very remarkable approach to the research of the origins of Christianity in general, and I have written this paper not only with the purpose of honoring one of the most prominent exegetic scholars of our time, but also with the intention of bringing to the fore a work that has been little known to laymen and rather neglected even among contemporary scholars.

EPILOGUE

THE SCHOLAR'S DILEMMA

By

George Sarton, D.Sc., L.H.D. (hon.), LL.D. (hon.)
Professor of the History of Science, Harvard University

CHAPTER XXIII

THE SCHOLAR'S DILEMMA

By

GEORGE SARTON

In the very complex personality of Albert Schweitzer nothing impresses me more than his downright criticism of the thoughtlessness of our age. Many people, good people too, congratulated themselves (at least before the war) on their ability to live in such a civilized age as ours. Not so Schweitzer, who remarked "Two perceptions cast their shadows over my existence. One consists in my realization that the world is inexplicably mysterious and full of suffering; the other in the fact that I have been born into a period of spiritual decadence in mankind."* The fantastic progress of physical science and the incredible multiplication of man's power over nature have caused many evils, not the least of which are pride, self-complacency, spiritual nonchalance and sterility. In spite of scientific progress, or rather because of it, nothing is more needed to-day than humility and reverence,—humility induced by the ever-increasing mysteries of life, by our ignorance of fundamentals, by our lack of appreciation of the infinite beauty surrounding us; reverence for the accomplishments of good men and good women throughout the centuries all over the world.

To be sure there is also an infinite amount of misery, much of which is partly unavoidable, while many evils, the worst ones, are caused by man's inhumanity, but almost everywhere there are found compassionate people to help the poor, the sick, the suffering. We should realize as strongly as Schweitzer does, that there

---

* This quotation and others are taken from the epilogue of his autobiography *My Life and Thought* (London, Allen & Unwin, 1933).

is another kind of misery, now spreading faster than ever, which needs healing. That misery is not of the body but of the soul; it does not affect only the poor and the downtrodden, but also— and even more so—the rich and powerful. Spiritual laxness and thoughtlessness.

Modern science is so deep and wide that even the most intelligent men can only master a small part of it. For the rest, if they are not too conceited, they are willing to consult experts. Nobody who is not an astronomer or a physician is obliged to know the details of astronomical knowledge, or of medicine, but everybody who is a citizen must think out in some measure the problems of his community, or he cannot be a good citizen, everybody who is a man must think out in some measure the problems of his relationship to God and neighbor, or he cannot be a good man. The difficulties of any science are so great that we may, nay that we must, be excused from investigating those which are outside of our own field; the difficulties of private and public life are perhaps equally great but no thinking man can abandon entirely to others their consideration without grave peril. However, the scientific limitations have caused a shrinking from spiritual responsibilities, and the result is the combination of skepticism, cynicism and complacency, which is impoverishing the modern world.

The scientist and the scholar deem it their duty to search for the truth in their own field, but sometimes their devotion, great as it may be, appears selfish to others and if they be sufficiently sensitive and imaginative, to themselves. Hence their anxious dilemma. Dr. Schweitzer solved it in his own saintly way, but his solution is personal not universal. The great majority of scholars must continue their main task. They are imprisoned in their tower, but it should not be an ivory tower nor a hopeless prison. For the accomplishment of their task they need solitude and silence, much of it yet not too much; retirement is justified but not aloofness.

Is the scholar devoting all of his time and energy to his self-appointed task doing the whole of his duty? It is clear that such doubting cannot be solved in a general way; for a man's duty is defined by so many contingencies, that it can never be the same as another man's, except perhaps during temporary emergencies. The twinges of our conscience originate from the fact that we always have many duties, some of which conflict with others; in any case it is not possible to fulfill them all; one must choose.

Very often the choice lies between things which are urgent and others which are less urgent, or not urgent at all, yet necessary. Nothing can be more urgent every day than to eat and drink; for if we don't, we soon die, but clearly our other duties, though less urgent, are all of them more important. Now look at it from a social point of view. What must we do for our fellow-men? We must feed, house, heal, comfort, teach and amuse them and give their bodies and spirits the strength to go and the joy to live. One of the main duties, not urgent but essential, is to help them see themselves and others as they are, without lies or prejudices,—to see everything in its true light and its proper perspective. Men of science have developed excellent methods for the discovery of material truth, but those methods must be applied as far as possible, not only to physical realities but also to human events of the past and the present, and that is, I take it, the scholar's task and his main duty.

One has often opposed human history to natural history without realizing that the distinction is to a large extent artificial. However, the history of human events is infinitely more complex, and hence infinitely more difficult. It will always be far more troublesome to understand the stars of Hollywood than the stars of heaven. In fact, human history is so hopelessly complicated that it can never be investigated completely, nor without bias; for it concerns ourselves too closely—yet it must be investigated as thoroughly and as honestly as possible. That is the duty of some scholars.

[463]

Deeply shaken as we all have been by the insane mysticism which has invaded Germany and the incredible perversions of truth which that mysticism has veiled, Schweitzer has openly declared "One belief of my childhood I have preserved with the certainty that I can never lose it: belief in truth. I am confident that the spirit generated by truth is stronger than the force of circumstances" and again, "I acknowledge myself to be one who places all his confidence in rational thinking."

And yet, he fully knows as well as any scholar that we can never be entirely rational, for rationalism cannot deal properly with the feelings and emotions, nor with infinity of any kind. We should carry rational methods to the limit being fully aware of the fact that mystical ideas permeate our thinking from beginning to end. Love is the source of our spiritual energy. We cannot understand men without love, nor anything indeed without desire.* We cannot love properly without knowing, and the available knowledge can only be obtained by scientists for physical matters or by historians or other humanists for human ones.

We don't need as many historians as we need engineers, doctors, bakers or chemists, and our need of them will never have the same urgency. Yet we need them if we wish to know mankind and to know ourselves.

It is very edifying for a sinful man to contemplate Albert Schweitzer's graduation from theology to music, from music to medicine and missionary work in the African jungles, but we may conceive and justify other evolutions, for example, that of man saying to himself "Nothing is more important than the gathering of objective and verifiable truth, for we cannot see any other ground upon which men can ever agree and unite. Truth is less urgent but more necessary than bread. It is thus necessary to

---

* This old commonplace was beautifully expressed by Nicholas of Cusa (1401-64) in one of his sermons "*Mens sine desiderio non intelligit et sine intellectu non desiderat. Mens igitur est principium intellectus et affectus: Mens est vis simplex nobilissima in qua coincidunt, intelligere et diligere*" (*Opera*, Basel, 1565, Liber V, p. 504). The whole chapter is very beautiful. See also Edmond Vansteenberghe: *Autour de la Docte ignorance* (p. 56, Münster i.W., 1915).

obtain the truth for them, to come as close to it as is possible, and to develop eventually better methods of reaching it and of purifying it. The task is always difficult; in the historical field it is supremely difficult and in some cases it may seem hopeless. The difficulty increases our duties and increases our devotion to them."

Alas—these duties will never be as tangible as those of the ferryman helping his brethren to cross the river, of the miller preparing flour for their bread, of the doctor healing their illnesses. Yet they exist, they must be fulfilled, and the men fulfilling them well deserve a modest livelihood. The ferryman, the miller, the doctor can, as it were, measure their usefulness; scholars cannot, for their labor is so complex and full of pitfalls that they can never be sure of its goodness. Sometimes they may be tormented with doubts and wonder whither to aim next.

We may fail to distinguish our Lambaréné, or having distinguished it we may fail to reach it, or having reached it, we may lack perseverence and be discouraged, but if God grant us to recognize it, to attain it, and to stay as long as the task may require or unto death, we shall have done our duty, as much of it as was in our feeble power, and no one can do more.

A TENTATIVE BIBLIOGRAPHY

OF

ALBERT SCHWEITZER

By

A. A. Roback, Ph.D.

Department of Education, Commonwealth of Massachusetts

A TENTATIVE ALBERT SCHWEITZER BIBLIOGRAPHY

COMPILED BY

A. A. ROBACK

NOTE: The titles presented here are by no means exhaustive, but they constitute a working basis, fairly complete so far as the books and longer articles are concerned. The rewording of the original titles in translation is apt to confuse the student of Schweitzer's writings. Even the English and American editions do not always correspond in title.

I

BOOKS BY ALBERT SCHWEITZER

A

AUTOBIOGRAPHY

I

GENERAL

Aus meiner Kindheit und Jugendzeit. 1923. 1924. München: C. H. Beck. Pp. 64; 2d ed. 1925, pp. 73.

Memoirs of Childhood and Youth. 1924. London: Allen & Unwin. Transl. C. T. Campion. N. Y.: Macmillan. 1925. Pp. 103.

Souvenirs de mon Enfance. 1926. Lausanne, Editions La Concorde. Pp. 12+84.

Uit mijn jeugd. (Out of My Youth), 3d ed. 1928. Haarlem (Tjeenk Willink). Pp. 108 (*in Dutch*).

Uit mijn leven en denken (Out of My Life and Thought). 1932. Haarlem (Tjeenk Willink). Pp. vii+247 (*in Dutch*).

Fra min Barndom og Ungdom (Out of My Childhood and Youth). 1927. Jespersen & Pio. Pp. 88 (*in Danish*).

Selbstdarstellung. 1929. Leipzig: Felix Meiner. Pp. 44.

Reprinted from the series *Die Philosophie in der Gegenwart in Selbstdarstellungen* (Ed R. Schmidt) Leipzig (Felix Meiner) 1929.

Albert Schweitzer—Naar zijn waarde geschat (a translation of the above). 1934 (Kluver) v+56 (*in Dutch*).

Aus meinem Leben und Denken. Leipzig: Felix Meiner, 1931; 1932; 1933; 1935; 1937. Pp. 211.

My Life and Thought. [1933.] London: Allen & Unwin. Transl. C. T. Campion. Pp. 283. N. Y. Henry Holt ("Out of My Life and Thought").

Kurt Bergel is preparing an abridged edition of this book for the use of college students.

Minnen från min barnsdoms och ungdomstid (Out of My Childhood and Youth) 1926. Uppsala. Pp. 84 (*in Swedish*).

II

ACTIVITIES IN AFRICA

Zwischen Wasser und Urwald. 1921; 1923. Pp. 154. Bern: Paul Haupt. München: C. H. Beck: [1926.] Pp. 169.

There was also published in Groningen (Wolters) an abridged edition of the German text for school use. 1935. Pp. 124.

Mellan urskog och vatten (Between the Jungle and the Sea). 1921. Uppsala: Lindblad. Pp. 168 (*in Swedish*).

On the Edge of the Primeval Forest. 1922. London: A. & C. Black. Trans. C. T. Campion. 11th impression 1938. N. Y. Macmillan. Pp. 180.

Mellem Floder og Urskov. (Between the Sea and the Jungle). 1922. 3rd ed. 1928. Pp. 156. (*In Dano-Norwegian*).

Aan den zoom van het oerwood. (On the Edge of the Primeval Forest). 1922, 1926, 1928. Haarlem (Tjeenk Willink). Pp. 230; 1939. Pp. x+211 (*in Dutch*).

A l'orée de la Forêt Vierge, etc. Lausanne, Edition La Concorde, 1923. Pp. 192.

A l'orée de la Forêt Vierge, etc., récits et réflexions d'un médecin en Afrique équatoriale française. Paris, Rieder, 1929. Pp. 231.

Wśród Czarnych na Równiku. (Among the Blacks of the Equator) Trans. Z. Petersowej. Warsaw, "Swiat", [1934] Pp. 262 *(in Polish).*

The title of the Hungarian translation is the equivalent of *The Jungle Doctor.* There is also a Finnish translation of this book.

Mitteilungen aus Lambaréné. Three booklets. 1 and 2—1924-1925; 3—1925-1927. Bern: P. Haupt. München: Beck.

Nouvelles de Lambaréné du printemps à l'automne, 1924. Strasbourg (Libr. évangélique) 1925. Pp. 44.

Nya brev från Afrikas urskog. (New Letters from the African Jungle) 1927. Transl. by Greta Lagerfelt). Stockholm. Pp. 109 *(in Swedish).*

Nya Lambarenebrev. (New Lambaréné Letters) 1929. Transl. by Anna Taube. Stockholm. Pp. 77 *(in Swedish).*

Meddelanden från Professor Albert Schwéitzer. (News from Prof. Albert Schweitzer). 1926-1930. Stockholm *(in Swedish).*

Opnieuw naar Lambaréné. (Once more Lambaréné). 1927-28. Haarlem (Tjeenk Willink). Pp. 216 *(in Dutch).*

Bouwen in het oerwoud. (Building in the Jungle). 1928. Haarlem Tjeenk Willink). Pp. 106 *(in Dutch).*

More from the Primeval Forest. 1931. A. & C. Black. Transl. C. T. Campion. Pp. 169. N. Y. Henry Holt ("The Forest Hospital at Lambaréné" Pp. 191).

Afrikanische Jagdgeschichten. 1936. Strasbourg: Editions des Sources. Pp. 16.

Afrikanische Geschichten. [1938] Leipzig: Felix Meiner. Pp. 98.

From My African Notebook. [1938] London: Allen & Unwin. Transl. Mrs. C. E. B. Russell. Pp. 132. N. Y.; Henry Holt ("African Notebook".) [1939] Pp. 144.

B

BIOGRAPHICAL

Eugène Münch. 1898. Mulhouse, Alsace: Brinkmann. *(In French).*

Goethe Gedenkrede. 1932 München: C. H. Beck. Pp. 51. English translation published in *The Hibbert Journal.*

Goethe; (an address delivered by Dr. Schweitzer at the Goethe-Haus, Frankfort-am-Main, on receiving the Goethe Prize from the City of Frankfort, August 28, 1928). Translated by C. T. Campion. N. Y., Holt [1928] Pp. 8.
(Reprinted from *The Hibbert Journal,* pp. 684-90).

C

MUSIC

J. S. Bach, le musicien-poète. 1905. Paris: Costallat. Pp. xx+455. 4th edition 1924.

J. S. Bach, 1908. Leipzig: Breitkopf und Härtel. Pp. 828. 10th edition 1934. Pp. xvi+843; 12th edition 1937.

J. S. Bach. 1911. London: A. & C. Black. Transl. Ernest Newman. 2 vols. Pp. 428+500; 4th impression 1938. N. Y. Macmillan.
This work, at least in the English translation, is out of print.

Deutsche und französische Orgelbaukunst und Orgelkunst. 1906. Leipzig: Breitkopf und Härtel. Pp. 51; 2nd edition with supplement, 1927. Pp. 73.

J. S. Bachs Orgelwerke. (Kritisch-praktische Ausgabe). In collaboration with Charles Marie Widor. 1912-1914. N. Y. G. Schirmer. 4 vols.

RECORDINGS OF ORGAN MUSIC

Three Albums of Bach's Preludes and Fugues and Chorales (Columbia). Chorale No. 1 in E; by César Franck (Columbia).

D

PHILOSOPHY

Die Religionsphilosophische Skizze der Kritik der reinen Vernunft. 1899. Freiburg i/B.
This is a doctoral dissertation in theology which was elaborated and published as

Die Religionsphilosophie Kants. 1899. Freiburg i/B.: J. C. B. Mohr (Paul Siebeck). Pp. 325.

Kulturphilosophie I: Verfall und Wiederaufbau der Kultur. 1923: 5th edition 1931. Bern: Paul Haupt; München: C. H. Beck. Pp. 64.

Kulturphilosophie II: Kultur und Ethik. 1923; 1926. München: C. H. Beck; 3rd edition [1925] Pp. xxiii+280.

The Decay and the Restoration of Civilization. 1923. London: A. & C. Black. Transl. C. T. Campion. Pp. xvi+105. 2nd edition 1932. N. Y. Macmillan.

Kulturens degeneration och regeneration. 1924. Stockholm (Diakonistyr) xxiii+69 (*in Swedish*).

Kulturens Forfald og Genrejsning (The Decay and Regeneration of Civilization). 1925 (Jespersen & Pio. Pp. 90 (*in Danish*).
2nd edition (revised), transl. C. T. Campion. 1929. Pp. xxiv+287

Civilization and Ethics. 1923. London: A. & C. Black. Transl. J. Naish. 2nd edition (revised) transl. C. T. Campion, 1929. Pp. xxiv+287, N. Y. Macmillan.

Verval en weder-opbouw der cultuur. (The Decline and Restoration of Civilization). 1928. Haarlem (Tjeenk Willink). Pp. 115 (*in Dutch*).

Cultuur en ethiek. (Civilization and Ethics). 1931. Haarlem (Tjeenk Willink) Pp. viii+18+319 (*in Dutch*).

Die Weltanschauung der indischen Denker. (*Mystik und Ethik*). 1935. München: Beck. Pp. xi+201.

De wereldverschouwing der Indische denkers. 1935. Haarlem (Tjeenk Willink). xii+180 (*in Dutch*).

Les Grands Penseurs de l'Inde: (Etude de philosophie comparée). 1936. (Bibliothèque scientifique) Paris; Payot. Pp. 238.

Indian Thought and Its Development. [1936] London: Hodder & Stoughton. Transl. Mrs. C. E. B. Russell. Pp. xii & 272. N. Y. Holt.

E

PSYCHIATRY

Kritik der von medizinischer Seite veröffentlichten Pathographien über Jesus. 1913. Tübingen: Laupp, (Strassburg).
This is Schweitzer's dissertation for the degree of M. D., which was afterwards published under the title of

BIBLIOGRAPHY

Die psychiatrische Beurteilung Jesu. (Darstellung und Kritik). 1913.
Tübingen: Mohr. Pp. vii+46.

F

RELIGION AND THEOLOGY

Das Abendmahl. Part I. *Das Abendmahlsproblem.* 1901. Tübingen:
Mohr. Pp. 62. 2nd edition, 1929. Part II: *Das Messianitäts– und
Leidensgeheimnis.* 1901. Tübingen: Mohr. Pp. 109. 2nd edition
1929.

*Kritische Dartstellung unterschiedlicher neuerer historischer Abendmahls-
auffassungen.* Freiburg. 1901.

Von Reimarus zu Wrede. 1906. Tübingen: J. C. B. Mohr. Pp. 418.

The Quest of the Historical Jesus. A Critical Study of its Progress from
Reimarus to Wrede. 1910. London: A. & C. Black. Transl. W.
Montgomery. Pp. x+410, 2nd edition 1911. Reprinted 1922, 1926.
N. Y. Macmillan.

Geschichte der Leben-Jesu-Forschung. Enlarged edition of his earlier
Von Reimarus zu Wrede. Tübingen: Mohr. 1913. Pp. xii+659;
5th edition; 1933.

There was also a lithographed edition in 1926.

*Geschichte der paulinischen Forschung von der Reformation bis auf die
Gegenwart.* 1911. Tübingen: Mohr. Pp. xii+197; 2nd ed. 1933.

Paul and His Interpreters. 1912. London: A. & C. Black. Transl. W.
Montgomery. Pp. xiii+253. N. Y. Macmillan.

The Mystery of the Kingdom of God: the Secret of Jesus' Messiahship
and Passion, 1914. Transl. Walter Lowrie. N. Y. Dodd, Mead.
A. & C. Black: London 1925. Pp. 275.

Christianity and the Religions of the World. 1923: Allen & Unwin.
Transl. J. Powers. Pp. xix+86. N. Y. Doubleday, Doran. 2nd
edition 1939.

Das Christentum und die Weltreligionen. 1924 Bern: Paul Haupt. Pp.
60; 2nd edition 1928.

Kristendomen och världsreligionerna. (Christianity and the Religions of
The World) 1924. Uppsala: Lindblad. Pp. 83 (*in Swedish*).

Kristendommen og Verdensreligionerne. (Christianity and the Religions of the World) 1925. Jespersen & Pio. Pp. 62 (*in Dano-Nor-wegian*)

Het Christentum en de wereldgodsdiensten. 1927; 1930. Pp. 96 (*in Dutch*).

There is also a Japanese translation of this work.

EDITORIAL

Albert Schweitzer appears to have been a co-editor of the Dutch monthly, *Maanblad voor Evangelisatie,* between the years of 1916 and 1920, vols. 6–10. This periodical is not listed in the *Union List of Serials,* and the extent of his editing or contributing cannot at the present writing be established. The active editor was De Kandelaar.

II

ARTICLES BY ALBERT SCHWEITZER
on civilization, race problems, Christianity, music, and humanitarianism, in English, French, and German, chronologically arranged, up to 1945.

Die Philosophie und die allgemeine Bildung des neunzehnten Jahrhunderts, in *Das neunzehnte Jahrhundert.* 1900; pp. 61–68. Strassburg.
One of twenty-four essays on the nineteenth century.

Premiers Mois à Lambaréné. *Europe* (Paris), Sept. 15, 1927, pp. 61–68.

Our Pets at Lambaréné. *Everyland* (a children's annual), vol. iii; pp. 36–38, 88–90, 114–116, 150–151.

The Relations of the White and Colored Races. *The Contemporary Review,* Jan. 1928, vol. 133, pp. 65–70.

Selbstdarstellung: in *Die Philosophie in der Gegenwart in Selbstdarstellungen.* Leipzig, 1929, vol. 7, pp. 205-248.

Sunday at Lambaréné. *Christian Century,* March 18, 1931, vol. 48, pp. 373-376. *Spectator,* April 4, 1931, vol. 146, pp. 540-41.

Address Delivered on Receiving the Goethe Prize etc. *Hibbert Journal,* July 1929, vol. xxvii, pp. 684-690.
This was also reprinted as a pamphlet in 1929, Holt, N. Y.

Le Secours médical aux Colonies. *Rev. d. deux Mondes,* Sept. 15, 1931, Series 8, vol. V, pp. 390–404.

Nochmals Falkenjägerei. *Atlantis,* March, 1932. Berlin-Zürich. English translation in *The Animals' Friend,* Nov. 1932, pp. 319-320.

Der runde Violinbogen. *Schweizerische Musikzeitung,* 1933, No. 6. This article appeared also as an offprint in seven pages.

Busy Days in Lambaréné. *Christian Century,* March 14, 1934, vol. 51, pp. 355–357.

Sermon on Forgiveness. *The Christian World,* Nov. 1, 1934, p. 11.

Religion in Modern Civilization. *Christian Century,* Nov. 21, 28, 1934, vol. 51, pp. 1483-1484; 1519-1521.

Reverence for Life. *The Animals' Magazine,* Oct. 1935, pp. 3, 4.

Philosophy and the Movement for the Protection of Animals. *International Journal of Animal Protection,* Edinburgh. May, 1935. (In English and German).

"Dr. Schweitzer and His Work." *Spectator,* Sept. 6, 1935, vol. 155, p. 357. This happens to be a letter from Dr. Schweitzer. The caption was supplied by the *Spectator.*

The Ethics of Reverence for Life. *Christendom* (Chicago) Winter, 1936; pp. 225–239.

Letters from Lambaréné. *Living Age,* Sept. 1938, vol. 355, pp. 70–72.

[Letter from Albert Schweitzer]. *Christian Century,* May 30, 1945, vol. 62, No. 22, p. 655.

III

BOOKS ON ALBERT SCHWEITZER

Barthel, Ernst: *Elsässische Geistesschicksale.* 1928. Heidelberg (Carl Winter) pp. 219-279.

Buri, Fritz: *Christentum und Kultur bei Albert Schweitzer.* 1941, pp. 145. Bern.

Campion, C. T: *Albert Schweitzer; Some Biographical Notes.* 1928. London (A. & C. Black) pp. 31.

FACSIMILES OF SCHWEITZER'S HANDWRITING

(*slightly reduced*)

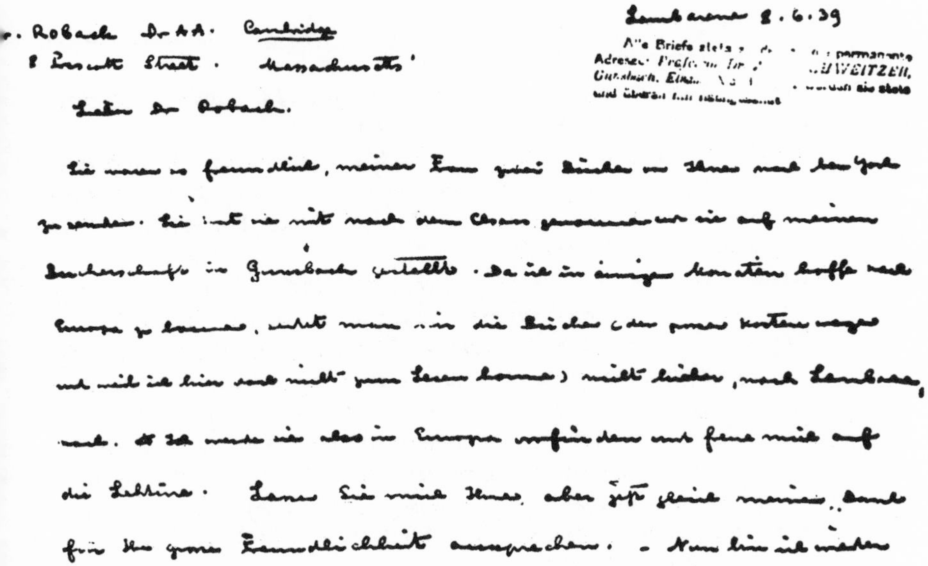

Prof. Roback Dr A.A. Cambridge
8 Prescott Street. Massachusetts

Lambarene 8.6.39

Lieber Dr Roback.

Sie waren so freundlich, meiner Frau zwei Bücher an Ihnen nach New York zu senden. Sie hat sie nicht nach dem Elsass genommen und sie auf meinem Bücherschrank in Günsbach gestellt. Da ich in einigen Monaten hoffe nach Europa zu kommen, erbitte man mir die Bücher (der grossen Kosten wegen und weil ich hier noch nicht zum Lesen komme) nicht hierher, nach Lambarene, nach. Ich werde sie also in Europa vorfinden und freue mich auf die Lektüre. Lassen Sie mich Ihnen aber jetzt gleich meinen Dank für Ihre grosse Freundlichkeit aussprechen. — Nun bin ich wieder

Part of a letter from Dr. Schweitzer, in German.

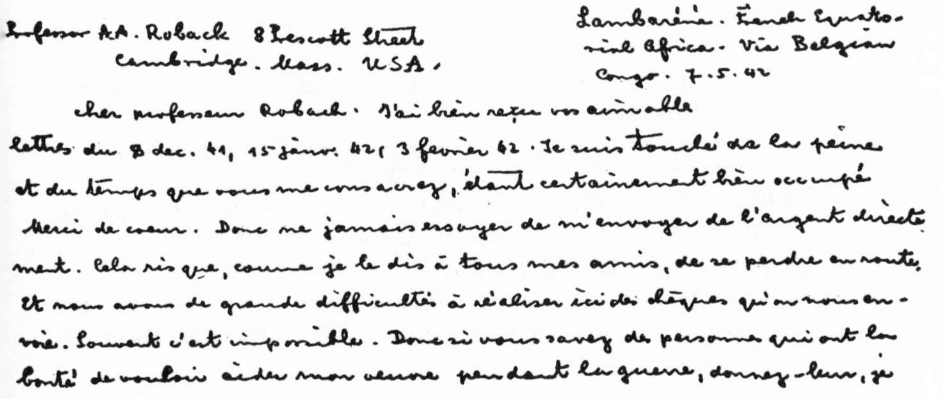

Professor A.A. Roback 8 Prescott Street
Cambridge. Mass. USA.

Lambaréné. French Equatorial Africa. Via Belgian Congo. 7.5.42

Cher professeur Roback. J'ai bien reçu vos aimables lettres du 8 déc. 41, 15 janv. 42, 3 février 42. Je suis touché de la peine et du temps que vous me consacrez, étant certainement bien occupé. Merci de coeur. Donc ne jamais essayer de m'envoyer de l'argent directement. Cela risque, comme je le dis à tous mes amis, de se perdre en route. Et nous avons de grandes difficultés à réaliser ici des chèques qu'on nous envoie. Souvent c'est impossible. Donc si vous savez des personnes qui ont la bonté de vouloir aider mon oeuvre pendant la guerre, donnez-leur, je

A Specimen of Dr. Schweitzer's handwriting, in French.

Eigenhuis, Jan: *Albert Schweitzer*. 1929. Haarlem (Tjeenk Willink) pp. 260 (*in Dutch*).

Henrich, Ruth: *They Thought He was Mad*. 1940. Eagle Books, No. 28, Friendship Press, N. Y., pp. 32.

Hunter, Allan Armstrong: *Three trumpets: Kagawa, Gandhi, Schweitzer*. 1939, pp. 156. N. Y. (Association Press).

Josselin de Jong, R. de: *De taak van den arts in verband met de persoon en het werk van Albert Schweitzer*. (The Task of the Physician in regard to the Person and Work of Albert Schweitzer). 1927. Utrecht, pp. 31 (*in Dutch*).

Kraus, Oskar: *Albert Schweitzer, sein Leben und seine Weltanschauung*. 1925. 2nd enlarged edition, 1929, pp. 78. Berlin (Metzner).

Kraus, Oskar: *Albert Schweitzer, his Work and his Philosophy* (with an introduction by A. D. Lindsay) 1944, pp. x+75. London: A. & C. Black.

Lagerfelt (Baroness) Greta and others: *Albert Schweitzer, Mannen och hans garning*. (Albert Schweitzer, The Man and His Work) 1938, pp. 239. Uppsala: J. A. Lindblad (*in Swedish*).

Raab, Karl: *Albert Schweitzer; Persönlichkeit und Denken*. 1937, pp. 95 Düsseldorf, Nolte.

Ratter, Magnus C: *Albert Schweitzer*. 1935. London: Allen & Unwin, pp. 260.

Regester, John Dickinson: *Albert Schweitzer, the Man and his Work*. 1931, pp. 145. N. Y. Abingdon Press.

Russell, Lillian M: *The Path to Reconstruction. A brief introduction to Albert Schweitzer's Philosophy of Civilization*. 1941. Pp. xii+68. London. Black.

Seaver George: *Albert Schweitzer; Christian Revolutionary*. 1945. Pp. 112. London, Clarke.

> From a recent letter, it may be gathered that this little book is to be expanded shortly into a large volume.

Snethlage, H.A.C: *Albert Schweitzer. De man die tot allen spreekt*. Albert Schweitzer—The Man Who Speaks to All) 1935. Pp. 100. Amsterdam, Lenkamp (*in Dutch*).

Strege, Martin: *Zum Sein in Gott durch Denken. Eine Darstellung der ethischen Mystik Albert Schweitzers*. 1937. Pp. 106. Bern: P. Haupt.

BIBLIOGRAPHY

Wegmann, Hans: *Albert Schweitzer als Führer.* 1928. Pp. 80. Zürich (Beer).

This was translated into Dutch as *Albert Schweitzer als Leidsman.* 1929. Pp. 104.

Werner, Martin: *Das Weltanschauungsproblem bei Karl Barth und Albert Schweitzer.* 1924. Pp. 136. München: Beck.

Werner, Martin: *Albert Schweitzer und das freie Christentum.* 1924 Pp. 31. Zürich: Beer.

UNPUBLISHED (in typescript)

[Sutherland, Gordon Alexander]: *The Schweitzerian heresy.* By "Alexander S. Wilson" (*pseud.*) 1940. Pp. 45, typewritten. Bowdoin Prize Essay, Harvard University.

The heresy referred to here concerns Schweitzer's views on the playing of Bach.

IN PREPARATION

Hagedorn, Hermann: *Albert Schweitzer.*
Seaver, George: *A Biography of Albert Schweitzer.* London (A. & C. Black).

It is worth noting that the late Stefan Zweig, shortly before the outbreak of the Nazi War, had planned to write a life of Albert Schweitzer. (See Alice Ehlers' reminiscences in this volume, pp. 233-234).

IV

ARTICLES ON ALBERT SCHWEITZER

Albers, A: *Münchner neueste Nachrichten.* 1925, No. 12.
Barber, B. A: Dr. Schweitzer's Autobiography. *London Quart. Review,* July 1933, vol. 158, pp. 395-401.
Barthel, E: Albert Schweitzer als Theologe. *Theologische Studien und Kritiken,* 1926, No. 3-4.
Barthel, E: Dr. Albert Schweitzer as Theologian. *Hibbert Journal,* July 1928, vol. 29, pp. 720-735.
Bie, O: *Dresdner Nachrichten.* July 1, 1925.

Bixler, J. S: Interpreter of Jesus and of Bach. *Christian Century*, Nov. 15, 1928, vol. 45, pp. 1935-1936.

Bixler, J. S: A Portrait of an Internationalist. *Christendom*, 1944, vol. 9, No. 1, pp. 35-39.

Breuer, R: "Rufer in der Wüste." *Aufbau*, Jan. 12, 1945, vol. ix, No. 2, p. 18.

Brock. E: *Logos*, 1923/1924, vol. 12, No. 3, pp. 415-418.

Clausen, B. T: Baffled Kindness. *Christian Century*, Sept. 27, 1939, vol. 56, pp. 1166-1167.

Cohn, Jonas: *Frankfurter Zeitung*, Sept. 9, 1924.

Deml, F: Die Ethik der Ehrfurcht vor dem Leben. *Deutsche Hochschulwarte*, vol. 2, No. 10.

Dodd, E. M: Kierkegaard and Schweitzer; an Essay in Comparison and Contrast. *London Quart. Review*, April 1945, vol. 170, pp. 148-153.

Dyrssen, Carl, *Didaskalia*, June 8, 1924.

Ellinger, A: *Münchner neueste Nachrichten*, Feb. 22, 1926.

Felis, Emmel: Albert Schweitzer. *Preussische Jahrbücher*, March, 1924.

Füssli, O: Prof. Dr. Albert Schweitzer und seine Tätigkeit im Urwald Aequatorialafrikas. *Illustrierte Wochenschrift*, April 18, 1925.

Heuschele, O: Albert Schweitzer. *Church Quart.*, Jan. 1935, vol. 8, pp. 29-34.

Hirsch, E: *Theologische Literaturzeitung*, 1924, No. 3.

Heym, H: Ein neuer Weg. *Protestantenblatt*, 1924, vol. 57, pp. 13-17.

Hogg, A. G: Philosophy of Civilization. *Internat. Review of Missions*, Jan. and April 1925, vol. 14, pp. 45-58; 237-251.

Kraus Oskar: Eine Albert Schweitzer Woche in Prag. *Deutsche Zeitung* (Prague) Jan. 5, 1923.

Kraus, Oskar: Epilog für eine Albert Schweitzer Woche. *Deutsche Hochschulwarte*, vol. 2, No. 10.

Kraus, Oskar: Albert Schweitzer. *Jahrbuch d. Charakterologie*, 1925, vol. 2/3, pp. 287-332.

Kraus, Oskar: *Hochschulwissen*. Jan. 1925, No. 1.

Kraus, Oskar: Wer ist Albert Schweitzer? *Prager Tagblatt*, Jan. 4, 1923.

Kraus, Oskar: *Das deutsche Buch* (Leipzig) 1928, No 11, 12.

Kunze, O: *Allgemeine Rundschau*. Oct. 8, 1928, vol. 25, p. 36.

Messer, August: *Philosophie und Leben*. March, 1925, No. 3.

Moehlman, C. H: Why a Genius Went to the Jungle. *World Tomorrow,* Oct. 30, 1930, vol. 13, pp. 418-49.

Montgomery, W: *The Expositor.* Aug. 1913.

Montgomery, W: Schweitzer as Missionary. *Hibbert Journal,* July 1914, vol. 12, pp. 871-885.

Montgomery, W: Schweitzer's Ethic. *Hibbert Journal,* July 1925, pp. 695-708.

Müller, H. C: Albert Schweitzer, seine Persönlichkeit und sein Werk. *Westermanns Monatshefte,* May 1926, vol. 140, pp. 309-313.

Muret, M: Le Christianisme Appliqué d'Albert Schweitzer. *Journal des Débats,* Oct. 21, 1932, vol. 39, part 2, pp. 675-678.

Niebuhr, R: Can Schweitzer Save Us from Russell? *Christian Century,* Sept. 3, 1925, vol. 42, pp. 1093-1095.

Ochs, S: *Vossische Zeitung.* March 12, 1927.

Paquet, A: Persons and Personages. *Living Age,* March 1935, vol. 348, pp. 43-46.

Peet, H. W: *Schweizerischen Jugendblätter.* July and Aug. 1925.

Pfister, O: *Neue Zürcher Zeitung.* April 17, 18, 1923. (Eng. transl. Albert Schweitzer—Missionary, Musician, Physician, *Living Age,* Aug. 2, 1924, vol. 322, pp. 229-233.

Rauch, K: Denker, Arzt und Helfer. *Westermanns Monatshefte,* Jan. 1935, vol. 157, pp. 482-484.

Russell, L. M. On Indian Thought and its Development. *Hibbert Journal,* July, 1935, pp. 630-634.

Sawicke, F: *Literarischer Handweiser.* 1924.

Seaver, G: Albert Schweitzer. *Spectator,* Jan. 12, 1945, vol. 174, p. 31. This was reprinted in pamphlet form.

Shillito, E: [Report on Schweitzer Commemoration in England]: *Christian Century,* Feb. 21, 1945, vol. 62, No. 8, p. 250.

Skillings, Mildred Davis: A Day with Albert Schweitzer. *The German-American Review,* Sept. 1935, vol. 2, No. 1, pp. 33-35, 52.

Smith, A: Albert Schweitzer. *Methodist Review,* Jan. 1931, vol. 114, pp. 24-29.

Spencer, M. A: Albert Schweitzer Honored at Edinburgh University. *Christian Century,* Aug. 10, 1932, vol. 49, p. 987.

Stamm, F. K: I Know Ten True Christians. *North American*, Dec. 1929, vol. 228, p. 676.

Steinbüchel, Th: Zur Problematik der Ethik der Gegenwart. *Berner Zeitschrift für Theologie und Seelsorge.* 1924, No. 3.

Suhrkamp, P: Albert Schweitzer zu seinem sechzigsten Geburtstag. *Neue Rundschau,* Feb. 1935, vol. 46, part 1, pp. 223-224.

Tasker, J. G: Dr. Albert Schweitzer's Work in Lambaréné. *London Quart. Review,* Jan. 1929, vol. 151, pp. 98-101.

Telford, J: Mysticism of Paul the Apostle. *London Quart. Review,* July 1932, vol. 157, pp. 393-400.

Trueblood, D. E: Philosophy in Action. *Christian Century,* April 1929, 1931, vol. 48, pp. 575-577.

Turner, V: Albert Schweitzer: His Work and His Philosophy. *Dublin Review,* July 1944, vol. 215, pp. 62-69.

Urmatt, F: La Vie étonnante d'Albert Schweitzer. *Revue Hebdomadaire,* May 22, 1937, pp. 409-423.

> In the footnote on page 409, we read *"d'un Français trop méconnu",* with reference to Schweitzer.

Veits, C: Albert Schweitzer als Musiker. *Deutsche Zeitung* (Prague) Jan. 5, 1925.

W. K: *Baseler Nachrichten.* Sept. 19, 1923.

Zweig, Stefan: *Neue Freie Presse* (Vienna). Dec. 24, 1932.

CHRONOLOGICALLY ARRANGED

Neue Zürcher Zeitung. March 29, 1923, May 17, Nov. 30, Dec. 1, 1924.

Münchner neueste Nachrichten. Jan. 1, 1925.

Berner Tageblatt. Jan. 14, 1925.

Doctor of Medicine, Music, and Theology. *Living Age,* Jan. 1929, vol. 335, pp. 352-353.

Schweizer Illustrierte Zeitung. July 30, 1930, pp. 1258-1265.

Die Musik (Berlin). Feb. 1931, pp. 334-337.

Schweitzer, his Black Brother's Keeper. *Lit. Dig.* March 21, 1931, vol. 108, pp. 18-19.

Among the Leopards *Lit. Dig.* Sept. 26, 1931, vol. 110, pp. 18-19.

The Animals' Friend. Nov. 1931, Jan., Feb., March 1933, March 1935, April 1936.

BIBLIOGRAPHY

Practical Internationalism. *The Aryan Path,* June 1932, pp. 429-431. Based on *Die Beziehungen zwischen den weissen und farbigen Rassen.*

Musik in Württemberg. 1932, No. 5, pp. 111-116.

Illustrierte Zeitung, (Leipzig). Dec. 8, 1932, pp. 668-669.

F. G. Arzt, Denker, Musiker. *Spectator,* Jan. 25, 1935, vol. 154, p. 119. Actually printed in German!

Manifold Life of Albert Schweitzer. *Lit. Dig.* Aug. 26 1933, vol. 116, p. 19.

L'Illustré. (Lausanne), Feb. 14, 1935, pp. 162-166.

The Aryan Path. (Bombay). June 1935, pp. 375-379.

War Catches up with Albert Schweitzer. *Christian Century,* Nov. 20, 1940, vol. 57, p. 1439.

Master in Darkest Africa. *Etude,* Jan. 1944, vol. 62, p. 10.

Dr. Schweitzer Reaches Seventy at Lambaréné. *Christian Century,* Feb. 14, 1945, vol. 62, No. 7, pp. 197-198.

FORTHCOMING

Walther, D: An Adventurer in Genius and Character. *London Contemporary Review,* [1946 ?].

INDEXES

REGISTER OF PERSONAL NAMES*

A

Abenguefit, 349
Acres, 390
Adam, 435
Aeschylus, 403, 408, 409, 422
Aetus, 342, 354, 455
Agreda y Vargas, Diego de, 330
Alarcon y Mendoza, Juan de
325-334, 336
Alarcon, Eugenio Salazar de, 335
Albers, A., 479
Albucasis, 347
Aleman, Mateo, 335
Alexander of Aphriodisias, 354, 355
Alexander of Tralles, 342, 347, 355
Alexander the Great, 280, 281
Alfanus (*Archbp.*) 348
Ali Abbas, 347, 348
Alkmaein, 349
Alonso de la Vera Cruz, (*Fray*), 335
Ambrose, (*See* St. Ambrose)
Anaximander, 400, 405-407, 411, 422
Anaximenes, 422
Andronicus III, (*Emp.*), 351
Angelus Silesius, 268 *note*
Angili da Scarperis, 352
Anselm, 435
Antyllus, 342
Apollo, 328
Aquinas, Thomas, 291-292, 427
Archigenes, 347
Archimedes, 59
Aretaeus, 342
Aristotle, 66, 75, 280, 316, 350, 353, 397, 402, 409, 410, 417-424

B

Augustine (*See* St. Augustine)
Augustinus, 423
Augustus, (*Emp.*), 283, 289
Aurelianus, C., 342-345
Aurispa, G., 352-353
Avancini, N., 318
Avicenna, 347, 349

Bach, J. S., 15, 38, 30, 42-44, 83-85, 89, 92, 104, 175-182, 186-195, 199-211, 218, 223, 225, 229-231, 233, 241, 304
emotion in Bach's music, 190-191
cantatas, 177—descriptive elements in, 179
passion music, 177
relationship to Wagner of, 191
Schweitzer's interpretation of, 175-195
Spitta's book on, 175
"symbolism" in thte music of, 177, 192, *note*
the chorale preludes of, 207-208
Bainton, R. H., 279
Balbuena, 335, 336
Balde, J., 317
Bandino, 352
Barber, B. A., 479
Barthel, E., 476, 479
Bartholdi (the sculptor), 32-33
Bartolome Frias de Albornoz, 335
Bartolomaeus, 348
Baur, F. Chr., 443, 444
Beck, C. H., 469-471, 473
Beethoven, 83, 182, 186, 304

* Names of characters in *belles-lettres* or of persons appearing as titles of books are italicized, as are also the names of mythological figures. Pseudonyms are flanked by quotes.

Begbie, H., 48
Benedict, (See St. Benedict)
Beneš, E., 17
Benzio, 353
Berganio, M. 351
Bergel, K., 108
Berlioz, 186
Bevan, 436
Bialik, Ch.N., *The Last Word*, quoted, 38 *note*
Biderman, J., 318
Bie, O., 479
Bismarck, (*Prince*) 296
Bixler, J. S., 51, 57, 101, 108, 117, 480
Bizet, G., 42
Blackwell, A. S., 38
Blake, Wm., 266 *note*, 272 *note*
Boccaccio, 351
Boecklin, 181
Boethius, 67, 261 *note*, 264 *note*
Bonaventura, 267 *note*
Bosanquet, 249
Bosco, J., 237
Bousset, W., 429, 430, 445, 447, 449
Bowne, 249
Bradley, 249
Brahma, 262 *ff.*
Brahms, 72, 178, 304
Breitkopf, 472
Brentano, C., 302
Bresslau, (*prof.*) 92
Bresslau, Helene, 92
Brett, G. S., 18
Brewer, R., 480
Brock, E., 480
Buri, F., 476
Burkitt, 430, 436, 438, 439
Burnet, J., 398, 416, 421
Butzer, 305

C

Caelius Aurelianus, 342
Caesar, J., 281-282
Campion, C. T., 469-473, 476

Careaga, Gutierre Marques de, 330
Carlyle, T., 58
Carmen Sylva, 60
Carossa, H., 299
Carpenter, E., 437
Cassiodorus, 343-344
Cassirer, E., 16, 18, 240
Cassius, Felix, 343
Cavaillé-Coll, 217, 220, 222-224, 226
Celsus, 342
Cervantes de Salazar, F., 335
Cetina (*see* Gutierre de Cetina), 335
Chamfort, 142
Chantepie de la Saussaye, 430, 433
Charlemagne, 290
Chesterfield, Lord, 142
Chesterman, C. C., 375, 390
Cheyne, 436
Chopin, 56
Chrisoloras, M., 352
Christ, 433, 316
Cicero, 281, 306, 351, 399, 422-423
Ciriaco, 353
Clark, A. C., 344
Clausen, B. T., 480
Clemenceau, G., 63
Cochrane, 390
Cohen, H., 240
Colmar, 32-33
Comte, A., 409
Compton, E. T., 242 *note*
Constantine (*Emp.*), 287-289, 348
Conybeare, F. C., 430, 437
Coomaraswamy, A. K., 17, 261
Cooke, E., 385, 387
Copho, 348
Cortes (*the Conqueror*), 335
Croce, B., 249

D

Dahlman, S., 17
Dale of Birmingham, 435
Damascene, 268

Dante, 67, 292
David, 437
Dehio, G., 303
Deichgraeber, K., 421
Deissman, 446-447, 449, 454
Deml, F., 480
Democritus, 345
Descartes, 45-46, 77, 240
Desiderius, 348
Diego Ruiz de Montoya (*Fray*), 329-330
Diels, 416, 420-421, 424
Dilthey, 139-140
Diogenes, 280
Dionysius, 354
Dioscorides, 342-344, 347, 353
Dives, 378, 381-383
Dodd, E. M., 480
Driver, 436
Droste-Hülshoff, A. *von,* 302
Droysen, 146
DuBellay, 317
DuBois, W. E. B., 18
Dyde, 252
Dryssen. C., 480

E

Eckhart (*see* Meister Eckhart)
Eerdmans, R. D., 429, 430
Ehlers, A., 108, 231
Eichendorff, J. von, 302
Eigenhuis, J., 478
Ellinger, A., 480
Emerson, R. W., 51, 249
Empiricus, M., 343
Erasmus, 292, 295, 308
Esau, 287
Eslava (*see* Gonzales de Eslava), 335
Eupate, 345
Euripides, 352, 423
Eusebius, 287
Ezra, 285

F

Faradj, 350
Felis, E., 480
Felix, C., 343
Feuerbach, 136
Fichte, J. G., 305
Filelfi, F., 353
Fischart, 312
Fisher, 390
Franchi, F., 328
Francisco de Terrazas, 335
Franck, C., 206, 219, 222, 225, 472
Freud, S., 141
Frias de Ilbornoz, 335
Füssli, O., 480
Fujinaga, E. (Rev.), 106

G

Galen, 341-345, 347-355
Galilei, 67
Galippus, 349
Galsworthy, J., 434
"Gariopontus," 348
Gerard of Cremona, 349-350
Gido da Magnala, 351
Gill, E., 272, *note*
Giordano Bruno, 67
Gluck, 137, 304
Goethe, 46, 58, 134, 141, 143, 181, 232, 240, 303, 317, 423, comparison of Schweitzer with, 106
Gomperz, T., 398, 402-403, 419, 421
Gongora, 328
Gonzales de Eslava, 335
Gore, C., 436, 437
Gottsched, 301, 314
Gottlieb, Th., 344
Green, T. H., 436
Grillparzer, 299, 302
Grimm, J., 314
Grotius, H., 294, 296

Guerra, G., (*Fray*), 330
Guilmant, 218-219, 224
Gundisalvi, 349
Güthel, C., 310
Gutierre de Cetina, 335
Guzman, A. de Saavedra, 335
Guzman, R. N. Felipez de, 331

H

Hagedorn, H., 479
Handel, 203-204, 206, 304
Hannibal, 282
Harris, R., 430
Härtel, 472
Haupt, P., 471, 473-474
Hawkins, J. (*Sir*), 431
Haydn, 304
Heard, G., 272 *note*, 274
Hegel('s), 71, 72, 248-257, 397, 443
   theory of unity of spirit, 134
   system, 248
   influence, 249
   optimism, 249
Heinsius, 317
Helmholtz, 179
Henrich, R., 478
Heraclitus, 397
Herder, 40, 317
Herman of Corinthia, 349
Hernando de Mendoza, 329
Hesiod, 283, 399, 401, 403, 405, 410
Hesse, 218
Heym, H., 480
Heuschele, O., 480
Hillel, 34
Hippocrates, 343-345, 347-354
Hirsch, E., 480
Hitler, A., 234
Hochland, 300
Hocking, W. E., 249
Hoffmann, E. T. A., 181
Hogg, A. G., 205, 480
Hölderlin, 240

Holtzmann, 430, 432
Homer, 266 *note*, 351-352, 402-405,
   407, 410, 412, 421
Horace, 316, 317
Humboldt, W. von, 136, 139, 240
Hume, D., 142
Hume, E. H., 108
Hunter, A. A., 478
Huxley, A., 274 *note*

I

Ibn al-Djezzer, 348
Ignatius, 308, 453
Innocent III (*Pope*), 291
Isaac Judaeus, 349

J

Jacob, 287
Jaeger, W., 16, 395
James, M., 346
James, Wm., 71
Janus, 446
Jeremiah, 285
Jesus, 30, 39, 40, 45, 58, 62, 79-81, 96,
   106, 115, 116, 122, 241, 286, 295,
   391, 430-433, 436-438, 444, 449, 452,
   453 (*see* also Christ)
Johannitius, 347
John, 431, 432
John the Apostle (*see* St. John)
John the Baptist, 432
Joseph II, 301
Josselin de Jong, R., 478
Jaun de la Cueva, 335
Joylon, 434
Julius Caesar, 281, 282
Jung, C., 141
Justin, 453

K

Kant, 60, 65, 122, 240
Kellersberger, 390
Keevill, 390

Kennett, 436
Kepler, 240
Kipling, R., 60
Klopstock, 301-302
Kleist, 240
Koch, J. L. A., 58
Kraus, O., 90, 478, 480
Kroll, W., 423
Krzenski, A. J., 272 *note*
Kuen, J., 316
Kuenen, 436
Kuijper, A., 428-430
Kunze, O., 480

L

Lagerfelt, G., 478
Lake, K., 17, 425
Lamartine, 181
Lamola, G., 356
La Rochefoucauld, 142
Lascaris, J., 354-355
Laupp, 473
Lavoisier, C., 65
Lazarus, 378, 380, 382, 383
Leibniz, 240, 249, 314
Leopold II of Belgium, 126, 127
Lessing, G. E., 240
Liddon, (*Cannon*), 435-437
Linton, O., 17, 441, 443
Liszt, F., 178
Livingstone, D., 121, 379
Lope de Vega, 325, 326, 328, 331, 332
Lorenzo de Medici, 353
Lotze, H., 179
Lowe, 390
Lowrie, W., 474
Lucifer, 285
Lucius Balbus, 423
Luis de Belmonte, 335
Luis de Leon, (Fray), 335
Luisa de Robles, 328
Luther, 293, 305, 307, 308, 310

M

Machiavelli, 296
Mahaut, A., 193 note
Maimonides, 347
Maldonado, P. G., (*Fray*), 329
Malebranche, F., 134
Manheim, E., 313
Mann, T., 108, 142
Manson-Bahr, P. (*Sir*), 17, 361, 365
Mansanares, 332
Marcellus Empiricus, 243
Marcus of Toledo, 350
Marheineke, 249, 254
Marius, 281
Mark, 431, 432, 437, 438
Masen, J., 318
Massenet, 64
Matthew, 430, 432
Maurus, R., 345
Mayer, R., 65
Mead, M., 268 *note*
Meissner, E., 272 *note*
Meister Eckhart, 269 *note*
Melanchthon, 307
Melissus, 416-417
Melkart of Tyre, 285
Mendelssohn, M., 240, 304
Meja, D., 335
Mendoza, A. de, 329
Mendoza, H. de, 329
Messer, A., 480
Mesue, 347
Metrodorus, 354
Michelangelo, 137
Micklem, Dr., 115-116
Mimnermus, 401
Mira de Mescue, 328
Mithridates, 282
Moehlman, C. H., 481
Mohr, J. C. B., 472-474
Montaigne, 142
Montgomery, W., 51, 431, 474, 481

Montoya, (*see* Diego Ruiz de Montoya), 329, 330
Montoya, G. R. de, 329
More, T., 296
Morris, Wm., 272 *note*
Moses, 284, 452
Mozarab, 349
Mozart, 42, 234, 304
Muelder, W., 108
Mueller, 354
Muir, 390
Müller, H. C., 481
Muret, M., 481
Muth, K., 299

N

Naish J., 473
Napoleon, 296
Nassau, R. H., 93
Nemesios, 348
Nehemiah, 285
Nestorius, 346
Newman, E., 176 note, 472
Niccolo de Deoprepio, 351, 354, 355
Nicetas, 346
Nicholas of Susa, 464
Nicolai, 301
Niebuhr, R., 481
Niekisch, E., 272 *note*
Nies-Berger, E., 106
Nietzsche('s) Fr., 63, 89, 144, 181, 316
    Biologistic philosophy, 34
    Creative ability, 145
    "Immoralism," 247
Nonnus, T., 354
Novalis, 134, 181

O

Occam, 292
Ochs, S., 481
Opitz, 301, 312, 313, 315, 317, 318
Oratianus O., 356

Oribasius, 342, 347, 354
Orr, 391
"Ossian," 302
O'Toole, G. B., 272 *note*
Ovid, 283

P

Paleologus, J. (*Emp.*), 352
Paquet, A., 481
Park, M., 121
Parmenides, 397, 399-401, 415-419
Pascal, B., 143
Pasteur, L., 67
Paul the Apostle (*see* St. Paul)
Paul of Aegina, 342, 347, 353-354
Payot, 473
Peet, H. W., 481
Peter the Apostle (*see* St. Peter)
Petrarch, 292, 317, 351
Petroncellus, 348
Pfeiffer, 268 *note*
Pfister, O., 27, 53, 481
Phemister, D. B., 341
Philagrios, 347
Philemon, 282
Philip IV, 325
Philo, 264 *ff*, 266
Philothenus of Alexandria, 354
Pijper, F., 429
Pindar, 403
Pisano, B., 351
Pirro, A., 192 *note*
Platearius, 348
Plato, 134, 240, 261 *ff*, 280, 351, 352, 397, 399, 403, 404, 417, 423, 424
Plato of Tivoli, 349
Pliny the Younger 343
Plutarch, 352, 402, 421
Poggio, 355
Pohlenz, 423
Polycrates, 400
Powers, J., 474
Priscianus, Th., 343, 356

Proust, M., 142
Publius Vegetius Renatus, 345
Pugh, 391
Pythagoras, 399-400

Q

Quintilian, 316
Quintus Serenus, 345

R

Raab, K., 45, 62 note ,478
Rabenus Maurus, 345
Ratinek, A., 356
Ratter, M. C., 117, 478
Rauch, K., 481
Rebecca, 287
Reger, M., 222
Regester, J. D., 45, 205, 207 *note*, 478
Reichenau, 345
Reiland, K., 30, 101
Reimarus, 430
Reinhardt, K., 415-416, 419, 421
Reitzenstein, 447, 449
Renan, E., 40
Renatus, P. V., 345
Reyes, Al., 17, 325
Rhazes, 347, 349
Richard of Bury, 345
[Richter], Jean Paul, 144
Riehl, A., 86
Rinuccio da Castiglione, P., 353
Rist, J., 315
Ritter, G., 296
Robert of Chester, 349
Robert, *King* of Sicily, 531
Roback, A. A., 29, 34, 51
Robertson Smith, 435
Ronsard, 317
Rosenberg, A., 62 *note*
Ross, E., 108
Rousseau, J. J., 58, 240
Royce, J., 249

Rufus, 342, 347, 355
Ruskin, J., 58
Russell, C. E. B., 27, 471, 473 (*see also the following entry*)
Russell, L. M., 478, 481

S

St. Ambrose, 288
St. Augustine, 288-289, 296, 398, 412, 423
St. Benedict, 343
St. John, 444, 445, 451, 453
St. Paul, 30, 79, 240, 286, 287, 289, 437, 443-455
St. Peter 433
Sabbadini, 351-352
Salazar de Alarcon, E., 335
Sallust, 282
Sanday, 437
Sarton, G., 17, 459, 461
Sassanidae, 346
Sawicke, F., 481
Scheler, M., 139, 143
Schelling, 181
Schering, A., 188 *note,* 192 *note*
Schiller, Fr., 181, 240
Schöffler, H., 320
Schopenhauer, A., 25, 79
Schrade, L., 17
Schubert, Franz, 186, 304
Schumann, R., 304
Schutz, 304
Schweitzer('s) Albert, *passim*
    aesthetics, 175-195
    and France, 62-63
    as author, 30
    aversion to nationalism, 64
    and the Nazi regime, 62
    character and personality, 51*ff*
    conflict of emotion and idea in, 71*ff*
    contribution to organ building, 215*ff*
    as critic of nineteenth century ethics, 241*ff*

defense of rationalism, 74
Dives and Lazarus, opinion of, 378, 383, 390
"elemental thought", of 45
eschatological interpretation of Jesus, 115
as ethical genius, 48
ethics, 27
foretells Nazi reign of terror, 47
as humanitarian, 67-68ff
imaginative power of, 207
influence in Holland and England, 431-435, 438-439
interest in Bach, 42
interest in organ-building, 42
interest in New Testament research of, 16
interpretation of St. Paul's Theology by, 446-455
as interpreter of Bach's music, 28, 176
a master of understanding, 133
as missionary, 27, 121ff
mysticism of, 57
as New Testament critic, 28
on Christianity, 58-59
on nationalism, 243
opinion of Russia, 63
as organist, 28, 30, 89, 200ff
as philosopher, 27
as philosopher of religion, 28
rationalism and optimism, 251, 256
recordings of Bach, 15
saintliness of, 105-105
scholar's dilemma, opinion on, 461, 464
search of historical Jesus, 241
self-discipline of, 49
studies medicine, 32, 84, 122
as surgeon, 28, 30
tension and polarity in, 51, 57, 71ff, 85
the man, 29-30
hardly a missionary, 32

the theologian, 27, 29
theory of civilization, 242
transcendentalism, 199ff
Schweitzer, H. B., 92, 231
Scipio Africanus, 283
Scipio Nascica, 282
Scotus, Duns, 292
Seaver, G., 478, 481
Seneca, 283
Serapion, 349
Shaftesbury, 240
Shakespeare, 106, 140
Shillito, E., (Rev.), 115, 481
Shorey, P., 274 note
Silbermann, 217-218, 220
Skillings, E., 20, 89
Skillings, M. D., 481
Smith, A., 481
Smits, M. J. C., 17
Smythe, J., 294
Snethlage, H. A. C., 478
Socrates, 67
Soederblom, 446
Solon, 402
Somervell, 391
Sonnenfels, J. von, 301
Soplillo, 327
Sophocles, 352
Soranus, 342, 345, 355
Spee, F. von, 315, 316
Spencer, M. A., 481
Spinoza, B., 29, 240
Spitta, P., 175, 176, 178
Spranger, E., 141
Stamm, F. K., 482
Stanley, H. L., 126
Steinbüchel, Th., 482
Stenzel, 407
Stephanus, 355
Stifter, A., 303
Stirner, M., 247
Strauss, D. F., 430
Strauss, R., 42, 178

Stravinsky, I., 108
Strege, M., 478
Stroux, 423
Sturm, J., 308
Suhrkamp, P., 482
Sulla, 281
Sutherland, G. A., 479

T

Tacitus, 351
Tasker, J. G., 482
Taube, A., 471
Telford, J., 482
Téllez, G. (*Fray*), 326
Terence, 306
Terrazas (see Francisco de Terrazas),
335
Terry, C. S., 205
Thales, 399, 406, 422
Theophrastus, 402, 419, 421
Theorodorus Priscianus, 343
Thompson, J. W., 344-345
Thucydides, 352
Timon, 401
"Tirso de Molina", 326
Tommasi, P., 353
Tovey, D. F. (Sir), 203, 210
Traversari, 353
Troeltsch, E., 134
Trueblood, D. E., 482
Turner, V., 482

U

Urmatt, F., 482

V

Vallejo, 328
Van den Bergh van Eysinga, 431

Van Manen, 429-431
Van Steenberghe, E., 464
Vauvenargues, 142
Veits, C., 482
Velasco, Luis de, 330
Venetiusm, J., 351
Veronese, G., 352
Vesalius, 357
Vetter, C., 315
Vi·etor, K., 17, 299
Villehardouin, 346
Vindicianus, 345, 356
Virgil, 283, 306, 317 351
Voltaire, 58

W

Wach, J., 17
Wackenroder, 181
Wagner, R., 42, 83, 178-179, 181, 185-
195, 304
Walther, D., 483
Wauchope, A. (Sir), 235
Weber, K. M. *v.*, 304
Wegmann, H., 479
Weiss, J., 432
Wellhausen, M., 436
Werner, M., 479
Wesley, J., 294
Wickram, 312
Widor, C. M., 31, 43, 44, 92, 104, 176,
199, 202, 210, 218, 219, 222, 222,
225, 472
Wieland, 302
Willstätter, R., 68
Winter, C., 476
Wolff, C., 314
Wolfskehl, M. L., 319
Wotton, 60
Wrede, 430
Wright, 436

X

Xenophanes, 397, 399-424

Y

YAHWEH, 284-285

Z

Zeller, E., 398, 416
Zeus, 282, 408-410
Ziebler, K., 192 note
Znaniecki, F., 272
Zweig, S., 233, 482

INDEX OF SUBJECTS

"ABSOLUTE MIND," 252
acholuric, 370
Acts, 444
Adequacy valence, 57, 58, 60
Aestheticism, 178
Aesthetics of music, 179, 183, 193-195
"Adiaphora," 305
Advertising, 73
Aesthetics, Schweitzer's, 175-195
Aetiology, 243-244
   factors in, 380
Africa, 28, 30-33, 53, 60, 91-94, 98, 99, 121, 126, 241, 282, 372, 397
Africans, 364
Age of the Antonines, 428
Age of the Flavians, 428
Air travel, 390
   progress in, 361
Albert Schweitzer Fellowship, 101, 102, 107
Albigensian Crusade in France, 428
Alsace, 30 63, 90, 97
Amazonia, Indians in, 387
Amoebic dysentery, 368
Anaemia, 370
   pernicious, 370
   splenic, 370
Anaximandrian cosmology, 413
Ancient manuscripts recovered, 355
Ancient Medicine, 398
Ancylostomiasis, 361
Anglo-Saxon monasteries, establishment of, 344
Anopheles Gambiae, 390
Antioch, community of, 445
Anthropomorphic deities, 405
   gods, 406
Anthropomorphism, 407, 410, 411

Apeiron, 411
Apostles, 443
Applied medicine, 390
Arabic, 349, 350
   medicine, 346
   translations, effects of, 350
   Transmission, 347
Arabs, 279, 349
Aramaic, 446
Arianism, 288
Art, 180
   romantic theory of, 181
   abstract, 182
   external signs in, 184
   of medicine, 341
Artist, imagination of, 180, 181
Artistic perception, 183
Association of ideas, aesthetic, 183, 184
Assyrians, 284
Astronomical knowledge, 462
Astronomy, 349
Atonement, 435
Atoning Death of Christ, doctrine of, 435
Austria, 301, 302

BACH SOCIETY, 199, 205
Barbados, 390
Baroque, 303, 314, 316, 219
   age, 178, 190
Being, 415
Being-in-Christ, 451
"Belles-lettres," 304, 315
Belief in truth, 464
Benedictine Monks, 316
Bible, the, 310, 311, 313, 436
Bilharziasis, 390-391
Blackwater fever, 363

Bladder and kidney diseases, 355
Bloodfilms, 370
Blood infections, 363
Bobbio manuscripts, 344
  monastery, 344
"Boundless," 407
Bread, 464
Bull of Mithras, 434
Byzantines, 279
Byzantium, 352

CALVINISTS, 307, 429
Calvinism, 293, 303, 305, 320, 433
Cantata, liturgical character of, 177
Capuchin monks, 316
Carthage, 282, 283, 288, 348
Cathedral libraries, 345, 353
  schools, 345
Catholic, 302, 303, 311, 435
  Church, 293, 306, 316, 431, 435
  Church, compared with Roman and
    Greek, 343
  literature, 301-303
  music, 304
  Standpoint, 303
Catholicism, 40
  German, 300, 304
Catholics, 299-301, 303, 304, 316, 318,
  429
Character, types of, 140
Chemists, 464
Chemotherapeutic research, 369
Chorale-melody, 188, 189, 193
Christendom, 279 ff.
Christ-mysticism, 451, 452
Christian,
  faith, 443, 355
  learning, 343
  mythology, 439
  practice, 439
  theology, 427
  theology, Hellenizing of, 453
  thought, 455
Christianity, 39, 40, 58-59, 97, 235, 279,

284, 286 ff., 302, 303, 310, 316, 387
  origins of, 455
Church, 302, 306, 307-309, 315
  as an institution, 438
  medieval, 289, 290
  libraries, 345
  of England, 435
  of the Counter-Reformation, 308
Orders, 318
Circumsion, 443
Citizen, 261, 262, 462
City of God, 263 ff., 296
Civilization, 243, 244, 261 ff.
Classical,
  learning, 343
  medical legacy, 345
  medical writings, recovery of, 341-357
Clinical,
  aspect, 369
  clerks, 369
  demonstration, 369
  examination of Lazarus, 379
Colitis,
  patients, 370
  mucous, 370
  ulcerative, 370
"Collective thought," 243
Cologne University, 356
Colonial imperialism, 121, 126
Colophon, 400, 401
Color bar, 391
Colored,
  folk, wretchedness of, 378
  races, 364
  student, difficulties of, 363
Comedy of manners, 331, 332
Common Law, 262
Composition, musical, 179, 180, 183
Communications, improved, aiding med-
  ical studies, 361
Comparative method, 369, 370
Complacency, 462
Comrades of the Way, 105
Concord, concept of, 280, 281

Conflict of duties, 463
Congo forest, 378
  Free State, 126
Conscience, 305
Conservative aristocrats in Holland, 429
Constantinople, drained of books, 355
Contributions to surgery, 342
Convictions, respect for, 243
Copper, ingots of, 381
Corinthians, 444
Cosmopolitanism, 279, 280, 287
Council of,
  Chalcedon, 435
  Constantinople, 435
  Ephesus, 435
  Nicaea, 435
Counter-Reformation, 302, 306, 307,
  311, 316-318, 320
Creation, conception of, 415
Criticism of New Testament, 437
Crusades, 291, 349
Cult of Roman Emperor, 433
Culture, 313
  bourgeois, 303
  Catholic and Protestant, 304
Custom, 253
Cynicism, 462
Czechoslovakia, 17

Dark Ages, 342, 346
Demonic world, 451
De natura deorum, 414
Dengue, 370
Desire, 464
Devil, 434, 435
Diabetes, 370
Dialectical philosophy of history, 443
Dialectic poem attributed to Xeno-
  phanes, 402
Dietetics, science of, 362
Difficulties of colored student, 363
Diffusion of medical knowledge, 348
Discoverers of manuscripts, 350
Diseases, virus, 363

Divine, 406, 407, 414
Divine boundlessness, as attribute of
  God, 413
Divine nature of Jesus, 438
Divinity of Jesus tempered, 431
Doctors, 464
Doctrine of Atoning Death of Christ,
  435
Dogmatics harmonized, 452
Dogmatism, 350
Donatist controversy, 208
Doxographers, 424
Doxographical attempt, 419
Doubts, 401, 465
Drugs, tolerance, spacing, toxicity, of,
  372
Dualism, 71, 75 ff., 85
Duodenal ulcer, 391
Duties, 463
Dysenteries, 361, 370, 382

Ecclesiastical doctrine about
  Jesus, 433
Ecclesiasticism, 427
Education, 72
Egoism, 247
Ekenosen, 437
Elea, 400, 415
Eleaticism, 415, 418
Eleatics, 415
Emotion(s), 185, 190, 464
  in Bach's music, 190, 191
  in Wagner's music, 190, 191
Emotion and idea, conflict of, 71
Emotion and knowledge, relation be-
  tween, 143
Empiricism, 398
Endocarditis, 370
Engineers, 464
England, 17, 293, 294, 311, 315, 345
English theologians, orthodox, 430
Enlightenment, German, 301, 319
  period of, 245, 246, 315
Epic theogonies, 410

Epicureans, 397
Epistemology, 75, 78
Epistle to Philemon, 447
Epistle to the Romans, 447
Erastian, 435
Erfurt University, 356
Errors in copying, detected, 356
Eschatological,
    mysticism, 447, 449
    pronouncements, 438
    solution, 449
Eschatology, 447, 452, 455
Establishment of Anglo-Saxon monasteries, 344
Ethical,
    acuity, 50
    Christian, 429
    genius, 47
    obtuseness, 50
Ethics, 255
    harmonized, 452
Europe, 342-245, 349, 351
European mysticism, 447
Exanthemata, 370
Existence, 133, 134
Experience, 135, 136
    expression of, 135, 136
    in tropical lands, 366
    objections of, 138
Explosives, 381
Expression
    of experience, 135
    types of, 135 ff.

FAITH, 81
    in Christ, 455
False authority, origin of, 401
Far East, 364, 368
Feelings, expressed in music, 184, 185
Feudalism, 290, 292
Fevers, differential diagnosis in, 355
Flesh and spirit, opposition of, 445
Food, qualities of, 355
Forced interpretations, 448

Foreign postgraduates wronged, 368
    students, 363
Form, 406
Fortune Magazine, 240
France, 62, 63, 292, 311, 320, 351
Free University, 429
Frustration or students, 364
"Fundamentalists," 429, 433

GALATIANS, 444
Gambia, 369
"Genicia," 356
German, 310-312, 317
German literature, 301, 302, 312, 314, 317, 320
Germany, 17, 62, 295, 301-304, 311, 314-316, 320, 365
    Catholic, 315
Gin, 381
Glycerine, 381
God, 76, 78, 284, 285, 305, 306, 308, 327, 406, 407
    as "all in all," 451
    as immobile, 407
    as 'Purpose,' 434
    conceptions of, 434
    Greek conceptions of, 407
    immanence of, 406
    immobility of, 408
    relationship to, 462
Gods, old conception of, 409
Golden Rule, 34
Gondisapor, 346
Gonorrhea, 355
Good Samaritan, parable of, 390
Gospel, 446
    of the Heathens, 446
Government medical services, 383, 366
Greece, 326
    intellectual history of, 398
Greco-Roman accomplishments, 341
Greek, 446
    artistic temper, 414
    city-state, 280, 412

INDEX OF SUBJECTS

Codices, 353
aspects of genius, 414
ground, 445
manuscripts, 344, 346, 348, 352
medicine, 342
  revival of, 347
medical literature, 342
medical schools, 341
mind, 446
Oriental culture, 445
philosophy, 397, 346
  two schools of, (Ionian, Italian
  school), 399
pluralism, 406
religion, mythical stage of, 412
spirit, 404
thought, 399
Greeks, 179-183, 341, 350
Greenite, 436
Gulf of Guinea, 122, 123
Günsbach, 32, 34-35, 90, 100, 104, 106,
  113, 232-233
Gynecology, 355

HARMONY, 189, 280, 414
Harvard, 439
  Glee Club, 202
Hate, 236
Heathens, 443
Hebrew language, 310
Hegelian system, 248, 253, 256
Helicopter, 390
Hellas, 404
Hellenes, 280—See also Greeks
Hellenism, 280, 281, 288
Hellenistic,
  age, 397
  cult, 445
  theory, 447
  world, 445
Hermeneutic principle, 134, 138, 139
Hermeneutics, 138, 139, 142, 145
Hero worship, 26
Heroism, 50

Hippocratic Corpus, 342
Historians, 304, 464
Historic-orthodox school, 433
Historical,
  century, 397
  field, 465
  interpretation of music, 180
  Jesus, 453
  truth, 433
"Historical Christian," 429
History, 144, 180, 182, 194
  European, 304
  of human events, complexity of, 463
Holland,
  Calvinistic, 303
  conservative aristocrats in, 429
  religion in, 428
Hollywood, 463
Homeric and Hesiodic Gods, 414
Hookworm, 382
Horae Synopticae, 431
Hospital and church, 388
Hostel idea, 365
Housing the student, 365
Human history vs. natural history, 463
Humanism, 306-308, 311, 317, 318, 320
Humanistic learning, 341
Humanists, 464
Humanity, concept of, 283, 286
Hungary, 301
Hypocrisy of Westerners, 364

IDEA, the, 251, 252
  of death, 445
Ideas, 183, 193
Ignorance of fundamentals, 461
Illness of modern culture, symptoms of,
  243
Images in Bach's music, 192, 193
Imagination, 142, 180, 185, 188, 207,
  208
Incarnation, 434-436
"In Christ," 445
"In the flesh," 451

Indians, 364
Indies, the, 326, 327
 Council of, 328, 331
Individual attention in teaching, 364
Individuality, 139
Infinity, 464
Inhumanity, 461
Inoculation, 369
Inquisition, the, 292
Intellect, 75
Intellect and emotion, dualism of, 72
Intellectual revolutionary, 404
International law, 294
Interpretation, forced, 448
Ionian,
 culture of nature, 401
 theories of nature, 412
Irish monasteries, 344
Italy, 282, 311, 320, 351, 352, 399

JANUS, 446
Jaundice, 370
Jesuit Order, 302, 308, 319
Jesuits, 307, 311, 315, 318
Jesus, historicity of, 430
Jewish,
 eschatology, 453
 Christian theology, 443
 interpolators, 438
 montheism, 446
 religion, 445
 transition, 445
Jews, 279, 282, 284, 286, 349
Johannine gospel, 431
Judaeo-Christian monotheism, 415
Judaism, 284-287,289
Justice, 262, 281
Justification of faith, 451

KALA-AZAR, 370
Kenotic theory, 437, 438
"Kingdom of God," 448
 doctrine of, 455

Knowledge, 74, 75, 81
Kyrios, 445

LABOR MOVEMENT in England, 294, 295
Lambaréné, 27, 31, 93, 98-100, 107-109,
 112, 122, 230, 241, 465
Language, 184, 310, 313
 "High German," 310
Latin, 310, 311, 316, 319, 345, 349, 351
 Ciceronian, 310
 manuscripts, 346
Latin America, 17
Laudatores Homeri, 404
Law-obedience, 443
 of Moses, 452
Learning, 72
 classical and Christian, 343
Leiden, theological faculty at, 429
Leprosy, 379, 390
Lethargy, 380
Liberals in Holland, 428, 429
Lingua franca, 364, 380
Liturgy, distinguished from art, 177
Liver abscess, 370
Livingstone College, 388
Logic, 85
Logical One, 418
Logos, the Mind of God, 435, 436
Love, 236, 286, 464
Lutheranism, 299, 301, 303, 305, 308,
 309

MACCABEAN struggle, 285
Macedonians, 280
Machiavellianism, 296
Madrid, 326, 328, 336
Magnanimity, 281
Malaria, 361, 363, 370, 382, 390
 cerebrospinal fluid in, 363
 sporozoite, 367
Malnutrition, 382
Manson method, 366
Manuscripts,
 discoverers of, 350
 recovery of, 351

Marcan picture, 438
Marian persecution in England, 428
Materialism of nineteenth century, 244, 255
Material One, 418
Mathematics, 82, 349
Matthew, Gospel of, 430
Mauritius, 390
Medes, 401
Medic invasion, 401
Medical, 341
  knowledge, popularization of, 344
  missionary, 390
  progress, 341
  science, cog in the machinery of, 366
  teaching influenced by War, 362
Messianic claim of Jesus, 448
Method, 366
  intuitive, 142
  synthetic, 142
Methodism, 295
Methodist revival, 294
Mexico, 326, 329, 330, 334-336
Middle Ages, 302, 305, 342-344, 347
Misery of the soul, 462
Missionaries, attitude of Negroes toward, 121
Missionary,
  doctor, standard of, 390
  effort, 388
  School of Medicine, 388
Missions, 383
  and healing, 383
Modern science, methodical abstractness of, 398
Modern theology, 455
Modernism, 429
Moderns in Holland, 428, 429, 431, 433, 434
Mohammedan religion, 123
Monastery, 343-346
Monistic philosophers, 415
Monks,
  Benedictine, 303, 316

Capuchin, 316
Monotheism, 284, 288, 406, 445
Morality, 253, 254
Moralization of the gods, 410
Mosaic,
  account of creation, 415
  law, 443, 445
Muses, 327, 328
Music, 82, 83, 137
  absolute, 178, 182, 184
  aesthetics of, 179
  aesthetical interpretation of, 180
  as art, 176, 177
  essence of, 182
  historical interpretation of, 180
  pictorial, 186
  poetic, 186
  poetry in, 179
  programmatic, 182
  relationship to poetry, 182
  symbolism of, 184, 185
Mysteries of life, 461
Mystery gods, 446
Mystic cults, 449
Mysticism, 57, 319, 334, 451
  eschatological, 447
  European, 447
  Pauline, 447
  of Nazi Germany, 464
Myth and religion in Greece, 398
  world of, 404
Mythical stage, 409
  theology, 414
Myths, 445

NATIONALISM, 243, 292
Nationality, idea of, 243, 244
Natural,
  law, 294
  philosophers, 400
  right, 254
  science, 82, 141
  theology, 399
Nazi regime, 17

INDEX OF SUBJECTS

Negroes, exploitation of, 125
  by whites, 124
  and world trade, 125, 126
Neighbor, relationship to, 462
Nestorian Christians, 346
New Testament, 436
  exegesis, 448
  research, 15, 448
  theologies, 444, 447
Norman Conquest, 345
Normans, 290
North Africa, 347
Nurses, training of, 372
Nutrition, science of, 362

OCCIDENTAL MEDICINE, advance of, 348
Objectification, stages of, 135-317
"Objective mind," 252, 253
Ogowe River, 30, 91
Old Testiment, 436, 445, 446
  "critical" position of, 436
Omnipotence as attribute of God, 408
On the Sublime, 415
"One World," 279
Optimism, 247, 249-251
Oriental,
  culture, 445
  ideas, 445
Origin of things, 401
Originality of Celsus, 342
Orthodox conservative theology, 455
Ossian fad, 302
Over-specialisation, 370
Overseas students, provision for, 364
Oxford Movement, 435

PAIDEIA, 404
Painting, 180
  and music, relationship between, 182,
    183
Pan American Highway, 361
Pantheist, 406
Papuan stretcher-bearers, 387
Parable of Dives and Lazarus, 378

Parasitological aspect, 396
Paris Missionary Society, 90, 122
Parmenidian ontology, 418
Particularism, 285
Pathological
  aspect, 369
  collections, deficiency of, 362
Patrons of learning, 350
Pauline
  Epistles, 430
  doctrine of "status quo," 452
  ethics, 452
  mysticism, 447
  problem, 449
  theology, 443, 447, 452, 454
    coherence of, 446, 450
Paulinism, 444, 446
Paul's theology, consistency of, 455
Pax Romana, 280, 282, 283, 287, 289-
  291
Peace, concept of
  among Greeks and Romans, 282, 283
  among Hebrews, 285
  transformation of, by Christianity, 286
Peace of God, 290
Persia, 346
Persians, 280
Personal solution, 462
Personality, 140, 143
Perversions of truth, 464
Philippians, 437
philosophical intuition, 405
philosophical theology, 414
  superiority of, 414
  truth of, 423
  universal validity of, 414
philosophical thinking in Greece, 404
Philosophy, 75, 78, 180, 245-257, 303,
  304, 306
  Indian, of work, 270
Physical science, 461
Pietism, 295, 311
Plague, 355
Plasmodium faliparum, 369

INDEX OF SUBJECTS

Pluralism
  Greek, 406
  in religion, 406
Pneumonia, 382
"Poetic harmonisation," 189
Poetry, 180, 303, 312, 316
  and music, relationship between, 179, 182
Polis, 413
  gods, 412
Politics, 261, 427
Polytheism, 288, 445
Popes, 291
"Positive" science, 409
Postgraduates foreign, wronged, 368
Prague University, 356
President of Harvard, 439
Pre-Socratic
  "materialists," 397
  philosophers, 398
  thinkers, 397
Pre-Socratics, 417
Prestige of Homer, 403
Pride, 461
Principle of all things, 406
Progress, 74
Propaganda, 73, 254
Prophets of Israel, 412
Proportation, 414
Protestant Reformation, 293
Protestantism, 40, 293, 303-305, 312, 314, 315, 319, 320
Protestant (s), 299-301, 303, 304, 311, 313, 317-320, 435
Psalms, 437
Psychological approach to Paul, 447
Public opinion, 255
Puritanism, 294
Pyrexia, 370

QUININE, 382

RATIONAL thinking, 464
Rationalism, 74, 246-252, 302, 464

Realistic point of view, 398
Reality, approach to, 414
Reason, 75, 249-252, 262
Reason and reality, 249, 251
Red blood corpuscles, 367
Redemption, 435
Reformation, 306, 307, 309, 311, 312
  German, 307
  Lutheran, 310
Religion, 40, 76, 84, 138, 141, 177, 304, 306
  a necessary element, 427
  as faith, 434
  blessings of, 428
  definition of, 428
  miseries of, 428
Religious
  genius, 446
  particularism, 412
  universalism, 412
Renaissance, 309, 312, 313, 320, 356
  European, 318
  German, 300
Renaissance, Age of, 292, 296, 305
Renal calculus, 370
Repose as attribute of God, 408
Republic, the, 414
Republican Party, 156
Respiratory diseases, 380
Resurrection, 450
  of Christ, 451
  with Christ, 445
Retirement, 462
Revelation, 433
Reverence, 413, 461
"Reverence for Life," 45, 46, 85, 96, 106
Revival of ancient learning, 350, 351
"Rhapsode," 402
Right, 253
Rococco, 303
Roman
  Empire, 279, 287, 341
  imperialism, 281

INDEX OF SUBJECTS

medical literature, 342
Romantic movement, 295, 296, 302
Romanticism, 180, 185, 300, 302, 310, 320
Romans, 444
Rome, 281-283, 287 ff., 351
Roundworms, 382
Royal Dutch Academy, 430
Rubber, raw, 381
Russia, 63, 295
Russians, 279

ST. BASIL on Mount Athos, 353
St. John, 445
St. Paul's theology, 452
Sacramental system, 431
Saint, 67, 68
Saintliness, 50
Salmonella group, 370
Salvation, 434
Samos, 400
Satires of Timon, 401
Satyriasis, 355
"Scepticism," 405 (see also skepticism)
Sceptics, 397.
Schaudinnian model, 367
Scholar's task, 463
Scholasticism, age of, 350, 427
School of Hygiene and Tropical Medicine, 371
Science, 73, 75
    of diabetics, 362
    of medicine, 341
    of nutrition, 362
Sciences, 302, 304
Scientific
    jargon, 373
    limitations, 461
    progress, 461
"Scientific spirit, awakening of," 398
Secularism, 292, 296
Self, (the), 263 ff.
    complacency, 461
    fulfillment, 279, 283

government, 262
"Sensual arts," 303
Sentimentalism, 57
Sermon on the Mount, 438
Sicily, 399, 350, 351
Silloi, 401-403
Sincerity in teaching, 364
Sittlichkeit, 253
Skepticism, 462 (*see* scepticism)
Skin diseases, 370
Slave trade, 121, 124, 390
    as an open sore, 379
Slavery, 383
Sleeping sickness, 380
Social and economic conditions, 244
Socialism, 295
Socialist Party, 156
Socialized state, 383
Society, 269
Society of Jesus, 319
South America, 361, 364
South Nigeria, 369
Spain, 311, 320, 325, 329, 330, 334, 335, 347, 350
Spanish language, tuition in, 365
Specimens, museum, 361
Speculative idealistic philosophy, 397
Spiritual
    decadence, 461
    energy, 464
    laxness, 462
    needs of students, 364
    nonchalance, 461
    responsibilities, 462
Splenomegaly, 370
State medical services, 391
State (the), 253, 309
    religion, 399
Sternal puncture, 363
Stoicism, 280, 283, 287, 294
Stoic,
    distinction, 414
    philosophy, 406
    trichotomy, 420

Stoics, 379, 415
Students, frustration of, 364
Studies, medical field, 361
Sublimity of the Divine, 413
Subtertian malaria, 368
Supppliants, The, 408
Surgery, contributions to, 342
Symbolism
  aesthetic nature of, 177
  and inadequacy of language, 184
  in Bach's music, 177, 192 not, 193
  of music, 184
  of the arts, 185
Symptoms of illness of modern culture,
  243
Synonymy in medication, 372
Synoptic criticism, 438 ffl
Synoptics, 444, 445

TABOO, 382
Teaching, *en masse,* 363
Temperate climates restore health, 369
Temperature charts, 370
Tension between life and thought, 86
Theater, 325, 326, 330
Theism, 427
Theocracy, 445
"Theodicy", 249
Theogenic epic, 399
Theologians, 304, 315
  contrasted with physicists, 399
Theological faculty at Leiden, 429
Theological trend in Greek philosophy,
  399
Theology, 398
  as distinct from religion, 427
  of physicists, 399
  of St. Paul, 443
  of the poets, 399
Theory of types, 140
Thirty Years War in Germany, 428
Thought, 74, 75, 77, 78, 85, 255
  and influence, 306

Thoughtlessness, 461
"Thread-spirit" Doctrine, 265
Threadworms, 382
"Tone-painting", 192
Totality of the arts, 183
Tragedies of Euripides, 414
Transaction between justice and mercy,
  435
Translations, 347, 349-351
Trinity College, 436
Tropical, 361
  fevers, 370
  dermatoses, 370
  lands, experience in, 366
  medicine, teaching and criticism of,
  373
  medicine, degree in, 366
  problems, 365
  schools, 365
Truce of God, 290
Truck, 381
Truth, 401, 405, 464, 465
  faith in, 256
  in Xenophanes, 403
Trypanosomiasis, 370, 390
Tse-tse flies, 380
Tuberculosis, 370, 379
Tuition in Spanish language, 365
Typhus, 370

UGANDA, mortality in, 380
Understanding, 133 ff.
  three-fold function of, 146
Unitarian Service Committee, 107, 114
United States, 348
Unity in philosophy and religion, 85
Unity of
  life, 134
  spirit, 134
  the arts, 181, 182
Universalism, 284, 285
Unknowable Creative Principle, 434
"Unmoved Mover", 408
Utrecht University, 429

INDEX OF SUBJECTS

V sign, 379
Validity, 405
Valuation
    of achievements, 151, 152
    activities, 153-160
    laws, 160-162
    persons, 162-168
Values, 81
Vatican, 353
Library, 354, 356
Von Reimarus zu Wrede, 431, 432

WELLCOME MUSEUM, 371, 372
Weltanschauung, 401, 427
"White man's scourge", 379
Will, 75
    of the state, 253

universal, 253
Will-to-action, 73
Will-to-live, 74, 77, 78
Witchcraft medicine, 382
Word and tone, relationship between, 179
World, 306
    -ground, 405
    of the footlights, 326
    -to-come, 450
World War, 246
Worms, 382
Wretchedness of colored folk, 378

YELLOW FEVER, 363, 390
Young Men's Christian Associations, 365

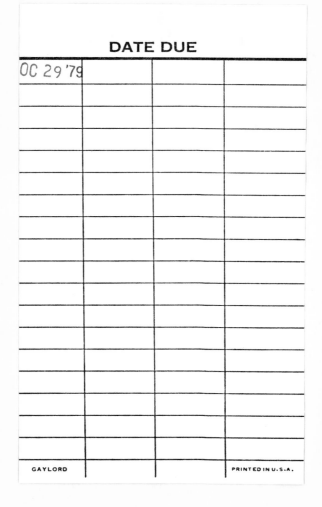

DATE DUE

OC 29 '79			
GAYLORD			PRINTED IN U.S.A.

Albert Schweitzer

THE ALBERT SCHWEITZER
JUBILEE BOOK